Counselling Ethics:
Issues and Cases

Counselling Ethics: Issues and Cases

William E. Schulz
Glenn W. Sheppard
Ron Lehr
Blythe Shepard

Canadian Counselling Association

Cover artwork by Dori Vanderheyden
with permission of the artist

Canadian Counselling Association
16 Concourse Gate, Suite 600
Ottawa, Canada K2E 7S8

ISBN 0-9697966-2-5

Printed in Canada

To

The Presidents of the Canadian Counselling
Association

John Evan Andoff	*1965-67*
Aurèle Gagnon	*1967-69*
Myrne B. Nevison	*1969-71*
John C. Paterson	*1971-73*
John Banmen	*1973-75*
Pierre Turgeon	*1975-77*
John R. Brosseau	*1977-79*
Kathie Swenson	*1979-81*
D. Stuart Conger	*1981-83*
Rod Conklin	*1983-85*
William Kennedy	*1985-87*
Walter Pawlovich	*1987-89*
Marcel Monette	*1989-91*
Sharon Robertson	*1991-93*
William Borgen	*1993-95*
Chris Cooper	*1995-97*
Karen Wright	*1997-99*
Renée Piché	*1999-2001*
Glenn W. Sheppard	*2001-2003*
Lorne Flavelle	*2003-2005*
David Paterson	*2005-2007*

Contents

Section One: Issues in Counselling Ethics..1

Chapter One: Introduction to Counselling Ethics 3
Chapter Two: Client Rights and Responsibilities......................21
Chapter Three: Confidentiality...49
Chapter Four: Boundary Issues and Violations in
                    Counsellor-Client Relationships...........................75
Chapter Five: Counselling in a Culturally Diverse Society 105
Chapter Six: Ethics of Research and Publication 145
Chapter Seven: Counsellor Education, Professional
                    Competence and Supervision 171

Section Two: Cases in Counselling Ethics...................................**203**

Chapter Eight: Case Studies in Professional Responsibility........205
Chapter Nine: Case Studies in Counselling Relationships........227
Chapter Ten: Case Studies in Consulting and Private
                    Practice 263
Chapter Eleven: Case Studies in Evaluation and Assessment 277
Chapter Twelve: Case Studies in Research and Publication.........295
Chapter Thirteen: Case Studies in Counsellor Education,
                    Training and Supervision 317

Appendices...**337**

Appendix A: CCA Code of Ethics...338
Appendix B: Association for Specialists in Group Work Best
                    Practice Guidelines...349
Appendix C: The Practice of Internet Counselling..................355
Appendix D: CCA Procedures for Processing Complaints of
                    Ethical Violations..361

ABOUT THE AUTHORS

William Schulz, PhD

Dr. Bill Schulz is a professor in counsellor education at the University of Manitoba. He has been the Chair of the Canadian Counselling Association Ethics Committee and is presently on the CCA Ethics Adjudication Committee. Bill revised the original CCA Code of Ethics in 1989 and, with Glenn Sheppard in 1999 and 2006, chaired the subsequent revisions of the CCA Code of Ethics. Bill is also the author of the first two casebooks on ethics for CCA. He wrote the initial certification guidelines and the *CCA Procedures for Processing Complaints of Ethical Violations.*

Glenn W. Sheppard, PhD

Dr. Glenn Sheppard is a past president of the Canadian Counselling Association (2001-2003) and has served as a CCA provincial director for a total of six years. He has been a professor of counsellor education at Memorial University of Newfoundland for 24 years, and 9 of these were as Chair of the Department of Educational Psychology.

Glenn was chair and editor for the CCA Committee on Standards of Practice for Counsellors and co-chair of the Committee for the 1999 and 2006 revisions of the CCA Code of Ethics. He chaired the CCA Ethics Committee from 1997 to 2001 as well as the first Ethics Adjudication Panel in 2005, and initiated and maintains the Ethics Notebook section of COGNICA. In addition to his university teaching, he works in private practice in St. John's, Newfoundland.

Ron Lehr, PhD
Dr. Ron Lehr, a graduate of Memorial University of Newfoundland (MUN) and the University of Alberta, currently teaches in the Counselling Program at Acadia University. In eighteen years as a counsellor-educator, he has served as President of the Counsellor-Educators Chapter of CCA and as the CCA Director for Nova Scotia, a position he currently holds. Ron's research interests in ethics are in the areas of informed consent, confidentiality, and ethical decision-making.

Blythe Shepard, PhD

Dr. Blythe Shepard is an assistant professor in Counselling Education at the University of Victoria. Previous to her work in Victoria, she was an elementary school teacher and community mental health worker. Her research interests focus on life-career development of rural youth and on families who have children with Fetal Alcohol Syndrome Disorder. Blythe has served as Vice-President of the Career Development Chapter of CCA and currently represents CCA on the working committee for counsellor regulation in British Columbia.

ACKNOWLEDGEMENTS

The authors would like to acknowledge a number of people for their help in writing this book: Max Uhlemann for his insights on counselling ethics; the many counsellors and counsellor-educators who provided counselling cases; Shelley Coveney for her word-processing skills, and Lorna Martin for her skills in language, book formatting and editing, as well as her knowledge of counselling and counselling ethics.

Introduction

Uses and Organization of this Book

Uses

During their professional careers, counsellors face many challenging ethical issues and dilemmas, and it is vitally important that they know about ethical principles, ethical articles and ethical decision-making. This book is intended to help counsellors in dealing with these areas.

Ethical Issues

Part One of this book examines key ethical issues and dilemmas that counsellors may confront. These issues, as presented in Chapters Two to Seven, provide current ethical challenges in the area of informed consent, confidentiality, boundary issues, diversity, research, and supervision.

Diversity Issues

In addition to Chapter Four on the issue of diversity, many of the cases and stimulus questions in the second part of this book are intended to make counsellors more contextually sensitive; taking into consideration the client's culture, race, religion, sexual orientation, disabilities, ethnic background and any other characteristics that are generally viewed as being somewhat unique.

Case Studies

The cases used in this book are from actual counselling situations. Positive and negative case examples are provided so that users of this book can see clearly the intention of each of the many articles in the *CCA Code of Ethics*.

Self-Assessment

At the beginning of each chapter, readers are encouraged to examine their attitudes toward the main issues in the chapter. It is often of interest to complete the self-assessment both at the beginning and at the end of an ethics course to see potential changes in attitudes.

Decision-Making

Ultimately, the purpose of an "issues and cases" book on ethics is to help counsellors make ethical decisions. Several decision-making approaches are suggested and readers are encouraged to use the processes for decision-making suggested later in this first chapter.

Stimulus Questions

Each of the 73 articles from the *CCA Code of Ethics* has relevant cases illustrating ethical and non-ethical behaviour by counsellors. Following these cases, readers are asked to read the commentary and to discuss the six questions written to promote further thinking about the ethical article and the sample cases.

Organization

The general intention of this CCA ethics casebook is to:

- Clarify major ethical issues in areas such as informed consent, confidentiality, boundary issues, diversity, research and publication, and supervision and training
- Promote discussion of ethical issues in the professional practice of counselling, on the counselling relationship, on testing and research, on consultation and private practice, and on counsellor preparation standards

- Demonstrate the willingness of our professional counselling association to regulate itself and to provide a process for self-regulation
- Protect our counselling association by setting standards of practice through case examples of both ethical and unethical behaviour in counselling
- Provide material that will assist the CCA Ethics Committee in dealing with complaints of ethical violations in a variety of situations
- Be a guide to counsellors in their everyday conduct and in the resolution of ethical dilemmas
- Help define and facilitate counsellors' relationships with employers and supervisors, and
- Provide examples that will help clarify each of the 73 ethical articles in the *CCA Code of Ethics* (2006).

This book is divided into two main sections: the issues section and the cases section. The seven chapters in the issues section deal with major ethical issues. Each of the chapters in this section begins with a self-assessment inventory designed to stimulate readers to begin analyzing their values and attitudes concerning key ethical issues. At the end of each chapter is a number of learning activities are listed, developed to help counsellors, counsellor-educators and counsellor-candidates apply the issues discussed in the chapter.

Overview

Section One

Chapter One

The three major topics discussed in the introductory chapter are:

- the professional counsellor
- values and ethics
- ethical decision-making

Professional counsellors have special competence and have the right to counsel individuals. Professional counsellors have clarified their own values on a number of issues and do not impose their values on clients. Professional counsellors are familiar with the process of ethical decision-making.

Chapter Two

Chapter Two deals with client rights, counsellor responsibilities, and informed consent. Included in the list of topics are:

- informed consent and ethics
- informed consent and Canadian law
- the process of informed consent
- content of informed consent forms

Chapter Three

Privacy, confidentiality, and privileged information are discussed in this chapter. Specific topics include:

- limits to confidentiality
- duty to warn
- suspected child abuse and confidentiality
- confidentiality and the school context

Chapter Four

Managing boundary issues and multiple relationships have been made more difficult because of differing viewpoints. Some of the issues considered in this chapter include:

- differing viewpoints on boundary issues
- maintaining appropriate boundaries
- role-blending
- bartering for counselling services
- research related to boundary issues

Chapter Five

Counsellors in the Canadian mosaic need to be familiar with issues involved in counselling culturally diverse populations. Some issues addressed include:

- the need for an emphasis on diversity
- multicultural/cross-cultural issues
- achieving culturally competent counselling
- implications for counsellor education related to culture-infused professional practices

Chapter Six

The ethics of research and publication are examined in this chapter. Specific topics include:

- gaining research approval
- responsibilities of the researcher
- voluntary, informed consent
- ethical research across cultures

Chapter Seven

The last of the chapters on ethical issues focuses on counsellor education, supervision, and professional competence. Some of the topics include:

- multiple roles of supervisors
- responsibilities of counsellor educators
- selection of trainees
- evaluation and remediation of counsellor-candidates

Section Two

In the next six chapters, ethical cases are presented, representing the six areas in the *CCA Code of Ethics* (2006). (Many of these cases were presented in the William E. Schulz casebooks entitled *Counselling Ethics Casebook* and *Counselling Ethics Casebook 2000*.) The cases vary both in style and length, reflecting the diversity of contributors. Every attempt has been made to reflect a variety of work settings for counsellors. Some cases have been altered to show more accurately the article under discussion. All names used in the cases are fictitious. Also, cases have been labelled "+" and "–" to designate whether the case reflects positive behaviour or negative behaviour based on the ethical article. No attempt has been made to specify the seriousness of any behaviour presented in the cases. As a result, some cases will exemplify very serious unethical behaviour while others will simply illustrate ignorance or questionable behaviour on the part of the counsellor.

Chapter Eight

Chapter Eight presents ethical cases based on professional responsibilities, followed by comments and questions relevant to the eleven ethical articles discussed in the chapter.

Chapter Nine

In this major chapter, 76 cases are presented that illustrate ethical and unethical behaviour by counsellors in the area of counselling relationships.

Chapter Ten
Chapter Ten focuses on ethical issues in the area of consulting and private practice counselling. Both positive and negative cases provide examples and clarification on the articles in the CCA Code of Ethics related to consulting and private practice.

Chapter Eleven
The eleven articles that constitute this chapter on evaluation and assessment are clarified through cases, commentary and questions.

Chapter Twelve
The thirteen articles in this chapter deal with ethical concerns in the area of research and publication.

Chapter Thirteen
Ethical cases on counsellor education, training and supervision are presented, followed by comments and questions relevant to the eleven articles discussed in this chapter.

Section One

———— ❖ ————

Issues in
Counselling Ethics

———— ❖ ————

In this section of the book, issues related to
the following areas are discussed: values
and ethics, ethical decision-making,
counsellor responsibilities and informed
consent, confidentiality, boundary issues,
diversity, research and publication, and
training and supervision.

Chapter One

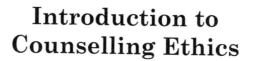

Introduction to Counselling Ethics

A real value in examining ethical dilemmas is
that, in the process of going through ethical
decision-making, counsellors can promote
their own professional growth.

Chapter Objectives

Following an overview of the background of counselling ethics in the Canadian Counselling Association (CCA) and the organization of this book, the major focus of the chapter is on the professional counsellor, on values and ethics, and on ethical decision-making. The specific objectives are to:

- Define the major characteristics of a counselling professional

- Clarify internal and external factors important for the ethical professional

- Describe the process to be taken when counsellor-client values conflict

- Identify personal values on issues such as abortion, assisted suicide and religion

- Use an ethical decision-making process for ethical dilemmas

- Clarify major aspects of virtue ethics

Self-Inventory

The items in this inventory are intended to begin the process of thinking about, discussing with others, and acting on ethical and professional issues in counselling. In this inventory there are no absolutely correct answers. This is consistent with ethical decision-making in general in that there seldom is only one correct response to ethical decisions.

Directions: For each statement in this inventory, indicate the response (or responses) that is (are) closest to your own beliefs.

_____ 1. When faced with an ethical issue or dilemma, the first thing to do it:
   a) identify the key factors in the issue or dilemma
   b) phone and consult with a lawyer
   c) read the CCA *Code of Ethics*
   d) quickly decide on what would be the best course of action
   e) _____

_____ 2. When a client threatens another person, the counselor must:
   a) phone the police
   b) convince the client to change his/ her mind
   c) warn the person threatened
   d) tell her/his supervisor/director
   e) _____

_____ 3. To be effective, counsellors must:
   a) like the client personally
   b) be free of any personal conflicts in the area in which the client is working
   c) have experienced feelings similar to those experienced by the client
   d) be of the same cultural group
   e) _____

_____ 4. Regarding the role of values in counselling, counsellors should:
   a) never impose their values on clients
   b) expose their values, without imposing them on clients
   c) keep their values out of the counselling relationship
   d) refer clients if their values are in conflict with the clients
   e) _____

_____ 5. Counsellors who work with culturally diverse groups without having cross-cultural knowledge and skills:
   a) are probably guilty of unethical behaviour
   b) could be practicing ethically
   c) are violating the civil rights of clients
   d) can compensate by being caring and respectful
   e) _____

_____ 6. Dual relationships that are likely to cause the most ethical concerns are:
   a) social relationships with clients,
   b) business arrangements with clients
   c) financial partnerships with clients
   d) supervisory responsibilities as a group facilitator
   e) _____

_____ 7. If counsellors determine that they cannot be helpful to a client, they should:
   a) refer the client
   b) terminate the counselling
   c) try to use different approaches
   d) should discuss the situation with the client
   e) _____

_____ 8. When counsellors provide counselling to two or more persons (e.g. parents and children):
   a) all persons in the counselling become clients and have the same rights
   b) the counsellor needs to clarify the nature of the relationship with each person

c) only the person who initiated the counselling is the client

d) the adults should determine the nature of the relationship

e) _____

9. The most important exception to client confidentiality occurs when:
a) a child is in need of protection
b) legal requirements demand that confidential material be revealed
c) a client threatens suicide
d) a client threatens to harm someone else
e) _____

10. Sexual intimacy with clients is:
a) illegal
b) always unethical
c) acceptable once the client/counsellor relationship ends
d) acceptable six months after the client/counsellor relationship ends
e) _____

11. When consulting with other professionals, counsellors:
a) can reveal the client's name if the counsellor trusts the other professional
b) must get consent from the client to consult with others
c) must keep the name of the client confidential
d) can reveal the client's name
e) _____

12. The counsellor's primary responsibility is to:
a) avoid ethical and legal violations
b) respect the client and to promote the welfare of the client
c) promote the goals and values of the agency for which she or he works
d) promote the values of the community/society
e) _____

Introduction

The CCA is a relatively new association, having its beginnings in 1965 as the Canadian Guidance and Counselling Association (CGCA). The first ethical guidelines for the CGCA were printed in 1981, and contained four sections (General, Counsellor-Counsellee Relationships, Measurement and Evaluation, and Research and Publication), with a total of 46 guidelines. The American Counseling Association (ACA), formerly the American Personnel and Guidance Association, had given the CGCA permission to adapt many of their ethical articles. This influence of the ACA has continued to the present time.

In 1987, William Schulz, Manitoba director of CCA, was asked to revise the Canadian counselling ethical articles, resulting in *Guidelines for Ethical Behaviour* (1989). The ethical articles were divided into five sections: general; counselling relationships; testing, research and publication; consulting and private practice; and counsellor preparation, with a total of 63 ethical articles. The CCA decided that to help educate their membership about counselling ethics, a casebook was needed that would provide examples of ethical and unethical behaviour as well as essays on key ethical issues such as boundary violations, confidentiality, and counsellor preparation.

In 1993, Schulz agreed to write an ethics casebook resulting in *Counselling Ethics Casebook* (1994). Many counsellors contributed case studies for the book and counsellor-educators from across Canada contributed a total of ten essays dealing with ethical issues.

In 1998, the CCA updated its 1989 *Code of Ethics*, and William Schulz and Glenn Sheppard, two CCA directors who were very involved in counselling and ethics, co-chaired an ethics committee that revised the *CCA Code of Ethics*. In May 1999, the CCA approved the new *Code of Ethics*. This present code has six major sections with a combined total of 73 articles. The six sections are:

A. Professional Responsibility

B. Counselling Relationships

C. Consulting and Private Practice

D. Evaluation and Assessment

E. Research and Publication

F. Counsellor Education, Training and Supervision

While the *CCA Code of Ethics* was being revised in 1999, William Schulz completed the second edition of the *Counselling Ethics Casebook 2000*. This casebook contains 280 cases exemplifying both positive and negative ethical behaviour of counsellors. The essay contributions of counsellor-educators from across Canada are expanded in the book, particularly in the area of counselling relationships, where the following essays provided much needed clarification on a number of ethical issues:

- Confidentiality: Dialogue and Discernment

- The Counsellor as Custodian: Protecting Our Clients' Personal Information

- The Duty to Protect

- Boundary Violations in Counsellor-Client Relationships.

In 2005, Glen Sheppard and William Schulz again revised the *CCA Code of Ethics*. This new *Code* (2006) revised the ethical principles and clarified the ethical decision-making process. Three new articles were added and each existing article was updated and edited to include a cross-referencing feature. The CCA Board of Directors approved the writing of a new casebook to accompany the 2006 Code of Ethics. The authors of this book decided to expand the issues section so that the book could be used by counsellor-educators, counsellor-candidates, and counsellors, not only as a casebook, but as a textbook for courses in counselling ethics. Major chapters were added in the following six areas:

1. Informed Consent and Client Rights Issues

2. Confidentiality Issues

3. Boundary Issues

4. Diversity Issues

5. Research and Publication Issues

6. Supervision and Training Issues.

Values and Ethics

It is important that counsellors know that their personal values can influence clients and that they avoid imposing their values on clients. This is often difficult since clients ask for advice; advice that then reflects the counsellors' values rather than the clients' values. It is difficult, maybe impossible, for counsellors not to communicate aspects of their values, both verbally and nonverbally.

Value conflicts between counsellors and clients can arise in many areas:

- abortion issues
- sex among young adolescents
- interracial marriages
- drug users
- use of condoms
- alcohol abusers
- care of the elderly
- euthanasia
- eating disorders
- child punishment (spanking)
- gang camaraderie
- cheating in schools
- the importance of achievement
- religious values
- assisted suicide
- gay marriage
- criminals
- the sanctity of marriage
- women's rights
- alternative lifestyles

It is worthwhile for counsellors to identify and discuss their attitudes and values on the list of issues listed above with a friend or colleague. The question each counsellor needs to ask is: "Are there values that I hold that could interfere with my ability to remain non-judgmental and objective?"

The following two cases are intended to point out the importance of counsellor values and ethics in counselling.

The Marsha Case

Marsha has had a reasonably successful career as an auditor for a large investment company. She is approaching her sixtieth birthday and realizes that she would like to fulfill her lifelong dream of getting her MBA. Marsha is concerned about whether she will be able to compete with students thirty or more years younger than she is. Maybe she should just stick with her present job.

As Marsha's career counsellor you may need to consider questions such as these:

Would you encourage a sixty-year-old person to begin study in a demanding MBA program?

Does your age influence what you would tell Marsha?

Do you believe you have some age biases?

The Albert Case

Albert has a counselling practice that attracts many clients. He advertises his practice as "Christian" counselling and he has strong religious fundamentalist beliefs. He sincerely believes that in a caring way he needs to let clients know what a strong belief in Jesus Christ will do for their lives. Recently, one of Albert's clients resented Albert's religious values becoming the major focus for his expressed problems with alcohol.

What should Albert say to his client?

What are the ethical implications of Albert's counselling practice?

Would you recommend that Albert drop "Christian" as one of the descriptors of his counselling practice?

To be professional, ethical helpers, counsellors need to be open to differing client values. Sue, Arrendondo and McDavis (1992) suggest three standards that are relevant for counsellors:

- awareness of personal values, biases and limitations

- understanding the worldview of culturally different clients

- development of a wide repertoire of appropriate intervention strategies

Albright and Hazler (1995) encourage counsellors to ask themselves a number of questions as they consider possible value differences with their clients:

- What are the important personal and moral values of the client?

- What type of support system does the client have?

- Does the client need a resource person or an advisor?

- Will clients receive compassion, acceptance and consideration no matter what their personal v a l u e s are?

- Will a referral help?

- Does anyone need to be informed about the client's issues?

- Will a declaration of counsellor values interfere with the counselling process?

In summary, counsellors cannot keep their own values out of the counselling relationship and counselling process. Counsellors need to accept the client's right to choose, but need not accept the client's values. When there is a difference between counsellors and clients on various values, it is important that the differences are discussed in order to see if the value conflicts will interfere with helping the client. If the value conflict does interfere, counsellors may have to prepare clients for referral to another counsellor.

The Professional Counsellor

Counselling is a professional career and many attempts continue to be made by counsellors toward greater professionalism. Professions modelled after law and medicine can be described as having a "specialized knowledge base or shared technical culture; a strong service ethic with a commitment to meeting clients' needs; and self-regulated collegial control rather than external bureaucratic control over recruitment and training, codes of ethics and standards of practice" (Goodson & Hargreaves, 1996, p. 5). Peterson and Nisenholz (1987, p. 167) identify several basic features of a profession.

- A profession determines its own preparation and education/training standards. In the field of counselling in Canada, the Canadian Counselling Association (CCA) has prepared accreditation guidelines for colleges and universities offering counsellor education programs. These were approved by the CCA Board in May, 2002. Curricular experiences that were outlined in the CCA accreditation document include:

  — professional identity

  — helping relationships

  — group counselling

  — human development

  — social and cultural foundations

  — career development

— appraisal

— research methods and program evaluation

Practicum requirements are seen as vital and include many required hours of supervision.

- A profession is recognized legally via licensure and certification using criteria defined by members of the groups. Canadian Counsellor Certification (CCC) and Quebec provincial licensure for counsellors are examples of certification standards undertaken toward this objective. Other provinces in Canada are also planning to introduce counsellor certification.

- A unique role of the profession in general and for each specialty within the profession must be determined by the members of the group. The individual counsellor exercises independent judgement, makes decisions and provides help. CCA members have defined specific roles for divisions with CCA; such as the private practitioners' chapter, the feminist chapter, school counsellors' chapter, career development chapter, and counsellor-educators' chapter. As well, there are a number of regional chapters including the Atlantic Chapter and British Columbia Chapter.

- A profession has its own professional ethics for its membership. CCA developed its first code of ethics soon after its formation in 1965. Since then the *Code* has been updated and revised three times (1989, 1999, and 2006). Casebooks (Schulz, 1994, 2000) were developed to clarify further the many articles in the *CCA*

Codes of Ethics. Additionally, Standards of Practice for Counsellors for each of the 73 articles in the *CCA Code of Ethics* were developed in 2001 to align with and to support the *CCA Code of Ethics.*

- A profession has procedures for disciplining those who behave unethically. In 1991, the *CCA Procedures for Professing Complaints of Ethical Violations* (see Appendix D) was adopted by CCA. These procedures have since been revised, adopted and updated in 2003, 2004 and 2006. Sanctions for ethical violations by CCA members include a formal reprimand with recommendations for corrective action; withdrawing membership for a specified period of time; placing the member on probation for a specified period of time, and expelling the member from CCA permanently.

- Generally, a profession is considered a terminal occupation, where a practitioner may be gainfully employed throughout her or his career.

In addition to these basic features of a profession, professional counsellors should also have a professional attitude. What does having a professional attitude encompass? It means devoting time and energy into furthering the profession. That is, counsellors need to initiate and to support initiatives for licensing and/or certifying, as well as to maintain close ties with agencies such as provincial departments of education and departments of health. A professional attitude means attending counselling conferences, workshops and in-service sessions. It means keeping current with counselling issues by reading new books, journals and counselling newsletters. A professional attitude also means being active in professional organizations such as CCA. CCA has made significant contributions to professional practice by providing guidelines for accreditation, certification, policy papers, continuing education units and ethical guidelines. In short, a professional attitude involves a commitment to continued personal and professional growth.

Remley and Herlihy (2005, pp. 4-5) comment on the importance of various factors in examining the professional counsellor and ethics. Internal elements that they consider are:

- intentionality
- moral principles of the helping professions
- knowledge of ethics and law
- decision-making skills and models
- the courage of personal convictions

Intentionality means wanting to do the right thing and is not unlike the ethical principle of beneficence, defined as being proactive in benefitting the client. In the *CCA Code of Ethics*, (2006) six moral principles have been outlined. These principles are intended to guide ethical reasoning and decision-making.

1. Beneficence—being proactive in benefitting the client
2. Fidelity—honouring client commitments and having integrity in client-counsellor relationships
3. Autonomy—respecting clients' freedom of choice
4. Nonmaleficence—not willfully harming others and refraining from actions that risk harm to others
5. Justice—respecting the equal treatment of all persons

6. Societal Interest—respecting the need to be responsible to society

The third internal area of ethical consideration by Remley and Herlihy (2005) is knowledge of ethics and the law. Counsellors need to familiarize themselves with codes of ethics and learn to apply their knowledge of ethical articles to counselling issues and dilemmas. The *CCA Code of Ethics* has 73 articles divided into the following six areas:

A. Professional Responsibility

B. Counselling Relationships

C. Consulting and Assessment

D. Evaluation and Assessment

E. Research and Publication

F. Counsellor Education, Training, and Supervision

Codes of ethics have also been developed for specific groups (e.g. school counsellors, group facilitators, employment and career counsellors and others) and for internet counselling.

The final internal ethical element, "the courage of personal convictions" is gaining more importance with the increasing emphasis on virtue ethics ("What would a virtuous person do with this ethical dilemma?"). It can take a lot of courage at times to do what the counsellor believes to be the right course of action, especially when others in positions of power disagree with the actions.

The external forces that Remley and Herlihy (2005, pp. 4-5) identify act as resources for the counsellor. Consultation with colleagues and others and seeking supervision are sound practices whenever counsellors face ethical dilemmas. Professional organizations encourage continuing professional development, and make professional development compulsory for counsellor certification.

The last three external ethical forces identified by Remley and Herlihy (2005): laws, codes of ethics, and system policies, all provide counsellors with guidelines for sound counselling practice and for assistance in ethical decision-making. Counsellors need to have some familiarity with laws such as the:

- *Charter of Rights and Freedoms*
- *Youth Criminal Justice Act*
- *Freedom of Information and Protection of Privacy Act*
- *Personal Health Information Act*
- *Personal Information Protection of Electronic Data Act*

The importance of codes of ethics has already been mentioned, and the need to understand and to apply the articles from codes of ethics in practice is vital. Finally, the system policy, meaning the policies of schools, institutions, or agencies where counsellors work, will have policies that can both challenge and support counsellors. For example, the drug and alcohol policy for most school boards asks that counsellors report any students suspected of using drugs and alcohol. Counsellors, in some instances, face problematic situations when they are counselling drug users who they feel can be helped with further counselling. With this issue, and many others, counsellors are left with an ethical dilemma; a dilemma in which they make a professional decision. Often, no one best, clear course of action is obvious.

Cottone and Tarvydas (2003) define these ethical dilemmas as conflicts that arise when competing standards of right and wrong apply to specific situations in counselling. For example, what ethical decision does the counsellor make in the following situations?

- A counsellor finds a client's issues beyond her expertise and refers the client to another counsellor who has far more expertise in the area. The client however, refuses the referral.

- A parent of a student whom the counsellor is counselling, phones and asks the counsellor for his daughter's files.

- A counsellor working in a small, remote community meets a client who has recently come to Canada. The client is having difficulty adjusting. The counsellor has never worked with a client from this ethnic group, and the client only speaks a little English. There are few social services in the community and there are not interpreters available.

Approaches to Ethical Decision-Making

Many counsellors would like perfect, right answers to their legal and ethical issues and dilemmas. Unfortunately, even the best codes of ethics, standards of practice and ethics casebooks cannot provide all the answers. Counsellors can, however, enhance their ethical decision-making by knowing some ethical decision-making models, and developing a model of ethical decision-making for their personal, professional practice. A number of authors and professional organizations have produced ethical decision-making model. These can be loosely divided into principle-based models and virtue ethics.

Principle-Based Decision-making Models

Many of the decision-making models in

this category emphasize rational, cognitive and behavioural aspects of decision-making and use similar steps in activating a decision plan. Keith-Spiegel and Koocher (1985) suggest these steps:

- Describe the parameters
- Define the potential issues
- Consult legal and ethical guidelines
- Evaluate the rights, responsibilities, and welfare of involved parties
- Generate alternate decisions
- Enumerate the consequences of each decision
- Estimate the probability for outcomes of each decision
- Make the decision.

Similarly, Corey, Corey, and Callanan (1998) suggest the following process:

- Identify the problem
- Identify potential issues involved
- Review relevant ethical guidelines
- Obtain consultation
- Consider possible and probably courses of action
- Enumerate consequences of various decisions
- Decide on best course of action.

In 1985, the American Counselors Association (formerly the American Association for Counseling and Development) provided funding for a series of videotape cassettes focusing ethical issues. These cassettes, *Confidentiality: The Professional's Dilemma* by Stadler (1985) and the subsequent work of Holly Forester-Miller and Thomas Davis (1995), and the casebook by Barbara Herlihy and Gerald Corey (1996), resulted in the following process suggested by the American Counseling Association:

1. ***Identify the problem***
   Counsellors determine what is the ethical issue or dilemma. They then gather information about the issue.

2. ***Apply the ACA Code of Ethics***
   If the code of ethics provides a clear direction, then the situation is an issue but not a true ethical dilemma. Sometimes different articles in the code are in conflict with each other, and then, it is necessary to go to the next step in the decision-making process.

3. ***Determine the Nature and Dimensions of the Dilemma***
   At this point counsellors are encouraged to read relevant literature (for example, the casebooks from the ACA). As well, the relevant ethical principles are considered:

   a) autonomy—allowing clients the freedom to make informed decisions and to plan their own action;

   b) nonmaleficence—doing no harm;

   c) beneficence—doing good;

   d) justice—acting fairly, and

   e) fidelity—upholding the clients trust.

   Finally, counsellors should consult their professional organizations and consult with other professional counsellors.

4. ***Generate Potential Courses of Action***
   What courses of action are possibilities? Is it appropriate to consult with the client? Continue to talk with colleagues.

5. ***Consider the Potential Consequences of all Options and Determine a Course of Action***

Here the question is: What will the consequences be for the client, others and the counsellor?

6. ***Evaluate the Selected Course of Action***

Generally, three tests are used to evaluate a course of action:

Test of Justice—Would you treat others in the same manner given the same situation?

Test of Publicity—Would you want your action reported to the media?

Test of Universality—Would you recommend this same course of action to another counsellor who was facing the same situation?

7. ***Implement the Course of Action***

To prepare for carrying out the action and to be aware of possible set-backs counsellors should consider the following:

What supports are needed to implement the selected course of action?

What could interfere with the implementation of the selected course of action?

What needs to be done to overcome any barriers to the implementation of the selected course of action?

In the Canadian Counselling Association model of ethical decision-making, two major features receive greater emphasis than in the three principle-based models just outlined. Schulz (2000) emphasizes a feeling/emotional dimension and focuses strongly on the six moral principles discussed earlier in this chapter.

The decision-making model that is briefly outlined in the recently revised *CCA Code of Ethics* (2006), now consists of six steps. Step Five of the decision-making process focuses on counsellor feelings and emotions, suggesting the consideration of virtue ethics (see next section for further details).

Step One: Identify the key ethical issues of a particular situation are identified.

Step Two: Examine the Code of Ethics is examined to see whether the ethical articles (e.g. on confidentiality or record-keeping) are relevant to the situation under question. If there are appropriate articles in the Code, following the articles may be sufficient to resolve the ethical dilemma. If not, the following additional steps may help.

Step Three: Examine the moral and ethical principles that are relevant and important in the situation. Briefly, these principles are:

a) Beneficence,

b) Fidelity,

c) Autonomy,

d) Nonmaleficence,

e) Justice, and

f) Societal interest.

Step Four: Choose the most important principles and relevant ethical articles and begin to implement some possible action by:

a) Generating alternatives and examining the risks and benefits of each alternative

b) Securing additional information and/or consulting with colleagues

c) Examining the probably outcomes of various courses of action

Step Five: Use emotional decision techniques. Until this point, decision-making has been mainly cognitive and rational. Time permitting, use strategies such as:

a) Quest – a solitary walk in the woods or park where your emotions are allowed to interact with the ethical dilemma being faced

b) Incubation – "sleep on it"

c) Time projection – projecting the ethical situation into the future and reflecting on the various fantasized scenarios

At this step counsellors can add some elements of virtue ethics, particularly considering all the options that may best help and may show consideration for the client.

Step Six: Take action. Follow a concrete action plan, evaluate the plan, and be prepared to adjust any negative or neutral consequences that might occur from the action taken.

A brief example shows how these steps work in practice. Guided questions follow the scenario to clarify the six-step, integrated approach.

A high school counsellor sees John, a seventeen-year-old, Grade 11 student on numerous occasions. Initially, these counsellor visits are a result of teacher referrals. Teachers find John to be "disruptive in the classroom." Over the months, a good relationship develops between the counsellor and John, and frequently John just drops in to chat. On one such occasion, John talks about his part-time job at a hardware store and how he makes quite a bit of extra money "lifting" the occasional article from the store and selling it. When the counsellor learns more details, he is convinced that considerable theft is involved. He doesn't know what to do, since he has assured John on more than one occasion that "Things said in my office will never leave this office."

Guided Questions:

1. What are the key ethical issues in this situation?

The counsellor had promised confidentiality, yet the student's actions are illegal. In the long term, the thefts would probably be discovered and John would be in serious trouble.

2. What ethical articles are relevant to this case?

The ethical articles relating to confidentiality provide for a respect for privacy, unless there is danger to the client or to others. The ethical articles also state that the counsellor's primary responsibility is to help the client. Furthermore, the counsellor needs to inform the client of the exceptions to confidentiality before the counselling begins.

3. What ethical principles are of major importance in this situation?

Six principles were identified earlier, and the principles of societal interest, autonomy, and beneficence are important in John's situation.

4. What are the most important principles and what are the risks and benefits of acting on principles?

The counsellor examines each one of

the principles and considers what would happen if he reported the theft, what would likely happen if he kept quiet and continued to work with John, and how he could best help John. Without identifying John, the counsellor discusses the situation with another counsellor, and is told that "to cover yourself you'd better tell the principal." The counsellor believes at this time that beneficence and responsibility to society are of greatest importance. Before acting, the counsellor asks himself a fourth question:

5. **Will I feel the same way about this situation if I think about it a little longer, and who shall I be in order to show the greatest integrity and caring for my client?**

The counsellor decides to "sleep on it" and think deeply about what would be best for the client.

6. **What plan of action will be most helpful in this situation?**

The counsellor makes an appointment with John and informs him that he will have to break confidentiality, since he feels that he would not be acting responsibly if he allows the stealing to continue. He tries to convince John that in the long term he might actually be helping him as well. John is given several options by the counsellor regarding the reporting of the theft himself, by the counsellor, or with the two of them seeing the appropriate authorities together.

Some counsellors like to develop a decision-making chart to help them with their ethical dilemmas. John's case could be presented as below:

Virtue Ethics Approaches

Most ethical decision-making models are based on principle ethics. Virtue ethics start from a different premise. According to Remley and Herlihy

Options for Action	Benefits	Risks	Probable Outcomes
Option 1 Avoid the issue	May be the easiest	The problem is not resolved.	Counsellor could lose his job.
Option 2 Keep counselling John and encourage him to make restitution.	Counsellor can keep using professional judgement as to what is best for John.	John comes for counselling but does not provide restitution.	Things might work out, but no consideration is made for the hardware store owner.
Option 3 After informing John of intended actions, report the activities to the appropriate authorities	In the long term, help John to act more responsibly.	Lose John as a client, and possibly other clients.	Initially, John would be angry, but would see that the stealing had to stop.

(2005), ethical decision-making involves more than moral actions based on principles; it also involves traits of character and virtue. Virtue ethics focus on the counsellor as a person. Virtue ethics then, are about subjective qualities, characteristics, habits and traits that lead a counsellor to a particular choice and subsequent action. With virtue ethics, counsellors do not follow established articles, rules or guidelines, but rather follow what a virtuous person would do under the circumstances. Ultimately, counsellors ask the question "Who shall I be?" Oakley (1996) outlines the main features of virtue ethics:

- An action is right if and only if it is what an individual possessing a virtuous character would do under the circumstances

- A description of admirable human traits is needed before a determination can be made about what is right in a given situation

- Virtues are valuable for their own sake and not for the outcome they may provide

- Virtues are objectively good. That is, being compassionate and caring is virtuous whether a person wants to be caring or not

Feminist ethics have also contributed a greatly to the issue of care in ethical decision-making. In the more than twenty years since Carol Gilligan's (1982) book, *In a Different Voice*, was printed, much has been written about the issue of care in relation to ethical issues. Ethical decisions are influenced by a concern for keeping and nurturing relationships. According to Gilligan, Ward and Taylor (1988), men are more likely to make ethical decisions based on justice. Justice implies that good solutions are found. Women see ethical decisions more in terms of care; namely, that clients be protected from harm. Thus, to women, relationships and care are more important than simple justice. Feminist ethics are far more likely to see ethical decision-making as a gray area, with many possible solutions. But what is first and foremost is the ethical article of how best to help and care for the client.

In summary, the virtue ethics model believes that counsellors are motivated to be virtuous and caring because they believe it is the right thing to do. The model recognizes the importance of emotions in decision-making. Finally, the virtue ethics model believes that counsellors must know themselves, their convictions, prejudice and attitudes.

Although a step-by-step methodology is much more difficult with virtue ethics, the following phases are an attempt to suggest some processes in using virtue ethics.

Phase One: Examine the Situation through Personal Awareness
Counsellors following a virtue ethics approach believe that emotion will inform their judgement. Counsellors might ask themselves questions such as:

- What emotions do I feel as I consider the ethical dilemma?

- How are these emotions influencing me (for example: emotions such as fear, responsibility, ambiguity and self-doubt)?

- What are my emotions telling me to do?

- Who do I want to be?

Phase Two: Examine the Situation through a Social/Cognitive/Emotive Process

Questions to consider during this phase include:

- How will my decision affect other stakeholders in this ethical dilemma?

- Do I need more information before I can make a decision?

- What are the positive, neutral, and negative consequences for each option that I have?

- What decision would I feel best about publicizing?

- Will my decision change if I share it with colleague?

Phase Three: Examine Competing Values

Counsellors need to prepare themselves to recognize their values and the implications of their values in ethical decision-making:

- What do I value most in my work as a counsellor?

- How can my values best show caring for the client in this situation?

- How can emotional decision-making exercises (imagery, incubation, vision quest, meditation) help me decide?

- What decision would best define who I am as a person?

- Am I willing to act on my values?

Phase Four: Plan and Take Action

The last question in Phase Two points to this action phase.

- What do I need to do to best plan and take action?

- What are some counter measures that I may have to take?

- How can I best evaluate my course of action?

In the final analysis, much of ethical decision-making depends on professional attitudes and judgment. Cottone and Tarvydas (2003, pp. 89-91) delineate several important counsellor attitudes in decision-making:

- Maintain an attitude of *reflection*. Counsellors reflect on their own issues and values and attempt to understand the issues and values of all others involved in the situation.

- Address *balance* between issues and parties to the ethical dilemma.

- Pay close attention to the *context* of the situation. Counsellors are aware of the client and community implications of their decision.

- Use a process of *collaboration* with all the parties in the situation.

Chapter Summary

Three major topics for this introductory chapter were discussed: counselling ethics, values, and virtue ethics.

The chapter began with a background summary of the *Canadian Counselling Association Code of Ethics*. Understanding the foundational principles of counselling clarifies subsequent ethics and standards of practice. Counsellors need to know that their personal values can influence their clients, and that they cannot keep their own values out of the counselling process. If values differences interfere with the counselling, counsellors may have to refer clients to other counsellors.

The second topic discussed in this chapter centred on the counsellor as a professional helper. Intentionality, the moral principles of the helping professions, knowledge of ethics and the law, decision-making skills and models, and the courage of personal convictions were the various factors examined as being related to the role of the professional counsellor. The final topic centered on ethical decision-making. The process steps of the CCA principle-based model were explored:

- examination of key ethical issues of a particular situation

- relationship of ethical articles from the *Code of Ethics* to the situation under question

- application of moral and ethical principles

- consideration of the consequences of possible action

- addition of emotional elements to the decision-making process, and action is taken.

Finally, key aspects of virtue ethics were considered:

- examination of the situation through personal awareness

- examination of the situation through a social/cognitive/emotive process

- examination of competing values

- planning and taking action.

Learning Activities

1. *Journal.* In your journal, write short responses to the following questions:
   a) What makes you think that you can help others?
   b) What concerns do you have as a beginning counsellor?
   c) Will you be able to leave your counselling in the office at the end of the day?

2. *Debate.* In small groups of two to four, debate the following issues:
   a) Can counsellors remain neutral to client values?
   b) Will counsellors' religious values influence how they counsel clients?

3. *Group Discussion.* In small groups, discuss how the life experiences of group members might help and/or hinder them in their counselling.

4. *Role-play.* Some counsellors have difficulty working with certain clients (e.g. sexual abusers, people from different religious groups, prisoners). In a role-reversal role-play, counsel (and be) a client that you believe you might have difficulty in counselling.

5. *Values Clarification.* Kinnier, Kernes and Dautheribes (2000, pp. 4-16) suggest the following list of universal moral values:
   — Commitment to something greater than oneself
   — Self-respect
   — Respect and caring for others
   — Caring for other living things and the environment.
   Do you agree with this list? Discuss these values with a partner.

6. *Self-Examination.* Examine your own values and biases from the following list of value-charged issues:
   suicide
   birth control
   assisted suicide
   cross-racial adoption
   sexual identity issues
   abortion
   religious beliefs
   unwed pregnancy
   discipline of children
   death and dying

dishonesty

same-sex marriages

drug use

welfare recipients

References

Albright, D.E., & Hazler, R.J. (1995) A right to die: Ethical dilemmas of euthanasia. *Counseling and Values*, 39 (3), 177-189.

American Counseling Association. (2000, 1995) *ACA Code of ethics and standards of practice*. Alexandria, VA: Author.

Canadian Counselling Association. (1989) *Guidelines for ethical behaviour*. Ottawa, Ontario: Author.

Canadian Counselling Association. (1999) *CCA code of ethics*. Ottawa, Ontario: Author.

Canadian Counselling Association. (2006) *CCA code of ethics*. Ottawa, Ontario: Author.

Corey, G., Corey, M., & Callanan, P. (1998) *Issues and ethics in the helping professions* (5th ed.). Pacific Grove, CA: Brooks/Cole.

Corey, G., Corey, M., & Callanan, P. (2003) *Issues and ethics in the helping professions* (6th ed.). Pacific Grove, CA: Brooks/Cole.

Cottone, R.R., & Tarvydas, V.M. (2003) *Ethical and professional issues in counselling* (2nd ed.). Upper Saddle River, NJ: Merrill Prentice Hall.

Forester-Miller, H., & Davis, T.E. (1995) *A practitioner's guide to ethical decision-making*. Alexandria, VA: American Counseling Association.

Gilligan, C. (1982) *In a different voice*. Cambridge, MA: Harvard University Press.

Gilligan, C., Ward, V., & Taylor, J. (1988) *Mapping the moral domain: A contribution of women's thinking to psychology and education*. Cambridge, MA: Harvard University Press.

Goodson, I. & Hargreaves, A. (Eds) (1996) *Teachers' professional lives*. London: Falmer Press.

Herlihy, B., & Corey, G. (1996) *ACA ethical standards casebook* (5th ed). Alexandria, VA: American Counseling Association.

Keith-Spiegal, P., & Koocher, G. (1985) *Ethics in psychology: Professional standards and cases*. New York: Random House.

Kinnier, R.T., Kernes, J.L., & Dautheribes, T.M. (2000). A short list of universal moral values. *Counseling and Values*, 45, 4-16.

Oakley, J. (1996) Varieties of virtue ethics. *Ratio*, 9, 128-152.

Peterson, J.V., & Nisenholz, B. (1987) *Orientation to counselling*. Boston: Allyn & Bacon.

Remley, T.P., & Herlihy, B. (2005) *Ethical, legal, and professional issues in counseling*. (2nd ed.). Upper Saddle River, NJ: Pearson.

Schulz, W.E. (1994) *Counselling ethics casebook*. Ottawa: Canadian Guidance and Counselling Association.

Schulz, W.E. (2000) *Counselling ethics casebook 2000*. Ottawa: Canadian Guidance and Counselling Association.

Stadler, A. (1985) *Confidentiality: The professionals' dilemma*. AACD Video Cassette Series. Alexandria, VA: AACD Foundation.

Sue, D.W., Arrendondo, P., & McDavis, R. (1992) Multicultural counseling competencies and standards: A call to the profession. *Journal of Counseling and Development*, 70, 477-486.

Chapter Two

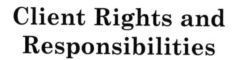

Client Rights and Responsibilities

Informed consent is an attempt to ensure
that the trust required of the patient is truly
justified, that the power of the therapist is not
abused intentionally or inadvertently, and
that the caring of the therapist is expressed
in ways that the patient clearly understands
and desires. (Pope & Vasquez, p. 75)

Chapter Objectives

The major focus of the chapter is on the rights and responsibilities of clients. The specific objectives are to:

- Help counsellors understand the concept of informed consent

- Promote a clearer understanding of how the counselling profession's Code of Ethics and Standards of Practice for Counsellors define informed consent in practice

- Increase understanding of the ethical nature of informed consent versus the legal nature of informed consent

- Distinguish between informed consent as a process and informed consent as a discrete act

- Gain a clearer understanding of informed consent as it relates to children and persons with diminished capacity

Self-Inventory

Directions: Before reading this chapter, please use the following scale to indicate your attitudes towards issues in this chapter. For each statement, indicate the response that most closely identifies your beliefs and attitudes. Use the following code:

5 = Strong agreement with this item
4 = Agreement with this item
3 = Undecided about this item
2 = Disagreement with this item
1 = Strong disagreement with this item

___ Informed consent is a process engaged in by the client and counsellor rather than a singular event at the beginning of counselling.

___ Informed consent is more closely related to legal issues than to ethical issues.

___ Every client has a legal right to give informed consent.

___ Obtaining informed consent from clients for counselling protects counsellors from future liability.

___ Minors living independently have the same legal right as mature minors to give consent.

___ The primary goal of informed consent is the protection of clients.

___ Informed consent allows clients to understand their involvement in counselling.

___ Clients may believe the counsellor is reticent to see them if the counsellor focuses too much on the hazards of counselling.

___ Mature minors have the legal right to give informed consent without parental involvement.

___ Record-keeping procedures should be part of the informed consent form.

___ Clients who are mentally disabled are generally competent to provide consent to counselling.

___ Signing a consent form is part of a counselling plan. It is one of many decisions made within a collaborative relationship.

Introduction

Clients' rights and responsibilities generally equate to the concept of informed consent. Daily, counsellors and clients engage daily in a process that requires considerable disclosure. Yet, informed consent and how it relates to the rights of clients, like confidentiality, is multi-layered and not as well-understood as it ought to be. Counsellors continue to address concerns related to informed consent such as requests from other parties to release or to share information, informing clients about the nature of the treatment in which they are about to engage, or informing clients about confidentiality and the limits imposed by the expectation to maintain absolute confidentiality. This chapter explores the rights and responsibilities of clients from the perspective of informed consent, and clarifies the importance of informed consent in the ethical counselling process.

What is Informed Consent?

The answer to this question might seem self-evident to counsellors who have yet to explore the complexities of the term; however, many counsellors agree that informed consent refers to rules or stipulations that govern how counsellors can interact with clients. Legally, consent is a contractual relationship. The consent agreement is premised on a special relationship of trust often called a "fiduciary" relationship. This means that the counsellor acts in a manner that benefits the client. Informed consent is required to establish an ethical counselling relationship. Effecting a proper consent necessitates completion of the so-called "consent process", which is somewhat more involved and detailed than simply getting a signature on a form.

O'Neill (1998) contends that the three main issues in informed consent include the sort and amount of information a client needs to make a truly informed decision. They are:

• specific consent

• information about alternative treatments, and

• information about the counsellor's conception of the problem and alternative conceptions.

Informed consent requires that clients make choices to enter or continue counselling knowingly, intelligently, and voluntarily. And, because the idea of informed consent has both ethical and legal expectations, counsellors must consider possibilities of litigation and sanctions. These potential sanctions may be imposed if counsellors deviate from the expectations of their professional associations as well as those of society at large. Counsellors must promote the ethical value of autonomy, and uphold their clients' right to self-determination in the counselling relationship with respect to treatment and on-going care.

The most important goals of informed consent are the protection of clients' interests and an endorsement of clients' autonomy. The *Standards of Practice for Counsellors* (CCA, 2001) states that informed consent is essential for the rights of clients to self-determination. Central to informed consent are:

- autonomy

- freedom from external constraints, and

- the right to determine life direction.

The principle of autonomy, enshrined in many professional codes of ethics, is hampered when it interferes with others' rights to self-determination, as in the *Tarasoff* case described in Chapter Three. In this case, a psychologist considers the rights of a third party not to be injured by his client.

Making self-governing decisions does not necessarily mean that decisions are made independently of others. At times, an ideal for individual freedom exists that might contradict the culture and society to which an individ-

ual may be linked. Self-determination or autonomy is a complex principle and in some ways, respecting autonomy may be more complicated in practice than once assumed. Counsellors must consider how people relate to others, and how their interests often reflect social values rather than self-interest. These relationships may reflect a truer picture of how people operate in everyday life.

In making informed choices, people demonstrate their ability to self-legislate and to self-govern. Emmanuel Kant believed that the ability of people to self-legislate made them unique. By exercising their wills, their self-ruling capacities, this ethical ideal of the intrinsic worth and dignity of persons is proven. It is a quality that is explained in terms of each individual's unique ability to be autonomous.

Whenever people make decisions or choices, they are influenced by outer and inner checks (Am I doing the right thing? Do I have enough information? Do I have enough experience? What are my fears?). Although clients cannot freely opt for something they do not understand, when given intelligible information pertinent to their counselling decisions, they can decide whether to consent to the implementation of a therapeutic plan. Consent as self-governing approval then, is justified both by respect for the autonomy of clients and as a means of protecting their individual well-being.

Informed consent is a process during which counsellors inform individuals about the nature of the counselling experience. O'Neill (1998) stated, "The two main ways of protecting the public from the healer are oversight and consent. Throughout most of the history of healing, the emphasis was on oversight:

monitoring of professional activity by professional associations, regulatory bodies, or the courts. The *Nuremberg Declaration* gave a new privileged position to consent, putting control into the hands of the client" (p. 13-14). The declaration specified that "voluntary consent of the human subject is absolutely essential in medical research and treatment" (p.13).

Beahrs and Gutheil (2001), in their review and synthesis of the history of informed consent in the United States recommend that counsellors convey to prospective clients, information that is material to personal decision-making. They warn that, in America, "informed consent is in the process of becoming mandatory for psychotherapeutic practice because the law says so under penalty of liability judgements of seven to eight figures" (p. 5). In contrast, though health practitioners are required by law to seek informed consent, litigation on this issue in Canada is minimal at the time of this writing. This issue appears to be related to the requirement that claimants must prove that harm resulting from treatment must relate to not having been adequately informed, a legal stipulation which can be very difficult to prove.

Pope and Vasquez (1991) comment on the decision-making involved in consent. Sumarah, Lehr and Wheeldon (2000) also discuss this as dialogue and discernment, a process, which involves the "right time" to discuss consent. The *CCA Code of Ethics* (2006) suggests that counsellors inform clients as soon as possible, but does not detail how this should be accomplished. For example, perhaps an initial session requires an immediate intervention as in the case of suicide. Or, perhaps the client is in tears, is distraught, or wants to talk

about abuse issues. When would be an appropriate time to talk about consent? Consent as an ongoing process needs to take these issues into account. Sumarah et al. also stresses the nature of this ongoing need to provide information to the client at various points throughout the counselling process.

Informed Consent and Professional Ethics

Most professional codes of ethics discuss consent, and the process used to elicit it. For example, both the Canadian Counselling Association (CCA) and the American Counselling Association (ACA) codes of ethics cover many areas in which consent are important. The concept permeates The *CCA Code of Ethics* (2006), and covers all areas in which people have to be informed when they agree to engage in a counselling relationship. This includes a general responsibility to obtain consent as well as obtaining consent in the following specific situations:

- when counselling minors or persons unable to give voluntary consent

- when a dual relationship cannot be avoided

- when participating in assessment, and

- when participating in research.

Although the focus of this chapter is from the Canadian perspective, counsellors might find the differences between American and Canadian perspectives interesting. Counsellors are also alerted to the fact that Canadian and American law, and hence possible litigation, can be quite different. For those interested in pursuing this topic further, Corey, Corey and Callanan (2003) provide a good American perspective on informed consent, as well as counsellor and client rights and responsibilities.

Clients' Rights and Counsellors' Responsibilities

Counsellors need to inform clients of their rights and responsibilities before entering into the counselling process or as soon as possible once the process has begun. Clients value counsellors who go through this process with them. For example, research by Sullivan, Martin, and Handelsman (1993) shows higher ratings from participants to therapists who use an informed-consent procedure, and more willingness to recommend them to friends, and to go to these therapists themselves. Professionals who use informed consent are rated as more expert and trustworthy than those who do not. In addition to the ethical and legal obligations to obtain consent, these findings contribute to therapeutic rapport, which can be effective in promoting the effectiveness of counselling.

The role of informed consent in the professional work of counsellors is outlined in the *CCA Code of Ethics* (2006), which articulates the ethics of informed consent, and in the *Standards of Practice for Counsellors* (CCA, 2001), which interprets the various articles of the *CCA Code of Ethics*. Beginning with Article B4, "Clients Rights and Informed Consent" the *CCA Code of Ethics* states:

> When counselling is initiated, and throughout the counselling process as necessary, counsellors inform clients of the purposes, goals, techniques, procedures, limitations, potential risks and benefits of services to be per-

formed, and other such pertinent information. Counsellors make sure that clients understand the implications of diagnosis, fees and fee collection arrangements, record-keeping, and limits to confidentiality. Clients have the right to participate in the ongoing counselling plans, to refuse any recommended services, and to be advised of the consequences of such refusal.

From the outset, Article B4 establishes informed consent as a process rather than a single event. On an ongoing basis, counsellors continue to inform and remind clients about their rights as well as their responsibilities. Counsellors tell clients at the beginning of the counselling process why they are together and the possible outcomes that might result from engaging in a therapeutic conversation. They also discuss how they will achieve those particular outcomes, and equally important, they discuss limitations, risks and benefits of participating in counselling. Informed consent does not stop there. It makes transparent the whole process. There should be no surprises for the client. Cottone (2001) and Lehr and Sumarah (2004) state that the counselling process is one of dialogue, collaboration, and consensus-making so that both the client and the counsellor are aware of all expectations and assumptions.

Despite the requirement to inform, many beginning and experienced counsellors often fall short of a full disclosure of information necessary to defend having fully informed the client. Frequently, counsellors are silent on the issue or, at best, discuss only limitations, which generally relate to limits placed on confidentiality. Although important, this is only a small portion of the information clients need to make informed decisions.

Voluntarily, Knowingly and Intelligently

The *Standards of Practice for Counsellors* (CCA, 2001) provides additional information about the process of informed consent, starting from the premise that potential clients must give consent voluntarily, knowingly, and intelligently. Voluntarily means clients freely agree to participate in any professional service their counsellor provides. People cannot be forced to accept the services of a counsellor. This is consistent with Canadian law discussed later in this chapter, which works on the principle that everyone has a right to agree to or to refuse treatment unless specific legislation or a court order/directive removes that right. For example, even individuals who are incarcerated have a right to consent to or to refuse treatment. People cannot be coerced into accepting treatment. Rozvosky (2003) cites R.V. *Sookochoff* (1985), in which the Saskatchewan court of Queen's Bench declares that partaking in a treatment program cannot be imposed as a condition of a probation order without the offender's consent.

Voluntarily giving consent implies there are no powerful incentives for people to participate in counselling, such as promotion, monetary gains, or pressure (such as threatening a student to accept the services of a school counsellor).

Counsellors fully disclose information that is vital to clients to understand the services they will receive. This disclosure allows the client the opportunity to give consent knowingly. This knowledge includes:

- the type of information that has to be reported to a third party such as information related to child abuse in any form

- note-taking policies

- protection of client information

- retention of records

- accessibility of records

The list of information provided to clients should be inclusive.

The concept of consenting intelligent consent, expanded upon in a separate section in this chapter, refers to the client having the capacity to understand what treatment entails, the possible benefits of this treatment, and the possible consequences of the treatment. Clients need to have the ability to sufficiently comprehend information provided to them to make their decision. When the client's rights to voluntarily, knowingly and intelligently engage in the counselling process are respected, counsellors promote an open and honest counselling climate.

The *CCA Code of Ethics* (2006) and the *Standards of Practice for Counsellors* (CCA, 2001) extensively outline the rights of clients and responsibilities of counsellors. Together, they specify that counsellors seek full and active participation from clients in decisions that affect them, respecting and integrating as much as possible their opinions and wishes. The client and counsellor recognize that informed consent is a process of reaching agreements to work collaboratively, rather than simply having a consent form signed. The Canadian Psychological Association's (CPA) *Code of Ethics* (2000) also addresses the role of the community of people that are often involved in a person's life such as family and significant community members, and includes them by stating that psychologists respect the expressed wishes of persons to involve others in their decision-making regarding informed consent. This includes respect for written as well as clearly expressed unwritten advance directives. Both counsellors and psychologists ensure that clients understand:

- the purpose and nature of the activity in which they are about to engage

- responsibilities of each party

- confidentiality protections and limitations

- likely benefits and risks

- alternatives

- the likely consequences of non-action

- the option to refuse or withdraw at any time, without prejudice

- over what period of time the consent applied, and

- how to rescind consent if desired.

Informed Consent and Canadian Law

The legal environment in Canada is changing. The *Standards of Practice for Counsellors* (CCA, 2001) quote R. Solomon, a Canadian law professor, who comments on a shift from paternalistic to rights-based principles of education and treatment, and to a recognition that the young, the mentally ill and the elderly who are competent, can make their own health and care decisions, independent of others. Canadian law now regards improper consent as a negligence issue (i.e., negligently obtaining consent). The law on consent relates to all types of procedures and treatments, and can be given orally, in written form

or as a combination of both. Communication between the counsellor and the client is vital in the process of obtaining consent. The client may remain silent because of uncertainty about the counselling process. Agreement to treatment may seem to be affirmed because of linguistic difficulties related to professional language or simply because the client's first language is not the language of the counsellor. Necessary weight must be given to the process of informed consent in both of these cases, before assuming that a person's conduct signifies consent.

Criteria for a valid consent

To ensure that counsellors have the legal consent of clients to engage in a counselling relationship, all criteria for proper authorization must be observed, otherwise the consent process and the authorization for counselling is negated. Rozvosky (2003), writes extensively on consent to treatment in the health professions. He puts forward the following criteria that clients need to meet for consent to be valid:

- Clients must be legally competent to consent to treatment.

- Clients must possess the mental capacity to authorize care.

- Clients must receive a proper disclosure of information from the caregiver.

- Client authorization should be specific to the procedure to be performed.

- Clients should have an opportunity to ask questions and to receive understandable answers.

- Client authorization should be free of undue influence and coercion.

These criteria and conditions have implications for counsellors who request informed consent for treatment or other aspects of counselling. To ensure that the criteria and conditions are met, counsellors who enter into a counselling relationship should also keep in mind the importance of documenting their process for informed consent. The importance of this will be covered later in this chapter.

Legally Competent: Children and Adolescents

There is a misconception among some counsellors that the age of majority is the age of consent. This is not generally the case in Canada, but many counsellors still insist on the signature of parents or guardians for youth who are eighteen or nineteen years old. Counsellors who continue to act in this manner probably do so because of a lack of knowledge of the issues or to protect themselves from liability suits. School counsellors are especially frustrated with the lack of direction given to them regarding the age of consent.

In actuality, the law presumes that all persons, including children, have a legal right to give an authorization for treatment. This presumption however, is not absolute, since it can be removed by legislation as well as by judicial directives. Schools are interesting places in terms of valid consent because they are often involved with parents, who care about their children and often want to know what is happening to them. This situation complicates matters for school counsellors who are also faced with administrators who must consider what they perceive as the rights of parents. It could be helpful for counsellors if they were familiar with provincial legislation regarding consent

in their region, especially since the age of consent may differ depending on the province or territory.

The *Standards of Practice for Counsellors* (CCA, 2001) offers a similar position on this issue:

> The parents and guardians of younger children have the legal authority to give consent on their behalf. However, the parental right to give consent diminishes, and may even terminate as the child grows older and acquires sufficient understanding and intelligence to fully comprehend the conditions for informed consent. Counsellors should be vigilant to keep themselves informed of their statutory obligations with respect to the rights of children, including their right to privacy and self-determination commensurate with their ability to do so and with regard to their best interests. (p. 11)

This particular standard raises many questions related to children's ability to give consent to treatment. Counsellors, especially school counsellors, struggle daily with the issue of an appropriate age and ability to give consent, and though there are no definitive answers available for counsellors, the process of determining whether a minor can give consent has become clearer. Rozvosky (2003) summarizes some of the available legislation on this issue, citing the *Medical Consent of Minors* legislation in New Brunswick and the *Health Care Directives Act* in Manitoba, which specifically establishes the age of consent to treatment for minors at sixteen years.

In New Brunswick, following the common law by which younger children may be capable of consenting, the statute allows consent under the age of 16-years-old. Interestingly, the *Medical Consent of Minors Act* in New Brunswick states that only a doctor or a dentist can give the required opinion regarding the patient's capacity to consent. This would mean that a 16-year-old individual might consent to counselling; however, for youth under 16 years of age, a physician or dentist must be involved.

In Quebec, the Civil Code of Quebec legislation sets the age at fourteen years. In Alberta, a mature minor can refuse or consent to treatment, but if the child were to be placed under child welfare legislation as a child in need of protection, that right would be lost. British Columbia counsellors are directed to the *Infant's Act*, which validates the common law by stating that a minor can legally consent to health care without any consent from a parent or guardian as long as the individual has met the legal conditions of informed consent. Counsellors in various parts of the country should become familiar with the legislation they need to consider when seeking the consent of minors.

Mature Minor
The Canadian Counselling Association's *Code of Ethics* (2006) states in article B5, that:

B5 **CHILDREN AND PERSONS WITH DIMINISHED CAPACITY**
Counsellors conduct the informed consent process with those legally appropriate to give consent when counselling, assessing, and having as research subjects children and/or persons with diminished capacity. These clients also give consent to such services or involvement commensurate with their capacity to do so. Counsellors understand that the parental or guardian right to consent on behalf of children diminishes commensurate with the child's growing capacity to provide informed consent.

This particular article allows counsellors to make judgements about what they ought to do, but does not specify an age at which a person could give informed consent. The *Standards of Practice for Counsellors* (CCA, 2001) refers to the principle of responsible caring, and indicates that this responsibility diminishes with age, without saying which age would be appropriate for independent thinking and decision-making. In addition, article B5 uses the phrase "...legally appropriate to give consent". This creates confusion since there are no established laws stating a legal age for giving consent in most regions of Canada. Legal precedent can, for example, allow adolescents much younger than the age of majority to give consent.

Tim Bond (1993), a leading ethicist in the field of counselling cites the legal precedence setting of the Gillick case in the United Kingdom, which establishes a common law position that as long youth under 16 years of age understand the nature of the issues and consequences involved, they are deemed competent, and therefore have a legal right to make an autonomous decision. This view is consistent with a review of literature of children's problem-solving abilities, which found that around age twelve, most minors had attained the formal operations stage of cognitive development that predominated in the general population and therefore, intellectual capacity was not a valid argument for denying minors over twelve years of age, as a group, the right of independent consent to treatment or veto of parental consent (Grisso & Vierling, 1978). The experimental studies by Keith-Spiegel and Mass (1981), and Weithorn and Campbell (1982) independently support this conclusion. Another study by Leathley (1990), and later supported by Beeman and Scott (1991) reports that 42 percent of psychologists in the New Zealand study, support the right of a 12-year-old child to privacy over the right of his or her parents to have access to information shared in the therapeutic context.

The concept of *Mature Minor Consent* relates closely with the legal age of consent. A sufficient body of common law in Canada states that, regardless of age, minors are capable of consenting or refusing consent to treatment if they are able to appreciate the nature and purpose of the treatment, and the consequences of giving or refusing consent. In these situations, the parents' consent is neither required nor can it override the minor's decision. If children are capable of consenting, this could suffice, and the consent of the parent is not needed. A counsellor might have valid reasons for requesting parental consent and sometimes it is wise to insist on parental agreement and involvement however, obtaining the agreement of parents should not be seen as parental consent which authorizes counselling. Except in unusual cases when a child is not a mature minor, the parents have exclusive decision-making authority.

The Court of Queen's Bench in Alberta (*Chiniliar v. Chiniliar*, 2001) defines the mature minor as "one with the capacity to understand the nature and consequences of medical treatment". Rozvosky (2003) states that the mental capability of consenting is really the capacity to understand the information which has to be given to the person

seeking treatment in order to obtain a valid consent. The law, he believes, seems to now favour the *Mature Minor Rule*, and considers the uniqueness of each case to determine if a child is capable of understanding the nature and consequences of a treatment decision.

Under the *Mature Minor Rule*, when a minor is considered to be a mature minor, counsellors treat that person as an adult as far as making a decision regarding care or treatment. No parental consent is required. Rozvosky states, "Any disagreement between a mature minor and his or her parent is irrelevant. Parents cannot overrule decisions made by their mature minor children. If a child is not a mature minor, then except in unusual cases, the parents have exclusive decision-making authority" (p. 82). The intent here is not to exclude parents from the process. Counsellors often encourage parental involvement in their children's counselling, and include this as part of the informed consent process.

The *Mature Minor Rule* places responsibility upon counsellors and other health care providers to get to know their client; just as it does in the adult treatment context. It requires counsellors to establish strong communication links with prospective clients. Some children are capable of understanding the nature and consequences of treatment decisions at age twelve, whereas some children at the age of fifteen years remain too immature to understand the nature of issues like abortion or birth control, concerns which school counsellors often address. If a particular 15-year-old youth is considered immature, his or her consent to treatment would not withstand legal scrutiny, whereas in another case, a counsellor could respect the decision of a 12-year-old child, an age which is often considered appropriate by psychologists to ask for consent. Counsellors and other health professionals, therefore, need to address the age at which children may consent on their own behalf quite apart from their parents, and whether children who can consent on their own behalf are still subject to a government agency under child welfare legislation in their province or territory.

From a counselling perspective, if a client, especially a minor, is not mentally capable of understanding issues related to their involvement in counselling, someone else's consent to counselling should be substituted. Clements and Uhlemann (1991) point out the difficulty of following the legally correct approach of the mature minor rule. They believe that it might be difficult to apply in practice because of pressure from parents and employers: "...school counsellors may not be able to counsel students without parental consent or may not be able to maintain client confidentiality because school board polices permit disclosures to parents" (p. 210). In many cases, however, neither school boards nor schools have developed policies regarding consent to treatment and access to school records. Counsellors and school administrators, despite the Mature Minor Rule, appear to favour talking to and obtaining permission from parents or guardians.

Emancipated Minor

Counsellors who work with children and adolescents also need to become familiar with the concept of the emancipated minor. This is especially true of school counsellors who often appear confused about issues related to an emancipated minor, or more simply put,

a young person who lives independently of his parents, who may even be married, or who might be in the military, but who has not yet reached the age of majority. In many cases, the rule of the emancipated minor might deem these young persons as adults for consent to treatment.

In Canada, some professionals in the helping or health professions sometimes rely upon the Emancipated Minor Rule to rationalize a young person making treatment choices without having to involve parents. The basic rule of informed consent remains for the emancipated minor as it does for everyone: the law presumes that all persons are legally and mentally capable of giving consent in the absence of contradictory proof. In other words, counsellors assess each case independently against the criteria required for consent as they would under the Mature Minor Rule. Clements and Uhlemann (1991) add that, in practice, Canadian health care professionals usually apply a combination of both the Emancipated Minor Rule and Mature Minor Rule when making decisions.

Mental Capacity to Consent

Persons seeking treatment must possess the mental capacity to provide authorization for treatment. The law assumes that everyone has the mental capacity to consent until found otherwise under the appropriate legislation. Potential clients therefore, need to possess the ability to reach a reasoned choice about treatment. In some instances, counsellors could be faced with individuals who are highly suicidal. These circumstances might be considered exceptional; however, the onus would still be on the counsellor to assess and determine whether or not this person had the mental capacity to make a decision.

The *Standards of Practice for Counsellors* (CCA, 2001) addresses mental capacity with respect to children and persons with diminished capacity. It recognizes that the young, the mentally ill, and the elderly who are competent, can make their own health and care decisions independent of others. Counsellors need to avoid mistakenly preventing persons who are competent to agree to their own treatment, and failing to prevent those not competent from the harmful effects of their own decisions. Although to date no uniform standard of competency exists, the ability of older adults to provide informed consent voluntarily depends upon their level of competency and their ability to comprehend their circumstances. A person's competency might be assessed by determining whether the person demonstrates a reasonable choice based upon rational reasons, whether the person has the ability to understand information vital to the decision-making process, and whether the person has a real understanding of that information.

Another interesting component of consent that counsellors need to consider is the linguistic ability of their clients. Counsellors need to ensure that individuals seeking treatment have the ability to understand the language in which they are being informed, and upon which they base consent. This continues to be an interesting dilemma for some counsellors. In the Canadian context, counsellors most often counsel in either the French or English language. However, given the diversity of the Canadian population, it is not uncommon for individuals to receive service in their first language. If, for example, an English speaking counsellor seeks consent from someone whose first language is not English, the counsellor must assess the level of comprehension of that individual. A person may demonstrate adequate functional language to buy groceries or gasoline for their car, and probably to travel on the local bus, however, to understand the complexities of the counselling process and the context of counselling requires that clients understand at a different level of comprehension; that of the counsellor's professional language. People whose first language is not that of the counsellor may need greater explanation of the counselling process and what it requires. The onus is on the counsellor to guarantee that the client understands what is being discussed, and to which processes they are giving their consent.

An interesting Canadian legal case, Schanczl v. Singh (1987), was influential in establishing the basis of language in informed consent. In this case, the liability was placed upon the physician to ensure that the patient, whose first language was not that of the physician's, adequately understood the information provided by the physician in order to obtain consent. In *Schanczl v. Singh*, the Alberta court of Queen's Bench imposed liability on a physician for failure to disclose material risks, and in so doing emphasized the plaintiff's difficulty in understanding English. The court surmised that this difficulty "placed a special duty on [the defendant] to be certain that his patient understood the alternatives available to him". In Rozvosky's (2003) summary of this case, he said: "The key to consent is communication and therefore the language used must achieve that objective" (p. 13). The implications for counsellors would, in all likelihood, be similar to those of physicians or any other health service provider.

Adequate Disclosure of Information

The last two decades have seen a shift away from a paternalistic attitude towards consent, where health professionals simply provided information to patients or clients to the degree that it was acceptable by other professional standards, to a more person-centred approach. In the landmark case of *Reibl v. Hughes* (1980), the ruling on the expectation of informed consent states that "...what the average prudent person, the reasonable person in the patient's particular position, would agree to or not agree to, if all material and special risks of going ahead with the surgery or foregoing it were made known to him" (Rozvosky, 2003, p. 13). This ruling establishes the principle of providing information that a layperson would need to make a decision. Practioners now have to consider whether a reasonable person other than the client would consent if advised of those risks. If the answer is "yes", it means in all likelihood that the client has been advised appropriately. If the answer is "no", the client's rights may have been denied; a position counsellors need to avoid.

As a result of the *Reibl* decision, physicians and other health providers now take more time to provide information, and to make sure that persons seeking treatment, which includes counselling, understand the nature of the service or treatment being provided. This has been very favourable for the rights of people receiving treatment, and though physicians and other health care workers may be ensuring consent to prevent litigation, the reality exists

that there have been very few cases of negligence arising out of failure to provide informed consent.

Although no current summative information pertaining to *Reibl* appears to exist, 10 years after the Supreme Court of Canada doctrinal rulings, Robertson (1991) reviewed cases involving *Reibl*, and concluded that the true significance of the changes that were introduced by the Supreme Court of Canada may be more symbolic in nature in that they reflect a fundamental change in the doctor-patient relationship and the power and authority underlying that relationship. Robertson cites 82 percent of informed consent claims were dismissed, and of 23 cases recorded for 1990 and 1991, the informed consent claims failed. He believes they failed causation (that risks of treatment were not adequately disclosed), which was proving to be a formidable impediment for plaintiffs. In interpreting and applying *Reibl* for a decade, the courts carefully balanced the full disclosure standard against the objective standard of causation. As a result, in the majority of cases, the doctor, or other health professional was absolved of liability even when his disclosure was inadequate.

It seems, therefore, that the courts are applying the causation requirement in a way that is extremely favourable to defendants (physicians, counsellors), contributing to a growing acceptance by Canadian Courts that the greater confidence and trust (which a patient has in a physician or in other health care workers) the less likely a reasonable person in that patient's position would be to decline treatment recommended by the physician, even if full disclosure of material risks and alternatives were made. Informed consent plays only a minor role in malpractice proceedings, and the fundamental doctrinal changes introduced by the Supreme Court of Canada, far from expanding professional liability, have in fact restricted it.

The responsibility for health care professionals to provide adequate information is the cornerstone of what Rozvosky (2003) refers to as the most important key to a valid, "informed" consent. Questions addressed in legal cases now reflect whether or not someone received sufficient information upon which to make a decision. Even though persons receiving treatment could agree either orally or in writing to a particular treatment, if there were negative outcomes, the complaint of the patient is usually in the form of someone who saying, "If I had known that, I never would have consented to the procedure". The courts therefore, established rules to deal with the issue of what constitutes adequate disclosure, and if there is not adequate disclosure, whether the patient's rights have been infringed.

Opportunity to Ask Questions and to Receive Understandable Answers

This criterion, covered more extensively in the discussion on the process of negotiating consent, stipulates that counsellors should not make the process of consent a "rush job" prior to the client's treatment decision. They need to give people who come for counselling an opportunity to discuss the counselling process, and what is involved in that process. Issues regarding other forms of treatment also need to be addressed. An example might be that of drug therapy versus talk therapy. Some people may ask their counsellor about anti-depressants: Should I stay on the medication if things start to get better for me? Should

I also take anti-depressants while I am in treatment with you? These and other questions may arise. Counsellors give clients an opportunity to seek answers to questions regarding therapeutic relationships. This exchange of information might help the caregiver determine if the person truly understands the nature and consequences of the treatment.

Undue Influence and Coercion

The ability of people to consent to treatment depends in part on their ability to understand that they have the right to consent to or to refuse treatment. Children and adolescents often fall into this category, as discussed above. Counsellors are frequently unsure about "the court-mandated client", and how this might affect the process of consent. This is an example where, as part of sentencing, someone's right has been removed by the court so that they might receive treatment (Criminal Code of Canada, 1999), and counsellors would not need the person's consent to counselling. However, all counsellors realize the importance of engaging in a therapeutic relationship. The respect shown to non-court-mandated clients should also be provided to court-mandated persons. In all cases, counsellors need to be aware of the rights of individuals with whom they work.

Consent of the mentally disabled.

The *Standards of Practice for Counsellors* (CCA, 2001) states:

> A small number of adults with developmental disabilities, critical illnesses, serious injury, or other disabling conditions may be declared by a court to be legally incompetent. Each province has legislation which provides for the

conditions and procedures for such a determination. Counsellors should seek informed consent for individuals declared incompetent from their legal guardians. (p. 11)

It is important to note that "a small number of adults..." could be considered legally incompetent and therefore, would need a guardian to provide consent to treatment. Another perspective is that the individual's inability to agree to or to refuse treatment does not automatically follow if a person has a mental illness. Some people living with a mental illness, disability or other instances of diminished ability may be capable of consenting to treatment, whereas others may not. Because a 'one rule fits all' cannot be established, counsellors might, in the case of persons who are mentally disabled, proceed as they would with a mature minor, emancipated minor, or someone who might have linguistic difficulties.

Some clients may be able to understand and consent to some forms of treatment but not to others. Likewise, as in the case of people who may be experiencing hallucinations, they may be able to give consent when not having psychotic episodes but might not be able to give consent if they are. Again, the onus is on the counsellor to determine competency. The law is more concerned with whether or not a person with a mental disability has the rational facility to make a decision about their own health care. Counsellors are advised to become familiar with various provincial legislation that will assist them in determining ability to provide informed consent. One of the most comprehensive legislative acts is found in Ontario's *Health Care Consent Act,* (1996).

The Process of Informed Consent

Although it is important to discuss informed consent from the perspective of which information should be included on a form, it is vitally important to examine informed consent as a process, including the initial form counsellors might wish to have clients sign. This section of Chapter Two explores how informed consent can be integrated into the counsellor-client relationship in a manner that respects both the idea of informed consent and the imperatives of clinical care.

Many researchers and professionals agree that consent is multifaceted, and often involves more than a one-time explanation of treatment. There is a growing consensus that consent should involve a process, which is ongoing throughout the counselling contract rather than an immediate one-time explanation of treatment regardless of the actual situation. O'Neill, (1998) describes consent as ongoing and negotiated throughout the counselling process. Sumarah, Lehr and Wheeldon (2000) discuss the process as collaborative, whereby the counsellor and client enter into a dialogue around issues that are important in the counselling relationship, such as confidentiality. They believe this discernment is not something counsellors engage in from time to time, but that it ought to be a regular part of the therapeutic process. They believe a discussion of confidentiality, and hence informed consent, does not simply occur at the onset of counselling, but recurs as new circumstances warrant.

Informed consent is a process that requires a degree of shared decision-making between counsellor and client.

It resembles decisions in other aspects of life such as letting mechanics fix your car; contractors paint your house or install your plumbing. Berg et al. (2001) offer what they call a practical procedural framework that addresses consent as an event and consent as a continuous model. The model of consent as an event is based on the notion that it is atypical in counselling contexts for counsellors and clients to make a single decision with respect to consent, or for all necessary information to be available when a decision could be made. The event model of consent promotes "one-shot" education of clients with little opportunity for reflection and integration of information into people's underlying scheme of values, particularly since the decision must be made imminently, when a client's anxiety is likely to be at a peak.

In practice, the event model of consent, or what O'Neill (1998) refers to as specific consent, might be the model most widely assumed by counsellors. In specific consent, counsellors inform clients what they intend to do and outline the possible risks and benefits. Counsellors do not always inform clients about possible risks either because they do not fully appreciate these risks themselves or they do not want to upset their clients. These issues are covered in more detail below. Sometimes situations arise when counsellors believe that discussing risks might not be understood by clients or if understood, clients might refuse to engage in counselling. In other words, when clients come for counselling, counsellors might simply discuss the limits to confidentiality, and ask their clients if they have any questions they want to ask. At other points during the counselling process, these issues could arise

again as discrete items that needed to be addressed. Even if clients are easily able to assimilate information on a one-time basis, a single discussion is still not a good way of involving clients in the decision-making process.

Informed consent as negotiation

O'Neill (1998) gives the issue of informed consent considerable thought, and promotes the idea that informed consent is an ongoing negotiation between the helper and the client. In his study of 92 Canadian therapists over a five-year period, he asked therapists what they believed should be part of consent, and why? When did they obtain consent, and how did they decide when it should be renegotiated? How did clients experience the process? O'Neill concludes that discussion between therapist and client is not only an ethical issue but also one with therapeutic value. As an example, he indicates that therapists dealing with survivors of sexual abuse were likely to see active negotiation as a way of giving control of the process to a client whose history was marked by traumatic loss of control. Negotiating can have a general therapeutic value because therapists have an opportunity to clear up their own and their clients' misconceptions about causes for their trouble, as well as misconceptions about therapy and what they might expect from it.

Counselling changes over time. The client's initial concern changes as counselling progresses. In a collaborative approach, therapists negotiate the focus of counselling with clients over a period of time. Consent, although given initially for a specific issue, has to evolve as the nature of the counselling changes. Sometimes, at the outset of counselling, an issue is unclear to both therapist and client. As counselling proceeds, the initial presenting issue often changes. In short, counsellors may and should obtain general consent before starting therapy. However, because of the uniqueness of particular individuals, problems, and interventions, consent evolves over the course of therapy.

Informed consent as process

During the dynamic process of informed consent, counsellors and clients have opportunities to ensure they adequately understand their shared venture. The following important questions might be helpful for counsellors to consider in this process:

- Do I possess at least a sufficient initial understanding of why this person wants my help?

- Do I know what the client expects, hopes or fears from counselling?

- Does the client really understand the approach I will use in my counselling to address this problem?

- Does the client know the common effects of using such an approach, and alternative approaches to this problem?

Other questions relate to decision-making such as:

- When is the right time for me to discuss informed consent?

- When would be a good time for me to introduce and talk about informed consent?

Up to this point, the focus has been on questions and comments that might be useful for counsellors to consider in the informed consent process. However, even when given an opportunity, clients do not always come forward with questions for counsellors. Often, they do not

know what questions they should ask or which questions they are entitled to ask. They trust the counsellor. To be more inclusive of clients in this process of informed consent, Pomerantz and Handlesman (2004) posed a list of questions counsellors could provide to clients to help them seek answers to become more informed about the therapeutic process. The list is adapted and revised from an earlier one by Handelsman and Galvin in 1988:

- What is the name of your kind of therapy?

- How does your kind of therapy compare with other kinds of therapy?

- How does your kind of therapy work?

- What are the possible risks involved (like divorce, depression)?

- What percentage of clients improves? In what ways? How do you know (e.g. , published research, your own practice experience, discussions with your colleagues)?

- What percentage of clients improves or get worse without this therapy?

- How do you know?

- What should I do if I feel therapy isn't working?

- What other types of therapy or help are there (like support groups)?

- What are the risks and benefits of these other approaches?

- What kind of records do you keep? Who has access to them (e.g., insurance companies, supervisors, etc.)?

- How much influence does the insurance company have on the therapy?

- Who do I talk to if I have a complaint about therapy which we can't work out?

This list of questions also alerts counsellors to information about which they need to be knowledgeable. The interested reader is directed to the above authors for a more comprehensive list of questions that counsellors can provide to clients to help them become more informed about the counselling process.

Berg et al. (2001) presented a practical way of integrating informed consent into everyday clinical care; a model in which informed consent is rooted in the helping relationship, simultaneously empowering clients and strengthening the therapeutic relationship. In this model, there is a two-way transfer of information in which counsellors share information with clients as it becomes available, and clients share their concerns with counsellors. These authors articulate a continuous process model, which they refer to as "mutual monitoring" because it allows each party to be sensitive to and to monitor factors that are entering into the other's thinking at any given time.

The process model of informed consent assists counsellors in gaining a better understanding of how to proceed in the process of obtaining consent. In the first step of this model, counsellors and clients establish a working relationship. As a guiding principle, counsellors convey to prospective clients information that is related to their particular decision. Providing useful information helps clients become more active agents on their own behalf, and directs them to contribute to changes they might need to make in therapy. At this point, clients might also be determining whether they would want to work with or trust this counsellor. Sometimes (not often), they ask counsellors about their credentials. They might enquire: What professional degree do you have? How often have you worked with this particular problem? They might want to know the "kind of person" the counsellor is. Encouraging this line of questioning permits the client to participate more fully in subsequent treatment decisions.

The second step of the process of obtaining consent has to do with defining the problem. This might be difficult for some theoretical counselling approaches. Some approaches indicate that whatever the client says *is* the problem *is not* the problem. Others say the problem *is not* the problem, but how people try to solve their problems *is* the problem. And on it goes. The intention of this step in the process however, is not to get into lengthy explanations of theory. Instead, it provides a forum for counsellors and clients to agree upon issues that need to be defined and addressed. Negotiation of counselling problems can be complex, and counsellors who ignore clients' definitions of their problems could find themselves with people who are dissatisfied, and who do not want to participate wholeheartedly in the counselling process. Meichenbaum and Turk (1987) advocate that, to the degree that patients are committed to definitions of their problems, and thus to particular treatment approaches, their inclinations to follow through with treatment approaches are likely to be increased. Because problem definitions often change during treatment, flexibility in the counselling process, and a commitment to on-going negotiation of client problems are needed.

The next step in this process of obtaining consent involves consensus about treatment goals. Put succinctly,

"What are the reasonable goals of therapy for the problem we have discussed?" The counsellor and client must collaborate to identify what would need to happen in order for counselling to have successful outcomes. Without adequate and well-defined goals, it is difficult to determine whether the client has benefitted from the services offered by the counsellor. In fact, in his discussion of informed consent, Plante (1999) argued that the movement toward empirically supported treatments has become so important to contemporary psychotherapy that "patients seeking treatment should be informed that empirically supported treatments exist, and the psychologist must let them know if they intend to use them (or not use them) in the treatment of the patient" (p. 400).

In the next step of the consent process, the counsellor discusses with the client the proposed approach to helping them with their problem. To meet all the legal requirements of an informed consent, the counsellor must convey to the client the nature, purpose, risks and benefits of treatment, along with alternatives and their risks and benefits. Providing adequate information to clients to obtain consent for treatment was and continues to be ignored by many practising professionals. This neglect to inform clients may relate to the notion of trust; an attitude that "doctor knows best" or "trust me" because I am trained to know what to do. However, clients need to know whether or when there are risks.

Although one of the ethical principles upon which the *CCA Code of Ethics* (2006) is built states "Do no harm", some counsellors do not possess the training to engage in certain practices or work with particular problems. If, for example, a counsellor has not taken any graduate training or post-graduate training in family therapy or couple counselling, they should not engage in this type of work. If they find themselves working in new territory, they might not be aware of potential risks or situations that might cause clients to experience emotional trauma, and would be unable to communicate this to their clients. In addition, they would not be able to adequately meet the other conditions of informed consent since they have not had the appropriate exposure to this particular area of counselling. In other words, there is the potential for harm because they are unaware of the possible effects of their interventions. Counsellors must also become knowledgeable about alternatives to the proposed counselling option or whether other therapeutic approaches to specific problems are more appropriate. Some problems, for example, may need specialised training such as sexual abuse counselling or post-trauma counselling. Clients with sleep disorders, anxiety, depression and other presenting problems may ask about a medication route. Counsellors should be prepared to discuss these and other options or alternatives with their clients.

The final step in the ongoing consent process is follow-up. When all other steps are taken, the counsellor ensures that the client continues to be informed about what is or is not happening in counselling. In nearly any counselling process, neither the counsellor nor the client knows from the outset the precise course that the therapy might travel. Some goals might be achieved or new issues might come to light; some potential for harm could arise as a result of some aspect of the counselling process;

the client or the counsellor might need to introduce new information into the process. Whatever the reason, follow-up ensures that the informed consent process remains dynamic, allowing for an ongoing collaborative relationship between counsellor and client.

Some recommendations that should be helpful to counsellors who want to improve their own informed consent process include the notion that information sharing is best done verbally with the counsellor documenting the client's level of interest and understanding in their written file. This does not have to be overly or obsessively comprehensive. Bloom (1992) believes that written contracts "run the risk of sacrificing clinical rapport so essential to positive therapeutic outcome, and fail to address new questions that emerge" (p. 8). Consistent with the notion of consent as a process, counsellors should not replace written forms for ongoing verbal consent.

Informed consent as an event

O'Neill (1998) states that, in specific consent, counsellors tell clients what they intend to do and outline the possible risks and benefits. He also cites two main reasons that practitioners fail to inform clients about risks: either they did not fully appreciate these risks themselves, or they worried about upsetting the person seeking treatment. The first instance, the issue is a question of practitioner competence. In the second instance, the issue is related to therapeutic privilege, which a court would more than likely not recognize. He warns practitioners against the latter on the grounds that it abandons the "reasonable doctor" standard (it might upset the client; the client might refuse treatment on learning of the risks; the

client might not understand the information; or most clinicians would not provide the information, an attitude that was more reflective of an outdated paternalistic perspective of professional relationships).

Counsellors often rely upon consent forms to document that specific information has been provided and understood by the client. However, counsellors need to be aware of the risks of not taking the appropriate time necessary to elicit informed consent. There is more to the process than getting a client's signature on a form in order to have a valid consent. A piece of paper can never be an effective substitute for the interpersonal exchange of information and two-way communication that is characteristic of the consent process. With emphasis upon informed consent as a process, not as a discrete act, Berg et al. (2001) stated:

> Informed consent is a process, not a form —without the process, the form is just a piece of paper. In the absence of the elements of informed consent, a signed consent form is largely useless. If appropriate disclosure was not made, if the form's signatory was not competent to understand the disclosure and make a decision, if the signatory signed the form but did not make a decision or understand what she signed, or if her signature was unduly pressured —the signed consent form will not serve any purpose. (pp. 188-189)

Consent forms are helpful to the degree that they supplement or aid the process of informed consent. They support the treatment of the client, and only secondarily protect the counsellor. Although counsellors are faced more frequently with issues of liability, good counselling practices are generally more helpful than a signed consent form. In an era of litigation, people are generally used to signing forms or contracts of one sort or another, often with an understanding that their signature might probably mean signing away their rights, and that their role in the decision-making is over. It could be helpful to the therapeutic relationship, as well as good ethical practice, if counsellors told clients that the contents of a consent form largely benefit the client, and promote their interests by facilitating the process of informed consent. Informed consent, of which the consent form is a part, protects the well-being of the client. It ensures that action taken by the counsellor is understood and intended to benefit the client.

A written form can serve to document important parts of the shared decision-making dialogue between the counsellor and the client. The form needs an outline of the expected treatment plan, and the responsibilities of the counsellor and the client with respect to this treatment plan. It may serve to document important parts of their dialogue. Signing a consent form is part of a therapeutic plan, and is considered to be one of many decisions made within a collaborative relationship.

Documenting consent

To reiterate an earlier point, consent forms ought to be used in conjunction with written notes in the client's file; notes which summarize the information conveyed to the client and their agreement to engage in the counselling process. They are a written account of what transpires between counsellor and client. Similar to the ethical standard of

keeping notes on progress in counselling, a written account of consent is important, since it provides counsellors with an historical record of the client's understanding of treatment. Written documentation also allows the counsellor to substantiate advice given to the client regarding risks should a client later allege that advice was not given. The detailed note is perhaps the most effective means for documenting consent.

A written form does not need to be long. In all likelihood, the degree of client understanding of information on a consent form diminishes as the length of the form increases. In addition to a form, much of what a counsellor would communicate to a client could be put into a brochure, which could clearly define confidentiality and the ethical and legal issues associated with it. The brochure could assist clients in making an informed consent to counselling. Figure 1 provides an example of a typical counsellor consent form. The form is written in simple, easy to understand language. Providing space for written notes allows the counsellor an opportunity to answer and record questions the client might have. It is recommended that counsellors expand further upon the space for written comments. If the form is an addition to direct discussion, there is little need for them to be all-inclusive. Brevity is best, since an encyclopaedic form may simply be overwhelming to clients. Counsellors should also omit unnecessary, irrelevant, and potentially misleading information from the consent form.

Counsellors need to be cognizant of the readability of forms they might use, keeping in mind that they are intended primarily for the benefit of the client. Therefore, they should keep any form readable, allowing for differences in the reading comprehension of clients. Consent forms tend to be written at a higher reading level than are suitable for the intended clientele. Intake forms, based upon clinical concepts and jargon, could be difficult for many clients to understand. Dialogue between counsellor and client regarding the contents of the form, such as issues in counselling and confidentiality, allows the client a thorough understanding of the process. Keep sentences short with simple readable language, and avoid words that are more than three syllables in length. Many newspapers aim their readability index to a grade six level yet many forms used by clinicians could be aimed at a university level audience.

Reading a form does not necessarily mean that a client understands the form or that they will remember the contents of it throughout their contact with the counsellor. In fact, some clients may not even remember the contents of the form at the end of their first session. Counsellors may consider personalizing written informed consent forms to aim language to the literacy level of each client. These forms could be used to develop rapport and clarify client expectations.

The manner and means of presenting consent forms are important. Rather than thrusting consent forms into the hands of clients in a waiting room or when they first enter the counselling office, clients may be given the form to read before the oral disclosure and subsequent discussion. This allows clients to ask questions and clarify any information orally. Counsellors should avoid making light of the importance of the consent form and the consent process. During the discussion with clients, avoid saying things like "I am

required to ask you to sign this." Make the informed process more than simple paperwork. Counsellors could ask clients to sign the form in their presence rather than at a receptionist's desk or elsewhere. This permits counsellors a greater opportunity to gain increased understanding of clients' concerns and informational needs.

In conclusion, it might be worthwhile for counsellors to consider Rozvosky's (2003) list of general rules for informed consent, depending on the context. A few rules that might be applicable to the counselling context include items such as:

- Do not obtain the patient's signature until the consent process has been completed

- Do not obtain consent from someone who is under the influence of medication or alcohol that might affect their mental ability to make a decision regarding services

- Make certain the form is complete before it is signed

- Answer all questions the person may have before signing the consent form

- Keep the language simple to understand

- Be certain that information on the form is correct.

- Remember to keep consent forms simple. They are intended to supplement the informed consent process rather than replace it.

Situations requiring consent

In addition to consent to treatment, counsellors are often faced with many other situations requiring consent from their clients. Issues arise related to ethical information sharing. Access, storage, release of records, and situations requiring a breach of confidentiality generally top this list. Counsellors should understand in advance the circumstances under which they are allowed to release information about clients to third parties. If they have not agreed to these circumstances, the client's consent to treatment is not legitimately informed. For example, no client can be genuinely informed of the counsellors' responsibilities to breach confidentiality related to harm to self or others if they are not told in advance.

When counsellors seek professional consultation, they make every effort to do so in ways that protect the identity of the client. If counsellors cannot protect their clients' identities, then informed consent from clients must be sought before the consultation begins. Informed consent to share information with third parties generally involves the use of consent forms stipulating the details regarding the person to whom information will be shared; the type of information to be shared (such as educational, social/emotional, or psychological details); a date stipulating the length of time for which the consent is valid; and signature spaces for the client and a witness.

Chapter Summary

This chapter provided a Canadian perspective on issues related to informed consent within a counselling relationship. There is agreement in the literature that informed consent is a process that happens throughout the counselling contract, not a one- or a two-time event. Although much of the research to date, as well as much of the legislation and case law relates to physicians, the issues pertaining to these health care professionals are also applicable to counsellors. In this chapter, informed consent was contextualized to the perspective of that which clients need to know in order to consent to treatment or to engage in a counselling relationship. Information counsellors provide in obtaining consent takes into account what any reasonable person would agree to if that person was in the client's position, rather than the traditional paternalistic perspective of the professional deciding what the client needs to know.

From the point of view that all Canadians, regardless of age, have a legal right to give consent, this chapter discussed exceptions to this legal right, and included a discussion of children and others who might not have the mental capacity to truly understand the consequences of the service being provided to them, as well as legislation and/or directives that would limit a person's right to give consent. The chapter concluded with a discussion of written consent forms, and how counsellors might use these forms as an adjunct to the process used in obtaining and maintaining consent in counselling.

Figure 1: Sample Consent Form

Sample Consent Form

➤ This form will help you understand the counselling process and assist you in feeling more comfortable about counselling, its benefits, risks, and possible outcomes.

➤ We will go through this form together. If there is anything you do not understand, please let me know and I will try to help you to understand it better.

➤ About me... l am a trained high school counsellor with 15 years of experience. I work with students, just like you, who need someone to talk to. I believe talking can help people sort out their feelings, and help them do things that are more positive. I know that each person is unique and special, and has something to offer. I want to help you discover your strengths and help you learn to build upon them. I am willing to help you to talk about whatever you feel will help you — even tough stuff. My approach is to provide a safe and comfortable environment for us to get to know each other better so you gain trust and the courage to work on your issues. I know many support services we can access if we need additional help.

➤ The time we spend together will provide you with an opportunity to work through challenging situations. I will keep everything you tell me in the utmost of confidence except:

  o If you give me permission to tell your personal information to others, who may be able to help you (i.e. teachers, parents, other professionals).
  o If there is a risk of you harming yourself or someone else (I will seek appropriate assistance for you).
  o If you tell me or I suspect someone is hurting you physically, sexually, or emotionally (I will contact appropriate services and/or the police).
  o If I am legally obligated to do so (court ordered to testify).

➤ What's not so great about counselling – the possibility of dealing with intense emotions like helplessness, insecurity, fear and anger. Also, other people may not support your efforts, nor is there a guarantee that counselling will successfully change the problems you are having.

➤ What's positive about counselling –the possibility of feeling better about yourself and your life; learning how solve your own problems; and, getting along better with other people. Counselling is voluntary. If you prefer to see one of the other counsellors at any time, I will help you do this.

➤ I also want you to know that I keep written records of all the students I talk to, with a few details about what we talk about. These records are available for you to see upon written request. All records are kept for seven (7) years after which they are destroyed.

Other issues regarding consent that was discussed (Use back of form as well):

_____
_____
_____
_____

I have read this form and I understand what it means. I agree to receive counselling from Mr. Thomas.

Signed _____   Date_____

Witness _____   Date_____

Learning Activities

1. *Learning groups.* In pairs, create a brochure for counselling services for one of the contexts listed below. Include information you believe is important to a client for consent purposes. Be comprehensive in your approach.

   a. Child and family counselling

   b. Counselling adolescents privately/ in a school context

   c. Counselling women who have been abused

   d. Addictions counselling

   e. Counselling perpetrators of domestic violence

   f. Counselling adults

   g. University or college counselling centre

   In the brochure, include:

   • a description of the service you or your agency/school offers

   • a description of any possible risks and benefits of the service offered

   • alternative approaches/services that might also be available

   • issues regarding confidentiality, including limits to confidentiality, note taking, record keeping and file storage

   • other information you believe might be helpful for clients seeking counselling services.

   Include a list of questions you would give to your clients that they might ask you to answer. Discuss in large group format issues arising during this assignment.

2. *Interview/Survey.* Divide the class into three groups (at least three members in each group). Each group will be responsible for conducting three or four (telephone or in-person) interviews with one of the following counselling groups regarding their informed consent practices: 1. School counsellors; 2. Private practioners; 3. Agency-based counsellors. Use the informed consent issues listed in the first exercise above as topics around which to structure the interview. Following the interviews, members will get together with their respective groups, and compare information they gleaned from their interviews, identifying themes that arose within each of the three groups; problems with informed consent issues in the contexts surveyed; and recommendations related to informed consent arising out of the interviews.

   Prepare a one- to two-page summary that can be shared with your classmates and with people you interviewed. Use these summaries as a forum for in-class discussion.

3. *Triadic Role-play.* Divide the class into triads. One person in each triad role-plays a counsellor, a client, and an observer. Each person plays each of the three roles during this exercise. The purpose of the exercise is to practice what should be said during the initial counselling session with a client.

   Using topics listed in exercise one, role play what you, the counsellor would say to a client coming in for counselling. As a client who has identified a specific reason for coming into counselling (depression, eating disorder, relationship difficulties, etc.), think of questions you think you ought to ask, questions to which you would genuinely like to know the answers prior to engaging in counselling with this counsellor. At the end of each interview, the observer provides feedback to each of the two other participants. Rotate so that everyone has an opportunity to play each role.

4. *Discussion.* In groups of 4 or 5 people, discuss the implications of informed consent for the profession of counselling. Is it a worthwhile process? What are the advantages/benefits of engaging in a "process" of informed consent? What issues do you anticipate during this process, and how would you handle these issues? What concerns do you have regarding a focus on informed consent? What reactions might you anticipate from your client in this process? During your discussion, note any concerns that you might like to bring back to the larger group for discussion and/or clarification.

5. *Workshop.* As a class, prepare and deliver a three-hour interactive workshop to local counsellors on the topic of informed consent. Use topics included in this chapter as well as other sources for your presentation.

References

American Counselling Association (2005). *ACA code of ethics.* USA: Author.

Beahrs, J.O. & Gutheil, T.G. (2001). Informed consent in psychotherapy. *American Journal of Psychiatry*, 158, 4-10.

Beeman, D.G. & Scott, N.A. (1991). Therapists' attitudes toward psychotherapy informed consent with adolescents. *Professional Psychology: Research and Practice*, 22 (3), 230-234.

Berg, J. W., Appelbaum, P. S., Lidz, C.W., & Parker, L. S. (2001). *Informed consent.* Oxford. Oxford University Press.

Bloom, B.L. (1992). Planned short-term psychotherapy: Current status and future challenges. *Applied and Preventive Psychology*, 1, 157-164.

Bond, T. (1993). *Standards and ethics for counselling in action.* London: UK. Sage.

Canadian Counselling Association (2006). *CCA code of ethics.* Ottawa, Ontario: Author.

Canadian Counselling Association (2001). *Standards of practice.* Ottawa, Ontario: Author.

Canadian Psychological Association (2000).*CPA code of ethics.* Ottawa, Ontario: Author.

Chiniliar v. Chiniliar (2001, 11 WW.R.386, 94 Alta. L-R. (2d) 338 at 347 (Q.B.)])

Clements, W. G. & Uhlemann, M. R. (1991). Informed consent, confidentiality and access to information. In David Turner and Max Uhlemann (Eds.) (1991). *A legal handbook for the helping professional.* Victoria: BC. The Sedgewick Society for Consumer and Public Education, School of Social Work, University of Victoria.

Cnsl Code of Quebec, S.Q. 1991, c.64, Title two, c. 1, S.14.

Corey, G., Corey, M.S. & Callanan, P. (2003). *Issues and ethics in the helping professions.* Pacific Grove: CA. Brooks-Cole.

Cottone, R.R. (2001). A social construction model of ethical decision-making. *Journal of Counseling and Development*, 79. 39-45.

Criminal Code of Canada (1999), 133 C.C.C. (3d) 532, 176 Sask. R. 106 (Q.B.).

Grisso, T. & Vierling, L. (1978). Minors consent to treatment: A developmental perspective. *Professional Psychology*, 9, 412-427.

Keith-Spiegel, P. & Maas, T. (1981). *Consent to research: Are there developmental differences?* Paper presented at the annual meeting of the American Psychological Association. Los Angeles.

Leathley, C. (1990). Ethical issues and dilemmas in New Zealand psychological practice. Unpublished thesis. Psychology Department, University of Waikato. Hamilton: NZ.

Lehr, R. & Sumarah, J. (2004). Professional judgment in ethical decision-making: Dialogue and relationship. *Canadian Journal of Counselling*, 38 (1), 14-24.

Medical Consent of Minors Act, C.S.N.B. c. M-6.1, S.2.

Meichenbaum, D. C. & Turk, D. (1987). *Facilitating treatment adherence: A practitioner's guidebook.* New York: Plenum Press.

O'Neill, P. (1998). N*egotiating consent in psychotherapy.* New York: University Press.

Ontario's Health Care Consent Act S.O. 1996, c.2, Sched. A.

Plante, T. G. (1999). Ten strategies for psychology trainees and practicing psychologists interested in avoiding ethical and legal perils. *Psychotherapy*, 36, 398-403.

Pomerantz, A.M. & Handelsman, M. M. (2004). Informed consent revisited: An updated written question format. *Professional Psychology: Research and Practice*, 35 (2), 201-205.

Pope, K.S. & Vasquez, M.J.T. (1991). *Ethics in psychotherapy and counseling.* San Francisco: Jossey-Bass.

R.V. Sookochoff. R.S.C. 1985, c. C-46, s. 742.3(1)(e).

Reibl v. Hughes, supra, note 1, 14 C.C.L.T. at 21. (1980)

Robertson, G. (1991). Informed consent ten years later: The impact of Reibl v. Hughes. *Canadian Bar Review*, 70(3), 423.

Rozovsky, L.E. (2003). *The Canadian law of consent to treatment.* Markham, Ontario: Butterworths.

Schanczl v. Singh (1987).

Sumarah, J, Lehr, R. and Wheeldon, L. (2000). Confidentiality: Dialogue and discernment. In W. E. Schulz. *Counselling ethics casebook.* Ottawa: Canadian Counselling Association.

Sullivan, T., Martin, W. L. & Handelsman, M. M. (1993). Practical benefits of an informed-consent procedure: an empirical investigation. *Professional Psychology: Research and Practice*, 24 (2), 160-163.

The Health Care Directives Act, C.C.S.M. c. H27, S4(2).

Weithorn, L. & Campbell, S. (1982). Informed consent for treatment: An empirical study of children's capacities. *Child Development*, 53, 413-425.

Chapter Three

Confidentiality

The social ethics question, "What should be done?" generally must be answered in a categorical way: confidences should be kept. Of course! But then there are singular circumstances in which a different sort of question arises: "Yes confidences should be kept, generally, but now, faced with the uniqueness of this present situation, what should I do?" (Bok, p. 129)

Chapter Objectives

The major focus of the chapter is on confidentiality. The specific objectives are to:

- Help counsellors understand confidentiality in a Canadian context

- Promote a clearer understanding of how the counselling profession's *Code of Ethics and Standards of Practice for Counsellors* define confidentiality in practice

- Understand limitations to confidentiality

- Gain a clearer understanding of confidentiality with minors

- Increase counsellors' understanding of confidentiality as a collaborative process

Self-Inventory

Directions: Before reading this chapter, please use the following scale to indicate your attitudes towards issues in this chapter. For each statement, indicate the response that most closely identifies your beliefs and attitudes. Use the following code:

5 = Strong agreement with this item
4 = Agreement with this item
3 = Undecided about this item
2 = Disagreement with this item
1 = Strong disagreement with this item

____ Legal considerations in counselling take precedence over ethical considerations.

____ Confidentiality provides assurance of trust or confidence in the person to whom private matters are shared.

____ Counsellors who are truly concerned with their clients' confidentiality and privacy should keep secret notes.

___ When trust in the therapeutic relationship is compromised, counsellors should refer their client to another counsellor.

___ It is well known that breaking confidentiality because of suspected harm or abuse inevitably damages the client-counsellor relationship.

___ It is common courtesy to inform a referral source on progress a client is making in counselling.

___ Counsellors have a legal obligation to protect the client's privacy at all costs.

___ Counsellors in Canada should act as if they have privilege, not releasing any client information without exhausting all legal avenues first.

___ Counsellors must immediately hand over their files if subpoenaed.

___ When counsellors are persuaded to breach confidentiality without the benefit of informed consent, they can be found negligent.

___ Counsellors should always inform police and the intended victim if a client threatens harm.

___ When clients requests information from their file, counsellors must promptly provide a copy.

___ Clients have a right to receive copies of other professional reports that are kept in their counselling file.

___ Counsellors should use every means possible to protect themselves when a client lays a complaint about them, including using information contained in the client's file.

___ Confidentiality in a school context should be treated in the same manner as confidentiality in any other context.

___ Parents have a legal right to be informed about their child's counselling until the child reaches the age of majority.

___ Counsellors must immediately release all confidential information contained in the file of a minor upon written request from a parent or guardian.

___ It is the counsellor's duty to discuss limits to confidentiality at the start of counselling only.

Introduction

Confidentiality is probably the single issue that raises the greatest number of difficulties for counsellors and this, according to Bond (1993), is due mainly to uncertainty about what counsellors think their optimum practice ought to be and arises from problems they experience in implementing ethical practice. Confidentiality raises the anxiety level of all counsellors. In addition to being central to the profession of counselling, the ability of counsellors to maintain confidentiality often reflects the integrity of the work they do.

Counsellors work in diverse settings, some of which have policies around confidentiality and some that have unique challenges related to confidentiality. Like other aspects of ethical practice, confidentiality is built upon principles that reflect important underpinnings of counselling. Those principles most closely related to confidentiality include 'integrity in relationships' and 'respect for self-determination'. Both of these principles coalesce and speak to the autonomy of persons, the right for people to live their lives, and to have information pertaining to their well-being kept in confidence. Autonomy, however, is not absolute. Since confidentiality is a priority in the counselling relationship, it should be part of the negotiation of the counselling process. For example, negotiation needs to include situations in which other parties fund counselling or when other contractual obligations are imposed upon the counsellor. At times, counsellors may feel it is in the best interest of their client to breach confidentiality while at other times ethical and legal issues demand that the counsellor breach confidence.

People who come to counsellors significantly value confidentiality yet some research indicates that guarantees for privacy and confidentiality are actually decreasing (Bersoff, 1997). Issues around harm to oneself and to others are continually being highlighted, which may in part be attributed to threat of liability placed on counsellors to report probable harm to oneself and others, a situation that has been the focus of ethical and legal discussions since the well-known Tarasoff case in the 1980s. Despite increased education of counsellors in graduate school and the introduction of stronger and more ethically aware counselling programs, issues related to breaches of confidentiality abound. In the past decade, there have been calls from professional associations and by the public at large to reduce ethical violations involving confidentiality, and a need to improve ethics education in professional counselling programs. Interestingly, Fly, Van Buck, Weinman, Kitchener and Lang (1997) suggest more is needed than simply introducing ethics courses at the graduate level, since their research finds that an ethics course does not necessarily deter students from making ethical violations as practicing counsellors. Perhaps what is needed is the continued lobbying of professional associations to legislate the counselling profession in Canada as well as a requirement for ongoing supervised practice of professional counsellors. This is currently happening in several Canadian provinces, and there is a national movement to legislate the profession of counselling.

Related to breaches of confidentiality in counselling relationships is professional judgement. Confidentiality requires that counsellors use sound professional judgement in the discernment of their professional practice (Daniels & Ferguson, 1998; Lehr & Sumarah, 2004). This is sometimes complicated as evidenced in school contexts where a school counsellor may work in the dual role of teacher and counsellor, or where others who may be as equally concerned about a student's well-being can request information. For some counsellors, being conscious of situations where they could be compromising a client's confidentiality is also an important consideration. This could occur with counsellors who might be challenged by having a private practice in the home where they see clients who continually come and go; where their business telephone and their residential telephone is the same; where others have access to their "confidential" voice messaging system; or where files might lay on their desk for other family members to see. The list of possible challenges to confidentiality contributes to the importance of a counsellor's professional judgement in the discernment of confidentiality. It clearly advocates that laws and codes of ethics provide guidelines for practitioners so that counsellors know what to do, and commit to doing it.

Counsellors face many other challenges related to confidentiality, such as when to release information to others, in what manner should they release information, and to whom should they release information. Answers to these and other questions appear simplistic, yet they are as diverse as the many contexts in which counsellors work, and the many situations they confront on an ongoing basis. Some confidentiality challenges faced by counsellors however, can be addressed if counsellors follow the counselling profession's code of ethics. In general, most counsellors follow this line of thinking. Nonetheless, in the majority of situations, counsellors are conflicted about what to do, especially when needed answers cannot be readily found. Throughout this chapter, ideas and questions related to confidentiality arise and hopefully, might serve as discussion points within a classroom setting or in the workplace.

Confidentiality: What does it mean?

The Oxford dictionary defines ethics as "relating to morals, treating of moral questions, honourable, set of principles of morals, rules of conduct" and confidence is defined as "firm trust, assured expectation, telling of private matters, allowed to know private thoughts or affairs." Confidentiality then, relates to a set of principles assuring trust or confidence. Confidentiality provides assurance of trust or confidence in the person with whom private matters are shared.

Trust in a confidential therapeutic relationship is the cornerstone of the counselling profession. Without it, effective therapeutic conversations with people are not possible. Individuals for example, who have recently lost trust in a relationship might comment, "I trusted her. I never believed for an instant she would do that." "I shared my soul with him. How could he do this to me?" Clients enter counselling with varying degrees of trust. Some have absolute trust that what they share with their counsellors is confidential. Others slowly share the deeper and more intimate concerns they have. Professional counsellors maintain and develop the trust bestowed upon them because of the position they hold in relation to the person seeking help.

Who owns confidentiality?

An important question that needs answering is: "Who owns confidentiality?" Phrased differently, counsellors can ask: "If someone tells me something, does that information belong to me, and is it my ethical duty to protect that information?" Although seemingly straightforward, issues around confidentiality, especially in settings where numerous people share concern for or who are in positions of caring for the person's welfare, can cloud the issue making it difficult manoeuvring for the counsellor.

Issues such as third party billing and guardianship often complicate confidentiality, leaving counsellors confused as to whom they are providing service. From the beginning, it is important that counsellors determine who their clients are. This, as mentioned above, can be negotiated since the person to whom the counsellor owes confidentiality may not always be evident. In many instances, loyalties or responsibilities to third parties or organizations may lead counsellors to betray the valid or mistaken expectations they have regarding confidentiality; a situation that may be exacerbated by confusion regarding who the client is. When counsellors receive referrals from third parties, such as an employee and/or family assistance program, the referring source often pays for the counsellors' service. This referral often comes with a reporting protocol which counsellors follow. In most instances however, when counsellors accept a referral, the person referred to them becomes their client. Similar but different are referrals from a court or lawyer requesting a family assessment. In both cases, counsellors might be paid by a third party to perform counselling-related tasks, but in the latter case the court or the lawyer becomes the client. In all cases, it would be appropriate to clarify expectations of all parties around issues of reporting and confidentiality.

No matter how grateful counsellors might be to referral sources, whether they are friends, colleagues, or others, the referral source has no right to learn that a particular individual has scheduled an appointment, has met with the counsellor, or what might or might not have been discussed, unless the counsellor obtains written informed consent from the client to discuss information with the referral source. Even a small act such as sending the referral source a "thank you" note or thanking them in person could be an inadvertent breach of their clients' confidentiality.

Once counsellors determine who their clients are, they protect confidentiality of all information given to them unless authorized or required to release this information. Confidentiality belongs to the person who consults with the counsellor. When counsellors take an oath of confidentiality, they are in effect agreeing to hold 'in trust' information that has been shared with them. This information 'belongs' to someone else; it should not be given away, nor can counsellors store it somewhere where other people might easily access it. One of the authors often uses the example of asking a friend to safely care for something of value for him until he needs it. The expectation of trust is given to this other person to keep the possession, not to give it anyone else, and to keep it safe. With his agreement she can share with others, but he trusts she will have it in her possession when he needs it. Without consent, the other person is bound by a promise to protect his possession. Confidentiality works in a similar manner. People are entrusting someone else, a counsellor, to protect confidential and private information for a limited period of time. Counsellors have a commitment, a fiduciary responsibility or duty to protect this information.

Confidentiality and Professional Codes of Ethics

Snook (2003), who worked as a school counsellor and as a school principal, professes that all professional groups have a dominant virtue (e.g. justice in law, truth in scholarship, and honesty in business), and that the central virtue of counselling is trust. With a promise of confidentiality, counsellors agree to hold in confidence and in trust, information or revelations clients share during the counselling experience.

Codes of ethics generally make strong statements about confidentiality. For example, article B2 of the Canadian Counselling Association's

Code of Ethics (2006) puts forth the following:

> Counselling relationships and information resulting therefrom are kept confidential. However, there are the following exceptions to confidentiality: (i) when disclosure is required to prevent clear and imminent danger to the client or others; (ii) when legal requirements demand that confidential material be revealed; (iii) when a child is in need of protection.

The *Standards of Practice for Counsellors* (CCA, 2001) also includes a standard for the release of information "when a client files a complaint or claims professional liability by the counsellor in a lawsuit". This latter point is often not communicated by counsellors in their disclosures probably because most counsellors trust that their clients will not charge them with an offence. The reality exists however, that counsellors can face litigation and/or ethical violations related to breaches of confidentiality. When people complain to the CCA ethics committee, they probably hear for the first time that personal information which they shared with their counsellor can now be used be used in the counsellor's defence. Counsellors are advised to fully disclose all limitations to confidentiality, a topic covered in more detail later in this chapter.

The New Zealand Association of Counsellors' *Code of Ethics* (2003) takes the issue of confidentiality further and states that "Counsellors shall treat all communication between counsellor and client as confidential and privileged information unless the client gives consent to particular information being disclosed". NZAC's *Code of Ethics* does not use "privileged" in a legal sense, but emphasizes confidentiality as the primary basis of the counselling relationship. The term "privileged" means that confidentiality belongs to the client, and except for the typical exceptions to confidentiality, counsellors are encouraged to pursue the status of privileged communication in accordance with the client's wishes until all legal avenues are exhausted.

"Privilege" and "privileged communication", are legal terms involving the right to maintain confidentiality in a legal proceeding. Treating information as privileged means counsellors have to "go the extra mile" to protect the integrity of the person with whom they are working. Privilege, which belongs to clients, means *they* are protected by law, *not* the counsellors with whom they share their information. The clients own the information shared with the counsellor, and have the right to say who can have access to it and who cannot. Ethical codes, statutes, and court decisions establish the principle that people are entitled to keep some things private.

To keep some things private might mean that counsellors consult with others such as with the head of their agency, institution, or school. They might have to meet with a client they no longer see to inform them about the possible impact of sharing specific private information with others. Clients may be unaware that some information in the counsellors' written notes might be embarrassing if shared with others. At other times, keeping some information private might require that counsellors delay the release of information when subpoenaed, and appeal to the court to quash a subpoena. This could mean procuring the services of a lawyer who might then try to convince a court judge that certain information in their file is sensitive and/or not relevant to the case at hand.

Canadian law clearly does not recognize many instances of privileged professional communications, apart from the well-known privilege between lawyers and their clients and, unlike their American counterparts where statutory privileges are quite common, in Canada there is no privilege between health care professionals and their patients, including clergy and their parishioners (Clements & Uhlemann, 1991). In fact, in *Meyer v. Rogers* (1991), an Ontario court ruling specifically states that there is no defence of therapeutic privilege in Canada. The client and the professional could however, argue to prevent access to a file. In most cases however, judges generally stipulate in an access order that counsellors make photocopies of their records, certify them as being true copies of the originals, and send them to the lawyer who made the application in court. The lawyer is usually given the right to inspect the original records to ensure that everything has been copied. Counsellors also need to be aware that it is illegal to strip files of information once it has been subpoenaed. This warning is extended to counsellors who mistakenly believe they should keep secret files to protect their clients; something frowned upon both legally and ethically. The *CCA Standards of Practice for Counsellors* (2001) states that "counsellors never destroy records or counselling notes after they receive a subpoena or have reason to expect receiving one. This action could be judged to be an obstruction of justice and it could result in being held in con-tempt of court".

In Canada, judges typically apply the Wigmore (1961) conditions to determine if confidentially obtained information should be disclosed during a legal proceeding. In other words, *privileged communication* must convince the court that the following conditions are met:

- Did the communication originate within a confidential relationship?

- Is the element of confidence essential to the full and satisfactory maintenance of the relationship?

- Is the relationship one which the community believes should be actively and constantly fostered?

- Will the injury done to the relationship by disclosure be of greater consequence than the benefit gained to the legal proceedings by disclosure?

These conditions allow counsellors to have their voices heard in a meaningful way in the judicial system. In the end, of course, counsellors need to adhere to the judge's final pronouncement. However, in many instances counsellors know with greater confidence that they acted in what they believe are the best interests of their client. Clements and Uhlemann (1991) stressed that "... judges will sometimes refuse to hear evidence of confidential communications between laypersons and professionals when they feel that the value or relevance of the evidence is small compared to the value of confidentiality to the professional relationship" (p. 214).

Inevitably, at some point in most counsellors' careers, they will be subpoenaed. Some helpful tips to deal with these subpoenas are provided by the American Psychological Association (1996), which recommends the following strategies:

- Determine whether the request for information carries the force of law.

- Contact the client.

- Negotiate with the requestor.

- Seek guidance from the court.

- File a motion to quash the subpoena.

In other words, counsellors are required to act in a manner deemed in the best interests of the client; in a manner that benefits the client. The strategies outlined above are consistent with acting "as if" counsellors had privilege; counsellors taking all necessary steps to protect the privacy of their client. Counsellors are also advised to read the *Standards of Practice for Counsellors* (CCA, 2001), which outlines in more detail how counsellors should deal with subpoenas.

Sometimes counsellors are persuaded that they must breach confidentiality without the benefit of informed consent, such as when a client is suicidal or intending harm to self or others. When this happens, counsellors could be protected from liability under the *Doctrine of Qualified Immunity* (CCA, 2001). This *Doctrine* requires that counsellors meet specific conditions:

- The action was taken in good faith.

- There was a demonstrative duty or interest to be fulfilled by the disclosure.

- The disclosure was limited in scope to this duty or interest.

- It was done on a proper occasion.

- The disclosure was made in an appropriate manner, and to the appropriate parties only.

The limits to confidentiality discussed below generally represent reasons why counsellors might properly disclose information without informed consent. Despite these limitations, in some cases counsellors might be prudent to inform clients of their obligation to report information given to them. This might allow counsellors and clients opportunities to maintain positive counselling relationships.

Limits to Confidentiality

Bond (1993) believes that the myth that all counselling is totally confidential needs to be clarified through ongoing discussion with the client. He claims that many clients enter counselling believing that anything and everything they tell counsellors is confidential. The general population (including those who have been in counselling) do not always have an accurate view of ethical limitations regarding the confidentiality of information discussed in counselling. Since ethics and confidentiality are professional issues in counselling, clients should not be expected to be well-versed on the topic. Clients often believe that everything discussed in the context of counselling is considered confidential, and there should be no exceptions. It is incumbent upon counsellors to apprise clients of exceptions to this important part of their relationship.

Counsellors sometimes find themselves in situations in which they realize they have not adequately negotiated the confidentiality agreement with their client. When clients talk about abuse, suicidal intentions, or other issues needing a breach of confidentiality, and counsellors realize that possible exceptions to confidentiality have not been discussed, how should they handle these particular situations? Should they stop the client and say, "I should advise you that you may be starting to tell me something that I cannot keep to myself? Can we stop here for a moment and discuss confidentiality?" Or, should they continue, allowing the client to share issues that placed them in a dilemma? These are important questions that are addressed in Chapter Two.

Ethical principles underpin codes of ethics, and state in one way or another, the need to respect and to care for the client and for others. Depending upon the profession in which counsellors are members, or by which their practices are regulated, they are ethically obligated to adhere to a professional code of ethics. When there is a conflict or dilemma, counsellors examine their code's principles, and assess if one takes precedence over the other. Article B1 of the *CCA Code of Ethics* (2006) addresses counselling relationships and the importance of confidentiality:

> Counsellors have a primary responsibility to respect the integrity and promote the welfare of their clients. They work collaboratively with clients to devise integrated, individual counselling plans that offer reasonable promise of success and are consistent with the abilities and circumstances of clients.

By promising confidentiality, counsellors fulfill this pledge, realizing that this obligation can be overridden if there is sufficient justification for doing so. When engaged with a client in a counselling relationship, the *Standards of Practice for Counsellors* (CCA, 2001) emphasizes that counsellors should inform clients about confidentiality and its limits, that confidentiality is not absolute, and that disclosure could be necessitated by any of the following circumstances:

- When there is an imminent danger to an identifiable third party or to self.

- When counsellors suspect abuse or neglect of a child.

- When a disclosure is ordered by a court.

- When a client requests disclosure.

- When a client files a complaint or claims professional liability by the counsellor in a lawsuit.

Imminent Danger and the Duty to Warn

The premises upon which confidentiality is based can be overridden when secrecy allows violence to be done to an innocent person, or involves someone as an unsuspecting accomplice in crime. At such times, the special relationship between the counsellor and the client cannot legitimise non-action. Counsellors cannot promise silence unless they realize that if given, there are situations where it can be breached. When counsellors become aware of a client's intent or potential to place others in clear or imminent danger, they use reasonable care to give threatened persons such warnings necessary to avert foreseeable dangers. 'Imminent' means counsellors ascertain a high probability of danger to oneself or to someone else in the near or foreseeable future. Clients have been known to say things similar to the following: "I'm so angry, I could kill him." or "I've often thought of committing suicide." In these cases, counsellors clarify the client's intention, even though there are no strong indications that a dangerous act is pending. If they clearly intend or plan to harm themselves or others; say they had a means to do this; and, indicate it is in the near or foreseeable future, prudence dictates that counsellors take an appropriate action.

Whether, how and when to warn others can be difficult for many counsellors. They are often confused by what constitutes harm. Threatening to physically harm someone by a specific means is clearer to counsellors as constituting harm than whether it might be harmful for a pregnant teenager to engage in unhealthy behaviour such as drinking alcohol. Some typical questions that might arise for counsellors related to 'harm' are:

- Is smoking drugs or taking alcohol reason enough to break confidence since it could cause harm, especially for a 14-year-old person?

- A client says he is going to do 'serious harm' to his brother the next time he sees him.

- A client is talking about suicide, should she/he be reported?

The questions are numerous, and are often disguised or vague. Like many other issues covered by the *CCA Code of Ethics* (2006), no clear answers to these and other questions exist, thus making it even more important that counsellors converse with others about what they should or should not do.

Probably the most recognized case in counselling is an American case; that of *Tarasoff v. Regents of the University of California* (1976), where a University of California student named Prosenjit Poddar was seeing a psychologist at the university's student health centre because a young woman, Tatiana Tarasoff, had rejected his affections. The psychologist concluded that Poddar was dangerous because of his patholog-

ical affection for Tarasoff, and because he intended to purchase a gun. The psychologist notified the police both verbally and in writing. However, when the police questioned Poddar, they concluded he was rational, and made him promise to stay away from Tarasoff. Two months later, Poddar killed Tarasoff. When the young woman's parents attempted to sue the University of California's health centre staff members and the police, the courts dismissed the case. Upon appeal, the Supreme Court of California did not find the police liable, but decreed instead that therapists do have a duty to use reasonable care to protect third parties against dangers posed by patients. The Supreme Court of California imposed an affirmative duty on therapists to warn a potential victim of intended harm by the client, stating that the right to confidentiality ends when the public peril begins. This particular case has been influential in helping to understand the concept of the counsellor's duty to warn. It also continues to generate litigation, legislation, and controversy in both the United States and Canada.

Fine and Ulrich (1998), in reference to *Tarasoff* (1976), argue that the majority of justices ruled the case on utilitarian grounds that in certain circumstances, a clinician's social responsibility supersedes a client's right to confidentiality, that counsellors do not have the right or the absolute duty to protect confidentiality in all cases. They state that a rebuttal to this position would suggest that one should maintain confidentiality in *all* cases because an individual's right to privacy is more absolute, and should never be violated. Fine and Ulrich conclude that "an action is ethically appropriate when it leads to the greatest possible balance of good consequences or to the lesser possible balance of bad consequences in the world as a whole" (p. 543). In a sense, they posit that a utilitarianism perspective considered a cost-benefit aspect of *Tarasoff*, the idealism that puts people in a double-bind, pinned between two moral imperatives. In a later discussion, Fine and Ulrich argue again for a utilitarian approach, a cost benefit weighing of breaching confidentiality when an HIV client was having unprotected sex with a partner, relying on withdrawal as a "safe" measure. They believe that knowing the lethal effects of HIV infection, a utilitarian approach allowed mental health practitioners to make appropriate decisions. With respect to counselling persons who are HIV positive and who engage in at-risk sexual behaviour, the *Standards of Practice for Counsellors* (CCA, 2001) states:

> Counsellors may be justified in breaching confidence with clients who are HIV positive and whose behaviour is putting others at risk. However, counsellors should make every effort to encourage such clients to take responsibility for informing their sexual or needle-sharing partners of their HIV status. With the client's informed permission, counsellors should contact the client's physician and seek the consultative assistance of another counsellor, and legal assistance maybe needed. (p. 9)

Tarasoff (1976) has been debated for many years, both in the United States and in Canada. In the latter case, counsellors have acted 'as if' *Tarasoff* applied to case law in Canada, although at the time of this writing, no known

cases of *Tarasoff* have been applied litigiously in this country. Canadian-based counsellors continue to act 'as if' this might some day apply to them. Fine and Ulrich (1998) state, "The courts have been very clear that in Canada there is no duty to make information available voluntarily to the police who would normally first have to obtain a search warrant or subpoena" (p.212). Clements and Uhlemann (1991) concluded, however, that although not explicitly recognized by a Canadian court, legal pundits believe that Canadian courts would eventually adopt the same reasoning as that of *Tarasoff*. Under the equivalent of a "Tarasoff Duty", they caution that counsellors should recognize ethically and legally that warning the intended victim or advising the police might save someone's life. This reasoning is similar to the ethical position advocated by the *Standards of Practice for Counsellors* (CCA, 2001), which posits the following:

> When counsellors believe that their clients might harm an identifiable person, then they should take steps to warn the individual of the potential danger. Depending on the particular circumstances, counsellors may be justified in taking any number of steps, including; ensuring vigilance by a client's family member, reporting to the police, voluntary or involuntarily hospitalization. Counsellors should consult with colleagues when making such decisions and may need to seek legal assistance. (p. 9)

Counsellors in Canada, therefore, are asked to act in a manner consistent with the ruling of *Tarasoff*. Without legal precedent, counsellors would be wise to inform police about probable harm to a third party, but they should also warn others that they might be in harm's way. In a sense, Canadian counsellors who warn a third party are acting ethically instead of legally even though the latter may eventually happen.

Suspected Child Abuse

In all provinces and territories of Canada, as well as in many other countries of the world, the law obligates counsellors to report suspected child abuse. This abuse might include psychological, emotional, physical, and sexual abuse or neglect. Because of different reporting protocols, and different provincial and territorial legislation related to child protection, counsellors need to familiarize themselves with the laws that govern their particular jurisdiction. A child, in most provinces and territories of Canada, is any person under the age of majority. This age, which is mandated by an act of legislation, varies from province to province but is generally either 18 or 19 years of age.

Reporting children in need of protection is mandatory, and is often contradictory to the therapeutic mandate to which counsellors subscribe. It is important that counsellors consistently provide detailed information about confidentiality limits to clients early in therapy, especially since some research indicates that clinicians who typically provide more frequent and more specific information about confidentiality limits are also more likely to report abuse (Nicolai & Scott, 1994). Reporting suspected child abuse or neglect can be stressful for counsellors. In some cases, they counsel clients who report that they have physically or sexually abused a child. Sometimes an adult client, who says they were sexually abused by a parent, tells a counsellor they now suspect the same parent might be sexually abusing an underage sibling who is still at home. When counsellors deliberate about reporting child abuse such as in this example, they consider the counselling relationship, the help they could offer this person and how this offer of help might be jeopardized if they report the person to the authorities. Counsellors can proceed in a manner that might increase the likelihood of the person remaining in counselling, although there is no guarantee the person will remain once a disclosure has been reported. At other times, especially in school contexts, a child in counselling may report having been hit or abused in other ways by a parent. Sometimes the parent of the abused child has friendships with other teachers on staff or they work in rural, remote or small communities where "everybody knows everybody". In these situations, confidentially consulting with, and obtaining support from authorities with Child and Family Services is helpful. Maintaining overall confidentiality is crucial to the health and welfare of the child.

Court-Ordered Disclosures

Counsellors at some point in their professional practice will be ordered to release confidential information. The inevitability of this dictates that they keep up-to-date counselling records, and write in a manner that is helpful to clients. Some counsellors believe 'no notes are good notes' however, in a court of law counsellors can be reprimanded for not keeping notes. The courts, as well as the *Standards of*

Practice for Counsellors (CCA, 2001), expect that professionals in the health professions keep notes that allow them to track the progress of persons with whom they work. In trying to protect the client by not keeping notes on counselling sessions, the counsellor might unintentionally be less helpful to their client in court.

When subpoenaed by a court to release confidential information, counsellors have the right to challenge the court order. As mentioned earlier, counsellors should take all necessary precautions to protect the confidentiality of their clients. Lawyers often go on "fishing trips", throwing a broad net to see what they can catch to help them with their case. Subpoenas are sometimes part of that broad net approach. If counsellors believe that releasing information to a court might be detrimental to the health and well-being of clients, or if they believe their notes or parts of their notes are not relevant to the case, they can challenge the subpoena in court. This often means that counsellors appear before a judge and appeal to protect records from disclosure. It is often wise to be represented by a lawyer when doing this. In the end, the judge assesses whether the notes should be released, often applying the conditions of Wigmore (1961). In many instances, judges have been known to dismiss subpoenas or remove information not related to the case at hand from the counselling record. By engaging in this process, counsellors take reasonable and necessary steps to ensure the confidentiality of their client's records.

Client-Requested Disclosure

It may appear self-evident that when clients request that counsellors release information contained in their file to a third party, then counsellors fulfill their obligation and release the requested information. In New Brunswick, in the case of *McInerney v. MacDonald* (1992), the Court of Queen's Bench ruled that, in the absence of legislation, a patient is entitled upon request to examine and copy all information in her medical records, which the physician considered in administering advice or treatment, including records prepared by other doctors that the physician may have received. Although the case was based upon a physician-patient relationship, in all likelihood this would also apply to counsellors. The court ruled further that information arising outside the doctor-patient relationship does not apply, that the patient is not entitled to the records themselves; that the physical medical records of the patient belong to the physician. This would mean clients have a right to all information contained in counselling records. However, there are instances when it might not be prudent to release information when requested, at least not without taking some further action. It is sometimes impossible to cover the range of possible reasons why clients would want counsellors to release information however, the examples below might help counsellors institute a process that could be helpful in their own future discernment.

Lawyers, parents and other third parties often request client records. This request is generally accompanied by a 'Release of Information' form signed by the client. In many instances, clients do not know the possible impact of releasing information from their file since they generally have limited knowledge of the contents of what a counsellor may have written. They might remember many topics discussed in counselling, but this may not reflect comments written by the counsellor, which are often in short form, and intended to reflect the client's progress. At other times, the 'Release of Information' form may have no expiry date yet, many months after the client signs the form, a lawyer or some other party decides they might now ask for information ('fishing trip'). In these cases, counsellors ought to take reasonable care to protect the information of their clients. They might want to discuss reasons for requesting a copy of their records with clients. Counsellors could also share the contents of information written in their clients' records, allowing clients a more informed decision on releasing their information.

When counsellors are asked to release records to persons who have been assessed by them, it is important to determine who the client is. The counsellor may have been hired by the court to conduct an assessment, in which case counsellors need to refer the person to someone who can help them. Sometimes requests come from parents or guardians. Counsellors can sometimes record information that could put their minor client at risk with a parent or guardian (see Chapter Two). Though clients have the right of access to their own confidential information, it is important that counsellors set up protocols that allow them time to investigate requests to release information. The *Standards of Practice for Counsellors* (CCA, 2001) summarizes the main points counsellors need to consider in setting up a procedure to release information to interested parties.

Client Complaints
Counsellors have a right to protect themselves. With litigation and ethical complaints on the rise against Canadian counsellors, (although not as frequently as their American counterparts), it is important that counsellors inform clients that, if a lawsuit or ethical complaint is lodged against them by the client, the counsellor can use notes from counselling sessions for their own protection. This particular limitation to confidentiality, covered in the *Standards of Practice for Counsellors* (CCA, 2001), states that a counsellor may break confidence "when a client files a complaint or claims professional liability by the counsellor in a lawsuit". This practice might sound rather harsh given counsellors' responsibility to protect the confidentiality of the client. Some counsellors may feel they would not compromise the confidentiality of the client even to protect themselves. Other counsellors might act in a manner that would minimize the impact of releasing client information to protect themselves. The context, and perhaps the severity of the complaint, will inform counsellors about action they need to take.

Most counsellors agree that without trust it is unlikely that the counselling experience would proceed very far. Some hold the first principle of respect for the client's privacy as sacramental in nature, a sign of the unique and special nature of this relationship. The limits to confidentiality, which cover harm, legal obligation, and the protection of children while appearing clear, can often require interpretation. For example, if there is a "suspicion" of harm, sufficient reason is given to breach confidence.

Counsellors prefer to place emphasis on privacy and respect but are less comfortable with the need for limitations. Counsellors prefer to facilitate private conversations, not to restrict them. Lehr and Sumarah (2004) discuss what they believed is a serious ethical tension: if counselling sessions were private with limitations then both counsellors and clients must work within a tension, which should concern them both. On the one hand, these authors contend that counsellors promote clients to be open, honest and truthful, and then reveal that they are obligated to breach confidence about particular disclosures. In a sense, this might be interpreted as cautioning clients about being too open, honest and truthful.

To complicate matters, the courts can disagree with one another. One court ruling can argue that public peril is a more important concern than confidential conversations while another court can rule in the opposite direction. Some courts and some professionals, as in the Tarasoff case, argue that public concern took precedence over respecting certain professional relationships (Bersoff, 1997). On the other hand, it can be argued that some professional relationships require that confidentiality takes precedence over the duty to warn. Counsellors work with conflicted notions about the promise of confidentiality albeit within limits.

Confidentiality and the School Context

School counsellors often find themselves working in contexts with other professionals who are likewise concerned with the welfare of children. In many Canadian schools, counsellors are often considered by their teachers' associations as "teachers" and an expression often heard is, "A teacher is a teacher, is a teacher, is a teacher." Although many school administrators and union personnel often define counsellors as teachers, school counsellors identify themselves primarily as counsellors, and must adhere to a professional code of ethics that might be, in many ways, different from teachers' codes of ethics. In Nova Scotia for example, it is stipulated in the Comprehensive Guidance and Counselling Program for Nova Scotia Schools that, when counsellors teach they are teachers, but at all other times they are counsellors. The dual role encountered by many school counsellors who teach presents particular problems for confidentiality and perceived confidentiality. In some instances, counsellors teach students they counsel; they are required to help students, yet they are also required to balance confidentiality of the students with the needs of teachers and parents. School counsellors operate in an environment where their role is different, and often more complex than that of others with whom they work. The school counsellor, probably more than any other counsellor, is guided by the ethical principle of "responsible caring". Although "responsible caring" is a principle common to all counsellors, the school context brings it to the foreground because of the younger age of the persons who seek counselling.

It has often been acknowledged that children and adolescents are most isolated from society's protection and resources, and because of their greater social vulnerability, they are entitled to the most strenuously offered protections possible under the law (Rankin, 1990). Schools, and in particular counsellors, offer protection and safety to children, and typically rely upon the common law concept of in *loco parentis* to exemplify the duty of care relationship, which exists between school personnel and students. Counsellors sometimes approach situations similar to that of a reasonable parent. In other words, how would a reasonable parent respond to this particular situation? It is not unusual in a graduate practicum seminar, for example, to hear a counsellor in training to make comments like the following: "As a parent, I would certainly want to know that my 15-year-old daughter was having unprotected sex. I believe the school counsellor has to inform the parent." Counsellors have a responsibility to the larger societal context, which might include teachers, parents, and others responsible for the welfare of children. It also considers the cultural norms of the larger cultural and societal contexts, identifying that which is acceptable and that which is not acceptable, and that which is harmful or that which is not harmful.

The *Standards of Practice for Counsellors* (CCA, 2001) states that counsellors' duty to protect or care for children who are growing physically, psychologically, emotionally, and spiritually diminishes as children get older, and become more autonomous and more self-directed. However, the age at which school counsellors might feel confident that students are self-sufficient, and can make decisions on their own behalf is still in question. This might be true of the 15-year-old student described in the above example. This inevitably leads to a variety of counselling practices in different school systems. Drodge (1997) discusses the balancing act required by counsellors in many Canadian schools to maintain confidentiality and their duty to protect children. He acknowledges the dilemma of how actions intended to serve the public interest in school safety might jeopardize the confidential relationship between students and counsellors.

Dilemmas sometimes arise in work with minors because of limits on keeping information private, and because confidentiality could limit helping. In coping with such dilemmas, it is sometimes necessary for counsellors to go beyond minimally meeting reporting requirements or deciding when it is in the client's best interests to breach confidences. The counsellor's focus should be on how to empower clients to take the lead in sharing information when this is deemed necessary, and to work to minimize negative consequences that could result from such sharing. School counsellors and school personnel need to strike a balance between the duty to protect students from harm, and the need to preserve student confidentiality.

School counsellors are aware that any disclosure of student information without consent can endanger the trusting relationship they have with students. In related research, Sullivan, Ramirez, Rae, Razo and George (2002) surveyed psychologists' decisions to break confidentiality with risk-taking adolescent clients in order to report potentially dangerous behaviours to the parents, and found that psychologists fear that once confidentiality is broken, the adolescent will no longer trust them and will therefore disclose less information during therapy sessions. Taylor and Adelman (1989), in their research, provide useful guidelines to help counsellors resolve the ethical dilemma of breaking confidentiality with minor clients such as (a) explain to the client exactly why confidentiality must be broken, (b) discuss some of the possible consequences that could result from breaking confidentiality, and (c) determine how confidentiality might be broken in a way that minimizes negative outcomes for the client. They believe these guidelines could help counsellors incorporate the act of breaking confidentiality into the therapeutic process, and increase the likelihood that the therapeutic relationship would be maintained.

Teachers, Administrators, and Other Professionals

Counsellors often find themselves in a quandary over teachers' and principals' requests for information. The following comments, which come from school counsellors at an ethics workshop given by one of the authors, reflect this perplexity:

- "What rules apply to sharing information with principals?"

- "How do I tactfully deal with teachers who want to know things that I am not able to tell them?"

- "I need to more clearly know my role as a member of a school team in sharing confidential information about specific students when asked; the issues surrounding this are somewhat difficult for me. What are the general guidelines?"

- "What are the ethics of sharing information about a child's counselling/ therapy sessions with a concerned and involved teacher/principal/parent?"

- "You are counselling a student who has been referred to you by a teacher in your school. The teacher follows up, and wants an update on the progress of the student. How much do you reveal?"

- "Should information in confidential files be shared with teacher aids?"

The myriad of concerns expressed by school counsellors, who often feel isolated in their professional contexts, raise the inevitable question that as professional counsellors, how can student confidentiality be respected while responding to the demands of a school environment where different people/professionals all work for the well-being of the student?

The *CCA Code of Ethics* (2006) challenges counsellors' ethical responsibility to respect and to safeguard their clients' right to confidentiality, and to protect from inappropriate disclosure, any information generated within the counselling relationship. The team approach of a school context requires that counsellors consult with teachers and administrators regarding what they believe might be in the student-client's best interest. It may be in the best interests of good counselling practice and the well-being of some students that counsellors share some information about the counselling in a controlled way with colleagues. Counsellors foresee this aspect of their work, and inform students that there are times when talking to teachers might be helpful to their work together. When school counsellors talk about limits to confidentiality, they might consider negotiating with the student what they can and cannot share with others within the school and beyond. They might enter into a dialogue with students regarding information that is private, which will not need to be shared, and information that is confidential, which might need to be shared because it is in their best interests. Information shared with school counsellors belongs to students; counsellors need to seek permission to share it with teachers, administrators, and others.

A question often posed by school counsellors pertains to their obligation to release confidential student information to requests (demands) from outside agencies. As discussed in Chapter Two, information about students which does not require permission to release, should only be shared with others if consent has been given by their parents'/guardians' or if clients give their consent. In the case of police, any of the exceptions to confidentiality might apply, but the exception that might be more likely is a subpoena, a situation that requires the cooperation of the counsellor. In situations where records are subpoenaed, counsellors should cooperate with the authorities, but take steps to protect the confidentiality of students. They may feel more supported if they have a school-based committee in place to help them, and it might also be advisable for the school or the committee to seek a legal opinion. To avert compromising the integrity of counselling relationships, counsellors might find it useful to enter into a dialogue on confidentiality with the student early in the counselling relationship.

Parents

The *Standards of Practice for Counsellors* (CCA, 2001) recommends that counsellors take responsibility to set up school-based procedures for responding to requests for access to information. Having well-communicated protocols in place should prove helpful to counsellors, and might help safeguard the confidentiality of students. Counsellors who work with children have the difficult task of protecting the minor's right to privacy while at the same time respecting the parents' or guardians' right to information.

Parents and guardians do not have an absolute right to know all the details of their children's counselling. In order to address any request for information, schools and other institutions dealing with children use established protocols, which involve counsellors and other appropriate persons in adjudicating parental or guardian requests for information about their child's counselling information. When counsellors believe that disclosure of children's counselling information is not warranted. The *Standards of Practice for Counsellors* (CCA, 2001) recommends the following helpful steps:

- Invoke the protocol established within the workplace for dealing with such requests.

- Discuss the parental/guardian request with the child and seek his/her attitude with respect to disclosure.

- If the child is not willing to disclose, then explain to the parents/guardians the merits of respecting their child's desire for privacy.

- A joint meeting between the child and parents/guardians and managed by the counsellor may be an appropriate step.

- If a counsellor must disclose, inform the child beforehand, and limit disclosure to the parameters of the request.

- In some cases, such as in cases of suspected abuse, the counsellor may not wish to comply with a parental/guardian request for disclosure. In such circumstances, counsellors may need to seek legal advice and, in exceptional circumstances, be prepared to have their decision challenged in court.

To date, few schools appear to have a formalized protocol for parental access to children's confidential files. Across Canada, a few government departments of education are currently in the process of developing guidelines that might help schools in this process.

Many provinces now have freedom of information and protection of privacy legislation, which oversee or make decisions on third party requests for information. Sheppard (2003) in his regular contribution to the ethics section of *COGNICA*, CCA's newsletter, reported on a *British Columbia Freedom of Information and Protection of Privacy Act* ruling on a case where a mother attempted access to her children's elementary school counselling records after she had been contacted by child protection personnel. The mother wanted to know what her children had said to the counsellor. The school refused the request and the file was given to the Commissioner. In his ruling, the Commissioner refused the mother access to her children's school counselling records, and provided some guidelines that are helpful to school boards and others when making such challenging decisions. They are:

- There must be a careful distinction between the right of a parent to access information on 'behalf of a child' and a parent's desire to access their child's record at arms-length from the interests of the child.

- Despite the decision in this case, school counsellors' counselling notes are not, as a class of records, exempt from disclosure under the Act.

- Counselling notes, as in this case, can contain personal information as defined under the *Act*, and disclosure would invade children's right to personal privacy.

- Children, as in this case, can have a reasonable expectation of confidentiality when they share personal information with their school counsellor.

- A parent's 'right to know' must be balanced against the reasonable expectations of the benefits and risks when there is request to invade their children's privacy.

Negotiating Confidentiality: A Collaborative Approach

How and when do counsellors inform clients about the nature of counselling; what is confidential? What is not confidential? How do counsellors work with clients and what are their rights? What are alternative approaches that might work as well or better than the proposed counselling offered by counsellors? What other issues are important to the counselling relationship and the counselling process?

This section addresses the work of Sumarah, Lehr and Wheeldon (2000) who discuss confidentiality as a negotiation process that revolves around dialogue between counsellors and clients. Rather than eschewing a hierarchical perspective, which places counsellors in a position of 'all knowing' and knowledgeable of what is in the best interests of clients, these authors believe counsellors need to be more proactive and mutually active in their approach to confidentiality. They advocate, as does Prilleltensky (1994) that, "A commitment to treating persons fairly, equitably and with respect demands that a collaborative approach be used" (p.210).

In the collaborative approach discussed by Sumarah, Lehr and

Wheeldon (2000), counsellors engage in a therapeutic conversation with their clients on the subject of confidentiality, and actively and regularly revisit this conversation as part of the counselling process. The following diagram shows this collaborative approach, which portrays counsellors' responses to confidential information (p.84):

A Continuum of Sustained Concern

Professional/Personal Disquiet →→→	Counsellor Confusion →→→	Professional Supervision →→→	Counsellor Incompetence →→→	Threat to Self/Others Protection of Child

Counsellor Choice   **Professional Duty**

Counsellors, after some discernment, determine where on the continuum the issue of conflict is located as well as how to talk with clients about appropriately breaking the vow of confidentiality.

Sumarah, Lehr and Wheeldon argue that, in addition to the traditional process of informing clients about confidentiality, counsellors should also engage in a dialogue with clients on the whole issue of confidentiality. The first part of this conversation, they state, might sound like this:

Counsellor: Before we continue with our session today, I would like you to know that what happens between us is confidential. By that I mean that anything you tell me is held in strictest confidence, and will not be communicated to anyone else without your written permission. However, you also need to be aware that there are circumstances under which I will have to break this confidence. If I believe you were going to hurt yourself or someone else, or if I believe a child is in need of protec-

tion, I will need to break my confidence with you. In addition, you should know that I keep a written record of our meetings and if subpoenaed, I will have to release my records to others.

Although this is an abridged version, for most practising counsellors, this would probably contain the essential elements of an acceptable standard of practice, and would explain in part how they would inform clients in order to obtain consent for counselling. This consent should be obtained in advance, and cover not only the intervention, but also any related issues regarding record-keeping, reporting and other disclosures of information.

Sumarah, Lehr and Wheeldon contend that it is the responsibility of counsellors to actively revisit the issue of confidentiality on a regular basis with the client, not merely "as the need arises". In this dialogue, the authors states that counsellors should balance the right to privacy with the need to know:

Counsellor: I've really appreciated talking with you about how anger has been getting you into trouble with your grade 7 teacher and your classmates. In our time together, you've worked really hard at not allowing it to have such an unhappy influence upon you. Today, your teacher, Mr. S., asked me to meet with him regarding your progress so I was wondering if you and I could talk about what is important for him to know as well as things we talked about that you would prefer that he not know.

Bob: Does he need to know that I don't like that he never asks me to answer questions in class? He always asks Melissa and Tommy but never me even when I raise my hand!

Counsellor: You and I have discussed your disappointment about not being called upon to answer questions in class, and how this is one of those things that gives anger an edge over you. If Mr. S. knew this, do you think that his co-operation might help you?

Bob: Yeah. Well, okay but don't tell him that I am jealous of Melissa. Does he need to know things I told you about my family?

Counsellor: You and I have talked a lot about your family. What are some of the things that you would prefer that I not share with Mr. S.? (p 85).

This conversation would continue to engage the counsellor and the client in an on-going, active collaboration and negotiation around issues of confidentiality.

Protecting Confidentiality

Counsellors can take steps to actively protect clients' confidentiality, and recognize traps they can avoid that will also serve to protect their client's confidentiality and someone's privacy. Norma Drosdowech (1998b) lists tips in the *Manitoba Journal of Counselling*, which she believes might be helpful to school counsellors. Many of these tips are also applicable to counsellors outside the school system. In summary, she states that counsellors have to "be careful" and "be conscious" of what they are doing: Do not leave information lying around on the desk or the computer for others to see. Do not talk to others in situations where they might be overheard such as in hallways, on the telephone, or in staff rooms. Above all, protect client names. This might include paging students to the counsellor's office, consulting with other professionals, and engaging in collegial supervision.

At a basic level, counsellors should neither give nor receive information regarding a professional contact without permission, which might prove difficult in multidisciplinary agencies or schools. In this situation, it is important that counsellors discuss the nature of the agency or institution and request the appropriate consent for disclosure. A general rule regarding confidentiality is to say nothing or as little as possible without permission from clients. Comments such as the following are often heard: "I know you are seeing my friend, how is she doing?" or "I asked my friend to contact you and was wondering if he did." Sometimes the comments come from unexpected sources. For example, counsellors might be contacted by other professionals or the police, and asked if they are counselling or have ever counselled a particular person. In all cases, it is prudent to say little or nothing at all. Counsellors may simply comment, "I'm sorry, I cannot say whether someone is seeing me or not. I cannot divulge information without written consent." This might be quite intimidating if the person asking is an RCMP officer or a member of the local constabulary. Counsellors need to remember they are not obligated to talk to the police, and should resist all attempts to do so unless they have the client's consent.

Counsellors are also cautioned about issues like leaving phone messages for clients. It is generally wise to seek permission to leave messages either on voice mail or with a third party. The same holds true for faxes, email and any other means of communicating. Counsellors should avoid "on the run" consultations, staff room consultations, elevator consultations, or any other public area where someone might recognize the person about whom counsellors were talking (Pope and Vasquez, 1991). Counsellors also need to treat the client's right to confidentiality when consulting as they would with any disclosure of information, to only use professional language when talking about a client and to protect the integrity of their clients and their personal issues *as if* they were in the room listening to everything being said about them.

On the basis of true examples, Woody (1999) also reveals pitfalls associated with issues arising from having an office in the home: unsecured documents in the home, the telephone answering machine in the home, the family internet account, the family computer, the shared fax machine, the shared mail box, the family dining table, the accidental revelation, the

errant spouse, and exposure through litigation. Woody does not favor counsellors having an office at home but suggests that extra safeguards would have to be put in place to ensure client confidentiality.

Forgetfulness or lack of consciousness and gossip are other culprits that favour breaches of confidentiality. Forgetfulness (and gossip) might happen at the photocopier, in the staff room, or some other place where counsellors might momentarily lay a client file to rest. Misplacing or forgetting files has probably happened to most counsellors at some point in their career, and for many, it can be one of the most anxiety-producing situations they could encounter. Counsellors' files should be kept in a filing cabinet that has limited access. It should be double locked, meaning counsellors would be prudent to have a locksmith put an extra security bar on the filing cabinet. Security of filing cabinets bought at an office depot is generally easily breached. The extra security bar is designed to keep people out.

Gossip could be the difference between "need to know" and "fun to know". For example, when informed consent has been given to consult with other colleagues, counsellors might want to reveal client identity simply because this person is a celebrity or is a well-known person in the community. It is easy to let information slip that is not relevant to the conversation. Even in general conversation with friends, counsellors might let slip that "so and so" was once a client of theirs. At other times, clients who were once seen by a counsellor have died. It is important that information on individuals, whether alive or dead, be treated in a similar confidential manner. The urge to say things might be overwhelming at times. Counsellors are very careful about breaching confidential information about clients.

In summary, counsellors are cautious in or away from their workplace. It is easy to have a lapse in memory. Avoid pit stops while transporting files from one area to another. Never discuss cases except under supervisory conditions where information about client identity is protected.

Chapter Summary

Counselling relationships are based upon trust. Confidentiality is vital to the maintenance of this trust. This chapter discussed the concept of confidentiality as it applies to Canadian counsellors. Special emphasis was placed upon ways in which counsellors could maintain a healthy working relationship with clients while at the same time acknowledging the need or the requirement to break confidence without the client's consent. Counsellors discuss confidentiality with clients early in the counselling relationship as part of the informed consent process. Where possible, when it becomes necessary for counsellors to divulge information without the client's consent, counsellors take steps to reduce the fallout from this disclosure, and work with the client in a manner that protects the integrity of the therapeutic relationship.

This chapter also emphasized confidentiality as a negotiated process. In reference to Sumarah and his colleagues, this chapter presented scenarios that were reflective of how counsellor and client discuss and negotiate the intricacies of confidentiality, which were reflective of the client's best interest. The chapter concluded with a commentary on steps and tips counsellors

could take to maximise confidentiality of a client's information.

Learning Activities

1. *Small Group Discussion.* In small groups of three of four people, discuss ways in which people develop trust in various kinds of relationships, business, teacher-student, siblings, parents, long-term relationships.

2. *Case Study.* A counsellor in a rural, elementary school has been counselling Melissa.

Melissa, a 10 year old on issues related to trauma she experienced as a result of a dog attack one year earlier. Up until recently, both parents have been quite supportive of your work with their daughter, often coming into your office to talk with you regarding their observations. During your work with Melissa, discussions were held related to the conflict at home with her parents. This long lasting conflict between the parents ended in their recent marital separation. In the ensuing struggle for custody of Melissa, your notes have been subpoenaed by the father's lawyer who believes they contain information that might help his client in court. Both Melissa and her mother prefer that you not release your counselling notes. You believe releasing the notes could be detrimental to the progress you have been making with Melissa.

In groups, discuss the following questions:
a) Can the counsellor keep the notes from being used in court?
b) If the counsellors were reluctant to testify, what might he or she say to the court prior to testifying?

c) How should counsellors prepare for testifying in court?

3. *Role-play.* Develop and role-play several of the following confidentiality situations:

a) A principal in a school asks to see the file of a student with whom the counsellor is working.

b) A teacher asks you to update her about the student that she referred for academic counselling.

c) A male counsellor from another school asks you for information about a student that has transferred to his school.

4. *Panel Discussion.* As a class, arrange for a panel representative from other professions who deal with issues of confidentiality. Professions that could be considered include lawyers, doctors, massage therapists, chiropractors, financial advisors, and teachers. As a class, create a list of questions for the panelists.

5. *Triads.* In triads, with one person being the counsellor, one a client, and one an observer, role-play situations in which you tell a client that you must break confidentiality. Each member of the triad role-lays one of the following situations:

a) a client is a danger to others

b) a client reports that he has stolen some items from his place of work

c) parents have been given permission to see counselling notes for their child.

References

American Psychological Association (1996). American Psychological Association (1996). Strategies for private practitioners coping with subpoenas or compelled testimony for client records or test data. *Professional Psychology: Research and Practice*, 27(3), 245-251.

Bersoff, D. (1997). *Ethical conflicts in psychology*. Washington: American Psychological.

Bok, S. (1984) *Secrets*. New York: Vintage.

Bond, T. (1993). *Standards and ethics for counselling in action*. London: UK. Sage.

Canadian Counselling Association (2006). *Code of ethics*. Ottawa, Ontario: Author.

Canadian Counselling Association (2001). *Standards of practice for counsellors*. Ottawa, Ontario: Author.

Clements, W. G. & Uhlemann, M. R. (1991). Informed consent, confidentiality and access to information. In D, Turner and M. Uhlemann (Eds.) (1991). *A legal handbook for the helping professional*. Victoria: BC. The Sedgewick Society for Consumer and Public Education, School of Social Work, University of Victoria.

Daniels, T. & Ferguson, D. (1998). Key ethical issues for counsellors. *Guidance and Counselling*, 14(2), 3-7.

Drodge, E. (1997). Confidentiality and the duty to protect. *Canadian Journal of Education*, 22 (3), 312-322.

Drosdowech, N. (1998a). Consent, negligence and confidentiality in the school system. *Manitoba Journal of Counselling*, 24(3), 20-23.

Drosdowech, N. (1998b). Ten tips for guarding confidentiality. *Manitoba Journal of Counselling*, June, 25.

Fine, M. & Ulrich, L. (1998). Integrating psychology and philosophy in teaching a graduate course in ethics. *Professional Psychology: Research and Practice*, 19, 542-546.

Fly, B., VanBuck, W., Weinman, L., Kitchener, K. & Lang, P. (1997). Ethical transgressions of psychology graduate students: Critical incidents with implications for training. *Professional Psychology: Research and Practice*, 28(5), 492-495.

Lehr, R. & Sumarah, J. (2004). Professional judgment in ethical decision-making: Dialogue and relationship. *Canadian Journal of Counselling*, 38 (1), 14-24.

McInerney v. Macdonald (1992). 66 D.L.R. (4th) 736 (N.B.C.A.).

Meyer Estate v. Rogers (1991), 2.O.R. (3d)356, 6 C.C.L.T. (2d)102, 78 D.L.R. (4th)307 (Gen. Div).

New Zealand Association of Counsellors (2003), *New Zealand code of ethics*.

Nicolai, K.M., Scott, N.A. (1994). Provision of confidentiality information and its relation to child abuse reporting. *Professional Psychology: Research and Practice*, 25 (2), 154-160.

Pope, K.S. & Vasquez, M.J.T. (1991). *Ethics in psychotherapy and counseling*. San Francisco: Ca. Jossey-Bass.

Prilleltensky, I. (1994). *The morals and politics of psychology*. New York: State University of New York Press.

Rankin, W.W. (1990). *Confidentiality and clergy: Churches, ethics, and the law*. Harrisburg: PA. Morehouse.

Sheppard, G. (2003). Parent denied access to counselling notes. *COGNICA: Notebook on Ethics, Legal Issues, and Standards in Counselling*. Ottawa: ON.

Snook, I. (2003). *The ethical teacher*. Palmerston North: NZ. Dunmore Press.

Sumarah, J, Lehr, R. and Wheeldon, L. (2000). Confidentiality: Dialogue and discernment. In W. E. Schulz. *Counselling ethics casebook*, Ottawa, Ontario: Canadian Counselling Association.

Sullivan J.R., Ramirez, E., Rae, W.A., Razo, N.P. & George, C.A. (2002). Factors contributing to breaking confidentiality with adolescent clients: A survey of pediatric psychologists. *Professional Psychology: Research and Practice*, 33 (4), 396-401.

Tarasoff v. Regents of the University of California (1976). 17 Cal. Bd. 425, 551 p. 2a, 131 Cal. Rptr. 14.

Taylor, L. & Adelman, H. S. (1989). Reframing the confidentiality dilemma to work in children's best interests. *Professional Psychology: Research and Practice*, 20, 79-83.

Wigmore, J.H. (1961). *Evidence. Vol. 3. Sec. 2285*. (3rd Ed.). Boston: Little, Brown.

Woody, R.H. (1999). Domestic violations of confidentiality. *Professional Psychology: Research and Practice*, 30 (6), 607-610.

Chapter Four

———— ❖ ————

Boundary Issues and Violations in Counsellor-Client Relationships

———— ❖ ————

An ethical decision-making approach has considerable utility for assisting counsellors with the sometimes difficult issues associated with those circumstances likely to lead to boundary violations.

Chapter Objectives

The major focus of the chapter is on boundary violations in counselor-client relationships. The specific objectives are to:

- Define the major categories of boundary relationship violations

- Clarify the role of professional ethics in understanding and addressing boundary issues in counselling relationships

- Describe challenges to maintaining appropriate boundaries for counsellors

- Identify unique ethical prohibitions related to sexual boundary violations

- Provide suggestions for addressing ethical issues and challenges related to the maintenance of appropriate boundaries in counseling

- Explain dual and multiple relationships and related ethical issues and challenges

- Examine boundary violations in higher education and provide suggestions as to how to avoid them

Self-Inventory

Directions: Before reading this chapter, please use the following scale to indicate your attitudes towards issues in this chapter. For each statement, indicate the response that most closely identifies your beliefs and attitudes. Use the following code:

5 = Strong agreement with this item
4 = Agreement with this item
3 = Undecided about this item
2 = Disagreement with this item
1 = Strong disagreement with this item

___ If I were to be served by a client in his place of work I suspect that, like most people, he would know that on such an occasion I am only his customer rather than his counsellor.

___ Since counselling is only a special version of a friendship relationship, the ethical concern about the risks of dual or multiple relationships seems misplaced.

___ As a counsellor I would have a firm prohibition against accepting gifts from clients since to do otherwise would complicate appropriate boundaries.

___ In a small, remote, rural community, I would have no hesitation in accepting for counselling, the person who does work on my car at the local garage or who does my hair at the local hair salon.

___ If I knew that a client was romantically or sexually attracted to me, I would immediately take steps to refer the client to another counsellor.

___ As a counsellor, I could accept as a client, my colleague's adolescent son since I would have very little difficulty setting appropriate boundaries.

___ Touching, such as hugging a client, presents very little problem for me since I am comfortable with it and many clients will be reassured by that degree of closeness and acceptance.

___ I would be inclined to accept an invitation from a client to have a celebratory drink at a loud bar following a particularly productive counselling session.

___ Dual relationships are not inherently unethical or harmful.

___ As a general principle, the counselling profession should adopt the ethical motion, "once a client, always a client", meaning all post-counselling relationships with clients are ethically unacceptable.

___ As both a school counsellor and a teacher in a high school, I know that with my personality I would have little difficulty keeping these roles separated.

___ If I had an unemployed electrician as a client, I would see no problem with offering the client paid work on my home renovation project.

___ When a counsellor sees a client in a public place, such as a shopping mall, it is both natural and appropriate to take the initiative to greet the client.

___ For those counsellors who specialize in seeing clients with sexual dysfunctions, there may be occasions when a healthy sexual experience between the counsellor and client would be both therapeutic and ethical.

___ The reality of dual relationships presents a significant ethical challenge for all counsellors.

___ It is not unusual for a counsellor to be sexually attracted to a client.

___ The professor leading the personal growth group in my counselling program is also teaching me another graduate course and I have no doubt that she can make independent judgements about my performance in each of those courses.

___ As a general rule, it is discourteous and inappropriate for a counsellor to decline a gift from a client since the giving of a gift is an accepted way to express appreciation.

___ According to some published reports, dual relationship problems seem to constitute the most frequent type of ethical complaint brought against counsellors.

___ A concise and unequivocal prohibition against all dual relationships is best, both in principle and in practice, for all counsellors.

Introduction

Boundary violations are acts that breach the core intent of the professional-client association. They happen when professionals exploit the relationship to meet personal needs rather than client needs. Changing that fundamental principle undoes the covenant, altering the ethos of care that obliges professionals to place clients' concerns first. In fact, all of the boundaries in a professional-client relationship exist in order to protect this core understanding. (Peterson, 1992, p. 75)

Peterson uses the term "boundary violations" to refer to a wide range of behaviours, all of which constitute a violation of the ethical codes of conduct which are intended to set boundaries for relationships between human service professionals and their clients. A boundary can be viewed, metaphorically, as a membrane around the counsellor-client relationship, or as a set of constraints and limits, intended to maintain a sense of safety for clients and to protect the integrity of the relationship. In her book, *At Personal Risk: Boundary Violations in Professional-Client Relationships*, Peterson elaborates on four broad categories of boundary relationship violations. They are:

- *A reversal of roles.* This refers to situations in which the professional helper, to satisfy his or her personal needs, switches places with the client so that the client becomes, to a significant degree, the caregiver. Such role reversals violate the primary ethic of care in which the client's needs must remain paramount. They also blur the relationship boundaries between the client and helper, and leave the client vulnerable to abuse.

- *The secret.* Here, Peterson refers to the professional's act of withholding information which is vital to the client and the concealment of which may be damaging to the client's well-being in the relationship. The lack of disclosure may also compromise the client's ability to exercise informed consent. Typically, in such circumstances, the helper has dual agendas which contribute to maintaining the secret.

- *The double bind.* This type of boundary violation occurs whenever the client is placed in "a no-win" situation because of some request or demand by the professional helper. These are situations which present a conflict of interest for the client who feels trapped as a consequence of such a request because there are uncertain implications for the therapeutic relationship by refusing or acceding to it.

• ***The indulgence of personal privilege.*** Violation of this nature occurs whenever the professional decides to use his or her authority or position in the relationship to fulfil a personal agenda. This indulgence could range from using information gained from the client to pursue some personal benefit outside the relationship to establishing a sexual relationship with a client.

Relationship Boundaries and Professional Ethics

Whether or not one accepts precisely Peterson's conceptualization of ethical boundaries and their violations within professional relationships, it is clear that the boundaries are grounded on the fundamental principles upon which a professional code of ethical conduct is based. These ethical principles, according to Kitchener (1984, 1985) who has analyzed many human service ethical codes, are: do no harm; benefit others; respect autonomy; be fair; and be faithful. In the *Code of Ethics* of the Canadian Counselling Association (2006) these fundamental ethical principles are stated as follows:

Beneficience—being proactive in promoting the client's best interests.

Fidelity—honouring commitments to clients and maintaining integrity in counselling relationships.

Nonmalificence—not wilfully harming clients and refraining from actions that risk harm.

Autonomy—respecting the rights of clients to self-determination.

Justice—respecting the dignity and just treatment of all persons.

Societal interest—respecting the need to be responsible to society.

Most human service professional associations give supremacy to the ethical concept of nonmalificence which has its origins in the history of medical ethics (Beauchamp & Childress, 1979; Childress, 1981). This principle is more commonly stated as "above all do no harm". It obligates professional helpers not only to avoid inflicting harm intentionally, but to refrain from engaging in any activities in which there is a high risk of harm to their clients without any offsetting benefits. Clearly, when professional relationship boundaries are violated, clients are vulnerable to abuse, and helpers may fail to keep their ethical obligation to "do no harm".

These ethical principles and concepts are now receiving increased attention within the counselling profession and are reflected in the various ethical codes and standards of practice of national counselling associations (ACA, 2005; BAC, 2002; CCA, 2006). Also, many scholars are making significant contributions to advancing our understanding of this critical dimension of professional life (Davenport, 2004; Eberlein, 1988; Erickson, 2001; Goldsteiin, 1999; Herlihy and Corey, 1997; Hill and Mamalaksis, 2001; Kitchener, 1988, 1996; Koocher and Keith-Spiegel, 1998; Pope and Vasquey, 1998; Syme, 2003; Tomm, 1991). This attention may be an indication of the growing maturity of the profession as well as a response to the public demand for accountability in the provision of quality mental health services. Whatever its origin, it is consistent with Gibson and Mitchell's (1990) observation that, "A profession's commitment to appropriate ethical and legal standards is critical to the profession's earning, maintaining, and deserving the public's trust" (p. 45).

Historically, the counselling profession was quick to express publicly an understanding of its legal and ethical obligations. The American Personnel and Guidance Association produced the first code of ethics for counsellors in 1961, just ten years after its founding. In fact, it established an ethics committee just one year following its formation as a professional association (Gibson & Pope, 1993). This first code was published in three revised editions after 1961 (ACDA, 1988) and later, as the American Counselling Association, it published a *Code of Ethics and Standards of Practice for Counsellors* (1995) which was recently revised (2005). The much younger Canadian Guidance and Counselling Association adopted its first code of ethics in 1981 and approved a revised code in 1989 (CGCA, 1981, 1989). This Association has also taken a new name, and as the Canadian Counselling Association (CCA), it approved a new code of ethics in 1999 and a revised edition in 2006.

Maintaining Appropriate Boundaries: A Continuing Challenge

The *CCA Code of Ethics* (2006) acknowledges that the determination of appropriate ethical behaviour must frequently be made when issues are not clear cut and in circumstances in which conflict between several competing ethical principles must be resolved. For this reason, the *Code* contains a brief introduction to the process of ethical decision-making by providing an abbreviated sequence of steps which counsellors may follow as an aid to resolving ethical dilemmas. An ethical decision-making approach has considerable utility for assisting counsellors with the sometimes difficult issues associated with those circumstances likely to lead

to the boundary violations highlighted by Peterson (1992).

Although all professional ethical codes address boundary violations, maintaining clear and appropriate boundaries around relationships with clients continues to challenge helping professionals (Davenport, 2004; Faulkner and Faulkner, 1997; Hermansson, 1997; Johnson and Farber, 1996; Kolbert, Morgan and Brendal, 2002; Somer and Saadon, 1999; Syme, 2003; Vallally, 1995). Lamb and Catanzaro (1998) define boundary behaviours as, "...those behaviours or activities that mark the limits or parameters of appropriate, good, and ethical practice, including both structural (e.g., roles, time, place-space) and process (e.g., gifts, language, self-disclosure, physical contact, interactional patterns) dimensions" (p. 498). Smith and Fitzpatrick (1995) point out that there can be at least two aspects to non-sexual boundary concerns. They are "boundary crossings" and "boundary violations". A boundary crossing is a departure from usual counselling practice that may not necessarily place a client at risk. However, violations are those behaviours that place the client and the counselling process at risk of harm. Nevertheless, all boundary crossings should be of concern to counsellors and be kept to a minimum, since some researchers have concluded that sexual misconduct by helping professionals is typically preceded by a number of inappropriate non-sexual behaviours. This, they believe, contributes to the gradual erosion of a commitment to the maintenance of an ethical professional relationship (Folmon, 1991; Simon, 1989; Somer and Saadon, 1989; Strasburger, Torgensen, Sutherland, 1992).

The determination of appropriate

boundary behaviour within professional helping relationships can be quite complex and may be influenced by factors such as the counsellor's theoretical perspective, the client's presenting problem, and the client's behaviour. Despite this complexity, the competent management of relational boundaries is essential to the maintenance of professional safety and integrity in the counselling process (Epstein, 1994). Boundaries must be established within a process which, by its nature, is intimate and private and includes all the challenges connected to balancing closeness with maintaining appropriate physical and psychological distance (Wilmer, 1991).

Clients are often in their most vulnerable state when they seek out counselling. As clients share the most private details of their lives, counsellors listen empathically to their clients' pain, confusion, anxieties, and failures as well as to their hopes and dreams. Such sharing can result in feelings of intimacy and closeness. The individual attention and understanding of a counsellor may be unique in the life of a client. It is not surprising then, that this may engender strong feelings which may distort the client's view of the counsellor. In fact, some theoretical constructions of counselling acknowledge such distortions as an expected and normal transference phenomenon (Corey, Corey and Callahan, 2003; Miller and Stiver, 1997; Pope and Vasquey, 1998).

Transference usually means the transfer by the client to the counsellor and to the counselling relationship of emotions, needs, and conflicts experienced with significant others in their lives. These writers believe that counsellors must learn to recognize the many manifestations of transference and manage this phenomenon for the benefit of client insight and growth. Transference, it is assumed, can be evident in a wide range of strong client feelings towards the counsellor, such as love, anger, and ambivalence. Clients, for example, may develop an excessive need to please their counsellors in order to feel liked or valued by them.

From this theoretical perspective, there is also the complementary counsellor process of "countertransference". This refers to the counsellor transferring to the client feelings, thoughts, and behaviours which stem from the counsellor's life experiences. Such transfer might result from unresolved personal issues or from unmet needs in the counsellor's life. Gerald Corey (1986) writes about the potential in counselling for countertransference to occur:

> I found that when I began counselling others, old wounds opened and feelings that I had not explored in depth came to the surface. Being a therapist forces us to confront our unexplored blanks related to loneliness, power, death, sexuality, our parents and so on. (p. 362)

Counsellors who work with children and adolescents may face unique challenges with respect to the maintenance of appropriate professional boundaries. Children and young adolescents share concerns with adult counsellors which often centre around interpersonal conflicts and hurtful experiences with parents, teachers, and other adults. Counsellors may violate relationship boundaries by an excessive need to be over-protective of their young clients. Children may also distort the counselling relationship out of their need to receive nurturance and care from the counsellor that are lacking from other adult caregivers in their lives. Clearly, it is the responsibility of counsellors to protect children from abusive experiences. However, this responsibility can be extended beyond acceptable relational boundaries when counsellors, out of their unmet needs, unwittingly develop unhealthy dependency upon their clients and the dynamics of their counselling are transformed into those of a needy, overprotective parent.

Eliana Gil (1991) cautions about the strong risks of countertransference when counsellors work with abused children:

> I have alluded to countertransference issues throughout the book but deal with them at length here to emphasize the relevance of countertransference to work with abused children. These children are extremely vulnerable, with tumultuous histories of abuse, neglect, and deprivation. Consequently, they elicit a multitude of responses from the therapist, including intense hostility, sadness, protective impulses, and/or feelings of helplessness.

> Occasionally, a child's plight demands special attention, and highly qualified professionals may find themselves behaving in unexpected ways. For example, one clinician treating an abused child got herself licensed as a foster parent and entered into a dual role with the child. Another clinician, whose rescuing instinct was strongly evoked, adopted a child. While these may be extremes, the clinician must carefully assess any personal conduct that threatens to develop outside the bound-

aries of a strict therapeutic relationship. (p. 192)

Of course, working with adult clients who have been sexually abused as children may be just as challenging. Briere (1992), author of a number of publications focusing on therapy for sexually abused adults, is cognizant of the risks of boundary violations when doing this work. It is his view that:

> Perhaps the most dangerous form of abuse-related countertransference is that of boundary violation. Examples of therapist boundary confusion include any type of sexual behaviour with clients, obviously inappropriate personal disclosures during therapy, excessively intrusive questions or statements, and most generally, the therapist's use of the client to gratify the therapist's own needs. (p. 160)

Whether or not one accepts the theoretical constructs of transference and countertransference, most counselling practitioners and theorists would agree that the counsellor's unmet needs can sometimes be so enmeshed in the counselling relationship that they obstruct his or her objectivity. Most individuals who enter the counselling profession have a strong motivation to help others and they receive satisfaction from being instrumental in helping others to make positive personal changes. These are acceptable and even desirable motivations, but it requires that counsellors be "...aware of their own needs, areas of unfinished business, potential personal conflicts, defences, and vulnerability" (Corey, 1996, p. 369). By continuing to develop their self-understanding, counsellors minimize the risks of relationship violations and avoid abuse of their power within counselling. Erickson (1993) succinctly captures the importance of avoiding boundary violations for those seeking counselling;

> Perhaps the main problem with boundary violations is that they replicate for the most susceptible their experiences with role reversal in their families of origin. Thus, instead of a corrective emotional experience, our conduct with those clients offers a replication of these early, familiar, very damaging encounters. It should be noted that many boundary violations are initiated by clients who consciously or unconsciously try to reduce the window of their own vulnerability by equalizing the power differential in the relationship. These situations, too, are our responsibility to manage appropriately to prevent the client's having yet another experience with being hurt by those who are supposed to help. (p. 87)

Sexual Boundary Violations: An Unequivocal Prohibition

One of the most serious boundary violations which continues to be of grave concern to counsellors, clients, and the general public is sexual contact between helpers and their clients. Such unethical behaviour continues to occur despite the fact that ethical codes of conduct for all the helping professions explicitly prohibit it (Haspel, Jorgenson, Parsons & Wincze, 1997; Kolbert, Morgan and Brendal, 2002; Russell, 1993; Rutter, 1990; Somer and Saadon, 1999; Syme, 2003; Vasquey and Kitchener, 1988). Very early in the history of the helping professions, sexu-

al contact between helpers and their clients was considered to be unacceptable. In fact, the medical profession has had this prohibition since it was included in the Hippocratic Oath over two thousand years ago (Edelstein, 1943). Despite this longstanding taboo, sexual exploitation continues to occur within all helping professions (Gabbard, 1989; Lamb and Catanzaro, 1998; Layman and McNamara, 1997; Somer and Saadon, 1999; Pope, 1990; Screenivasan, 1989; Wilson, 1993).

The *CCA Code of Ethics* (2006) states the prohibition against sexual contact between counsellors and clients in Section B, Article B12 as follows:

B12 **SEXUAL INTIMACIES**
Counsellors avoid any type of sexual intimacies with clients and they do not counsel persons with whom they have had a sexual relationship. Counsellors do not engage in sexual intimacies with former clients within a minimum of three years after terminating the counselling relationship. This prohibition is not limited to the three year period but extends indefinitely if the client is clearly vulnerable, by reason of emotional or cognitive disorder, to exploitative influence by the counsellor. Counsellors, in all such circumstances, clearly bear the burden to ensure that no such exploitative influence has occurred, and to seek consultative assistance.

This ethical Article is similar in intention to those found in the ethical codes of other professions. For example, in its position paper (Screenivasan, 1989), the Canadian Psychiatric Association states, "Erotizing the physician/patient relationship is unacceptable under any circumstances and cannot be rationalized as therapy" (p. 234). The *Code of Ethics* (1996) of the

National Association of Social Workers stipulates, "The social worker should under no circumstances engage in sexual activities or sexual contact with current clients, whether such contact is consensual or forced." In several additions to the principles of medical ethics adapted by the American Psychiatric Association (APA, 1985), practitioners are alerted to the potential for sexual misconduct, "...the necessary intensity of the therapeutic relationship may tend to activate sexual and other needs and fantasies on the part of both patient and therapist, while weakening the objectivity necessary for control" (p. 4). Also, like most codes, it states that, regardless of the behaviour of the client, it is the clear and unequivocal responsibility of the professional under all circumstances to maintain this fundamental relationship boundary.

Article B12 of the *CCA Code of Ethics* (2006) also addresses the issue of post-termination sexual relationships between counsellors and their former clients. There is not an absolute prohibition against such a possibility. However, it does set a time limit of three years after the ending of the counselling relationship and presents a general criterion which must be met in order to make any such sexual contact ethically acceptable. Also, the counsellor is held responsible for ensuring that there is no risk of exploitation and other psychological harm because of the previous professional contact and/or the mental health status of the former client.

CCA's ethical position is similar to that taken by the American Psychological Association (1995), although the APA sets a shorter time limit of two years. Professional contact between a counsellor and a client can be for any of a wide range of services which can vary considerably with respect to duration and intensity. A contact can be as brief as one session with limited client self-disclosure and little possibility for the development of a transferential relationship. In such a circumstance, it may be inappropriate to have an absolute prohibition against any future non-professional contact between the counsellor and client. However, this ethical point of view remains controversial and the American Psychiatric Association has an absolute ban on sexual contact with former patients (Gabbard, 1994; Lamb and Catanzaro, 1998).

According to a study by Gibson and Pope (1993) as well as others (Borys, 1994; Anderson and Kitchener, 1996), counsellors continue to support this basic ethical standard and disapprove of a wide range of behaviours which they consider to be a violation of this relationship boundary. These researchers report that one-fourth of the 21 behaviours judged to be unethical by the 579 certified counsellors in their study were of a sexual nature. These findings are encouraging however, since they indicate a growing public and professional awareness of the disturbing extent of sexual abuse within society in general including abuse within professional-client relationships.

Sexual Boundary Violations: The Extent of the Problem

The prevalence rates for this most serious boundary violation are difficult to establish. However, a number of national surveys based on self-reports conducted in the U.S. have been summarized by Pope and Bouhoutsos (1986). They conclude that sexual intimacies between clients and male therapists happen at a rate of from nine to twelve percent and from two to three percent between female therapists and their clients. Another U.S. study conducted by Bajt and Pope (1989) reports that an alarming proportion of sexual contact between therapists and clients include children and adolescents. They report that 56 percent of the victims in this study were young clients including girls between the ages of three and 17 years with a mean age of 13 years and boys ranging from seven to 16 years with an average age of 12 years. In a study by Parsons and Wincze (1995), therapists were asked whether they had treated in the past three to four years, any clients who report having sexual contact with a previous therapist. As many as 22 percent reported that they had done so. Garrett (1994) based his study on 1000 clinical psychologists in Great Britain and reports that four percent admitted to sexual contact with current or previous clients with an additional two percent reporting sexual intercourse with clients and two percent having some other type of erotic relationship. The Ethics Committee of the Canadian Counselling Association reports that in 2005 it dealt with complaints against two of its members for alleged sexual relationships with their clients (Hendricken-Eldershaw, 2005).

Somer and Saaden (1999) conducted a study in which they "undertook to enhance our understanding of the process of leading to sexual boundary violation in psychotherapy from the perspective of former exploited patients" (p. 504). They conclude that the offending psychologists were well regarded but typically worked alone and that there was a gradual sequence of ethical boundary crossings that eventually led to the sexual misconduct. Many of the clients had been sexual

abused as children. Their initial positive response to the sexual activity was later seen by those clients as exploitation and re-victimization. The authors make the very well-founded recommendation that professionals working with victims of sexual abuse avoid working in isolation from other colleagues and that they seek out peer consultation and support.

Some writers, particularly feminist therapists, have expressed the view that sexual contact within counselling, the victims of which are largely female clients, can only be properly understood within the context of larger societal problems which result in the abuse of women (Gartell, Herman, Olarte, Feldstein, Localio, 1986). Others believe that counsellors and counsellor-educators should be particularly well qualified and committed to the advancement of the recognition, understanding, and processes required to change societal structures which lead to the victimization of women (Frazier and Cohen, 1992).

What Can Be Done?

Regardless of the reasons for sexual misconduct by professional helpers, clearly this critical problem requires urgent attention. In the counselling profession, as in other human service groups, it demands increased recognition as an issue of immediate concern and requires the attention of individual practitioners, counsellor-educators and professional organizations.

One strategic element in an overall initiative to address the risks of sexually-based boundary violations has been proposed by Corey (1991). He argues that counsellor education programs do not adequately prepare counsellors to deal appropriately with sexual feelings which they may experience towards their clients. Corey proposes that, "Educational programs must provide a safe environment in which trainees can acknowledge and discuss feelings of sexual attraction. If counsellors do not learn how to deal with these feelings, they are more likely to become involved in seductive exchanges. Ideally, practitioners will be able to accept their sexual feelings and desires toward certain clients and at the same time see the distinction between having these feelings and *acting* on them" (p. 68).

The Canadian Counselling Association in its *Standards of Practice for Counsellors* (CCA, 2001) provides the following guidelines to counsellors to assist them in avoiding boundary violations with respect to intimate and sexual matters in their counselling:

1. Be vigilant about setting and maintaining counsellor-client boundaries in counselling.

2. Seek out consultation or supervision whenever a sexual attraction to a client is likely to interfere with maintaining professional conduct.

3. Avoid making sexualized comments about a client's appearance or physical attributes.

4. Be alert and sensitive to client differences and vulnerabilities with respect to their sexuality.

5. Avoid exploring client sexual history or sexual experiences unless it is germane to the goals or counselling for the client.

6. Avoid disclosures about the counsellor's sexual experiences, problems or fantasies.

7. Respond to any seductive or sexualized behaviour on behalf of clients in a professional manner consistent with the goals of counselling and seek consultation or supervision when needed.

Counsellors may experience feelings of sexual or romantic attraction towards clients more frequently than has been previously acknowledged (Gottlieb, Sell, Schoenfeld, 1988). In a U.S. survey, 87 percent (95 percent of men, 75 percent of women) of the 575 psychotherapists responding to a questionnaire reported that they had been sexually attracted to their clients on at least one occasion (Pope, Keith-Spiegel, Tabachnick, 1986). Pope and his associates (Pope, Sonne, Holyroyd, 1993) have published a book entitled *Sexual Feelings in Psychotherapy: Explorations for Therapists and Therapists-in-Training*. This publication is based on the author's research on sexual attraction in therapeutic relationships. It should serve as a useful resource in responding to Corey's call to deal with this important dimension of counselling in graduate training and in continuing professional development programs.

Some professionals, (e.g., Gartell, Herman, Olarte, Feldstein, Localio, 1987) advocate that professional human service associations should adopt a policy of mandatory reporting to ethics committees or licensing boards of all complaints heard from clients of being sexually abused by their counsellors. In fact, a number of U.S. states have legislated such mandatory reporting (Appelbaum, 1990). In Canada, two provincial commissions examining sexual misconduct in the medical profession have each recommended mandatory reporting by medical practitioners whenever patients allege that they were sexually abused by a member of that profession (Hardy, 1993; Wilson, 1993).

In the United States, five states have enacted legislative prohibitions against therapists' sexual misconduct. The Minnesota statute, for example, provides the following conditions for civil action against any offending therapist:

> A cause of action against a psychotherapist for sexual exploitation exists for a patient or former patient for injury caused by sexual contact with the psychotherapist, if the sexual contact occurred: (1) during the period the patient was receiving psychotherapy from the psychotherapist; or (2) after the period the patient received psychotherapy from the psychotherapist if (a) the former patient was emotionally dependent on the psychotherapist; or (b) the sexual contact occurred by means of therapeutic deception.
>
> The patient or former patient may recover damages from a psychotherapist who is found liable for sexual exploitation. It is not a defence to the action that sexual contact with a patient occurred outside a therapy or treatment session or that it occurred off the premises regularly used by the psychotherapist for therapy or treatment sessions. (Minn. Stat. 148A.02. 1996. In Haspel, Jorgenson, Wincze and Parsons, 1997, p. 64).

Non-Sexual Dual and Multiple Relationships

In addition to the increased attention to sexual dual relationships between counsellors and clients, there has been a dramatic increase in professional concerns over non-sexual dual relationships (Anderson and Kitchener, 1996; Borys, 1994; Davenport, 2004; Erickson, 2001; Gibson and Pope, 1993; Hill and Mamalaksis, 2001; Kagle and Giebalhausen, 1994; Pearson and Piazza, 1997; Pope, Tabachnick and Keith-Spiegel, 1987; Pope, 1991; Syme, 2003). Dual or multiple relationships are present whenever counsellors have non-professional relationships with clients, supervisees, research participants, or students. Such relationships can occur before, during and after professional relationships and many of them have the potential to compromise counsellors ethical obligations to their clients.

The *CCA Code of Ethics* (2006) addresses dual relationships in a number of sections of the *Code*.

B8 **DUAL RELATIONSHIPS**
Counsellors make every effort to avoid dual relationships with clients that could impair professional judgment or increase the risk of harm to clients. Examples of dual relationships include, but are not limited to, familial, social, financial, business, or close personal relationships. When a dual relationship cannot be avoided, counsellors take appropriate professional precautions such as informed consent, consultation, supervision, and documentation to ensure that judgment is not impaired and no exploitation occurs.

B11 RELATIONSHIPS WITH FORMER-CLIENTS

Counsellors remain accountable for any relationships established with former clients. Those relationships could include, but are not limited to those of a friendship, social, financial, and business nature. Counsellors exercise caution about entering any such relationships and take into account whether or not the issues and relational dynamics present during the counselling have been fully resolved and properly terminated. In any case, counsellors seek consultation on such decisions.

C7 CONFLICT OF INTEREST

Counsellors who engage in consultation avoid circumstances where the duality of relationships, or the prior possession of information could lead to a conflict of interest.

F7 RELATIONAL BOUNDARIES

Counsellors who work as counsellor-educators, trainers, and supervisors establish relationships with their students, trainees, and supervisees such that appropriate relational boundaries are clarified and maintained, and dual relationships avoided.

Anderson and Kitchener (1996) report that psychologists identify eight distinct types of non-sexual, non-romantic relationships with clients. They are: personal-friendship, collegial-professional, supervisory-evaluative, religious, collegial-professional plus social, and workplace. They further divide these contacts into those that are either circumstantial and or intentional.

Pearson and Piazza (1997) have made a very helpful contribution to this challenging ethical area by proposing a comprehensive classification of dual relationships based on their review of

previous efforts appearing in the literature, including Anderson and Kitchener's analysis. As they point out, often well-meaning and ethically motivated counsellors and other professionals can be unaware of the ethical implications inherent in the duality of relationships. The following excerpt from their classification system helps to heighten awareness of this problematic area:

Circumstantial Multiple Roles

At times, dual relationships occur out of pure coincidence. Examples would include a counsellor who is returning defective merchandise to a store where the only clerk is a current client, or a counsellor whose child befriends the child of a client. As noted by Smith and Fitzpatrick (1995), such incidents are inevitable in small communities. The risk in these cases seems to be primarily a misinterpretation of which relationship is in effect at the time, and therefore which relationship "rules" are in effect. For example, the aforementioned store clerk could interpret his or her customer's complaints or demands as personal attacks, thereby affecting the client-counsellor relationship.

Structured Multiple Professional Roles

Dual relationships often occur because they are integral to a professional's job. They can occur between professional colleagues or between a professional and a non-professional, such as a student or a client. What is essential to this type of dual relationship is that the nature of all the relationships is professional. Structured multiple professional roles are prevalent in counsellor education and supervision. Kurpuis, Gibson, Lewis, and Corbet (1991) pointed out that faculty and supervisors can hold multiple roles simultaneously, including those of instructor, advisor, supervisor, administrator, employer, and mentor. These roles are typically perceived as complementary and are not necessarily thought to create conflicts of interest for the professional. However, problems can arise if the professional loses sight of, or takes advantage of, the power differential inherent in his or her role (e.g., the faculty member who requests first authorship of an article when the student co-author deserves it). The supervisee or student may give in to the professional's wishes due to the power differential of one relationship, even if the nature of the other relationship is peer-like.

Shifts in Professional Roles

Dual relationships can occur when there is a change or shift in organizational structure, thereby changing the relationships of those within the organization. An example of such a shift would be two therapists in an agency who have developed a close friendship. Because there is no power differential (they are both at the line staff level), this creates no difficulty. The supervisor of their program then resigns, and one of them successfully bids for the position, gaining supervisory authority over the other. Other examples of this are when clients become co-workers or former students are hired as faculty in programs from which they graduated, suddenly becoming educators to former peers and peers with former educators.

Personal and Professional Role Conflicts

In this type of dual relationship, there may be a pre-existing professional relationship that is followed by a personal relationship, or the parties may have already developed a personal relationship that is followed by a professional

one. Circumstances in which a professional relationship becomes complicated by the development of a subsequent personal relationship seem to have received the most notoriety, primarily because of increasing attention to sexual dual relationships between professionals and their clients, students, or supervisees. However, this type of dual relationship does not have to be sexual or romantic in nature. Social or peer-like dual relationships, such as collaborating on publications or engaging in a shared pastime (such as a sport or a hobby), are also examples of mixing personal and professional roles.

The Predatory Professional

This final type of dual relationship occurs "when professionals exploit the relationship to meet personal needs rather than client needs" (Peterson, 1992, p. 75). Predatory professionals deliberately seduce or exploit others, unconcerned with anything but their own needs. (Pearson and Piazza, pp. 92-97)

The dual relationship clauses in the *CCA Code of Ethics* (2006) implicitly recognize that counselling relationships are characterized by a significant power differential. Clients are typically at their most vulnerable state when seeking help. They are expected to be open and self-focused in the counselling encounter. However, this is not the emotional status or behaviour expected of the counsellor. Indeed, such openness and self-preoccupation by the counsellor could very well constitute ethical misconduct. It is this inherent power imbalance that can make dual relationships so challenging to the maintenance of appropriate relational boundaries.

Typically, studies of the beliefs and experiences of helping professionals with respect to dual relationships have involved asking participants to respond to an inventory of behaviours presented by the researchers (Anderson and Kitchener, 1996; Borys, 1988; Gibson and Pope, 1993). The results of these studies suggest a lack of consensus for some of the behaviours at the lower end of the duality scale, but there appears to be an agreement that certain behaviours are never acceptable, such as: selling a product to a client, engaging in sexual activity with a client during counselling or after termination, inviting a client to a personal party or social event, accepting more than a small token gift from a client, accepting an invitation from a client to attend a social event, inviting a client to an office party or open house. In a Canadian study, Tracey Nigro (2000, Nigro and Uhlemann, 2004) obtained from counsellors who were members of the Canadian Counselling Association in British Columbia their beliefs about, and actual experiences with, dual relationships. Participants reported having experienced a wide range of challenging dual relationship circumstances. However, it appears that many of these were circumstantial. The study used a survey instrument with 39 dual relationship activities to assess the counsellors' views about the ethicality of such activities. The following are the five items, in descending order, that received the highest disapproval rating:

- Having a sexual relationship with a client

- Going into business with a client

- Having a sexual relationship with a previous client six months after termination

- Inviting a client to a personal party or social event

- Hiring a client.

With our heightened awareness of this area of ethical concern, it is not surprising that a variety of behaviours are consistently identified because of their problematic duality. St. Germaine (1993) adds to this list of counsellor behaviours those which, in her view, constitute a dual relationship with clients:

- buying a product or service from a client

- selling a product to a client

- entering into a business or financial arrangement with a client

- attending social events of a client or inviting client to social events

- developing a friendship or social relationship with a client or former client

- accepting gifts from a client

- counselling a clients close friend, family member, or lover

- counselling a close friend or family member or the lover of a friend or family member

- counselling an employee or student, or a close friend or family member of an employee or student. (p. 29)

Boundary Issues Within Higher Education

During the past decade there has been increased attention to dual and multiple relationships within higher education (Biaggio, Paget and Chenoweth, 1997; Bowman, Hatley and Bowman, 1995; Davenport, 2004; Johnson and Nelson, 1999; Kolbert, Morgan and Brendal, 2002; Rupert and Holmes, 1997). Some writers have focused, in particular, on the multiple roles integral to the work of those educators in professional preparation programs (Congress, 1996; O'Conner, Slimp and Burian, 1994). Counsellor-educators and others are urged to increase their attentiveness to the multiple roles which they might be expected to fulfil, and whenever possible to avoid the duality of relationships that might result in contradictory goals and expectations and have the potential for harm to their students. In addition to Article 7 in Section F of the *CCA Code of Ethics*, this obligation is addressed in two additional articles:

F4 CLARIFICATION OF ROLES AND RESPONSIBILITIES

Counsellors who engage in counselling supervision of students or trainees take responsibility for clarifying their respective roles and obligations.

F8 OBLIGATION TO INFORM

Counsellors who work as counsellor-educators, trainers, and supervisors take steps to inform students, trainees, and supervisees, at the beginning of activities associated with these roles, of all reasonably foreseeable circumstances under which confidentiality may be breached during such activities.

Counsellor-educators may be particularly at risk of unwittingly entering into dual relationships since they often fill many roles, including supervisor, administrator, teacher and mentor. As others have pointed out (Bowman, Hatley and Bowman, 1995; Congress, 1996; Corey, Corey and Callahan, 1998; O'Conner, Slimp and Burian, 1994; Pearson and Piazza, 1997), counsellor-educators and supervisors need to be alert to the potential ethical pitfalls of dual relationships before they engage in counselling with their students or supervisees. The risks of blending these

roles, according to Kitchener (1988), are that "...confidentiality may be compromised, student autonomy sacrificed, the therapy process impaired, and objectivity damaged..." (p. 217).

Some scholars have expressed the view that multiple relationships are not entirely avoidable within educational settings since professionals in such workplaces are expected to play multiple roles (Biaggio, Paget, Chenoweth, 1997). If so, this is all the more reason to pay close attention to such relationships in order to avoid any harmful effects. Some students have identified unfairness and favouritism as the main harmful risks of dual relationships in academia (Sullivan and Ogloff, 1998). In a recent study (Kolbert, Morgan and Brendal, 2002) the researchers found some differences between the potential harm attributed to relationships by professors and the concerns expressed by students. The educators limit the possible risks to the effect on their objectivity while the students express additional apprehension about the possibility of exploitation. However, both groups recognize the inherent power differential in faculty-student relationships and assigned the primary responsibility to faculty members for ensuring appropriate boundaries.

The British Association of Counselling in its various codes of ethics addresses the ethical concern over dual relationships (BAC 1986, 1990, 1993). For example, in the *Code of Ethics and Practice for the Supervision of Counsellors* (1986) it states:

> Supervisors and counsellors are both responsible for setting and maintaining clear boundaries between working relationships and friendships or other relation-

ships, and making explicit the boundaries between supervision, consultancy, therapy and training. (2.3, p. 175)

The British codes recognize the potential for a conflict of interest when those with managerial responsibility for counsellors also serve as supervisors. It sets out the following ethical guideline to avoid the potential risks in such duality of roles:

Counsellors who have line managers owe them managerial accountability for their work. The counselling supervisor role should be independent of the line manager role. However, where the counselling supervisor is also the line manager, the counsellor should also have access to independent consultation support (B.3.3, BAC, 1990)

There is also a growing recognition of the potential for boundary violations associated with the experiential components of programs to prepare group counsellors as well as with the personal growth experiences required in some counsellor education programs (Davenport, 2004; Forester-Miller, Duncan, 1990; Kottler, 2004). There is the concern that the multiple roles of counsellor-educators who teach and supervise these important components of counsellor education programs can unwittingly have a negative consequence for students. Therefore, the *CCA Code of Ethics* (2006) contains the following two clauses intended to alert counsellor-educators, trainers, and supervisors to these concerns and of the need to take the necessary precautions.

F10 DEALING WITH PERSONAL ISSUES Counsellors responsible for counsellor education, training, and supervision recognize when such activities evoke significant personal issues for students, trainees, and supervisees and refer to other sources when necessary to avoid counselling those for whom they hold administrative, or evaluative responsibility.

F10 SELF GROWTH ACTIVITIES Counsellors who work as counsellor-educators, trainees, and supervisors ensure that any professional experiences which require self-disclosure, and engagement in self-growth activities are managed in a manner consistent with the principles of informed consent, confidentiality, and safeguarding against any harmful effects.

In addition, counsellor-educators and others would do well to heed the advice of Bowman, Hatley and Bowman (1995) who state the following, based on their study of this complex ethical area:

The findings of this study support the need for continuing professional debate and research regarding ethics within the area of faculty-student relationships. More important, the focus should be expanded to include more student input, because mentoring, friendship, and social interaction often have a profound influence on a student's overall graduate training experience. Students and faculty can benefit from exploring the issues of what constitutes a dual relationship, what unethical behaviours are, and how the abstractness of any ethical code on faculty-student relationships should be interpreted. (p. 241)

The Association for Specialists in Group Work also address the dual relationship issues in its *Ethical Guidelines for Group Counsellors* (ASGW, 1989). To minimize the risks to students, it set the following standard of conduct for educators:

> Students who participate in a group as a partial course requirement for a group course are not evaluated for an academic grade based upon their degree of participation as a member in a group. Instructors of group counselling courses take steps to minimize the possible negative impact on students when they participate in a group course by separating course grades from participation in the group and by allowing students to decide what issues to explore and when to stop. (#9 [g])

Managing Dual Relationship Challenges

School counsellors need to be particularly cognizant of the ethical challenges associated with the duality of roles, since they frequently have to balance their responsibilities to students, parents, colleagues and the community (Hardy, 1986). Ethical dilemmas can emerge when the expectations of these groups are in conflict. For example, if school counsellors are expected to accept school disciplinary functions, it may compromise their obligations to place the welfare of clients first, since it is difficult to reconcile the dual roles of disciplinarian or informant and counsellor. In a position statement on the potential for role duality inherent in the position of school counsellor, Michael Dougherty (Herlihy and Corey, 1997) takes a firm position:

> I believe that school counsellors should avoid roles such as disciplinarian, substitute teacher, and lunchroom/bathroom/bus monitor that conflict with their primary role as counsellors to students. The unique role of the counsellor in the school makes the taking on of such roles highly questionable as they are likely to violate some of the basic tenets of the counselling relationship (e.g., confidentiality). As a consequence, new counselling relationships with students may be inhibited and existing ones may be compromised. (p. 175)

School counsellors can avoid some of these ethical dilemmas by being sensitive to and anticipating the potential complications arising from attempting to fulfil multiple roles. They can, in collaboration with their professional colleagues, reach a shared view of their role and responsibilities and ensure that it is clearly communicated to students, teachers, administrators, and parents.

Of course, as many authors acknowledge, helping professionals who work in small communities and in institutions such as schools and hospitals, cannot always avoid dual and multiple relationships with clients (Brownlee, 1996; Erickson, 2001; Faulkner and Faulkner, 1997; Horst, 1989; Keith-Spiegel and Koocher, 1985; Schank, 1998; Schank and Skovholt, 1997; Stockman, 1990). Schank and Skovholt (1997) conducted a study of the dual relationship dilemmas experienced by psychologists working in rural and small communities. They identify these four categories of dual relationship ethical dilemmas that are likely to occur for counsellors and other mental health practitioners who work in small, rural communities:

- overlapping social relationships
- overlapping business or professional relationships
- the effects of overlapping social relationships on the counsellor's family
- working with more than one family member or clients or with others who have friendships with individual clients. (p. 46)

They appear to share the view of Smith and Fitzpatrick (1995) that:

Overlapping relationships are inevitable in rural and other small communities where community involvement lessens suspicion and increases approachability and where "denying help to a potential client because of a pre-existing relationship could mean that the person gets no help at all." (p. 502)

Syme (2003) also acknowledges that non-sexual dual relationships are not always avoidable, and not just in rural communities. In her engaging and fact-filled book, *Dual Relationships in Counselling and Psychotherapy* (2003), she provides many guidelines for navigating this challenging ethical terrain and gives the following sage advice:

Broadly a dual relationship arises in any situation where a therapist assumes more than one significantly different role either simultaneously or sequentially with a client, supervisee or trainee. These relationships are not necessarily harmful, or unavoidable, but there is always the potential for a conflict of interest and of exploitation of the person seeking help. This makes it critical that whenever there is a possibility of a dual relationship the therapist, who is the person who knows the difficulties that could arise in such relationships, must think about and perhaps discuss with a supervisor the potential conflicts of interest and exploitation before entering into such a relationship. (p. 8)

Hill and Mamalakis (2001) address the unique ethical challenges confronting family therapists who work with religious communities as leaders, employees, or community members and, in particular, the need to negotiate the dual relationships that they are likely to encounter. They propose the following set of reflective questions to be used by individuals who find themselves confronted with the associated ethical dilemmas:

- What are the expectations, obligations, or interests of my role in the dual relationship?
- Do these expectations, obligations, or interests conflict with those of my role as therapist?
- Why, of all other available options, am I considering this therapeutic or dual relationship?
- Might a role I serve outside of therapy keep someone from coming to me for therapy?
- Might I experience a conflict of interest by beginning therapy or a dual relationship?

Kitchener (1988) proposes a number of guidelines to help counsellors, counsellor-educators, and other helpers, regardless of type of work environment, to recognize dual relationships with a high probability of ethical difficulties. She suggests the use of these three guidelines:

First, as the incompatibility of expectations increases between roles, so will the potential for misunderstanding and harm; for example, the incompatibility of the expectation of a therapist and a supervisor.

Second, as the obligations of different roles diverge, the potential for divided loyalties and loss of objectivity increases.

Last, as the power and prestige between the professional's and consumer's roles increases, so does the potential for exploitation and an inability on the part of the consumers to remain objective about their own best interests.

These three taken together suggest that the relationship has a high potential for misunderstanding, confusion and damage. (p. 219)

Herlihy and Corey (1997) conclude their comprehensive treatment of dual relationships in counselling with the following succinct thematic summary of the state of current understanding of this complex area of ethical concern:

- Multiple relationship issues affect virtually all mental-health practitioners, regardless of their work setting or clientele.

- All professional codes of ethics caution against dual relationships, but newer codes acknowledge the complex nature of these relationships.

- Not all multiple relationships challenge us to monitor ourselves and to examine our motivations for our practices.

- Whenever you consider becoming involved in a dual or multiple relationship, seek consultation from trusted colleagues or a supervisor.

- There are few absolute answers that can neatly resolve dual or multiple relationship dilemmas.

- The cautions for entering into dual or multiple relationships should be for the benefit of our clients or others served, rather than to protect ourselves from censure.

- In determining whether to proceed with a dual or multiple relationship, consider whether the potential benefit outweighs the potential for harm.

- It is the responsibility of counsellor preparation programs to introduce boundary issues and explore multiple relationship questions. It is important to teach students ways of thinking about alternative courses of action.

- Counsellor education programs have a responsibility to develop their own guidelines, policies, and procedures for dealing with multiple roles and role conflicts within the program. (pp. 223-228)

This inventory of key beliefs about the nature of role duality in counselling is a cogent reminder of the dynamic and emerging nature of our ethical strivings within the counselling profession. It also underscores the necessity for counsellors to exercise a high level of ethical reasoning and concern in fulfilling their obligation to maintain appropriate relational boundaries with clients. In fact, most instructional models advocated for the teaching of professional ethics emphasize the need to teach a process of ethical reasoning and decision-making (Gawthrop & Uhlemann, 1992; Elliot, 1991; Kitchener, 1984).

The *CCA Code of Ethics* (2006) declares that members, counsellor-educators, as well as others, have a responsibility to induct students into the ethical standards of the profession. It states:

F4 **ETHICAL ORIENTATION**
Counsellors who are responsible for counsellor education, training, and supervision have an obligation to make their students, trainees, and supervisees aware of their ethical responsibilities as expressed in the CCA *Code of Ethics*, and *Standards of Practice for Counsellors*.

This ethical requirement is intended to ensure that the counselling profession meets a fundamental condition of professionalism: having a membership with a thorough understanding of and adherence to a shared code of ethical conduct. Although such codes are essential to the maintenance of the integrity and accountability of the profession, boundary violations as well as other ethical misconduct, can only be prevented when counsellors have the ability and courage to exercise a high level of ethical judgement. As Pope and Vasquey (1991) express it:

> Such codes...cannot do our thinking, feeling and responding for us. [They] can never be a substitute for the active process by which the individual therapist or counsellor struggles with the sometimes bewildering, always unique, constellation of responsibilities, contexts, and competing demands of helping others. (p. xi)

Chapter Summary

The maintenance of appropriate boundaries in counsellor-client relationships has emerged during the past several decades as a significant ethical challenge for the counselling profession. This chapter reviewed the reasons for this development and explained how insufficient attention to the management of boundaries can lead to violations of the longstanding ethical principle of nonmalficence, sometimes expressed as, "above all else do no harm". There was also an examination of the various categories of boundary violations and the challenges faced by counsellors in maintaining the constraints and limits necessary to protect the integrity of counselling relationships.

The prohibition by all human service professions against sexual, dual relationships with clients was addressed with attention to the considerable harmful effects of such serious ethical violations. As well, there was an identification of the many different types of nonsexual dual and multiple relationships that can confront and challenge counsellors and with the potential to compromise their fiduciary duty to their clients. Although not all dual relationships can be avoided, suggestions were provided with the intent to empower counsellors to make ethically informed decisions when confronted with such problematic circumstances. This discussion also extended to the potential for boundary violations in higher education, their harmful effects, and how to avoid them. The chapter concluded with the acknowledgement that ultimately counsellors will act ethically only when they have the intention, awareness, and knowledge to do so, combined with the capacity to make ethical decisions in what can sometimes be challenging dilemmatic circumstances.

Learning Activities

1. *Small Group.* Generate two or three specific examples of counsellor behaviour that might constitute boundary violations in each of Peterson's four categories: a reversal of roles, the secret, the double bind, and the indulgence of personal privilege.

2. *Discussion.* Generate several examples of boundary crossings that might not be boundary violations. Explain why. Now give several examples of those that would very likely be boundary violations. Discuss the difference.

3. *Small Group.* Generate a list of six examples of counsellor inappropriate non-sexual conduct that might begin the erosion of the counsellor's commitment to the maintenance of appropriate boundaries.

4. *Role-play.* In pairs, with each of you taking turns as counsellor and client, simulate a dialogue that you think should take place between you about the duality of roles in each of the following circumstances:

   a) You are the only counsellor in a small, isolated community and you have decided to accept the local automobile mechanic as your client.

   b) You have seen a client for three sessions and you have just discovered that he/she is a very close personal friend of your first cousin with whom you have frequent social contact.

   c) One of your current clients has just registered for your Saturday program, Nature's Rules for Health Living, that you offer in the community.

   d) As a school counsellor you also have to teach Social Studies to one of Grade 10 classes. Several students in the class are also seeing you individually for counselling concerning some very significant personal and familial issues.

   e) Since your last session with her, this client has left two phone messages for you. In one she invites you to a local concert for which she has a free ticket. The second message invites you to her home to attend her birthday party.

   f) As a school counsellor you saw today for counselling a 16-year-old (daughter) of a parent who is also the local hockey coach. Your daughter is also on the team and you are also very involved as a parent. While standing next to the coach while watching the game, she says "Joan said she dropped by to see you today. I was quite surprised and I am concerned. Can you tell me what's bothering her?"

5. *Pair-share.* Discuss how you would handle the following circumstances:

   a) You are seeing a client for the first session. He discloses that he was seeing another counsellor (someone you know to be a CCA member) for some time but their relationship in his words "has blossomed into a romantic relationship and so since we obviously stopped the counselling relationship, we are now dating and I need a new counsellor".

   b) You have been seeing a client for five or six sessions. In the last four weeks the following has been happening: you have had several intimate dreams about this client; you are particularly excited about seeing this client on the days of his/her appointment; just yesterday you checked his/her counselling file for the address and on your way home you took a detour to drive by his/her house.

6. *Small Group/Pairs.* Discuss how you might handle the following circumstantial challenges as a counsellor:

a) Your young adult daughter just brought her new friend to the family holiday party. You immediately recognized him as a client with whom you worked intensely several years ago as a school counsellor to help him deal with years of sexual abuse by his brother.

b) As a counsellor you had a client terminate counselling with you prematurely after 4-5 sessions. She did not say why. She has now graduated and is now a temporary clerical employee in the student services division where you also work.

c) Last year you saw an unemployed man for a number of counselling sessions. You knew that he was certified as an electrician. You just received a telephone call in which he told you that he has started a new electrical business and was wondering if you would hire him for electrical work needed on your major house renovations project.

In pairs simulate the conversation you might have in each of these circumstances.

7. *Guest Speakers.* Invite counsellor(s) to class from different work environ-

ments (i.e., schools, private practice, community clinics, etc.) and ask them to identify the type of challenges to boundary maintenance that they experience in their work.

8. *Survey.* Construct a dual relationship survey, or use, with permission, a survey already published (i.e., Nigro, 2004; Borys and Pope, 1989) and administer it to colleagues in your graduate program and/or to a number of practising counsellors.

References

Adler, J., and D. Rosenberg (1992). Psychotherapy. *Newsweek*, April 13, 53-58.

American Counselling Association (2005). *Code of ethics.* Alexandria, VA: Author.

American Counselling Association (1995). *Code of ethics and standards of practice.* Alexandria: VA: Author.

American Counselling and Development Association (1988). *Code of ethics.* Alexandria: VA: Author.

American Psychiatric Association (1985). *Principles of medical ethics with annotations especially applicable to psychiatry.* Washington, DC: Author.

American Psychiatric Association (1995). *Ethical principles of psychologists and code of conduct.* Washington, DC: Author.

American Psychological Association, Ethics Committee (1988). Trends in ethics uses, common pitfalls, and published resources. *American Psychologist*, 43(7), 564-572.

Anderson, S.K. & Kitchener, K.S. (1996). Nonromantic, nonsexual posttherapy relationships between psychologists and former clients: An exploratory study of critical incidents. *Professional Psychology: Research and Practice*, 27(1), 59-66.

Appelbaum, P.S. (1990). Statutes regulating patient-therapist sex. *Hospital and Community Psychiatry*, 41, 15-16.

Association for Specialists in Group Work (1989). *Ethical guidelines for group counsellors*. Alexandria, VA: Author.

Bajt, T.R. & Pope, K.S. (1989). Therapist-patient sexual intimacy involving children and adolescents. *American Psychologist*.

Beauchamp, T.L. & Childress, L.F. (1979). *Principles of biomedical ethics*. Oxford: Oxford University Press.

Beck, M., K. Springen, D. Foote (1992). *Newsweek*, April 13, 53-58.

Biaggio, M., Paget, T.L. & Chenoweth, M.S. (1997). A model for ethical management of faculty-student dual relationships. *Professional Psychology: Research and Practice*, 28, 184-189.

Borys, D.S. (1994). Maintaining therapeutic boundaries: The motive is therapeutic effectiveness, not defensive practice. *Ethics & Behaviour*, 4, 267-273.

Bowman, V.E., Hatley, L.D. & Bowman, R.L. (1995). Faculty-student relationships: A dual role controversy. *Counsellor Education and Supervision*, 34, March, 232-242.

Briere, J.N. (1992). *Child abuse trauma: Theory and treatment of the lasting effects*. Newbury Park, CA: Sage Publications.

British Association for Counselling (1990). *Code of ethics and practice for counsellors*. Rugby: England. Author.

British Association for Counselling (1986). *Code of Ethics and Practice for the Supervision of Counsellors*. Rugby: England. Author.

British Association for Counselling (1993). *Code of ethics and practice for counsellors*. Rugby: England. Author

British Association for Counselling and Psychotherapy (2002). *Ethical framework for good practice in counselling and psychotherapy*. Rugby: England. Author.

British Columbia Association of Clinical Counsellors (2005). *Code of ethical conduct and standards of clinical practice for registered clinical counsellors*. Victoria: British Columbia.

Brownlee, K. (1996). The ethics of nonsexual dual relationships: A dilemma for the rural mental health professional. *Community Mental Health Journal*, 32, 497-503.

Butler, M.H., & Gardner, B.C. (2001). Ethics and the ideal helping relationship: Response to Hill and Mamalakis. *Family Relations*, 50, 209-214.

Canadian Counselling Association (2006). *Code of ethics*. Ottawa. Ontario: Author.

Canadian Counselling Association (2001). *Standards of practice for counsellors*. Ottawa, Ontario: Author.

Canadian Guidance and Counselling Association (1989). *Guidelines for ethical behaviour*. Ottawa, Ontario: Author.

Canadian Guidance and Counselling Association (1981). *Guidelines for ethical behaviour*. Ottawa, Ontario: Author.

Canadian Psychological Association (2006). *A Canadian code of ethics for psychologists*. Old Cheben, Quebec: Author.

Catalano, S. (1997). The challenges of clinical practice in small or rural communities: Case studies in managing dual relationships in and outside of therapy. *Journal of Contemporary Psychotherapy*, 27(1), 23-35.

Childress, L.F. (1981). *Priorities in biomedical ethics*. Philadelphia: Westminister Press.

Congress, E.P. (1996). Dual relationships in academia: Dilemmas for social work educators. *Journal of Social Work Education*, 32, 3, 329-338.

Corey, G., M.S. Corey & Callahan, P. (2003). *Issues and ethics in the helping professions* (6th ed.). Pacific Grove, CA: Brooks/Cole.

Craig, J.D. (1991). Preventing dual relationships in pastoral counseling. *Counseling and Values*, 36, 49-54.

Davenport, D.S. (2004). Ethical issues in the teaching of group counseling. *The Journal for Specialists in Group Work*, 29, 43-49.

Eberlein, L. (1988). The new CPA code of ethics for Canadian psychologists: An education and training perspective. *Canadian Psychology*, 29(2), 206-212.

Edelstein, L. (1943). *The Hippocratic Oath: Text, translation and interpretation. Bulletin of the History of Medicine, Supplement 1*. Baltimore: John Hopkins Press.

Elliot, M.M. (1991). *Ethical decision-making and judgements of psychologists: An exploratory study*. Unpublished doctoral dissertation, University of Alberta, Edmonton.

Epstein, R.S. (1994). *Keeping boundaries: Maintaining safety and integrity in the psychotherapeutic process*. Washington, DC: American Psychiatric Press.

Erickson, Beth M. (1993). *Helping men change: The role of the female therapist*. Newbury Park, CA: Sage Publications Limited.

Erickson, S.N. (2001). Multiple relationships in rural counseling. *Family Journal: Counseling and Therapy for Couples and Families*, 9(3), 302-304.

Faulkner, K.K., & Faulkner, T.A. (1997). Managing multiple relationships in rural communities: Neutrality and boundary violations. *Clinical Psychology Science and Practice*, 4, 225-234.

Folman, R.Z. (1991). Therapist-patient sex: Attraction and boundary problems. *Psychotherapy*, 28, 168-173.

Forester-Miller, H. & Duncan, J.A. (1990). The ethics of dual relationships in the training of group counsellors. *The Journal for Specialists in Group Work*, 15(2), 88-93.

Frazier, P.A. & Cohen, B.B. (1992). Research on the sexual victimization of women: Implications for counsellor training. *The Counselling Psychologist*, 20, 141-158.

Frick, P.E. (1994). In L.M. Oldham and L.M. Riba (Eds.), *American psychiatric press review of psychiatry*, Vol. 13 (pp. 415-432). Washington, DC: American Psychiatric Press.

Gabbard, G.O. (1994). Reconsidering the American Psychological Association's policy on sex with former patients: It is justifiable? *Professional Psychology: Research and Practice*, 25, 329-335.

Gabbard, G.O. (1989). *Sexual exploitation in professional relationships*. Washington, D.C.: American Psychiatric Press, Inc.

Gartell, N., Herman, J., Olarte, S., Feldstein, M. & Localio, R. (1986). Psychiatrist-patient sexual contact: Results of a national survey I: prevalence. *American Journal of Psychiatry*, 143, 1126-1131.

Gartell, N., Herman, J., Olarte, S., Feldstein, M. & Localio, R. (1986). Reporting practices of psychiatrists who knew of sexual misconduct by colleagues. *American Journal of Orthopsychiatry*, 57, 287-295.

Gartrell, N.K. (1992). Boundaries in lesbian therapy relationships. *Women and Therapy*, 12(3), 29-50.

Garrett, T. (1994). Sexual contact between psychotherapists and their patients. In Clarkson, P. and Pokorny, M. (Eds.), *The Handbook of Psychotherapy*. London, Routledge.

Gawthrop, J., & M. Wilemann (1992). Effects of the problem-solving approach in ethics training. *Professional Psychology: Research and Practice*, 23, 1, 38-42.

Gibson, W.T. & Pope, K.S. (1993). The ethics of counselling: A national survey of certified counsellors. *Journal of*

Counselling and Development, 71, 330-336.

Gibson, R.L., & Mitchell, M.H. (1990). *Introduction to counselling and guidance* (3rd. ed.). New York: Macmillan.

Gil, E. (1991). *The healing power of play: Working with abused children.* New York, NY: Guildford Press.

Goldstein, H. (1999). On boundaries. Families in Society: *The Journal of Contemporary Human Services*, 80, 435-438.

Gothell, T.G. & Gabbard, G.O. (1993). The concept of boundaries in clinical practice: Theoretical and risk-management dimensions. *American Journal of Psychiatry*, 130, 188-196.

Gottlieb, M.C. (1993). Avoiding exploitative dual: A decision-making model. *Psychotherapy*, 30, 41-48.

Gottlieb, M.C., Sell, J.M. & Schoenfeld, L.S. (1988). Social/romantic relationships with present and former clients: State licensing board actions. *Professional Psychology: Research and Practice*, 19, 459-462.

Green-Vasan, U. (1989). Sexual exploitation of patients: The position paper of the Canadian Psychiatric Association. *Canadian Journal of Psychiatry*, 34, 234-235.

Hall, M.E.I., & Barber, B.A. (1996). The therapist in a missions context: Avoiding dual role conflicts. *Journal of Psychology and Theology*, 24, 212-219.

Hardy, G. (1993). Mandatory reporting of sexual abuse: Physicians say regulations go too far. *Evening Telegram*, January 7, p. 12.

Haspel, K.C., Jorgenson, L.M., Parsons, J.P., & Wincze, J.P. (1997). Legislative intervention regarding therapist sexual misconduct: An overview. *Professional Psychology: Research and Practice*, February, 28, 1, 63-72.

Hendricken-Eldershaw, C. (2005). *The ethics committee.* Canadian Counselling Association. Ottawa, Ontario

Herlihy, B. & Corey, G. (1997). *Dual relationships in counselling.* Alexandria: VA. American Counselling Association.

Herlihy, B., & Corey, G. (1997). *Boundary issues in counseling: multiple roles and responsibilities.* Alexandria, VA: American Counseling Association.

Hermansson, G. (1997). Boundaries and boundary management in counselling: The never-ending story. *British Journal of Guidance & Counselling*, 25, 133-143.

Hill, M.R., & Mamalakis, P.M. (2001). Family therapists and religious communities: negotiating dual relationships. *Family Relations*, 50, 199-208.

Hines, A.H. & Charg, A.S. (1998). Dual agency, dual relationships, boundary crossings, and associated boundary violations: A survey of military and civilian psychiatrists. *Military Medicine*, 163, 826-833.

Horst, E.A. (1989). Dual relationships between psychologists and clients in rural and urban areas. *Journal of Rural Community Psychology*, 10, 15-23.

Huey, W.C. (1986). Ethical concerns in school counselling. *Journal of Counselling and Development*, 64, 321-322.

Johnson, S.H. and Farber, B.A. (1996). Maintenance of boundaries in psychotherapeutic practice. *Psychotherapy*, 33, 391-402.

Johnson, W.B. and Nelson, N. (1999). Mentor-protégé relationships in graduate training: Some ethical concerns. *Ethics and Behaviour*, 9, 189-210.

Kagle, J.D., & Giebelhausen, P.N. (1994). Dual relationships and professional boundaries. *Social Work*, 39, 213-220.

Kathler, J.A. (2004). Realities of teaching group counseling. *The Journal for Specialists in Group Work*, 29, 51-53.

Keith-Spiegel, P. & Koocher, G.P. (1985). *Ethics in psychology*. Hillsdale, N.J.: Lawrence Eribaum.

Kitchener, K.S. (1996). There is more to ethics than principles. *The Counseling Psychologist*, 24(1), 92-97.

Kitchener, K.S. (1988). Dual role relationships: What makes them so problematic? *Journal of Counselling and Development*, 67, 217-221.

Kitchener, K.S. (1985). Ethical principles and ethical decisions in student affairs. In H.J. Canon & R.D. Brown (eds.), *Applied ethics in student services*. San Francisco: Jossey-Bass.

Kitchener, K.S. (1984). Intuition, initial evaluation and ethical principles: Foundation for ethical decisions in counselling psychology. *The Counselling Psychologist*, 12, 43-55.

Kolbert, J.B., Morgan, B., & Brendal, J.M. (2002). Faculty and student perceptions of dual relationships within Counselor Education: A Qualitative Analysis. *Counselor Education and Supervision*, 41, 193-205.

Koocher, G.P., & Keith-Spiegel, P. (1998). *Ethics in psychology: Professional standards and cases*. New York: Oxford University Press.

Koocher, G.P. (1994). The commerce of professional psychology and the new ethics code. *Professional Psychology: Research and Practice*, 25, 4, 355-361.

Kurplus, D., Gibson, G., Lewis, J., & Corbet, M. (1991). Ethical issues in supervising counseling practitioners. *Counsellor Education and Supervision*, 31, 48-57.

Lamb, D.H. & Catanzaro, S.L. (1998). Sexual and non-sexual boundary violations involving psychologists, clients, supervisors, and students: Implications for professional practice. *Professional Psychology: Research and Practice*, October 29, 5, 498-503.

Layman, M.J. & McNamara, J.R. (1997).

Remediation for ethic violations: Focus in psychotherapists' sexual contact with clients. *Professional Psychology: Research and Practice*, 28, 281-292.

Lerman, H. & Rigby, D.N. (1990). Boundary violations: Misuse of the power of the therapist. In H. Lerman & N. Porter (Eds.). *Feminist ethics in psychotherapy* (pp. 51-59). New York: Springer Publishing.

Lord-Nelson, L.G., Summers, J.A., Turnbull, A.P. (2004). Boundaries in family-professional relationship: Implications for special education. *Remedial and Special Education*, 25, 153-165.

Mamalchas, P.M., & Hill, M.R. (2001). Evaluating potential dual relationship: A response to Butler and Gardner. *Family Relations*, 50, 214-219.

Miller, G.M. and Larrabee, R.J. (1995). Sexual intimacy in counselor education and supervision: A national survey. *Counselor Education and Supervision*, 34, 4, 332-343.

Miller, J.B. & Stiver, I.P. (1997). *The healing connection: How women form relationships in therapy and in life*. Boston: Beacon Press.

National Association of Social Workers (1996). *Code of ethics*. Washington, DC: Author.

Nigro, T. and Uhlemann, M.R. (2004). Dual relationships in counselling: A survey of British Columbian counsellors. *Canadian Journal of Counselling*, 38, 1, 36-53.

Nigro, T. (2000). *Attitudes and experiences of British Columbian counsellors regarding dual relationships*. Unpublished Masters thesis, University of Victoria, BC.

O'Conner Slimp, P.A. & Burian, B.K. (1994). Multiple relationships during internships: consequences and recommendations. *Professional Psychology: Research and Practice*, 25, 1, 39-45.

Ontario School Counsellors Association (2003). *Ethical guidelines for Ontario school counsellors*. Bridgenorth: Ontario. Author.

Ontario Association of Consultants, Counsellors, Psychotherapists, and Psychometrists (2004). *Code of ethics*. Toronto: Ontario. Author.

Parsons, L.P., & Wincze, J.P. (1995). A survey of client-therapist sexual involvement in Rhode Island as reported by subsequent treating therapists. *Professional psychology: Research and practice*, 26, 171-175.

Pearson, B., & Piazza, N. (1997). Classification of dual relationships in the helping professions. *Counsellor Education and Supervision*, 37, December, 89-99.

Pettifor, J. & Pitcher, S. (1982). Ethics training in Canadian graduate schools. *Canadian Psychology*, 23(4), 235-242.

Peterson, M.R. (1992). *At personal risk: Boundary violations in professional-client relationships*. New York, NY: W.W. Norton & Co., Inc.

Pope, K.S. (1985). How clients are harmed by sexual contact with mental health professionals: The syndrome and its prevalence. *Journal of Counselling and Development*, 67, 222-226.

Pope, K.S. (1990). Therapist-patient sexual involvement: A review of the research. *Clinical Psychology Review*, 10, 477-490.

Pope, K.S. & Bouhoutsos, J.C. (1986). *Sexual intimacy between therapists and patients*. New York: Praeger Press.

Pope, K.S. & Vasquey, M.J.T (1998). *Ethics in psychotherapy and counselling*,(2nd. ed.). San Francisco: Jossey-Bass.

Pope, K.S., Sonne, J.L. & Holyroyd, J.(1993). *Sexual feelings in psychotherapy: Explanations for therapists and therapists-in-training*. Washington, DC: American Psychological Association.

Pope, K.S. (1994). *Sexual involvement with therapists*. Washington, DC: American Psychological Association.

Pope, K.S., Keith-Spiegel, P. & Tabachnick, B.G. (1986). Sexual attraction to clients: The human therapist and the (sometimes) inhuman training system. *American Psychologist*, 41, 147-158.

Rupert, P.A. & Holmes, D.L. (1997). Dual relationships in higher education. *Journal of Higher Education*, 68, 6, 660-678.

Russell, J. (1993). *Out of bounds: Sexual exploitation in counselling and therapy*.

Rutter, P. (1990). *Sex in the forbidden zone*. London: Unwin Paperbacks.

Ryan, C.J. and Anderson, J. (1996). Sleeping with post: The ethics of post-termination patient-therapist sexual contact. *Australian and New Zealand Journal of Psychiatry*, 30, 171-178.

Salisbury, W.D. and Kinnier, R.T. (1996). Post-termination friendship between counsellors and clients. *Journal of Counseling and Development*, 74, 495-499.

Sell, J.M., Gottlieb, M.C. & Schoenfeld, L. (1986). Ethical considerations of social/romantic relationships with present and former clients. *Professional Psychology: Research and Practice*, 17(6), 504-508.

Schank, J.A. (1998). Ethical issues in rural counselling practice. *Canadian Journal of Counselling*, 32 (4), 270-283.

Schank, J.A., & Skovholt, T.M. (1997). Dual-relationship dilemmas of rural and small-community psychologists. *Professional Psychology: Research and Practice,* 28 (1), 44-49.

Screenivasan, U. (1989). Sexual exploitation of patients: The position of the Canadian Psychiatric Association. *Canadian Journal of Psychiatry*, 34, 234-235.

Simon, R.I. (1989). Sexual exploitation of patients: How it begins before it happens. *Psychiatry Annual*, 19, 104-112.

Smith, D. & Fitzpatrick, M. (1995). Patient-therapist boundary issue: An integrative review of theory and research. *Professional Psychology: Research and Practice*, 26, 499-506.

Somer, E. and Saadon, M. (1999). Therapist-client sex: Clients' retrospective reports. *Professional Psychology: Research and Practice*, 30, 5, 504-509.

St. Germaine, J. (1996). Dual relationships and certified alcohol and drug counsellors: A national study of ethical beliefs and behaviours. *Alcoholism Treatment Quarterly*,14, 2, 29-44.

St. Germaine, J. (1993). Dual relationships: What's wrong with them? *American Counselor*, 2, 25-30.

Stadler, H.A. (1986). To counsel or not to counsel: The ethical dilemma of dual relationships. *Journal of Counselling and Human Service Professions*, 1(1), 134-140.

Stockman, A.E. (1990). Dual relationships in rural mental health practice: An ethical dilemma. *Journal of Rural Community Psychology*, 11(2), 31-45.

Strasburger, L.H., Jorgensen, I. & Sutherland, P. (1992). The prevention of psychotherapist sexual misconduct: Avoiding the slippery slope. *American Journal of Psychotherapy*, 46, 544-55.

Sullivan, L.E. and Ogloff, J.R. (1981). Appropriate supervision-graduate relationships. *Ethics and Behaviour*, 8, 229-247.

Syme, Gabrielle (2003). *Dual relationships in counselling and psychotherapy*. London: Sage Publications.

Thoreson, R.W., Shaughnessy, P. & Frazier, P.A. (1995). Sexual contact during and after professional practices and attitudes of female counsellors. *Journal of Counseling & Development*, 74(1), 84-89.

Tomm, K. (1991, Winter). The ethics of dual relationships. *The Calgary Participator: A Family Therapy Newsletter*, 1, 11-15.

Tymchuk, A. (1986). Guidelines for ethical decision making. *Canadian Psychology*, 27(1), 36-43.

Valentich, M., & Gripton, J. (1992). Dual relationships: Dilemmas and doubts. *Canadian Journal of Human Sexuality*, 1(3), 155-166.

Vallally, S.E. (1995). *Defining professional boundaries in therapeutic relationships*. Unpublished Master thesis, University of Calgary, Calgary, Alberta.

Vasquey, M.J.T. & Kitchener, K.S. (1988). Introduction to special issue. *Journal of Counselling and Development*, 67, 214-216.

Williams, M.H. (1997). Boundary violations: Do some contended standards of care fail to encompass commonplace procedures of humanistic, behavioural, and eclectic psychotherapies? *Psychotherapy*, 34, 238-248.

Wilmer, H.A. (1991). *Closeness in Personal and Professional Relationships*. Boston, Mass: Shambhala publications, Inc.

Wilson, D. (1993). B.C. doctors to adopt sex-abuse proposal. *The Globe and Mail*, July 9, p. 10.

Chapter Five

❖

Counselling in a
Culturally Diverse
Society

❖

"Based on the premise that all helping originates in a cultural context, the counselling
profession has been challenged to incorporate tenets of multiculturalism into its practices." (Arthur & Stewart, p. 3)

Chapter
Objectives

This chapter with its focus on the challenges of counselling in a culturally diverse society has the following objectives:

- to draw attention to the growing cultural diversity within Canadian society

- to understand the ethical imperative for counsellors to honour this human diversity by providing competent culturally responsive counselling

- to identify and explain some of the primary principles and concepts that can inform multicultural counselling

- to examine some of the differing perspectives on what constitutes cultural differences and multicultural competency, and their implications for counselors

- to draw attention to the considerable and growing Canadian literature on cultural diversity and cultural responsive counselling

- to advocate for the provision of culturally competent counselling services to individuals with specific cultural needs

- to provide an inventory of the counselling competencies necessary for the provision of culturally responsive counselling within Canadian society.

Self-Inventory

Directions: Before reading this chapter, please use the following scale to indicate your attitudes towards issues in this chapter. For each statement, indicate the response that most closely identifies your beliefs and attitudes. Use the following code:

5 = Strong agreement with this item
4 = Agreement with this item
3 = Undecided about this item
2 = Disagreement with this item
1 = Strong disagreement with this item

___ All counselling could be viewed as multicultural since it is likely to involve
significant counsellor-client differences.

___ Spirituality and religious beliefs are so diverse and are such private matters of faith that they are best avoided.

___ The concept of multicultural counselling should be restricted to differences of race, ethnicity, and nationality.

___ A female client whose husband died at sea after he was away from home for a month, said in her last session with you, "You know, he came to visit me on the night he died." This is obviously a client who is hallucinating.

___ Counselling is so culturally encapsulated that it is difficult to see its usefulness for
individuals outside the dominant white middle class Canadian society.

___ There is likely to be greater differences within various cultural groups than the degree
of differences between them.

___ Ethnocentrism is the natural capacity of most counsellors to see the world from the viewpoint of those with a different ethnic background from their own.

___ Counselling is likely to be successful only to the extent that the counsellor and client
share the same worldview.

___ From a counselling perspective, it makes sense to view ethnicity and culture as meaning one and the same.

___ Multicultural counselling should be understood from a broad perspective that includes client differences associated with gender, age, sexual orientation, spirituality and so forth.

___ It could be viewed as unethical to accept as a client someone whose cultural background is very different from your own.

___ Across different cultures, problems of individual human distress are typically attributed to one or more biological, experiential or supernatural causes.

___ The sooner those who immigrate to Canada adopt the cultural beliefs and values of
the host society the sooner they will feel adjusted to their new country.

___ The fundamental counselling competency of empathy, combined with the attributes of openness, genuineness and respect, should be sufficient to help counsellors deal with most culturally different clients.

___ Clients from Aboriginal communities are likely to have spiritual beliefs and a view of healing practices such that they are unlikely to be helped by the usual counselling practices.

Introduction

Based on the premise that all helping originates in a cultural context, the counselling profession has been challenged to incorporate the tenets of multiculturalism into its practices. (p. 3)

This view, expressed by Arthur and Stewart (2001), is now a central tenet for many who advocate for the importance of a multicultural approach to all counselling in our culturally diverse society (Arthur and Collins, 2005; Ishiyama, 1995; Ishiyama and Arvay, 2003; Pedersen, 2001; Sue and Sue, 2003). It is also expressed in virtually every ethics code of the various national counselling associations (ACA, 2005; BACP, 2002; CCA, 2006). For example, the Code of Ethics (2006) of the Canadian Counselling Association expresses it in the following Articles:

A9 **SENSITIVITY TO DIVERSITY**
Counsellors strive to understand and respect the diversity of their clients, including differences related to age, ethnicity, culture, gender, disability, religion, sexual orientation, and socio-economic status.

B9 **RESPECTING DIVERSITY**
Counsellors actively work to understand the diverse cultural background of the clients with whom they work, and do not condone or engage in discrimination based on age, colour, culture, ethnicity, disability, gender, religion, sexual orientation, marital, or socioeconomic status.

The Canadian Counselling Association gives additional emphases to the need for its members to embrace an understanding of cultural diversity in their professional practices, by dedicating, since 1995, three special issues of the *Canadian Journal of Counselling* to multicultural counselling (Arthur and Stewart, 2001; Ishiyama, 1995; Ishiyama and Arvay, 2003) as well as numerous articles that reflect its rich complexity. In the introduction to the third special issue, guest editors Ishiyama and Arvay (2003), make the following succinct case for cultural responsiveness in counselling:

Canadian society continues to expand in its richness and complexity of cultural diversity and pluralistic worldviews. We have an increasing number of new immigrants, refugees, international students, sojourners, returnees, intermarried couples, and children with so-called "mixed race" and multi-ethnic backgrounds. Helping professionals cannot be effective or ethical in their practice without recognizing the existence of ethnocultural diversity and various types of challenges inherent in intercultural communication and helping contexts. (p. 171)

This growing cultural diversity of Canadian society can be attributed, in large part, to immigration and differential birth rates. Aboriginal peoples currently comprise three percent of Canada's population and have the highest growth rate of all cultural groups. Within this population, the growth rate for individuals aged 15 to 24 is even higher (Statistics Canada, 1996). Using Statistics Canada as their source, Arthur and Stewart (2001), summarize the following changes to Canada's cultural mosaic:

Nearly 30% of the total population reports their ethnic origin to be other than the British Isles, French or Canadian. There are growing numbers of people with multiple ethnic origins due to intermarriage between people whose families have lived in Canada for several generations. Since the 1970s, more than half of Canada's immigrant population has been a member of a visible minority group, increasing to more than three quarters of the immigrant population in the 1990s. Visible minorities are currently 1 in 9 in Canada and are expected to reach 20% of the adult population and 25% of children by the year 2016. These changes in Canada's population mirror changes about the potential counselling clientele of the future. The rationale for multicultural counselling is now well documented. (p. 4)

The magnitude of these changes within the population is not unique to Canada. According to the United States Council of Economic Advisors (1998), by the year 2050 approximately one-half of the population of the United States is expected to be of African-American, Hispanic, Native American, and Asian-Pacific descent.

Lipsitz (1991) projected another aspect of these continuing changes to the American population 15 years ago, "Census estimates indicate that from 1985 to 2000 there will be 2.4 million more Hispanic children, compared with 1.7 million more African-American children, and 66,000 more non-Hispanic white children. If current population growth is sustained, Hispanic will become this country's largest minority by 2020." (p. 22)

As Canadian society continues to grow in its cultural diversity and social complexity, it is imperative that all counsellors learn to advance their ability to provide culturally responsive counselling services. The rapid and exponential growth in the counselling literature of articles and other publications dealing with multicultural counselling attest to the profession's preoccupation with this daunting challenge. Pedersen (1999) has, in fact, referred to the development of multicultural counselling as a "fourth force" in the profession, taking its place alongside psychodynamism, humanism, and behaviourism. Whether or not such a claim is justified, there is clearly a compelling need for counsellors to deepen their understanding of how culture influences both them and their clients. There is also an obligation for counsellors to acquire an insightful understanding of societal and relational power dynamics, and the nature of racism and prejudice, including any racist and prejudicial attitudes and behaviours they may have.

Multicultural Counselling: Assumptions, Concepts and Controversies

Cultural Encapsulation, Ethnocentrism and Culture

It appears that all humans have a natural propensity to view the world through their culturally based perspectives without regard for the reality that others see the world through a different cultural lens based on different cultural assumptions. This phenomenon was first applied specifically to counsellors and their behaviours when Wrenn (1962) used the concept of cultural encapsulation over forty years ago.

Others have used the term ethnocentrism to describe the same habituated behaviour (Albee, 1994). The primary attributes of this human phenomenological behavior are: viewing individuals and their behaviour and generally seeing the psychosocial world through one's own culturally determined beliefs, values and worldview; and being unaware of this inherent insensitivity and acting without being attuned to others' culturally constructed reality. Pedersen (Pedersen, Draguns, Lonner, Trimble, 2002) believes that some degree of cultural encapsulation or ethnocentrism exists whenever any of the following conditions occur:

- All persons are measured according to the same hypothetical "normal" standard of behaviour, irrespective of their culturally different contexts.

- Individualism is presumed to be more appropriate than a collectivist perspective in all settings.

- Professional boundaries are narrowly defined, and interdisciplinary cooperation is discouraged.

- Psychological health is described primarily in abstractions, with little or no attention to the unique manifestation in its cultural context.

- Dependency is always considered to be an undesirable or even a neurotic condition.

- A person's support system is not normally considered relevant to any analysis of that person's psychological health.

- Only linear, "cause-effect" thinking is accepted as scientific and appropriate.

- The individual is usually or always expected to adjust to fit the system.

- The historical roots of a person's background are disregarded or minimalized.

- The counsellor presumes her or himself to be free of racism and cultural bias. (p. 7)

Clearly, multicultural counselling will continue to be a challenge because of what Devereux (1951) calls our "unconscious cultural narcissism and ethnocentrism".

Undoubtedly, there is considerable individual variance amongst counsellors with respect to their encapsulated or ethnocentric awareness and their responses to clients with different cultural experiences from their own. In any case, multicultural counselling emerged as a positive and widespread development dedicated to practices intended to advance cultural awareness and responsiveness. According to Arredondo and her colleagues (Arredondo, Toporek, Brown, Jones, Locke, Sanchez, Stadler, 1996) "multicultural counselling refers to preparation and practices that integrate multicultural and culture-specific awareness, knowledge, and skills into counselling interactions." (p. 1)

It appears that multicultural counselling may be the preferred title from among the various labels with which it seems to be used interchangeably, such as, cross-cultural counselling, intercultural counselling, and transcultural counselling. According to Corey and his associates (Corey, Corey, Callanan, 2003),

We prefer multicultural because it more accurately reflects the complexity of culture but avoids any implied comparison. The multicultural perspective in human-service education takes into consideration the specific values, beliefs and actions conditioned by a client's ethnicity, gender, religion, socioeconomic status, political views, lifestyle, geographic region, and historical experiences with the dominant culture. (p. 111)

It is easy to see that the concept of culture embedded in the above definition of multiculturalism prepared by Corey and his colleagues is very broad and all-inclusive. However, as can be seen by a review of the sample of definitions of culture presented in Table 1, there is not a complete consensus as to what constitutes culture. This lack of agreement was very evident when Kroeber and Kluckholm found 150 definitions of culture in their review of the concept in 1952. Triandis (1996) has also noted this longstanding search for a common and succinct definition and he captures some of the rich definitional variety in the following way:

It has been defined as the human-made part of the environment, and thus it can be distinguished into objective culture (e.g., tools or roads) and subjective culture (e.g., categorizations, beliefs, attitudes, norms, role definitions, or values). It has been defined as a complex schedule of reinforcements, as being to humans what a program is to a computer. Some have emphasized shared behaviors, cognitive systems or meanings...others have argued it is a construct in the mind of the investigator. Other definitions have stressed that culture is to society what memory is to individuals...consisting of shared elements of subjective culture and behavioral patterns found among those who speak a particular language dialect, in a particular region, during a specific historic period. (p. 408)

Clearly, culture is a multidimensional and complex concept and at its core it includes shared traditions, normative values, beliefs, and behaviours, that account for the sense of belonging and association within a cultural group. Some of the more exclusive definitions may limit the meaning of culture to only the attributes of ethnicity or nationality (Daya, 2001).

Table 1: Selected Definitions of Culture

Culture: Some Selected Definitions

• Culture is a set of meanings, behavioral names, and values used by members of a particular society, as they construct their unique world. (Alarcon, Foulks, and Vakkur, 1998)

• "Culture defines reality for those who belong to (it)... The beliefs, values, and behaviors of a culture. It provides its members with some degree of personal and social meaning for human existence and are bound through tradition and transmitted from generation to generation. (Kagawa-Singer, M., & Chung, R.C.Y., 1994)

• Culture may be defined broadly to include such variables as: (a) ethnographic (ethnicity and rationality); (b) demographic (age, gender, and place of residence); (c) status (educational, social, and economic); and (d) affiliation (formal and informal). (Pedersen & Ivey, 2003)

- Culture is the shared values, beliefs, expectations, world views, symbols, and appropriate behaviors of a group that provide its members with norms, plans, and needs for social living. (Gladding, 2001)

- Culture refers to the widely shared ideas, videos, formation, and uses of categories, assumptions about life, and goal-directed activities that become unconsciously or subconsciously accepted as "right" and "correct" by people who identify themselves as members of a society. (Brislin, 1993)

- Culture means the shared history, practices and values of a racial, regional or religious group of people. (D'Ardenne & Mahtani, 1999)

- Culture is shared constraints that limit the behavior repertoire available to members of a certain sociocultural group in a way different from individuals belonging to some other groups. (Poortinga, 1990)

Ethnicity and Ethnic Identity

Ethnicity is a concept that is relevant to a multicultural counselling perspective. It is typically understood to be one of the components of culture. Santrock (2006) defines it as "a dimension of culture based on cultural heritage, nationality, race, religion, and language." (p. 411) Phinney (2000) views ethnicity as a dynamic and multidimensional construct. She believes that there can be considerable differences among individuals within the same ethnic groups, depending on the personal meaning they ascribe to their ethnicity and the role it plays.

Ethnic identity is another aspect of ethnicity. It is one part of the broader psychological construction of personal identity. Its contribution to the larger whole depends on the degree of an individual's identification with and sense of belonging to the ethnic group. Diller (1991) has examined the many intricate ways in which Sigmund Freud's ethnic identity is intertwined with his development of psychoanalysis. In so doing, he provides a succinct descriptive example of ethnic identity.

Ethnic identity in turn refers to that portion of personal identity that contributes to one's self-image as a member of a minority group, in this case, as a Jew. Thus, when we speak of Jewish identity, we refer to the individual's subjective experience of his or her own Jewishness, that is, what he or she feels about it both consciously and unconsciously, how it is conceived and how he or she reacts to it. Jewish identity formation, like that of personal identity, results from an integration of the various experiences one has had as a Jew. (p. 46)

There is some variation, however, in the ways in which ethnic identity can be understood and expressed. For example, Cross and his associates (2002) have proposed a way of conceptualizing Black identity within American society that they believe might have utility for counsellors and other professionals. They view Black identity as complex and dynamic and as a repertoire of everyday behaviours and feelings intended to achieve the following five different outcomes or transactions:

- identity-protection, or buffering against potentially negative, hurtful experiences.

* an identity "on/off" switch called code switching that allows movement in and out of Black and non-Black cultural settings

* identity connectivity enactments that make trans-racial friendships possible

* identity-belonging activities that promote a sense of bonding and attachment to the Black experience

* identity individuation activities that sustain the boundaries of a person's individuality. (p. 105)

Basic to this analysis is the understanding that individuals who are members of a minority group make every effort to manage their ethnic identity in an effort to avoid the hurtful consequences of prejudice and discrimination.

Acculturation

The process of acculturation should be understood and be part of the discourse about multicultural counselling, particularly in a nation like Canada, sometimes referred to as "a nation of immigrants". Despite the commitment in the *Canadian Multiculturalism Act* to the importance of encouraging different cultural groups to value and celebrate their cultural traditions, every newcomer is naturally influenced by the cultural values and practices of a new country.

Acculturation can be defined as the process by which immigrants adopt the cultural traits, behaviours, values and other attributes of the host society as well as the processes that change or moderate their traditional cultural values (Olmedo, 1979). So, acculturation could be viewed primarily as the process by which individuals relate to

the majority culture, whereas ethnic identity relates to the view individuals have of themselves compared to their primary cultural groups.

The process of adjustment to a new society can be quite challenging and stressful both for individuals and families. Merali (2004) has summarized some of these challenges for refugee families during their transition to Canadian society:

* adolescents being subject to different behavioural demands in the home and school contexts which may interfere with the development of a consolidated identity

* declines in perceived parenting efficacy due to problems in transmitting cultural values to children

* a reduction in perceived family support and cohesion (p. 92)

Some Differing Points of View: Etic and Emic?

Some advocates support a broad inclusionary view of multicultural counselling (Pedersen, Draguns, Lonner, Trimble, 2002). They seem to take the position that virtually all counselling is multicultural since, in most instances, there are likely to be some significant differences between the counsellor and the client such as age, gender, spirituality, social status, life experiences, ethnicity, and so forth. Some of those counsellor-client differences are even more likely to be present in Canada's culturally diverse society.

In Canada, and increasingly in other western nations, many of its citizens have co-existing multiple cultural identities. This is particularly true for immigrants who come from cultures different from the majority culture in the host society. New Canadians often find themselves in the challenging process of retaining, and sometimes celebrating, their cultural heritage while at the same time adopting some of the cultural behaviours, values, and attitudes of their new society. First generation children of immigrants often have the responsibility of explaining, or serving as cultural guides, to their parents. This role reversal can have significant implications for family relationships and can challenge the well established familial roles and responsibilities.

Those who advocate for a broadly based and orthogonal view of culture (Pedersen, et al., 2002; Oetting & Beauvais, 1991; Weinrach & Thomas, 1996) believe that their perspective is better suited to this reality of multiple and simultaneous cultural identities. Pedersen (2001) clarifies this point of view:

> We can actually belong to many different cultures at the same time. Sometimes within—group cultural differences actually seem to exceed between—group differences as we identify the complex and dynamic salience of culture moving from one situation to another (Cross, 1995). From this broadly defined perspective, all counselling and, in fact, all communication are inherently and unavoidably multicultural. (p. 18)

This broadly based and generic approach to multicultural counselling may also address one of the criticisms sometimes directed at it. The risk, or potential disadvantage, of seeing clients primarily from the perspective of their cultural identity or by focusing on selected cultural variables such as gender, ethnicity, sexual orientation, age, and so forth has been highlighted by

Arthur and Stewart (2001), "...defining multicultural counselling on the basis of specific cultural variable risks stereotyping and perpetuating the marginalization of diverse populations. Cautions are given against assuming that the needs of clients from specific cultural groups are uniform" (p. 4).

Although the broad, inclusionary view of multicultural counselling is both appealing and justified by some (Patterson, 1996; Pedersen, 2001), it is not without it critics. The controversy is sometimes seen as a choice between the *etic* and *emic* perspectives. These terms have evolved from the linguistic concepts of 'phonemic' and 'phonetic' (Pike, 1966). The *etic* view is that all counselling is to some extent multicultural because there are bound to be significant differences present in every counsellor-client encounter since all individuals carry a unique individual culture. It follows that counsellors must acquire a set of generic competencies in order to work effectively with diverse clientele. This view underscores the importance of avoiding stereotypical responses and gives prominence to the counselling relationships and the ability of counsellors to be open to each client's unique manifestation of cultural identity and individual differences.

Those who support an *emic* position argue that multicultural counselling must give importance to cultural and ethnic diversity, and that counsellors must acquire a competent knowledge of various cultural, racial, and ethnic groups. In other words, counselling must be informed from a culture-specific knowledge base. Understanding a client's cultural background is essential to the provision of culturally responsive counselling. Some say that the broad etic perspective runs the risk of equating significant cultural diversity to nothing more than individual differences. Locke (1990) expressed this position:

> A view of multicultural counseling that does not direct attention toward the racial/ethnic minority groups within that culture is but an attempt to eliminate any focus on the pluralistic nature of that culture. Such a system views cultural differences as no more than individual differences. (p. 24)

Some writers (Daya, 2001) have proposed that a common-factors approach to multicultural counselling might contribute to a resolution of the *etic/emic* controversy. A number of theorists (Fischer, Jones, Atkinson, 1998; Frank, 1961) have also proposed that there are core elements common to all effective therapies. Daya (2001) calls attention to Jerome Frank's contribution to an understanding of these core components. "He emphasized the importance of considering factors that are universal, relevant, and common to all psychological and spiritual healing encounters. The underlying premise of universal healing elements makes the common factor paradigm particularly suitable for multicultural counselling." (p. 53)

The Significance of Worldviews

A shared worldview between counsellor and client has been identified as one of the core elements essential to successful multicultural counselling (Fischer et al., 1998; Ibrahim, 1991; Torrey, 1986). A worldview can be defined as "...the way individuals perceive their relationship to the world, for example, nature, other people, animals, institutions,

objects, the universe, religion, and so forth." (Sue and Sue, 2003)

Some time ago Kluckhohm and Strodtbeck (1961) proposed a theoretical framework for understanding the diversity of cultural values that might constitute different worldviews. They elaborate on the following five value categories:

- human nature (bad, good and bad, good, neutral)

- social relations (linear-hierarchical, collateral group, individualism)

- people/nature relations (subjugation to nature/fate, harmony/coexistence, mastery over   nature)

- time focus (past/traditions)

- human activity (being, being-in-becoming, doing).

A scale to assess worldviews (Ibrahim and Kahn, 1987) has been developed based on Kluckhohm and Stordtbeck's conceptual schema and with sufficient reliability and validity for its use as a counselling and research tool.

Although this conceptual mapping may not capture all the diversity of cultural values or their complexity, it continues to have the utilitarian function of helping counsellors to begin the process of understanding both their own cultural values and the assumptive world of their clients.

Hofstede (2001, 1999, 1991) also sheds considerable light on cultural diversity and worldviews with his impressive multinational study. One of the core cultural differences found by him, and further investigated by Triandis (1996), is captured in the value constructs of individualism and constructivism. Triandis provides these definitions:

Collectivism

In some cultures the self is described as an aspect of a collective (e.g., family or tribe); personal goals are subordinated to the goals of this collective; norms, duties, and obligations regulate most social behaviour; taking into account the needs of others in the regulation of social behaviour is widely practiced. (p. 409)

Individualism

The self is defined as independent and autonomous from collectives. Personal goals are given priority over the goals of collectives. Social behaviour is shaped by attitudes and perceived enjoyable consequences. The perceived profit and loss from a social behaviour is computed, and when a relationship is too costly it is dropped. This construct is linked to the ideology of modernity. (p. 409)

Hofstede also elaborates on three other cultural dimensions evident in his data:

- power distance – the extent to which the less powerful members of institutions and organizations within a country expect and accept the power is distributed unequally

- uncertain avoidance – the extent to which people within a culture are made nervous by situations which they perceive as unstructured, unclear, or unpredictable, situations which they therefore try to avoid by maintaining strict codes of behaviour and a belief in absolute truths

- masculinity-femininity – masculinity pertains to societies in which social gender roles are clearly distinct (i.e., men are supposed to be assertive, tough and focused on material success whereas women are supposed to be modest, tender, and concerned with the quality of life); femininity pertains to societies in which social gender roles overlap (i.e., both men and women are supposed to be modest, tender, and concerned with the quality of life). (1991, p. 82)

Collectivism is the predominant value in the traditional cultures of Asia and African whereas individualism has been the primary value perspective in Euro-American societies. These values and others identified by Hofstede and by Triandis constitute a continuum of culturally based values or worldviews.

In Canada's culturally diverse society, many versions of these value orientations are present and are part of the cultural mosaic. Counsellors must appreciate that these are significant and potent variables in personal decision-making, interpersonal relationships, parenting, conflict resolution, and familial dynamics. They clearly have implications for the provision of culturally attuned counselling services to individuals, families, and communities. It is obvious that the Euro-American emphasis on individuality, personally determined educational and career goals, and individual responsibility, are likely to be at variance with values that give primacy to familial and communal influences, interdependence, and collective duties and responsibilities.

Even though the concept of cultural determinism had a difficult birth at the beginning of the twentieth century (Benedict, 1951), we now accept that many of our fundamental views about the world, how it functions, and our place in it, are culturally acquired. Goldschmidt (1969) sums up his anthropological perspective on the potency of culture as follows:

Anthropology has taught us that the world is differently defined in different places. It is not only that people have different customs; it is not only that people believe in different gods and expect different postmortem fates. It is, rather, that the worlds of different people have different shapes. The very metaphysical presuppositions differ: space does not conform to Euclidean geometry, time does not form a continuous unidirectional flow, causation does not conform to Aristotelian logic, man is not undifferentiated from nonman or life from death, as in our world. (p. 18)

One critical element in any client's worldview of particular significance for counsellors and counselling is the set of beliefs about the nature of human distress, or behavioural problems, their causation, as well as the range of culturally sanctioned practices intended to cure them or to bring relief. With respect to causation for example, human distress is attributed to one or more biological, experiential, or supernatural causes, the first two being more likely in traditional western societies and supernatural causes being more evident in other societies. However, this has never been a neat, discrete division and is particularly less so in the culturally diverse societies of Canada and the United States. In non-western cultures, the culturally sanctioned individuals who address what in western societies is considered to be "mental health problems" usually have one of the following titles: herbalist, healer, or diviner.

Torrey (1986) examines this salient aspect of different cultures in his book entitled, *Witchdoctors and psychiatrists: The common goals of psychotherapy and its future.* He concludes that there are four core elements necessary for successful therapy: a shared worldview, the personal qualities of the therapist, the expectation of the client, and the client's emerging sense of mastery (p. x). This is a version of the common factors-approach mentioned earlier. Fischer and his colleagues (1998) identify a somewhat similar set of necessary common attributes: a shared worldview, the counselling relationship, client expectations for a positive outcome, and the client's acceptance of the rituals of counselling. Rituals refers to the range of interventions and other practices employed by counsellors.

Speight and her associates (Speight, Myers, Cox and Highlen, 1991) propose a redefinition of multicultural counselling based on holistic, optimal theory. They believe that all counselling is multicultural and that optional theory provides an overarching theoretical framework that harmonizes a fragmented view of individuals into a more holistic one. This theory is seen as particularly well suited to multicultural counselling since it is consistent with the basic principle that "Every person is like all persons, like some persons, and like no other persons" (Kluckhohm and Murray, 1953) and therefore "Each counselling encounter possesses this mixture of sameness and differentness." (Speight et al., 1991, p. 32) A diagrammatic sketch depicts how, in this tripartite model, the three contributions of the attributes from human universality, individual uniqueness, and attributes from a specific cultural identity, can interact to shape each individual's unique worldview.

Figure 1: Influences on Worldview

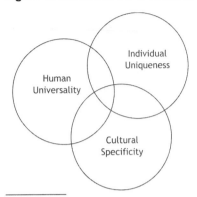

Reproduced with the permission of ACA.

Achieving Counseling Competence in a Culturally Diverse Society: An Ethical Imperative

Culture is not a vague or exotic label attached to far away persons and places, but a personal orientation to each decision, behavior, and action in our lives. (Pedersen, 1988, p. vii)

This view of culture as having a dynamic omnipresence in all human transactions is a core assumption of most of the contemporary perspectives on multicultural counselling. Consequently, all counselling can, to some extent, be seen as multicultural since it includes not only nationality, ethnicity, and race, but also differences associated with gender, sexual orientation, age, spirituality, religion, social class, and disability. So, all counsellors are challenged to become culturally competent practitioners.

In addition to the specific articles (A9, B9, D10) of the Code of Ethics of the Canadian Counselling Association (2006) that mandate this responsibility for its members, the following general

responsibilities underscore the basic need to maintain high standards of professional competence and the ability to work collaboratively with clients to increase the likelihood of positive counselling outcomes.

A1 GENERAL RESPONSIBILITY
Counsellors maintain high standards of professional competence and ethical behaviour, and recognize the need for continuing education and personal care in order to meet this responsibility.

B1 PRIMARY RESPONSIBILITY
Counsellors have a primary responsibility to respect the integrity and promote the welfare of their clients. They work collaboratively with clients to devise integrated, individual counselling plans that offer reasonable promise of success and are consistent with the abilities and circumstances of clients.

As Canadian society becomes more culturally diverse and socially complex, counsellors can expect to increasingly have clients with culturally determined beliefs and behaviours different from their own. The *Canadian Multiculturalism Act* (1988) advises human service providers to "make use, as appropriate, of the language skills and cultural understandings of individuals of all origins" (p. 2). Also, the 1988 Canadian Task Force on Mental Health Issues Affecting Immigrants and Refugees reported that there was a high rate of premature termination for, what it called, intercultural counselling. This finding is also consistent with reports in the United States. (Sue and Sue, 1999)

The counselling profession in Canada has not been insensitive to its mandate to ensure that its members are competent to work in a culturally diverse environment. In addition to its declared ethical aspirations in this respect, the Canadian Counselling Association (CCA) has produced a considerable body of literature addressing many of the immense varieties of issues within the broad scope of multicultural counselling through its scholarly publication, the *Canadian Journal of Counselling*. Table 2 presents an inventory of some of these articles relevant to multicultural counselling. The Canadian Counselling Associ-ation, through its policies for the formation of counselling chapters, has provided a focused, or dedicated, approach to some aspects of its broadly-based advocacy mandate.

Author(s)	Title	Source
General Perspectives		
Rungta, S.A. Margolis, R.L. Westwood, M.J.	Training Counsellors to Work with Diverse Populations: An Integrated Approach	1993, 27, 1, p. 50
Petersen, P.	The Cultural-based Counsellor as an Unintentional Racist	1995, 29, 3, p. 197
Ishiyama, F.I.	Introduction to the Special Issue on Intercultural Counselling in a Multicultural Context	1995, 29, 3, p. 194
Leclerc, C.	Les relations interethniques dans les services éducatifs et sociaux: au-delà de l'angélisme et de l'intransigeance, la construction de scénarios inédits	1997, 31, 2, p. 185
Arthur, N. Stewart, J.	Multicultural Counselling in New Millennium: Introduction to the Special Theme Issue	2001, 35, 1, p. 3
Pedersen, P.B.	Multiculturalism and the Paradigm Shift in Counselling: Controversies and Alternative Futures	2001, 35, 1, p. 15
Pettifor, J.L.	Are Professional Codes of Ethics Relevant for Multicultural Counselling?	2001, 35, 1, p. 26
Arthur, N. Januszkowski, T.	The Multicultural Counselling Competencies of Canadian Counsellors	2001, 35, 1, p. 36
Daya, R.	Changing the Face of Multicultural Counselling with Principles of Change	2001, 35, 1, p. 49
Peavy, V. Han, Z.L.	Social and Cultural Context of Intercultural Counselling	2003, 37, 3, p. 186
Pedersen, P.B. Ivey, A.E.	Culture-centered Exercises for Teaching Basic Group Microskills	2003, 37, 3, p. 197
Ishiyama, F.I. Arvay, M.	Introduction to Special Issues: Multicultural Counselling: Embracing Cultural Diversity	2003, 37, 3, p. 171

Author(s)	Title	Source
Familial Perspectives		
Rigazio-DiGilio, S.A. Ivey, A.	Individual and Family Issues in Intercultural Therapy	1995, 29, 3, p. 244
Grant, K.J. Henley, A. Kean, M.	The Journey After the Journey. Family Counselling in the Context of Immigration and Ethnic Diversity	2001, 35, 1, p. 89
Merali, N.	Family Experiences of Central American Refugees Who Overestimate Intergenerational Gaps	2004, 38, 2, p. 91
Adjustment/Transitional Perspectives		
Ishiyama, F.I.	Culturally Dislocated Clients: Self-Validation and Cultural Conflict Issues and Counselling Implementations	1995, 29, 3, p. 262
Arthur, N.	Preparing International Students for the Re-entry Transition	2005, 37, 3, p. 173
Sikh Perspectives		
Sanshic, J.S.	A Sikh Perspective on Life-Stress: Implications for Counselling	2005, 39, 1, p. 40
Mani, P.S.	Perception of Supports and Barriers: Career Decision-making for Sikh Indo Canadian Young Women Entering the Social Sciences	2005, 39, 3, p. 189
Aboriginal First Nations Perspectives		
Dolan, C.A.	A Study of the Mismatch Between Native Students' Counselling Needs and Available Services	1995, 29, 3, p. 234
McCormick, R.	Healing through Interdependence: The Role of Connecting in First Nations Healing Process	1997, 31, 2, p. 172
McCormick, R.	Ethical Considerations in First Nations Counselling	1998, 32, 4, p. 284
Poonowessie, A. Charter, A.	An Aboriginal Worldview of Helping: Empowering Approaches	2001, 35,1, p. 63
Smith, D.B. Morrissette, P.J.	The Experience of White Male Counsellors Who Work with First Nations Clients	2001, 35.1, p. 74
McCormick, R.	Aboriginal Traditions in the Treatment of Substance Abuse: Let Only Good Spirits Guide You.	2000, 24, 1, p. 25
Wyrostock, N. Pasban, B.	Traditional Healing Practices Among First Nations Students	2000, 34, 1, p. 14

Author(s)	Title	Source
Aboriginal First Nations Perspectives		
Morissette, P.J.	First Nations and Aboriginal Counsellor Education	2003, 37, 3, p. 205
Wihak, C. Merali, N.	Culturally Sensitive Counselling in Nunavut: Implications of Inuit Traditional Knowledge	2003, 37, 4, p. 243
Wihak, C. Merali, N.	A Narrative Study of Counsellors' Understanding of Inuit Spirituality	2005, 39, 4, p. 245
Gender Perspectives		
Cummings, A.L. Hallberg, E.T.	Women's Experiences of Change Processes During Intensive Counselling	1995, 39, 2, p. 147
Barlow, C.A. Cairn, K.V.	Mothering as a Psychological Process: A Grounded Theory Exploration	1997, 31, 2, p. 232
Sells, D.J. Martin, R.B.	Gender and Modality Differences in Experiencing and Emotional Expression	2001, 35, 2, p. 176
Stoltz, J.A.	Masculinity and School Violence: Addressing the Role of Male Gender Socialization	2005, 39, 1, p. 52
Cardu, H. Sanschagrin, M.	Agir suprès des femmes immigrants: analyse de reponsibilities identitaires pro-fessionelles des conseillers d'orientation	2005, 39, 4, p. 215
Sheppard, B.	Embedded Selves: Co-constructing a Relationally Based Career Workshop for Rural Girls	2005, 39, 4, p. 231
Chinese Perspectives		
Zhang, D.	Depression and Culture - A Chinese Perspective	1995, 29, 3, p. 227
Wong, C., O-N Piron, N.	Western Biases and Assumptions as Impediments in Counselling Traditional Chinese Clients	1995, 29, 2, p. 107
Japanese Perspectives		
Aldores, J.L.	Cross-cultural Counselling and Cross-cul-tural Meanings: An Exploration of Morita Psychology	1994, 28, 3, p. 238
Ishiyama, F.I.	A Bending Willow Tree: A Japanese (Morita Therapy) Model of Human Nature and Client Change	2003, 37, 3, p. 216

Author(s)	Title	Source
Career/Employment Counselling		
Amundson, N. Westward, M. Prefontaine, R.	Cultural Bridging and Employment Counselling with Clients from Different Contact Backgrounds	1995, 29, 3, p. 206
Diop, M.	Les éléments d'analyse pour une formation de conseillors d'orientation en intervention interculturelle	1995, 29, 3, p. 214
Career/Employment Counselling		
Alderson, K.G.	A Different Kind of Outing: Training Counsellors to Work with Sexual Minority Clients	2004, 38, 3, p. 193
Culture and Child Abuse		
Merali, N.	Culturally Informed Ethical Decision-making in Situations of Suspected Child Abuse	2002, 36, 3, p. 233

Prepared by Glenn W. Sheppard.

For example, it has four chapters that fall within the scope of a broad, inclusionary view of multicultural counselling. They are:

The Feminist Network Chapter
Its objectives are to promote appropriate counselling practices for girls and women, as stated in its charter:

* to educate counsellors about feminist therapeutic approaches

* to nurture feminist counsellors through mentoring and ongoing education.

Aboriginal Circle Chapter
This chapter, established in 2004, has the following purpose:

* to learn best practice approaches when working with Aboriginals

* to offer the opportunity for members to consult with one another

* to research

* to learn from First Nation people themselves

* to offer an opportunity to advocate.

The Pastoral Counselling Chapter
This chapter, established in 2005, has the following objectives:

* to provide a forum where in pastoral counsellors may encourage, share and exchange experiences and ideas that emerge from their work

* to encourage the exchange of knowledge and new developments in the field of pastoral counselling (including developments in psychology, sociology and spirituality and where these intersect)

* to serve as a direct link to association, universities, societies, and councils, thereby providing for the presentation of mutually sought aims and objectives in the field of pastoral counselling

* to promote a representational understanding of the pastoral counselling profession to others within and outside the counselling community

- to encourage the ethical use of spiritual models, religious values and assessment tools in the counselling process.

Gay, Lesbian, Bisexual, Transgender, and Two-Spirited (GLBTT) Chapter

This most recent chapter has the following objectives:

- to promote and educate counsellors of the importance of queer affirmative practice in Canada

- to enrich the multicultural competencies of current and future mental health practitioner through professional development (knowledge, skills, and awareness)

- to provide a forum of mentorship and support of GLBTT students, practitioners, and researchers, including allies

- to work in direct collaboration with the Canadian Counselling Association in meeting the overall shared goals and objectives between the chapter and the organization as a whole

- to consult and collaborate with other national and international associations working in the area of queer affirmative counselling and cultural competency

- to establish an association wide discussion surrounding the topic of sexuality, identity (issues and concerns) and the implications of being a GLBTT client or counsellor in today's multicultural millennium.

Counselling Competencies for a Culturally Diverse Society

The overall professional competence for working effectively and ethically in a culturally diverse society has been labeled in various ways including: cultural sensitivity, cultural attunement, cultural awareness, cultural responsiveness, cultural expertise. Whatever the label and the nuanced differences in meaning, the three core elements of this area of competence are:

1. Counsellor awareness and understanding of their own worldview, including an appreciation for the cultural and other life experiences that have influenced their values, beliefs, behaviours, as well as their stereotypical and prejudicial attitudes. It may very well be that being comfortable with one's own cultural identity and personal roots is a prerequisite to empathically understanding the cultural reality of another in a spirit of openness and a non-threatened manner.

2. Having cultural knowledge and understanding of different individuals and groups. This includes an understanding of their worldview and for the sexual, political, economic, and historical experiences, and other influences that may have shaped it.

   "Cultural knowledge includes information about the client's cultural roots, values, perceived problems and preferred interventions, as well as any significant within-group diversity, including differing levels of socioeconomic status, acculturation and racial identity commitment." (Arthur and Stewart, 2001, p. 7)

3. Having the skills and flexibility to work with culturally diverse clients including having an understanding of the cultural biases or assumptions

underlying their usual interventions and the ability to use interventions that are culturally attuned.

Cultural Empathy

The well-known and respected Canadian counsellor-educator, Dr. Vance Peavy (2004, 2001), held the view that counselling, when practiced at its best, can be a multicultural engagement since it is grounded on a respectful openness to the client's reality and capacity for personal meaning making. Drawing on the ideas of Kierkegaard, he presented the following advice to counsellors:

- Listen from the perspective of the other.

- Listen with a fresh ear and allow yourself to be amazed at what you hear.

- Exercise patience, respect, and equality.

- Begin where the other is, not where you expect, assume, or need them to be.

- Come to the helping situation in a state of not-knowing; let the other teach you.

- Restrain your own vanity, self-importance, and need to assert yourself. (Peavy, 2004, p. 33)

Another core and foundational competency aligned with these attributes, and long considered a necessary condition for effective counselling, is empathic understanding. Rogers (1957) was the first to identify empathy as having this significant role in facilitating therapeutic change. The following definition captures the essence of this concept.

Empathy in its most fundamental

sense, primary accurate empathy, involves understanding the experiences, behaviors, and feelings of others as they experience them. It means that helpers must, to the best of their abilities, put aside their own biases, prejudices, and points of view of their clients. It means entering into the experience of clients in order to develop a feeling for their inner world and how they view both this inner world and the world of people and things around them. (Rogers, 1980, p. 142)

Cultural empathy has been conceptualized as a particular expression of this Rogerian construct (Chung and Bemak, 2002; Ridley and Udipi, 2002; Washington and Kyi, 2003) and as a requisite for culturally responsive counselling. Chung and Bemak (2002) identified the following dimensions as significant contributors to effective cultural empathy:

- understand and accept the context of family and community for clients from different backgrounds

- incorporate indigenous healing practices from the client's culture when possible

- be knowledgeable about the historical and sociopolitical background of clients

- be knowledgeable about the psychosocial adjustments that must be made by clients who have moved from one environment to another

- be highly sensitive to the oppression, discrimination, and racism that are encountered by many people and often on a daily basis

- for those clients who feel underprivileged and devalued, it is essential for effective cultural empathy to facilitate empowerment for clients. (p. 138)

Ridley and Lingle (Ridley and Udipi, 2002) have presented a list of components that, in their view, constitute cultural empathy, including (a) verbally describing to the client the counsellor's understanding of the client's self-experience; (b) conveying an interest in learning more about the client's cultural values; (c) expressing navieté with regard to the client's cultural experience; (d) affirming the client's cultural experience; (e) clarifying language and other modes of cultural communication; (f) communicating a desire to help the client work through personal struggles, tensions, conflicts, and challenges; and (g) at an advanced level, helping clients learn more about themselves and how to become more congruent (p. 320).

Even though counsellors must acquire competencies particular to multicultural counselling, it is important to acknowledge the importance of, and to build on, the core generic counselling skills and attitudes that constitute a solid foundation for the challenging task of working with cultural diverse clientele.

Multicultural Counselling Competencies

Gerald Wing Sue was one of the earliest advocates for culturally centered counselling within the American counselling profession. He and his colleagues have made a tremendous contribution to advancing the goals of what as become known as multicultural counselling (Sue and Sue, 2003; Sue, Arredondo, McDavis, 1992). One of their major initiatives was the development of a com-

prehensive taxonomy of multicultural counseling competencies (Sue, Bernier, Durran, Feinberg, Pedersen, Smith and Noftall, 1982). These were later updated and revised by Sue and his colleagues (1992). More recently, Arredondo and her associates (1996) have presented a complete description of these competencies along with explanatory notes and dimensions of personality component. Because of the comprehensiveness and significance of this work by Sue, Arredondo and others, and because the competencies developed by them have been endorsed by the Association of Counsellor Education and Supervision (ACES) in the United States, they are presented here in the following form:

Multicultural Competencies and Objectives

I. Counsellor Awareness of Own Cultural Values and Biases

A. Attitudes and Beliefs

1. Culturally skilled counsellors have moved from being culturally unaware to being aware and sensitive to their own cultural heritage and to valuing and respecting differences.

2. Culturally skilled counsellors are aware of how their own cultural backgrounds and experiences and attitudes, values, and biases influence psychological processes.

3. Culturally skilled counsellors are able to recognize the limits of their competencies and expertise.

4. Culturally skilled counsellors are comfortable with differences that exist between themselves and clients in terms of race, ethnicity, culture, and beliefs.

B. Knowledge

1. Culturally skilled counsellors have specific knowledge about their own racial and cultural heritage and how it personally and professionally affects their definitions of normality–abnormality and the process of counselling.

2. Culturally skilled counsellors possess knowledge and understanding about how oppression, racism, discrimination, and stereotyping affects them personally and in their work. This allows them to acknowledge their own racist attitudes, beliefs, and feelings. Although this standard applies to all groups, for White counsellors it may mean that they understand how they may have directly or indirectly benefited from individual, institutional, and cultural racism (White identity development models).

3. Culturally skilled counsellors possess knowledge about their social impact on others. They are knowledgeable about communication style differences, how their style may clash or foster the counseling process with minority clients, and how to anticipate the impact it may have on others.

C. Skills

1. Culturally skilled counsellors seek out educational, consultative, and training experience to improve their understanding and effectiveness in working with culturally different populations. Being able to recognize the limits of their competencies, they (a) seek consultation, (b) seek further training or education, (c) refer out to more qualified individuals or resources, or (d) engage in a combination of these.

2. Culturally skilled counsellors are constantly seeking to understand themselves as racial and cultural beings and are actively seeking a nonracist identity.

II. Counselor Awareness of Client's Worldview

A. Attitudes and Beliefs

1. Culturally skilled counsellors are aware of their negative emotional reactions toward other racial and ethnic groups that may prove detrimental to their clients in counseling. They are willing to contrast their own beliefs and attitudes with those of their culturally different clients in a nonjudgmental fashion.

2. Culturally skilled counsellors are aware of their stereotypes and preconceived notions that they may hold toward other racial and ethnic minority groups.

B. Knowledge

1. Culturally skilled counsellors possess specific knowledge and information about the particular group they are working with. They are aware of the life experiences, cultural heritage, and historical background of their culturally different clients. This particular competency is strongly linked to the "minority identity development models" available in the literature.

2. Culturally skilled counsellors understand how race, culture, ethnicity, and so forth may affect personality formation, vocational choices, manifestation of psychological disorders, help seeking behavior, and the appropriateness or inappropriateness of counseling approaches.

3. Culturally skilled counsellors understand and have knowledge about

sociopolitical influences that impinge upon the life of racial and ethnic minorities. Immigration issues, poverty, racism, stereotyping, and powerlessness all leave major scars that may influence the counseling process.

C. Skills

1. Culturally skilled counsellors should familiarize themselves with relevant research and the latest findings regarding mental health and mental disorders of various ethnic and racial groups. They should actively seek out educational experiences that foster their knowledge, understanding, and cross cultural skills.

2. Culturally skilled counsellors become actively involved with minority individuals outside of the counselling setting (community events, social and political functions, celebrations, friendships, neighborhood groups, and so forth) so that their perspective of minorities is more than an academic or helping exercise.

III. Culturally Appropriate Intervention Strategies

A. Attitudes and Beliefs

1. Culturally skilled counsellors respect clients' religious and/or spiritual beliefs and values, including attributions and taboos, because they affect world view, psychosocial functioning, and expressions of distress.

2. Culturally skilled counsellors respect indigenous helping practices and respect minority community intrinsic help giving networks.

3. Culturally skilled counsellors value bilingualism and do not view another language as an impediment to counseling (monolingualism may be the culprit).

B. Knowledge

1. Culturally skilled counsellors have a clear and explicit knowledge and understanding of the generic characteristics of counselling and therapy (culture bound, class bound, and monolingual) and how they may clash with the cultural values of various minority groups.

2. Culturally skilled counsellors are aware of institutional barriers that prevent minorities from using mental health services.

3. Culturally skilled counsellors have knowledge of the potential bias in assessment instruments and use procedures and interpret findings keeping in mind the cultural and linguistic characteristics of the clients.

4. Culturally skilled counsellors have knowledge of minority family structures, hierarchies, values, and beliefs. They are knowledgeable about the community characteristics and the resources in the community as well as the family.

5. Culturally skilled counsellors should be aware of relevant discriminatory practices at the social and community level that may be affecting the psychological welfare of the population being served.

C. Skills

1. Culturally skilled counsellors are able to engage in a variety of verbal and nonverbal helping responses. They are able to send and receive both verbal and nonverbal messages accurately and appropriately. They are not tied down to only one method

or approach to helping but recognize that helping styles and approaches may be culture bound. When they sense that their helping style is limited and potentially inappropriate, they can anticipate and ameliorate its negative impact.

2. Culturally skilled counsellors are able to exercise institutional intervention skills on behalf of their clients. They can help clients determine whether a "problem" stems from racism or bias in others (the concept of health paranoia) so that clients do not inappropriately personalize problems.

3. Culturally skilled counsellors are not averse to seeking consultation with traditional healers and religious and spiritual leaders and practitioners in the treatment of culturally different clients when appropriate.

4. Culturally skilled counsellors take responsibility for interacting in the language requested by the client and, if not feasible, make appropriate referral. A serious problem arises when the linguistic skills of a counsellor do not match the language of the client. This being the case, counsellors should (a) seek a translator with cultural knowledge and appropriate professional background and (b) refer to a knowledgeable and competent bilingual counsellor.

5. Culturally skilled counsellors have training and expertise in the use of traditional assessment and testing instruments. They not only understand the technical aspects of the instruments but are also aware of the cultural limitations. This allows them to use test instruments for the welfare of the diverse clients.

6. Culturally skilled counsellors should attend to as well as work to eliminate biases, prejudices, and discriminatory practices. They should be cognizant of sociopolitical contexts in conducting evaluation and providing interventions and should develop sensitivity to issues of oppression, sexism, elitism, and racism.

7. Culturally skilled counsellors take responsibility in educating their clients to the processes of psychological intervention, such as goals, expectations, legal rights, and the counselor's orientation.

Source: Reprinted from *Developing and Managing Your School Guidance and Counseling Program*, 4th Edition, pp. 455-457. © ACA. Reprinted with permission. No further reproduction authorized without written permission of the American Counseling Association.

Providing Culturally Competent Services to Individuals with Specific Cultural Needs: Some Selected Examples

Children with Special Needs and their Families

Many educators and others (Brun and Fowler, 1999; Edyburn, 2000; Frame, 1997; Lamorry, 2002; Parette and Petch-Hogan, 2000) have made a plea for the provision of culturally competent services to students with special needs. For example, Lamorry (2002) reminds all professionals who work with exceptional children that "each culture has its own explanations for why some babies are born with disabilities, how these children are to be treated, and what responsibilities and roles are expected of family members" (p. 67). Understanding these differences in beliefs and expectations is a core element of cultural competence and it is essential if school counsellors, teachers, administrators and other professionals are to work effectively with all students and their families.

An understanding of and sensitivity to cultural and linguistic differences between home and schools can ease familial concerns and promote communication and home-school collaboration. It also has implications for many educational practices including, in particular, the selection of appropriate psychoeducational assessment measures and the language in which they are administered. Of course, this expectation for culturally sensitive assessment practices is quite compatible with the ethical obligations of professional counsellors as expressed in the following clause of the *CCA Code of Ethics* (2006):

D10 SENSITIVITY TO DIVERSITY WHEN ASSESSING AND EVALUATING
Counsellors proceed with caution when judging and interpreting the performance of minority group members and any other persons not represented in the group on which the evaluation and assessment instruments and procedures were standardized. They recognize and take into account the potential effects of age, ethnicity, disability, culture, gender, religion, sexual orientation and socio-economic status on both the administration of, and the interpretation of date from, such instruments and procedures.

Since working with parents and families is so essential to the work of school counsellors, school psychologists, and their educational colleagues, it is necessary to understand the familial structures and traditions of the families with whom they work. Cartledge and her colleagues (2000) provide the following

useful inventory of the cultural attributes of many minority families with whom those in education are likely to have professional relationships:

- The **extended family** consists of blood relatives that are multigenerational. The primary role of this kinship system is to ensure that the family provides for the welfare of all members of the kin network at all times (e.g., child care, supervision, parenting, material and monetary resources, and emotional support to children and family members).

- **Mutual aid** is a common element in the extended family life of culturally diverse families. Family members often pool resources for survival and growth.

- **Fictive kinship** among nonblood-related people exists in diverse communities because of common ancestry, social plight, and history. Fictive kin also provide mutual aid, caregiving, and family support.

- **Racial identity** is an awareness of the history of one's own cultural group. Individuals exhibit pride and dignity through the maintenance of customs and traditions.

- **Religious consciousness** is the active participation in the cultural group's religious beliefs and practices. Reliance on faith and the church to support family life is an attribute. (p. 33)

In order to establish culturally sensitive relationships and to offer interventions with any family of a child with special needs, it will be appropriate for the professional to reflect on the following questions:

a) What are the core cultural values of this family and how might they be different from mine?

b) How are various roles and responsibilities likely to be distributed in this family?

c) What beliefs might this family hold regarding human exceptionality? How might this influence their relationships with the affected child, in terms of expectations, parenting, disciplining and so forth?

d) What role does religion and other cultural institutions play in the life of this family?

e) What might the family's educational values be and how might they view the role and intervention of a mental health professional?

Gay, Lesbian, Bisexual, Transgender, and Two-Spirited (GLBTT) Clients

Much like cultural minority groups, gay, lesbian, bisexual, transgender and two-spirited (GLBTT) individuals often face the prejudices of society and even the biases of counsellors. Counsellors who work with GLBTT clients have the professional responsibility to learn about the concerns of these diverse groups. Since counsellors, like all citizens, have been influenced by the stereotypical and prejudicial attitudes of society they may have to seek out opportunities to understand and address any of their biases or homophobic responses. Counsellors who work with GLBTT clients are likely to be dealing with such client issues as: the personal, societal, and familial challenges associated with "coming out", safe-sex practices, and empowering clients to deal with the prejudicial and hurtful responses of others. In both public and private schools it is important that school counsellors join with their educational colleagues to ensure that their commitment to making the school a safe place for students includes the extra attention and effort necessary to ensure that this safety extends as well to GLBTT students.

Counsellors can help to determine their feelings toward GLBTT clients and their readiness to work competently and ethically with them by evaluating themselves against the expectations in the following documents: *Guidelines for Psychotherapy with Lesbian, Gay and Bisexual Clients* from the American Psychological Association (2000), and *Seeing the Rainbow: Teachers talk about Bisexual, Gay, Lesbian, Transgender and Two-Spirited Realities* from the Canadian Teachers' Federation (2002).

Although much has been done in recent years to deal with homophobia in schools, much needs to be done. Besides naming supportive adults in schools that students can talk to, other strategies to address homophobia could include:

- Providing resources for GLBTT students and their families.

- Changing language that assumes everyone is heterosexual.

- Dealing forthrightly with harassment and labelling.

- Including lesbian/gay concerns in all school prevention programs such as sexual harassment and suicide and anti-violence and safe school initiatives.

War-affected Clients

Culturally-appropriate counselling for clients who are war-affected involves being sensitive to issues that may include dislocation, trauma, grief, and culture shock combined with often disadvantaged socio-economic situations, and abbreviated, disjointed, or non-existent educational opportunities, particularly for those immigrants who have refugee status. The dominant culture and language of the new country are also often divergent from the country of origin.

According to MacKay and Tavares (2005),

> Families and learners from war-affected and interrupted schooling backgrounds and with ESL needs face many obstacles in adapting successfully and integrating to a new culture and educational system....(S)ome of the obstacles...if not overcome lead to

a loss of hope and limited opportunities for success. (p. 15)

Prior to counselling for specific issues then, it is important for the counsellor to take into account the context of the client's life and the many layers of stressors and cultural issues that may be affecting the likelihood of successful therapy. The table below highlights the importance of understanding the worldview of the client, beginning with whether the client is a refugee or an immigrant.

Despite the profound and unique issues that can confront refugees, as briefly outlined in the above chart, this in no way minimizes the challenges that may also face immigrants, including some of the acculturation and intergenerational difficulties detailed earlier

Immigrants	Refugees
Most personal business is taken care of before leaving home country	Personal business is unsettled; must leave in a hurry
Education of children is usually not interrupted	Interrupted education of children – due to waiting time in camps or while leaving home country
Adjustment to new culture may be easier due to choice in relocating	Adjustment to new culture could be very difficult due to traumatic experiences and forced relocation
Sense of loss is not necessarily traumatic	Sense of loss is profound; may include family members as well as personal property
Repatriation is a matter of personal choice	Repatriation is not an option unless the crisis situation has stabilized or ended

Adapted from: British Columbia Ministry of Education (2000). *Students who are refugees: A resource package for teachers – focus on the Kosovar refugees.* Victoria, BC: British Columbia Ministry of Education. In MacKay, T. & Tavares, T. (2005). *Building hope: Preliminary report for consultation and discussion.* Winnipeg: Manitoba Education, Citizenship, and Youth.

in the chapter. Counsellors must appreciate the significant and potent variables in the client's background that impact on personal decision-making, interpersonal relationships, parenting, conflict resolution, and familial dynamics. A culturally competent counsellor-client relationship relies on cultural awareness and empathy, and recognition of stressors and sensitivities for the individual to set the stage for effective therapy.

Implications for Counsellor Education and for the Counselling Profession

The attitudes, awareness, knowledge and skills essential to the competent and ethical provision of counselling in a culturally diverse society must be an integrated and omnipresent factor of counsellor education and supervision and continuing professional development. This is necessary if the counselling profession is to meet its obligation to ensure that counsellors provide culturally responsible counselling services to Canadians.

In addition to the societal and ethically compelling case for the counselling profession to embrace culture-infused professional practices (Arthur and Collins, 2005), there are also many positive and broadly based advantages to doing so, as Pedersen (2001) summarizes so well:

1. Recognizing that all behaviour is learned and displayed in a cultural context makes possible accurate assessment, meaningful understanding and appropriate interventions relative to that cultural context. Interpreting behaviour out of context is likely to result in misattribution.

2. People who express similar positive expectations or values through different culturally learned behaviours share the "common ground" that allows them to disagree in their behaviours while sharing the same ultimate positive goal. Not everyone who smiles at you is your friend and not everyone who shouts at you is your enemy.

3. Recognizing the thousands of "culture teachers," each of us has internalized from the friends, enemies, relatives, heroes, heroines and fantasies helps us understand and identify the sources of our individual identity. As we encounter problems we are likely to imagine how one or another influential figure we knew might act in a similar situation.

4. Just as a healthy eco-system requires a diversity in the gene pool so a healthy society requires a diversity of cultural perspectives for its psychological health. By considering many different perspectives in problem solving we are less likely to overlook the right answer.

5. Recognizing our natural tendency to encapsulate ourselves, cultural diversity protects us from imposing our self-reference criteria inappropriately by challenging our assumptions. We have been taught to "do unto others as you would have them do unto you," imposing our own wants and needs on others.

6. Contact with different cultures provides opportunities to rehearse adaptive functioning skills that will help us survive in the diversified global village of the future. By learning to work with those different from ourselves we already know

we can develop the facility for working with future cultures that we do not yet know.

7. Social justice and moral development require the contrasting cultural perspectives of multiculturalism to prevent any one dominant group from holding the standards of justice hostage. Every social system that has imposed the exclusive will of the dominant culture as the measure of just and moral behaviour, has ended up being condemned by history.

8. By looking at both similarities and differences at the same time according to the "quantum metaphor," it becomes possible to identify nonlinear alternatives to rigidly absolutist thinking. It is not just the content of our thinking but the very process of thinking itself which can become culturally encapsulated.

9. We are able to continue our learning curve to match the rapid social changes around us by understanding all education as examples of culture shock. We know we have learned something new when we experience a sense of surprise, making education metaphorically similar to a journey.

10. Spiritual completeness requires that we complement our own understanding of Ultimate Reality with the different understandings others have to increase our spiritual completeness. The well known metaphor that all trails lead to the top of the mountain may indeed apply to our sense of spiritual understanding.

11. The untried political alternative of cultural pluralism provides the only alternative to absolutism on the one hand and anarchy on the other. Our survival in the future will depend on our ability to work with persons who are different from ourselves without sacrificing integrity while at the same time finding common ground.

12. A culture-centered perspective will strengthen the relevance and applicability of psychology by more adequately reflecting the complex and dynamic reality in which we all live. The multicultural perspective resembles the fourth dimension of time as its complements our understanding of three-dimensional space.

Reprinted with the permission of the Canadian Counselling Association. Source: Pedersen, P.B. (2001). Multiculturalism and the paradigm shift in counselling: Controversies and alternatives futures. *Canadian Journal of Counselling*, 35, 1, 15-25.

Chapter Summary

As Canadian society becomes more culturally diverse it underscores the ethical imperative for the counselling profession to incorporate the principles and tenets of multicultural counselling into all aspects of its education and services. This chapter drew attention to the nature of this diversity and examines the ethical aspirations of the profession to acquire and promote the competencies necessary for culturally responsive counselling practices. Such foundational concepts as: culture, cultural encapsulation, ethnocentrism, ethnicity, and ethnic identity were defined and discussed. There was particularly attention to what constitutes a worldview and the significance of counsellor-client worldviews to the provision of appropriate and successful counselling.

The chapter examined the view that culturally responsive counselling can be limited to differences associated with race, ethnicity, and nationality. However, the primary focus was on the contemporary view that all behaviour occurs within a cultural context, and that culture should be broadly conceptualized to also include differences influenced by gender, age, disability, sexual orientation, religion and so forth. There was also a exploration of the differences between an etic perspective that suggested there are basic qualities of counselling that can be effective across cultural differences and the emic view that such differences may require cultural specific competencies. However, comprehensive culturally appropriate competency may require a blending of universal counselling attributes and culturally specific expertise.

This chapter included an inventory that samples the considerable number of articles dealing with many aspects of multicultural counselling from the *Canadian Journal of Counselling*, the scholarly journal of the Canadian Counselling Association (CCA). There was also a presentation of four CCA chapters, each dedicated to advocacy for a different aspect of a broadly defined culturally competent counselling mandate.

The concept of cultural empathy was presented as a core competency of multicultural counselling along with other foundational counsellor attributes considered necessary to effective counselling regardless of client differences. Since professional colleagues in the United States have developed and adopted the most comprehensive taxonomy of multicultural competencies to

date it seemed appropriate to present them in an abbreviated form in this chapter. The chapter concluded with a plea for culture to be infused in counsellor education and supervision and all counselling practices and an identification of the many potential professional and societal benefits for doing so.

Learning Activities

1. *Case Study*. Carefully review the following counselling scenario:

You are a counsellor working at an educational institution. A Vietnamese student, Tu Li, is assigned to you because of academic difficulties. You note that the student is a reluctant speaker and is slow in his conversational style.

In attempting to establish positive relationship with Tu Li, you lean toward him, look him straight in the eyes and ask him directly to tell you about the difficulties he is having in his academic work. When the student looks away and does not respond, you suspect that he has a language problem and that a class in English as a second language might help him to communicate more effectively.

In the course of your counselling sessions, Tu Li says that he is feeling mounting pressure from his father to major in the sciences in order to pursue a career in medicine. Tu Li feels he is not suited for medicine and is keen to study interior design. Besides, he is getting "B" and "C" grades in his biology course, which he fears will bring embarrassment and shame to his family. You reassure him that there is nothing to be ashamed of and encourage him to pursue his interest in interior design.[1]

(a) Identify and discuss the cultural issues evident in this scenario.

(b) Identify and discuss the examples of ethnocentric bias on the part of the counsellor.

2. *Role-play.* Develop a number of additional scenarios in which there are significant cultural differences between the counsellor and client. After some rehearsal, and in counselling dyads, role-play a counsellor who ignores these differences and acts from a culturally encapsulated perspective. Repeat the role-play with the counsellor responding in appropriate culturally responsive ways.

3. *Class Discussion/Debate.* In February 2006, an international crisis developed. Muslims worldwide were offended by cartoons of the Prophet Muhammad that appeared in a Danish newspaper. Violent reactions included the arson of the Danish embassy in Beirut and clashes with riot police, resulting in the deaths of some protesters. The crisis has been described as a clash between religious rights and the rights of a free press in a democratic society.

(a) Have a debate in your class taking each side of this important conflict.

(b) Invite a member of the Muslim community to class to explain the reasons for strong Muslim reaction to these cartoons.

---

[1] Thanks to Gail Benick for this scenario, taken, with CCA permission, from Ethics Notebook, *Cognica*, 34, 3, p. 10.

(c) Invite a member of the media to make the case for freedom of the press.

(d) Discuss the implications of this event for counselling.

4. *Guest Speaker/Discussion.* Invite elders from local first nations/aboriginal communities to discuss their cultural values with particular attention to healing practices and spiritual beliefs. Through these discussions, and other means, become familiar with such practices or sweet grass and sweat lodge ceremonies, and sentencing circles.

5. *Book Review/Discussion.* Read and discuss such books as:

(a) *Growing Up Métis, The Inuit Way, and Dancing with a Ghost.*

(b) Read and discuss such publications as: *Real Boys: Rescuing our Sons from the Myth of Manhood, In a Different Voice, The Concept of Man in Sikhism, Men are From Mars, Women are From Venus, Chicano Ethnicity, The Myths of Gender.*

6. Autobiography. Write a cultural autobiography that includes:

(a) Your reflections on the primary cultural learnings as you matured

(b) The salient influences on your cultural beliefs and values

(c) The experiences you have had with other cultures and how they have affected your multicultural understandings

(d) Some personal prejudices and biases of which you have become aware

(e) Cultural differences that remain most challenging for you

(f) Personal cultural learning goals.

7. *Article Review.* Review the *Guidelines for Psychotherapy with Lesbian, Gay and Bisexual Clients* (American Psychological Association, 2000, 1999) and *Seeing the Rainbow: Teachers Talk about Bisexual, Gay, Lesbian, Transgender and Two-Spirited Realities* (Canadian Teachers' Federation). Discuss these documents in class with particular attention to your attitudes and challenges with respect to these ideas.

8. *Research/Discussion.* Select one of the scales designed to access worldviews and administer it to classmates. Following appropriate procedures, have the scale(s) completed by individuals and groups with differing cultural backgrounds. Discuss the results in your class.

9. Guest Speakers. Invite representatives to participate in your class discussion from places such as the following:

   - the organization for international students at your university

   - the Centre for New Canadians

   - the Status of Women Council and other women's groups

   - the gay and lesbian associations and support/advocacy groups

   - the many religions in your community

   - the sexual health centres and the Right to Life organizations

   - the local Human Rights Association

10. *Brainstorming.* From communities with which you and your classmates are familiar, generate an inventory

of indigenous beliefs surrounding significant life events such as birth, death, tragic events and so forth.

References

Alarcon, R.D., Foulks, E.F., & Vakkur, M. (1998). *Personality disorders and culture: Clinical and conceptual interactions.* New York: Wiley.

Albee, G.W. (1994). The sins of the father: Sexism, racism and ethnocentrism in psychology. *International Psychologist,* 35, 1, 22.

Alden, L., & Ishiyama, F.L. (1997). Shyness and social phobias: Japanese and Western views. *Canadian Clinical Psychologist,* 7(3), 4-7.

Alderson, K. (2003). The ecological model of gay male identity. *Canadian Journal of Human Sexuality,* 12, 75-85.

Alderson, K. (2000). *Beyond coming out: Experience of positive gay identity.* Toronto: Insomniac Press.

Alderson, K.E. (2004). A different kind of outing: Training counsellors to work with sexual minority clients. *Canadian Journal of Counselling,* 38(3), 193-210.

Aldores, J.L. (1994). Cross-cultural counselling and cross-cultural meanings: An exploration of Morita psychotherapy. *Canadian Journal of Counselling,* 28(3), 238-249.

American Counselling Association (2005). *Code of ethics.* Alexandria, VA: Author.

American Psychological Association. (1991). *Guidelines for providers of psychological services to ethnic, linguistic and culturally diverse populations.* Washington, DC: Author.

American Psychological Association. (2000). Guidelines for psychotherapy with lesbian, gay, and bisexual clients. *American Psychologist,* 55, 1440-1451.

Amundson, N., Westwood, M., & Prefontaine, R. (1995). Cultural bridging and employment counselling with clients from different cultural backgrounds. *Canadian Journal of Counselling*, 29(3), 206-213.

Ancis, J.R., & Sanchez-Hucles, J.V. (2000). A preliminary analysis of counseling students' attitudes toward counseling women and women of color: Implications for cultural competency training. *Journal of Multicultural Counseling and Development*, 28, 16-31.

Ancis, J.R. (2004). *Culturally responsive interventions: Innovative approaches to working with diverse populations*. New York: Brunner-Routledge.

Arredondo, P., Toporek, R., Brown, S.P., Jones, J., Locke, D.C., Sanchez, J., & Stadler, H. (1996). Operationalization of the multicultural counseling competencies. *Journal of Multicultural Counseling and Development*, 24(1), 42-78.

Arthur, N., & Collins, S. (2005). *Culture-infused counselling: Celebrating the Canadian mosaic*. Calgary, AB: Counselling Concepts.

Arthur, N. (2003). Preparing international students for the re-entry transition. *Canadian Journal of Counselling*, 29(3), p. 173.

Arthur, N., & Stewart, J. (2001). Multicultural counselling in the new millennium: Introduction to the special theme issue. *Canadian Journal of Counselling*, 35, 1, 3-14.

Arthur, N. (1998). Counsellor education for diversity: Where do we go from here? *Canadian Journal of Counselling*, 32, 88-103.

Arthur, N. & Januszkowski, T. (2001). The multicultural counselling competencies of Canadian counsellors. *Canadian Journal of Counselling*, 35(1), 36-48.

Arthur, N., & Stewart, J. (2001). Multicultural counselling in the new millennium: Introduction to the special theme issue. *Canadian Journal of Counselling*, 35(1), 3-14.

Arthur, N., & Januszkowski, T. (2001). The multicultural counselling competencies of Canadian counsellors. *Canadian Journal of Counselling*, 35, 36-48.

Artz, S., Riecken, T., MacIntyre, B., Lam, E., & Maczewski, M.(2000). Theorizing gender differences in receptivity to violence prevention programs in schools. *BC Counsellor*, 22(1), 7-36.

Axelson, J.A. (1999). *Counseling and development in a multicultural society* (3rd ed.). Toronto, ON: Brooks/Cole Publishing Company.

Barlow, C.A., & Cairns, K.V. (1997). Mothering as a psychological process: A grounded theory exploration. *Canadian Journal of Counselling*, 31, 2, 232-247.

Benedict, R. (1950). Patterns of Culture. New York, NY: New American Library.

British Association for Counselling and Psychotherapy (2002). *Ethical framework for good practice in counselling and psychotherapy*. Rugby, England: Author.

Brislin, R. (1993). *Understanding culture's influence on behavior*. Orlando, FL: Harcourt Brace.

Brun, D.A., & Fowler, S.A. (1999). Designing sensitive transition plans for young children and their families. *Teaching Exceptional Children*, 31(5), 26-30.

Cahill, M., Philpott, D., Nesbit, W., & Jeffery, G. (2004). Understanding the importance of culture in career development. In Philpott, D.P., Nesbit, W.C., Cahill, M.F., & Jeffery, G.H. (2004). *Cultural Diversity and Education: Interface Issues*. St. John's, NL: Memorial University of Newfoundland.

Canadian Counselling Association (2006). *Code of Ethics*. Ottawa, Ontario: Author.

Canadian *Multiculturalism Act*. Government of Canada, Ottawa, Canada.

Canadian Psychological Association. (1996). *Guidelines for non-discriminatory practice*. Ottawa, Ontario: Author.

Canadian Teachers' Federation and Elementary Teachers' Federation of Ontario (2002). *Seeing the rainbow: Teachers talk about bisexual, gay, lesbian, transgender and two-spirited realities*. Ottawa, Ontario.

Canadian Task force on Mental Health Issues Affecting Immigrants and Refugees (1988). *A review of the literature on migrant mental health*. Ottawa: Health and Welfare Canada.

Cardis, H., & Sanschagrin, M. (2005). Agir auprès des femmes immigrantes: analyse des representations identitaires professionelles des conseillers d'orientation. *Canadian Journal of Counselling*, 39, 4, 215-230.

Cartledge, G., Kea., C.D., & Ida, D.J. (2000). Anticipating differences – celebrating strengths. *Teaching Exceptional Children*, 32(3), 30-37.

Chisholm, S. (1994). *Assimilation and oppression: The northern experience*. Education Canada, 34(4), 28-34.

Chung, R. C-Y., & Bemark, F. (2002). The relationship of culture and empathy in cross-cultural counseling. *Journal of Counseling and Development*, 80, 154-159.

Cobb, N.J. (2004). *Adolescence: Continuity, change and diversity*. New York, NY: McGraw-Hill.

Comeau, P., & Santin, A. (1995). *The first Canadians: A profile of Canada's Native People*. Toronto, ON: Lorimer.

Corey, G., Schneider-Corey, M., & Callanan, P. (2003). *Issues and ethics in the helping professions*. Pacific Grove, CA: Brooks/Cole.

Council of Economic Advisors for the President's Initiative on Race (1998). *Changing American: Indicators of social and economic well-being by race and*

Hispanic origin. Washington, DC: Government Printing Office.

Cross, W.E., Smith, L., & Payne, Y. (2002). Black identity: A repertoire of daily enactments. In P.B. Pederson, J.G. Draguns, W.I. Lonner, and J.E. Trimble (2002). *Counseling across cultures* (5th ed.). Thousand Oaks, CA: Sage Publications, Inc.

Cross, W.E. (1995). The psychology of microscience: Revisiting the cross model. In S.E. Porterotto, J.M. Cases, L.A. Suzuki & C.M. Alexander (Eds.), *Handbook of Multicultural Counseling*, pp. 93-122. Thousand Oaks, CA: Sage.

Crozier, S., Harris, S., Larsen, C., Pettifor, J., & Sloane, L.(1996). *Guidelines for non-discrimination practice*. Ottawa: Canadian Psychological Association.

Cummings, A.L., & Halberg, E.T. (1995). Women's experiences of change processes during intensive counselling. *Canadian Journal of Counselling*, 29, 2, 147-159.

D'Ardenne, P., & Mahtani, A. (1999). *Transcultural counselling in action*, (2nd ed.). London: Sage.

Darou, W.G. (1987). Counselling and the northern Native. *Canadian Journal of Counselling*, 21, 33-41.

Daya, R. (2001). Changing the face of multicultural counselling with principles of change. *Canadian Journal of Counselling*, 30, 1, 49-62.

Devereux, G. (1995). Three technical problems in psychotherapy in psychotherapy of Plains Indians patients. *American Journal of Psychotherapy*, 5, 411-423.

Diller, J.V. (1999). *Cultural diversity: A primer for the human services*. Toronto, ON: Brooks/Cole-Wadsworth Publishing Company.

Diller, J.V. (1991). *Freud's Jewish identity: A case study in the impact of ethnicity*. Mississauga, ON: Associated University Presses.

Dolan, C.A.(1995). A study of the mismatch between native students' counselling needs and available services. *Canadian Journal of Counselling,* 29(3), p. 234.

Diop, M. (1995). Des éléments d'analyse pour une formation de conseillers d'orientation en intervention interculturelle. *Canadian Journal of Counselling,* 29(3), p. 214.

Du, J.N. (1980). Pseudobattered child syndrome in Vietnamese immigration children. *Canadian Medical Association Journal,* 122(4), 394-395.

Edyburn, D.L. (2000). Diversity in the new millennium, *Teaching Exceptional Children,* 32(3).

Fischer, A.R, Jones, L.M., & Atkinson, R.A. (1998). Back to the future of multicultural psychotherapy with a common factors approach. *Counseling Psychologist,* 26, 602-606.

Fleras, A., & Elliott, J.L. (1992). *The challenge of diversity: Multiculturalism in Canada.* Scarborough, ON: Nelson Canada.

Foreman, K. (1991). A dramatic approach to native teacher education. *Canadian Journal of Native Education,* 18(1), 73-80.

France, M.H. (1997). First Nations: Helping and learning in the Aboriginal community. *Guidance & Counselling,* 12, 3-8.

Frank, J.D. (1961). *Persuasion and healing.* Baltimore, MD: John Hopkins University Press.

Ghuman, P. (1994). *Coping with two cultures: British Asian and Indo-Canadian adolescents.* Clevedon, England: Multilingual Matters.

Ghuman, P. (1994). Canadian or Indo-Canadian: A study of South Asian adolescents. *International Journal of Adolescence and Youth,* 4, 229-243.

Gladding, S.T. (2001). *The counseling dictionary: Concise definition of frequently used terms.* Upper Saddle River, New Jersey: Merrill Prentice Hall.

Goldschmidt, W. (1969). *Foreword to C. Castaneda, The teachings of Don Juan: A Yagac way of knowledge.* New York: Ballantine Books.

Grant, K.J. Henley, A. & Kean, M. (2001). The Journey after the journey: Family counselling in the context of immigration and ethnic diversity, *Canadian Journal of Counselling,* 35(1), 89-100.

Grewal, J.S. (1990). *The Sikhs of the Punjab.* New York: Cambridge University Press.

Hofstede, G. (2001). *Culture's consequences: Comparing values, behaviors, institutions, and organizations arms nations* (2nd ed.). Thousand Oaks, CA: Sage.

Hofstede, G. (1991). *Cultures and organizations: Software of the mind.* London: McGraw-Hill.

Hoskins, M. (1999). Worlds apart and lives together: Developing cultural attainments. *Child and youth care forum,* 28, 72-85.

Ibrahim, F.A., & Kahn, H. (1987). Assessment of worldviews. *Psychological Reports,* 60, 163-176.

Ibrahim, F.A. (1991). Contribution of cultural worldview to generic counseling and development. Special issue: Multiculturalism as a fourth force in counseling. *Journal of Counseling and Development,* 70(1), 13-19.

Innu Nation and Mushuau Innu Band Council (1995). *Gathering voices: Finding strength to help our people.* Vancouver, BC: Douglas and McIntyre.

Ishiyama, F.I. (1995). Intercultural counselling in a multicultural context. *Canadian Journal of Counselling,* 29(3), 194-277.

Ishiyama, F.I. (2003). A bending willow tree: A Japanese (Morita Therapy) model of human nature and client change. *Canadian Journal of*

Counselling, 29(3), p. 216

Ishiyama, F. (1995). Culturally dislocated clients: Self-validation and cultural conflict issues and counselling implications. *Canadian Journal of Counselling*, 29(3), p. 262.

Ishiyama, F.I. (1995). Introduction to the special issue. *Canadian Journal of Counselling*, 29(3), p. 194.

Ishiyama, F. I., Arvay, M. (2003). Introduction: Multicultural counselling: Embracing cultural diversity. *Canadian Journal of Counselling*, 37(3), p. 171.

Ishiyama, F.I. & Arvay, M. (2003). Multicultural counselling: Embracing cultural diversity. *Canadian Journal of Counselling*, 37(3), 171-232.

Kagawa-Singer, M., & Chung, R.C-Y. (1994). A paradigm for culturally based care in ethnic minority populations. *Journal of Community Psychology*, 22, 192-208.

Kaulback, B. (1984). Among native children: A review of the research. *Canadian Journal of Native Education*, 11(3), 27-37.

Kluckhohm, C., & Murray, H.A. (1953). Personality formation: The determinants. In C. Kluckhohm, H.A. Murray and D.M. Schneider (Eds.), *Personality in nature, society and culture* (pp. 336-370). New York, NY: Random House.

Kluckhohm, F.R., & Strodtbeck, F.L. (1961). *Variations in values orientations.* Evanston, IL: Row, Peterson.

Koens, P.R.(1989). Local control within a model of the sociology of knowledge: A study of curriculum. *Canadian Journal of Native Education*, 16(1), 37-44.

Korhonen, M. (2002). *Inuit clients and the effective helper: An investigation of culturally sensitive counselling.* Unpublished doctoral dissertation. Department of Psychology. Durham University. Durham, England.

Kroeber, A.L., & Kluckholm, C. (1952).

Culture: A central review of concepts and definitions. New York: Vintage Books.

Lamorry, S. (2002). The effects of culture on special education services: Evil eyes, prayer meetings and IEPs. *Teaching Exceptional Children*, 34(5), 67-71.

Larose, F.(1991). Learning processes and knowledge transfer in a native bush-oriented society: Implications for schooling. *Canadian Journal of Native Education*, 18, 81-91.

Leclerc, C.(1997). Les relations interethniques dans les services éducatifs et sociaux: au-dejà de l'angélisme et de l'intransigeance, la construction de scénarios inédits. *Canadian Journal of Counselling*, 31, 2, 185-204.

Lipsitz, J. (1991). Public policy and young adolescents: A 1990s context for researchers. *Journal of Early Adolescence,* 11(1), 20-37.

Locke, P.C. (1990). And so provincial view of multicultural counseling. *Counseling Education and Supervision*, 30, 18-25.

Mani, P.S. (2005). Perceptions of Supports and Barriers: Career Decision-making for Sikh Indo-Canadian young women entering the social sciences. *Canadian Journal of Counselling,* 39(3), 199-211.

McCormick, R. (1997). Healing through interdependence: The role of connecting in First Nations healing practices. *Canadian Journal of Counselling*, 31, 2, 172-184.

McCormick, R. (1997). An integration of healing wisdom: The vision quest ceremony from an attachment theory perspective. *Guidance and Counselling,* 12(2), 18-22.

McCormick, R., & France, H. (1997). The helping circle: Theoretical and practical considerations of using a First Nations peer support network. *Guidance and Counselling*, 12(2), 27-32.

McCormick, R. (1997). First Nations counsellor training. *Canadian Journal of Community Mental Health*, 16(2), 91-99.

McCormick, R. (1997). The significance of connectedness in First Nations healing. *Canadian Journal of Counselling*, 31(3), 172-184.

McCormick, R., & Amundson, N. (1997). Career life planning for First Nations people. *Journal of Employment Counselling*, 34(4), 171-180.

McCormick, R. (1998). Ethical considerations in First Nations counseling. Canadian Journal of Counselling, 32(4), 284-297.

McCormick, R.M. (1996). The facilitation of healing for First Nations people of British Columbia. *Canadian Journal of Native Education,* 21(2), 249-322.

McCormick, R., & France, H. (1995). Counselling First Nations clients on career issues: Implications for the school counselor. *Guidance and Counselling*, 10(2), 27-31.

McCormick, R., & Paterson, D.W. (1996). Student counselling in Canadian universities. *International Journal for the Advancement of Counselling*, 18(4), 235-243.

McCormick, R. (1996). Culturally appropriate means and ends of counselling as described by the First Nations people of British Columbia. *International Journal for the Advancement of Counselling*, 24, 31-42.

McCormick, R. (2000). Aboriginal traditions in the treatment of substance abuse: Let only the good spirits guide you. *Canadian Journal of Counselling,* 34(1), 25-32.

McRae, D. (1993). *Report on the complaints of the Innu of Labrador to the Canadian Human Rights Commission.* Ottawa, ON: Canadian Human Rights Commission.

Merali, N. (1996). *Immigrants' perceptions of the degree of acceptability of acculturated adolescent behaviour.* Unpublished master's thesis. University of Calgary, Calgary, AB.

Merali, N. (2002). Culturally informed ethical decision-making in situations of suspected child abuse. *Canadian Journal of Counselling*, 36, 3, 233-244.

Merali, N. (2004). Family experiences of Central American refugees who overestimate intergenerational gaps. *Canadian Journal of Counselling,* 38(2), 91-103.

Morrissette, P.I. (2003). First Nations and aboriginal counsellor education. *Canadian Journal of Counselling*, 29(3), p. 205.

Naidoo, J., & Davis, J. (1988). Canadian South Asian women in transition: A dualistic view of life. International *Journal of Comparative Family Studies,* 19, 311-327.

Nayar, K.E. (2004). *The Sikh diaspora in Vancouver: Three generations amid tradition, modernity, and multiculturalism.* Toronto: University of Toronto Press.

O'Connell, J.T. (2000). Sikh religion-ethnic experience in Canada. In H. Coward, J.R. Hinnells, & R.B. Williams (Eds.), *The South Asian diaspora in Britain, Canada, and the United States* (pp. 190-209). Albany: State of University New York Press.

Olmedo, E.L. (1979). Acculturation: A psychomotor perspective. *American Psychologist*, 34, 1061-1070.

Oetting, E.R., & Deauvais, F. (1991). Orthogonal cultural identification theory: The cultural identification of minority adolescents. *International Journal of Addictions*, 25, 655-685.

Parette, H.P., & Petch-Hogan, B. (2000). Approaching families: Facilitating culturally/linguistically diverse formal involvement. *Teaching Exceptional Children*, 33(2), 36-41.

Patterson, C. (1996). Multicultural counseling: From diversity to universality. *Journal of Counselling and Development*, 74, 227-231.

Pauktutit (1991). The Inuit way. Ottawa, ON: Pauktutit.

Peavy, R.V. (2004). *Sociodynamic counselling: A practical approach to meaning making.* Chagrin Falls, Ohio: Taos Institute.

Peavy, R.V., & Han, Z.L. (2003). Social and cultural context of intercultural counselling. *Canadian Journal of Counselling,* 37(3), 186-196.

Pedersen, P. (1988). *A handbook for developing multicultural awareness.* American Counseling Association, Alexandria: Virginia.

Pedersen, P.B. (2001). Multiculturalism and the paradigm shift in counseling: Controversies and alternative futures. *Canadian Journal of Counselling,* 35(1), 15-25.

Pedersen, P.B. (Ed.). (1999). *Multiculturalism as a fourth force.* Philadelphia: Brunner/Mazel.

Pedersen, P. (1995). The culture-bound counsellor as an unintentional racist. *Canadian Journal of Counselling,* 29, 197-205.

Pedersen, P.B. (1991). Special issue of multicultural as a fourth face in counseling. *Journal of Counseling and Development,* 70, 1, 4-250.

Pedersen, P.B., Draguns, J.G., Lonner, W.J., & Trimble, J.E. (Eds.) (2002). *Counseling across cultures,* 5th ed. Thousand Oaks, CA: Sage.

Pedersen, P.B., & Ivey, A.E. (2003). Culture-centered exercise for teaching basic group micro skills. *Canadian Journal of Counselling,* 37, 3, 197-204.

Pettifor, J.L. (2001). Are professional codes of ethics relevant for multicultural counselling? *Canadian Journal of Counselling,* 35(1), 26-35.

Phinney, J. (2000). Ethnic identity. In A.E. Kazdin (Eds.) *Encyclopedia of Psychology,* pp. 254-259. New York: Oxford University Press.

Pike, K.L. (1966). Etic and emic standpoints for the description of behavior. In K.L. Pike (Ed.), *Language in relation to a unified theory of the structure of human behavior* (pp. 152-163). The Hague: N.V. Uitgeverij Mouton.

Poonwassie, A. & Charter, A. (2001). An Aboriginal worldview of helping: Empowering approaches. *Canadian Journal of Counselling,* 35(1), 63-73.

Poortinga, Y.H. (1990). Towards a conceptualization of culture for psychology. *Cross-cultural Psychology Bulletin,* 24(3), p. 6.

Press, H. (1995). Davis Inlet in crisis: Will the lessons ever be learned? *Canadian Journal of Native Studies,* 15(2), 187-209.

Purich, D. (1991). *Inuit and Their Land.* Halifax, NS: Lorrimer.

Ridley, C.R., & Udipi, S. (2002). Putting cultural empathy into practice. In P.D. Pedersen, J.G. Draguns, W.J. Lonner, & J.E. Trimble (Eds.), *Counseling across cultures* (5th ed.), pp. 317-334. Thousand Oaks, CA: Sage.

Rigazio-DiGilio, S.A. & Ivey, A.E. (1995). Individual and family issues in intercultural therapy: A culturally centred perspective. *Canadian Journal of Counselling,* 29(3), p. 244.

Rogers, C.R. (1980). *A way of being.* Boston, MA: Houghton Mifflin.

Rogers, C.R. (1957). The necessary and sufficient conditions of therapeutic personality change. *Journal of Counselling and Psychology,* 21, 95-103.

Ross, R. (1992). *Dancing with a ghost.* Markham, ON: Reed Books.

Rungta, S.A., Margolis, R.L., & Westwood, M.J. (1993). Training counsellors to work with diverse populations: An integrated approach. *Canadian Journal of Counselling,* 27, 50-64.

Sells, D.L., & Martin, R.B. (2001). Gender and modality differences in experiencing an emotional expression. *Canadian Journal of Counselling*, 35, 2, 176-188.

Samson, C. (2000/2001). Teaching lies: The Innu experience of schooling. *London Journal of Canadian Studies*, 16, 84-102.

Sanchez, A.R.(2001). Multicultural family counseling: Toward cultural sensibility. In J.G. Ponterotto, J.M. Casa, L.A. Suzuki, & C.M. Alexander (Eds.), *Handbook of multicultural counseling* (2nd ed.) (pp. 672-700). Thousand Oaks, CA: Sage.

Santrock, J.W. (2002). *Adolescence* (11th ed.). New York, NY: McGraw-Hill.

Sandhu, J.S. (2005). A Sikh perspective on life-stress: Implications for counselling. *Canadian Journal of Counselling*, 39(1), 40–51.

Shepard, B. (2005). Embedded selves: Co-constructing a relationally based career workshop for rural girls. *Canadian Journal of Counselling*, 39, 4, 231-244.

Siann, G., & Knox, A. (1992). Influences on career choice: The responses of ethnic-minority and ethnic-majority girls. *British Journal of Guidance and Counselling*, 20, 193-204.

Smith, D.B. & Morrissette, P.J. (2001). The experiences of white male counsellors who work with First Nations clients, *Canadian Journal of Counselling*, 35(1), 74-88.

Speight, S.L., Myer, L.J., Cox, C.I., & Highlen, P.S.(1991). *Journal of Counselling and Development*, 70, 29-36.

Statistics Canada (1996b). *1996 Census: Ethnic origin, visible minorities.* Ottawa: ON: Government of Canada.

Statistics Canada. (1996). *1996 census: Aboriginal data.* Ottawa, ON: Government of Canada.

Statistics Canada.(1996). *1996 Census: Aboriginal data.* Ottawa, ON: Government of Canada.

Statistics Canada. (1995). *Projections of visible minority populations groups, Canada, provinces and regions, 1991-2016 (Statistics Canada Catalogue 91-541-XPE).* Ottawa, ON: Government of Canada.

Stoltz, J. (2005). Masculinity and school violence: Addressing the role of male gender socialization. *Canadian Journal of Counselling*, 39(1), 52-63.

Sue, D.W., & Bernier, J.E., Durran, A., Feinberg, L., Pedersen, P., Smith, E.J., & Nuttall, E.V. (1982). Position paper: Cross-cultural counseling competencies. *The Counseling Psychologist*, 10, 2, 45-52.

Sue, D.W., & Sue, D. (1999). *Counseling the culturally-different: Theory and practice.* New York: John Wiley & Sons.

Sue, D.W., & Sue, D. (2003). *Counseling the culturally diverse: Theory and practice* (4th ed.), New York: John Wiley & Sons.

Sue, D.W., Arredondo, P., & McDavis, R.J. (1992). Multicultural counseling competencies and standards: A call to profession. *Journal of Counseling and Development,* 70(4), 477-486.

Toohey, K., Kishor, N., & Beynon, J. (1998). Do visible minority students of Chinese and South Asian ancestry want teaching as a career? Perceptions of some secondary school students in Vancouver, B.C. *Canadian Ethnic Studies*, 30(2), 50-72.

Torrey, E.F. (1986). *Witchdoctors and psychiatrists: The common roots of psychotherapy and its future.* New York, NY: Harper and Row Publishers.

Triandis, H.C. (1996). The psychological measurement of cultural syndromes. *American Psychologist*, 407-415.

Waldram, J.B., Herring, D.A., & Young, T.K. (1995). *Aboriginal health in Canada: Historical, cultural, and epidemiological perspectives.* Toronto: University of Toronto Press.

Walters, D.(1995). Mandatory reporting of child abuse: Legal, ethical, and clinical implications within a Canadian context. *Canadian Psychology*, 36(3), 163-182.

Washington, C.D., & Kyi, W.W. (2003). *Cultural empathy, requisite for cross-cultural counseling.* Paper presented at the 2003 annual conference, American Counseling Association, Anaheim, CA.

Weinrach, S.G., & Thomas, K.R. (1996). The counseling profession's commitment to diversity-sensitive counseling: A critical assessment. *Journal of Counseling and Development,* 74, 472-477.

Westwood, M. (1982). A cross-cultural comparison of East Indian and Anglo-European expectations of counselling. *International Journal for the Advancement of Counselling,* 5, 283-289.

Wihak, C., & Merali, N. (2003). Culturally sensitive counselling in Nunavut: Implications of Inuit traditional knowledge. *Canadian Journal of Counselling,* 37, 243-255.

Wihak, C., & Merali, N. (2005). Narrative Study of Counsellors' Understanding of Inuit Spirituality. *Canadian Journal of Counselling,* 39, 4, 245-259.

Wilgosh, L., & Mulcahy, R. (1993). Cognitive educational models of assessment, programming and instruction for native learners. *Canadian Journal of Behavioral Science,* 20(1), 129-135.

Wilgosh, L., Mulcahy, R., & Watters, B. (1986). Assessing intellectual performance of culturally different Inuit children with the WISC-R. *Canadian Journal of Behavioral Science,* 18, 270-277.

Wong, O-N., C., & Pinon, N. (1995). Western biases and assumptions as impediments in counselling traditional Chinese clients. *Canadian Journal of Counselling,* 29, 2, 107-119.

Wrenn, G. (1962). The culturally encapsulated counsellor. *Harvard Educational Review,* 32, 444-449.

Wyrostock, N., & Pasban, B. (2000). Traditional healing practices among First Nations students. *Canadian Journal of Counselling,* 24, 1, 14-25.

Zhang, D. (1995). Depression and culture – A Chinese perspective. *Canadian Journal of Counselling,* 29(3), p. 227.

Chapter Six

Ethics of Research and Publication

"The topic of human subjects research ... involves a tenuous and often complicated balance between advancing scientific knowledge and ensuring adequate protection and benefits for the subject." (Sanyin, 1999, p. 1)

Chapter Objectives

The major focus of the chapter is on the ethics related to research and publication. The specific objectives are to:

- Explain the purpose of the *Tri-Council Policy Statement*

- Summarize the central responsibilities of the principal researcher(s) and members of the research team

- Explain the rationale for and the elements of obtaining informed consent

- Recognize the challenges in obtaining informed consent from vulnerable populations

- Describe how to resolve issues of confidentiality and anonymity in research

- Describe how counsellors can understand and work with diversity in research situations

- Define and describe the guiding ethical principles in research and publication

Self-Inventory

Directions: Before reading this chapter, please use the following scale to indicate your attitudes towards issues in this chapter. For each statement, indicate the response that most closely identifies your beliefs and attitudes. Use the following code:

5 = Strong agreement with this item
4 = Agreement with this item
3 = Undecided about this item
2 = Disagreement with this item
1 = Strong disagreement with this item

___ Research participants should be given a complete explanation of the purpose of data collection procedures including interviews, inventories, and tests.

____ Researchers should rely solely on the ethical guidelines in planning, conducting, and reporting on research.

____ As a research associate who has contributed to the research by transcribing interviews and coding transcripts, I should be acknowledged in any publications.

____ It is not necessary for a Social Sciences and Humanities Research Council (SSHRC)-funded doctoral student to acknowledge the source of funding at conferences or in publications.

____ Minors should be allowed to take part in research projects without parental consent or knowledge.

____ Special ethical guidelines are needed for researching with members of ethnic or cultural minority groups.

____ As a journal reviewer I can build on the arguments and ideas put forth by those who submit articles for publication.

____ Because of all the assistance given to me, my supervisor has the right to be first author on any publications based on my thesis.

____ I view it as unethical to employ monetary inducements aimed at recruiting participants to my study.

____ I believe that confidentiality can be maintained by giving research participants a pseudonym and a code to be used on all data.

____ I believe that it is ethical to give only partial information about my research when asking participants to fill out questionnaires to avoid biasing responses.

____ While I am obtaining informed consent from research participants, I also explain that I will be offering an honorarium for participation.

____ I would encourage participants to continue in the study even though they give me non-verbal indications of a desire to discontinue.

____ I would have no trouble in submitting a manuscript already under review to a second journal as long as I made some changes to it.

Introduction

Counsellors who do research may face particular ethical issues because of their training as counsellors (Etherington, 1996). Certainly the skills and theoretical knowledge that make it possible to work therapeutically with clients have an impact on how counsellors conduct research. Unlike the counselling practices of therapeutic interventions, assessment and evaluation, research, and the subsequent publication of results are not entirely aimed at directly benefiting those individuals who participate in it. In fact, historically, the rights of human subjects in research have been ignored and in some cases abused (Bersoff & Bersoff, 1999/2003; Rosenthal, 1994/2003), as evidenced in Milgrim's study of obedience (Milgrim, 1963). In Milgrim's study subjects were told that they were taking part in a learning experience in which the learner was given an electric shock whenever the learner erred. When subjects hesitated they were urged to continue raising the intensity level of painful stimulus to the highest point possible. Subjects were deceived into thinking they were actually delivering an electric shock and were left with profound feelings of shame. Tensions continue to exist between scientific inquiry and protection of the integrity of individuals. At the centre of research ethics are two main concerns: the prevention of harm and protection of the rights of research participants.

Ethical practice in research rests on two approaches: consequentialist and deontological (Beauchamp, Faden, Wallace, & Walters, 1982). Consequentialist approaches are goal-based and focus on the outcomes of research. According to consequentialist approaches, the rightness or wrongness of an action depends solely on its consequences. One should act in such a way as to bring about the best state of affairs, where the best state of affairs may be understood in various ways, for example, as the greatest benefit for the greatest number of people. In taking part in the research, have participants been harmed in some way? If they have been harmed, has this consequence been outweighed by the benefits of the research? In contrast, deontological approaches focus on respecting the rights of research participants to privacy, respect, and self-determination (Beauchamp et al., 1982). Deontological ethics hold certain acts as right or wrong in themselves, for example, promise-breaking or lying. In the context of research, fraud, plagiarism, and misrepresentation would be regarded as morally wrong in themselves, not simply because they tend to have bad consequences.

Specific principles associated with consequentialist approaches include non-maleficence, that is, avoiding harm to participants, and beneficence or the belief that research on human subjects should produce some positive and identifiable benefit to participants or to soci-

ety rather than research for its own sake. Deontological approaches emphasize two principles: autonomy and justice. Autonomy or self-determination entails respecting the values and decisions of research participants while the principle of justice requires the researcher to consider whether undue burdens are being placed on vulnerable groups when other groups of people could be accessed instead. The benefits of research should be available to all people regardless of status (Kitchener, 2000) and therefore, research necessitates a:

> [c]ommitment to... sensitive and reflexive understanding of the experience of others; respect for others as persons; listening to others in conditions of respect and care; mutuality of benefit and gratefulness for giving relationships; openness to criticism and the exposure of prejudice... (Bridges, 2002, p. 86)

Throughout the chapter, pay attention to how both consequentialist and deontological approaches inform current research-related ethical codes (Ford, 2001).

These sets of principles are embedded in the Canadian Counselling Association's (CCA's) *Standards of Practice for Counsellors* (2001) to guide research practice, including the planning, conducting, and reporting of research. They are designed to ensure respect for:

- human dignity
- vulnerable persons
- informed consent
- justice and diversity
- confidentiality and privacy

- the need to minimize harm and to maximize benefits.

Beyond these central issues in counselling research, the material in this chapter covers the topics of gaining research approval as outlined in the *Tri-Council Policy Statement* (2003); responsibilities of the researcher and the research team; the complex process of seeking informed consent, especially with children or adults with impaired capacity; threats to confidentiality and anonymity in community-based research and qualitative research; researching across cultures; research into one's practice; and student research and publication.

Gaining Research Approval

Conducting research is subject to guidance control through professional bodies such as the Canadian Counselling Association (CCA) and through academic institutions by a research ethics board (REB) that follow the standards and procedures outlined in the *Tri-Council Policy Statement: Ethical Conduct for Research Involving Human Subjects* (SSHRC 2003; hereafter referred to as the *Tri-Council Policy Statement*). Professional codes of ethics address research as just one of a number of ethical activities compared to the more detailed *Tri-Council Policy Statement*. However, the *Canadian Counselling Association Code of Ethics* (2006) is informed by the same overarching guiding principles. Further reading in this area is available in the *Tri-Council Policy Statement* (SSHRC, 2003).

Guiding principles adopted from the policies of the Medical Research Council (MCR), the Natural Sciences and Engineering Research Council (NSERC), and the Social Sciences and Humanities Research Council (SSHRC) to form the *Tri-Council Policy Statement* (SSHRC, 2003) provide common standards and values for counselling researchers. The overall guiding principle is respect for human dignity, "from bodily to psychological to cultural integrity" (SSHRC, 2003, p. i.5) and to avoid "treating persons as means (mere objects or things)" (p. i.5). Additional key principles include respect for free and informed consent; respect for vulnerable persons; respect for privacy and confidentiality; respect for justice and inclusiveness; balancing harms and benefits, and minimizing harm and maximizing benefit.

The *Tri-Council Policy Statement* (SSHRC, 2003) addresses the ever-changing societal context of an ethics framework by taking a subject-centered perspective.

Research subjects contribute enormously to the progress and promise of research in advancing the human condition. In many areas of research, subjects are participants in the development of a research project and collaboration between them and the researcher in such circumstances is vital and requires nurturing. Such collaboration entails an active involvement by research subjects, and ensures both that their interests are central to the project or study, and that they will not be treated simply as objects.... A subject-centred approach should, however, also recognize that researchers and research subjects may not always see the harms and benefits of a research project in the same way. Indeed, individual subjects within the same study may respond very differently to the information provided in the free and informed consent process. Hence, researchers and REBs must strive to understand the views of the potential or actual research subjects. (i.7)

Primary research issues are outlined in the *Tri-Council Policy Statement* including informed consent, privacy and confidentiality, conflict of interest, inclusion in research, and research involving Aboriginal peoples. Similar researcher responsibilities are also summarized in the *CCA Code of Ethics* (2006). The *Code* provides a description of behaviour which not only guides but also forms the criteria against which any complaints may be judged.

Responsibilities of the Researcher

Researchers enjoy, and should continue to enjoy, important freedoms and privileges. To secure the maximum benefits from research, society needs to ensure that researchers have certain freedoms.... However, researchers and institutions also recognize that with freedom comes responsibility, including the responsibility to ensure that research involving human subjects meets high scientific and ethical standards. The research er's commitment to the advancement of knowledge also implies duties of honest and thoughtful inquiry, rigorous analysis, and accountability for the use of professional standards. (SSHRC, 2003, i.8)

Counsellor-researchers need to be knowledgeable about the various research methodologies and data collection approaches that can be used to answer research questions professionally and ethically. Moreover, research studies and program evaluations need to be as well designed as possible as poor quality of the design may lead to inaccurate conclusions which can, at the very least, waste participants' time and may impact future funding for community-focused programs (Rosenthal, 1994/2003).

The manner in which researchers and participants treat each other as human beings in a research relationship is related to the ontological and epistemological foundations of research work (Murphy & Dingwall, 2001). Assumptions about the nature of reality, how individuals can come to know that reality, our understanding of what constitutes "truth" and so on, are critical to the assessment of responsibilities as researchers (Murphy & Dingwall). As social science researchers, counsellors need to be aware of their connection to the research situation and their effects on it. In quantitative approaches, procedures and techniques are promoted in an attempt to ensure objectivity. For example, interview scripts are used to expose each participant to the same stimulus so the results will be comparable and to limit the effect of the interviewer on the social interaction (Creswell, 2005). In qualitative approaches, the interaction between the participant and researcher is a key instrument for data collection and knowledge production (Creswell). Research methods, therefore, are flexible tools to be used to pursue the questions asked.

The *Tri-Council Policy Statement* acknowledges the complex and evolving nature of research approaches and consequent ethical considerations. Diversity in research approaches "requires a reasonable flexibility in the implementation of common principles" (SSHRC, 2003, p. i2).

> Counsellors plan, conduct, and report on research in a manner consistent with relevant ethical principles, professional standards of practice, federal and provincial laws, institutional regulations, cultural norms, and standards governing research with human subjects. (CCA, 2006, E1)

Embedded in this ethical principle is the need to design and conduct research that reflects cultural sensitivity and appropriateness. Some issues that are particularly germane to research with diverse groups include making use of culturally insensitive assessment instruments, conducting primarily problem-focused research, neglecting to form culturally diverse research teams, and failing to report to control group participants when the treatment-control model appears to be beneficial (Gil & Bob, 1999). Conducting culturally competent research is examined later in this chapter.

Principal Researcher Responsibility

Research may entail physical, psychological, or material risks to participants. Counsellor researchers have an obligation to foresee risks and to minimize any outcomes that may result from participation in the study (CCA, 2006, E2). Kelman (1982) classifies main areas of concern in social research including harms and benefits, privacy and confidentiality, and informed consent and deception. He suggests that the types of impacts on participants

consist of concrete interests (e.g., injury, public exposure, and impaired capacity for decision-making), the quality of interpersonal relationships (e.g., stress and indignity, reduced control over what is shared about oneself, and lack of choice and respect), and at the level of society through social values (e.g., contributing to negative stereotypes, eroding trust, and infringing on the private space of individuals and groups).

With these general areas in mind, consider the counsellor researcher's situation in the following example. Identify the main ethical issues and reflect on your stance if you were conducting this research:

The Monica Case

Monica's research focused on examining the high prevalence of obesity among adults in a small ethnic community. She utilized a mixed-method approach that incorporated semi-structured interviews and inventories. Once Monica had completed data collection she had no further contact with the community. When Monica was asked to discuss her findings on a local radio show, she highlighted the poor eating habits and lack of physical activity of participants. The radio discussion concluded with some remarks about the lack of leadership within the community.

- What impact might this research have on the participants?

- What ethical responsibilities does the researcher have in this situation?

- According to Kelman, what areas of concern need to be addressed?

• What would you have done differently, and why?

One ethical problem with this case is
the lack of regard for harmful effects on
subjects caused by the research.
Participants' responses were shared
publicly without the benefit of a follow-
up discussion of results with participants. Additionally, it is possible that
Monica's responses on the radio may
have supported negative stereotypes of
a cultural group. In this case, it might
have been best for the researcher to
return to the community after she had
analyzed the data. A pertinent discussion could then occur in regards to the
"fit" of the results with participants'
experience; how results can best be
used to assist participants in changing
practices that contribute to obesity; and
how appropriate and beneficial dissemination of research results can be developed.

In addition to the above areas of concern, the principal investigator (PI) of
the research project has specific responsibilities as outlined in the *CCA Code of
Ethics* (2006). The PI has the primary
responsibility for the research project.
Responsibilities include knowing if and
from whom approval is required (CCA,
2006, E3). In some cases approval may
have to meet the internal review
requirements for research of other public and private organizations as well as
by the research ethics board at the academic institution.

An M.Ed. student in counselling
plans to study how children who
have experienced the death of a
parent respond to a unique school
program on children and losses.
She hopes to run focus groups
before and after the program at
one school. Her supervisor in-

forms her that she will need
approval from the school district
as well as the university.

Applications for institutional review
must be accurate and approval obtained
before the research is conducted.
Research procedures must follow the
approved protocol. When methods,
informed consent procedures, compensation, and confidentiality protections
are modified during different phases of
the research, institutional approval
should be sought through amendments
to the original protocol. You may
become involved in a research project
while in your counselling program.
Undergraduate and graduate students
who form part of a research team also
share ethical responsibilities with the
primary investigator and must take
"full responsibility for their own
actions" and "share ethical obligations"
(CCA, 2006, E3).

Ensuring Consent is Informed and Voluntary

Gaining consent to participate in
research is a central concern in
research ethics codes (CCA, 2006, E5).
It is generally accepted that complete
informed consent includes a discussion
of the following elements: the purpose
of the research, expected duration and
procedures; participants' right to
decline to participate and to withdraw
from the research once participation
has begun; the anticipated consequences of refusing or withdrawing; log-
ically expected reasons that may impact
their willingness to participate, including potential threats to safety, anxiety,
or other adverse effects; any potential
research benefits; limits of confidentiality; incentives for participation; and the
contact person to reach to ask further

questions about the research and participant's rights (American Psychological Association, 2002, 8.02).

As might be expected, consent-seeking involves more than securing approval from the research ethics board or the signing of a consent form by participants. It is an ongoing process throughout the research, before, during, and after research in the writing of reports and the dissemination of results (Miller & Bell, 2002).

> Researchers should refrain from treating such ritualistic enactment of consent- seeking as the be-all and end-all of ethical considerations but should instead engage in a more reflexive approach to the types and levels of consent required before, during and after the act of research . (Sin, 2005, p. 290)

Informed consent is the participant's agreement to take part in a study after having obtained thorough information about the research process including the associated risks and benefits. To protect individual's autonomy and to comply with this standard of informed consent, counsellors must obtain and document written or oral consent by providing information in the participant's language and at a language level understood by potential participants. When research is conducted that involves children or adults with impaired capacity to consent or with families from diverse language populations, researchers should enquire into language preferences and proficiencies (Fisher et al., 2002).

The Bob Case
During his practicum, Bob, an M.A. student in counselling, completed a psychotherapy group

with children aged ten to fourteen years during his practicum. He was surprised at the children's ability to reason and problem-solve. He wants to conduct his research study with this age group on their experience of divorce in their families and to make a video of their interviews for psycho-educational purposes. Bob is convinced that children have the right to give their consent to research. He recalls that the *United Nations Convention on the Rights of the Child* (1989) advocates the right of every child to self-determination, dignity, respect, non-interference, and the right to make informed decisions. He also questions whether parents would contest their children's desire to participate, given the stories children might tell about their parents' divorce. Bob says that those parents who do consent are the families likely to have had an amicable divorce.

- What are your thoughts about Bob's ethics and rationale for obtaining informed consent only from the children?

- How would you respect the rights of both children and parents?

Typically, researchers are cautioned through ethical codes and guidelines to take care when interviewing children up to school-leaving age. The Canadian Counselling Association's *CCA Standards of Practice for Counsellors* (2001) suggests:

> Obtain informed consent from parents, guardians, or legally authorized persons for those who are legally incapable of giving

informed consent. Seek the assent of children and others for whom a proxy consent is given commensurate with their ability, unless they cannot reasonably be consulted because age or disability limits their ability to do so. (p. 30)

Children under the age of 13 years normally require parent or guardian consent to participate in a research study. Letters of consent need to be age-appropriate for children. For children aged seven and under, a simple verbal script can be used to introduce the researcher and the child's role in the study. Parents/guardians can ensure their child understands that they are free to choose whether the researcher can use their work or not. Although adolescents aged 13 to 16 years can provide their own consent in studies deemed minimal risk, parents/guardians are usually in-formed.

Strongly influenced by the developmental approach, researchers traditionally viewed young children as unable to give informed consent. This view has been challenged by a number of researchers (Ashcroft, Goodenough, Williamson, & Kent, 2003; Danby, 2002; Tobin, 1995; Wendler & Shah, 2003) who suggest that children are competent interpreters of their everyday worlds. Ashcroft et al. found when children (aged eight to eleven years) were asked concrete questions based on their personal experience, they were frequently able to articulate and reflect on a range of ethical issues related to the research project. Stanley, Sieber, and Melton (1995/2003) also argue that the competence of minors to consent to research is probably underestimated depending on the type of research being

conducted. Age, general cognitive ability, emotional status, and knowledge need to be considered when researching with minors. When the research is focused on significant emotional aspects of one's life, a normal, capable 16-year-old may not be able to give complete informed consent (Stanley et al.). Age alone is not sufficient to judge ability to consent. The responsibility is on the researcher to err on the side of caution. As a task becomes more intrusive or as a task reduces anonymity (as in case studies), there is an increasing need for informed consent.

This changing viewpoint leads to different ethical considerations than those that have addressed traditional understandings of children as pre-competent (Danby, 2002; Walkerdine, 1999). Researching with any individual deemed incompetent requires practitioners to be aware of the relevant ethical codes and guidelines, but further, to be able to judge the relative importance of conflicting ethical principles. To do this successfully requires not only further clarification of the ethical dilemmas which arise in research with those unable to give full consent, but also that researchers, as an ethical position, should ensure that they seek support and supervision from knowledgeable colleagues who will challenge their thinking and practice. While the age of informed consent remains contentious, an attempt should be made to explain the procedures and potential outcomes to the child and to make decisions with them, not just for them, ensuring that the child fully understands not only the short-term implications of the research but also the long-term implications (e.g. being in a video for educational purposes).

How much of the information on consent forms do participants actually understand? In order to address the rights of human research subjects as outlined in the *Tri-Council Policy Statement* (SSHRC, 2003), consent forms have increased in length (Baker & Taub as cited in Mann, 1994/2003). It is unclear however, if these statements about rights and confidentiality are understood by research participants. When Mann compared comprehension of two consent forms matched for readability – a long, detailed form and a short, general form, she concluded that the longer form was less well comprehended than the shorter form with fewer details.

The Roberto Case

Roberto wants to conduct research with older adults who live in a long-term care facility. As part of his research he will carry out naturalistic observations over a prolonged period of time. He believes that extended time with participants will give him a better picture of the challenges they face and supports available to them. An honorarium of forty dollars will be paid to each participant. He develops a consent form that includes the necessary information as summarized in the *Tri-Council Policy Statement*. His committee members suggest that he needs to rethink the process of informed consent and they present the following questions for him to consider.

- What might be some of the difficulties faced by participants in understanding his research?
- How might the researcher-partici-

pant role be misconstrued by participants?
- What expectations might participants form?
- What 'power-over' issues may be present in the research situation that may impact on voluntariness?

Roberto needs to assess potential participants' level of decision-making. He could present vignettes which require participants to make choices between high risk and low risk interventions. By engaging in a discussion about the pros and cons presented in the vignettes, Roberto can assess whether each individual is capable of making a decision to participate. Stanley et al. (1995/2003) argue that many adults have poor comprehension of consent information while Thompson (2002) suggests that "not only must an informed consent design be tailored to the research method, but, more importantly, it must respond to the circumstances of potential participants" (p. 97). In particular, Thompson points out three contextual realities that can have a bearing for people with developmental disabilities: institutionalization, lack of decision-making opportunities, and the desire to pass as 'normal.' Participants' sense of liberty may be impacted when they live in residential settings where they are monitored. Residential living decreases opportunities for decision-making and may lead to learned helplessness in those individuals (Lindsey, 1994 as cited in Thompson, 2002). In other words, individuals with developmental disabilities or long-term illness may defer to caregivers and others in authority when in a choice-making situation. In order to develop a 'friendship' or to be accepted, participants may hide the fact that they cannot read or understand the consent form by simply obeying the requests of the researcher.

Roberto's offer of compensation for participation must also be considered. Without some compensation, participants may be exploited for their time and receiving tangible rewards, such as money, can be fair payment for their participation in the research. However, coercion can occur with vulnerable populations. In this particular case, the forty dollars in addition to the long-term relationship may be viewed as a special benefit which will set participants apart from those who do not participate and which will provide them with the human contact they may lack. Many potential researchers may see it as a daunting task to take into account the various aspects of informed consent. At post-secondary institutions, research ethics boards and supervisory committees provide avenues for analyzing and discussing the steps involved in obtaining informed consent with assorted populations and across various situations.

Confidentiality and Privacy

Confidentiality refers to mutually agreed upon arrangements for use of participants' data. CCA's standard on confidentiality reads: "Counsellors ensure that research information on subjects is confidential and the identity of participants is protected unless otherwise authorized by them, consistent with all informed consent procedures" (CCA, 2006, E6). Respect for confidentiality is essential to maintain trust between the public and researchers. There is a strong public interest in maintaining confidentiality so that individuals will be encouraged, for example, to seek appropriate counselling and to share information rele-

vant to it. If members of the public become suspicious of researchers, they may choose not to take part in research in future.

As part of the process of informed consent, exceptions to confidentiality, possible threats to confidentiality, and ways to protect confidentiality need to be outlined. Section 3 of the *Tri-Council Policy Statement* (SSHRC, 2003) compels researchers to maintain confidentiality of any personal information disclosed in the context of a researcher relationship unless participants have given free and informed consent. Exceptions to respect and protection of privacy and confidentiality occur when public interest is at stake, as in the protection of life. University research ethics boards insist that access to counselling or psychological services is available to research participants who may be at risk for harming themselves or others (Sales & Folkman, 2000, p. 52). Violations of confidentiality can have serious outcomes for participants, particularly for those who belong to vulnerable populations. For example, Sales and Folkman note that "information divulged to an employer that an individual is HIV-positive can affect his or her career" (p. 51) while "a child's observations about a parent that are revealed to a parent can result in negative consequences for the child" (p. 51).

Although closely associated with the term confidentiality, anonymity does not have the same meaning. Anonymity pertains to the information that an individual has disclosed in a study with the expectation that the information has no identifiers linked to the participant and therefore cannot in any way be traced to the participant. Research should use unlinked or truly anonymized data wherever possible. If this is not possible, the amount of personal data stored by researchers should be kept to the minimum necessary to achieve the purpose of the study; that is, data kept should be adequate, relevant, and not excessive in relation to the project. Personal data should be modified as early as possible in the processing of data so that some or all of those who might see it cannot identify individuals. Anonymity can be achieved by masking the names of individuals through the use of pseudonyms and by obscuring identifying characteristics of individuals. While on the surface maintaining anonymity appears to be a matter of coding data and scoring protocols to avoid the use of participants' names and keeping all identifying materials in a locked filing cabinet, the process is not straightforward. Data collection methods and type of research approach taken can raise significant ethical concerns. In research that involves human participants, the greater the engagement with participants the more likelihood that ethical dilemmas will arise.

Ethical Challenges

Focus group interviews are useful approaches for capturing individuals' personal experiences, beliefs, and perceptions and for gathering multiple perceptions about an area of interest (Morgan, 1997) but are particularly challenging in terms of privacy and confidentiality. Marshall and Shepard (2006) were confronted with a number of ethical dilemmas when conducting focus groups with young people in community settings. Challenges to confidentiality included: sharing information gained in the focus group outside the group as gossip or as a way to retaliate against another group member and over-disclosing information as partici-

pants became comfortable in the group. The researchers discussed respecting confidentiality throughout the research process and took the opportunity to revisit the concept of confidentiality as the issue arose in the focus group. Possible scenarios were used to illustrate how a disclosure might be wrongfully used intentionally or by accident.

Community-based research presents other challenges (Murphy & Dingwall, 2001; Snyder, 2002). When research is carried out in a few selected settings, fieldnotes, and interview transcripts provide sufficient details to allow participants to be identified (Murphy & Dingwall). Protecting participants' anonymity becomes problematic when individuals can be identified by others who know them through the use of extensive direct quotations. Phrasing and choice of words or the details of personal narratives are not easy to disguise completely. As well, extended fieldwork necessarily means public visibility. The researcher is seen with specific individuals and it is relatively easy for "others to reconstruct identities... from published accounts" (Nespor, 2002, p. 547).

> [A]nonymization is likely to be most problematic precisely where it would be most useful—at the local level—and that it can do little to protect the identities of participants from intimates and associates or from midlevel officials and bureaucrats they deal with – the very people likely to be in positions to react or retaliate against them. (Nespor, 2002, p. 548)

Snyder (2002) recommends that counsellor-researchers clarify with each participant the nature of the research project including the limitations to guaranteeing anonymity of participants and the limits to maintaining confidentiality of their responses. Participants can be given the opportunity to read through the initial findings for accuracy and to remove any information that might identify them. In field-based approaches, researchers can negotiate active research relationships that embrace an ethics of responsibility, working with participants to identify and resolve issues of confidentiality and privacy.

Counsellors who are trained to be active listeners may find that when participants are given time to talk for prolonged periods of time, they speak of private manners or of difficult times in their lives. Researchers have a responsibility to protect the anonymity of participants and should assume that all information told to them in the research process is extremely confidential. It may be helpful for researchers to ask themselves, "What information in this interview would I not want to reveal to others?"

Duty of care requires researchers to ensure that information is stored securely so as not to be seen by others. According to the principle of care, when recalled life episodes produce strong emotional responses, researchers are obligated to allow sufficient time for the participant to debrief. If, after discussing the issues or events, the participant is still feeling some discomfort, the researcher can locate a counsellor who can support the participant to resolve the situation.

Ethical Research Across Cultures

The basic principles outlined in the *Tri-Council Policy* (SSHRC, 2003) and counselling ethical codes reflect the high value that the dominant Western tradition places on individual autonomy. Researchers need to be cognizant that this is not the only way in which human interaction and responsibilities are conceptualised. In many non-Western societies, and in some communities within Western societies, the rights and autonomy of the individual are complex and may be restricted to some extent by those individuals or groups who have some type of authority over that individual (Piquemal, 2001). Thus, researchers need to be aware of individuals' rights within specific local and national socio-cultural contexts (Bäärnhielm & Ekblad, 2002). Recent developments in social research practice emphasize the importance of community values as well as the values of the individual within that community (Bäärnhielm & Ekblad; Payton, 1994). Community-based research calls for researchers to balance individual values with collective values due to the variety of opinions likely to be encountered in the research setting (Snow, Grady, & Goyette-Ewing, 2000). This discussion about conducting research cross-culturally is not meant to overwhelm beginning researchers. Instead, the intention is to provide some basic information about the issues faced in doing this type of research and recommendations for conducting culturally competent research.

Research with diverse populations raises complex ethical issues in a number of areas starting with the researcher's values. Researcher biases influence the types of research questions asked, the researcher-participant relationship, and the interpretation of results (Pope-Davis, et al., 2001). Researchers working with diverse populations are frequently criticized for having their own research agendas and hypotheses (Pope-Davis, et al.). Additionally, the choice of data collection approaches, for example, survey instruments, may limit the ability "to fully capture the values, experiences, and worldview of a participant through one-sentence items (Pope-Davis, et al., 2001, p. 129).

Cultural and social disparities between participant and researcher may shape how ethical considerations are understood and construed. In a study of the meaning of mental illness among Swedish and Turkish born women, Bäärnhielm and Ekblad (2002) found that the "concepts of integrity, autonomy, nonmaleficence, beneficence, and justice can be given different meanings" (p. 478). In a research project aimed at understanding healthcare problems, a participant was given a diagnosis of major depression following the *Structured Clinical Interview for DSM-IV Axis 1 Disorders-Research Version* (2002). When the participant asked for and received the results of her diagnostic interview, she responded: "You are not allowed to say that [referring to depression]. I do feel depressed but I don't want anyone to know that. That is our secret."(Bäärnhielm & Ekblad, 2002, p. 476). The primary researcher noted that it's essential when accessing personal information through in-depth interviews to familiarize oneself with the meaning of the research situation for the participant. In recognition of the fact that values and norms cannot be generalized across cultural groups or from a cultural group to an individual, the researchers advocate taking the time to reflect on "one's own moral standpoints" and "to become well acquainted with the participants'

contextual understanding of the research situation – their expectations, hopes and fears" (p. 478).

One workable option to address these needs and to capture participants' worldviews and context is to conduct qualitative research as a first step (Pope-Davis et al., 2001). Qualitative methods are sensitive to context and present a detailed portrayal of participants' points of view, using their own words (Janesick, 2000). Gil and Bob (1999) add the caution that overlooking the strengths of minority populations and only focusing on social and psychological problems that exist in minority communities "only exacerbates existing negative stereotypes, creating distance between the perspectives of researchers on issues impacting minorities and actual problems based on reality and needs of the minority communities" (p. 50).

Participatory action research (PAR) is a logical response to make research more relevant to diverse populations and to apply outcomes in a way that directly benefits the participants and involves them in guiding the research project. In PAR, community-based organizations or groups (for example, neighbourhood organizations or community residents) help researchers to recruit participants and to play a direct role in the design and conduct of the research study by bringing community members into the study as partners; to use the knowledge of the community to understand local problems and to design activities to improve the situation; to connect community members directly with how the research is done and its outcomes; and to provide immediate benefits from the results of the research to the community. This involvement can help improve the quality of life in the community by putting new knowledge in the hands of those who need to make changes and to build capacity in communities for future collaborations by training community members in data collection and analysis.

Because PAR is negotiated at the local level, the sharing of leadership, control, power, and decision-making throughout the entire research process, from design to dissemination is ensured (Macaulay et al., 1997; Williams et al., 1996). With opportunities to discuss results with the community, joint interpretations can emerge. Cultural and internal validity are increased and harms are minimized (e.g., stigmatization of the individual and the community by "outsiders") and benefits are maximized. Within this "dynamic social space" (Potvin, et al., 2003, p. 1303), researchers are more likely in their written reports to "mention any variables and conditions that might affect the outcome of the investigation or the interpretation of results" (CCA, 2006, E10), including dissenting views of both researchers and the community, if no agreement can be reached on the interpretation.

Conducting Research with Aboriginal Peoples

There is growing recognition that some research involving Aboriginal individuals may also involve the communities or groups to which they belong. The Councils affirm that in developing ethical standards and practices, Aboriginal peoples have rights and interests which deserve recognition and respect by the research community. (SSHRC, 2003, 6.1)

Because PAR is based on a mutually respectful partnership between researchers and communities, the approach has been suggested as ethically appropriate for use with Aboriginal communities. The challenge of ethical research with Indigenous people involves freeing researchers from exercising intellectual arrogance and using paternalistic practices. Instead, Smith (1999) recommends that Indigenous people design or at the very least, be directly involved in the research process. According to Smith, current ethics review boards and professional codes of ethics presume that one model of research suits all research designs. Indigenous peoples have their own notions of ethics, research, the researched, and community review processes. Smith proclaims that research practices with Aboriginal people should be guided by moral and pedagogical imperatives, particularly since there is a power dynamic embedded in the relationship with the researcher due to the history of colonization. Researchers are in a position to extend knowledge or to perpetuate ignorance, therefore, research projects should be directed towards "acts of reclaiming, reformulating, and reconstituting Indigenous cultures and languages... to the struggle to become self-determining (Smith, p.142). Other characteristics of research with Indigenous populations present specific ethical challenges.

Since researchers may belong to a different culture, for example, debates may arise because of different definitions of public and private life. Notions of property will sometimes differ between the researcher, sponsors and the community. Language differences may impede clear communication and understanding that is instrumental to the informed consent process. A researcher may also be confronted by ethical dilemmas because of competing interests among different sections of the community. (SSHRC, 2003, 6.2)

The Tri-Council outlines four situations in which it is essential to take into account the concerns of the Aboriginal group rather than the individual (SSHRC, 2003, pp. 6.2-6.3):

- Property or private information belonging to the group as a whole is studied or used.

- Leaders of the group are involved in the identification of potential participants.

- The research is designed to analyze or describe characteristics of the group.

- Individuals are selected to speak on behalf of, or otherwise represent, the group.

Piquemal (2001) notes that ethical codes recommend that cross-cultural research be conducted in a manner that is sensitive to participants' rights yet provide few, if any, concrete suggestions. Piquemal (2000) outlines four guiding principles for research with Aboriginal people:

to establish a partnership before seeking such consent; to consult with relevant authorities, who may be both individuals and the collective; to continually confirm consent to ensure consent is ongoing; and to provide the participants with all the information and data that might be useful or beneficial to them, and to do so prior to completion of the final report. (p. 49)

Best practices for working with Aboriginal communities are outlined by the Tri-Council (SSHRC, 2003), in the *Journal of Aboriginal Health* (Schnarch, 2004), and through invited papers to the *National Council on Ethics in Human Research* (McPherson, Nelson, & Rabb, 2004). The following best practices have been taken from the Tri-Council Policy Statement (pp. 6.3-6.4):

- Respect the culture, traditions and knowledge of the Aboriginal group.

- Conceptualize and conduct research with Aboriginal group as a partnership.

- Consult members of the group who have relevant expertise.

- Involve the group in the design of the project.

- Examine how the research may be shaped to addresses the needs and concerns of the group.

- Make best efforts to ensure that the emphasis of the research, and the ways chosen to conduct it, respect the many viewpoints of different segments of the group in question.

- Provide the group with information respecting the following: protection of the Aboriginal group's cultural estate and other property; the availability of a preliminary report for comment; the potential employment by researchers of members of the community appropriate and without prejudice; researchers' willingness to cooperate with community institutions; and researchers' willingness to deposit data, working papers and related materials in an agreed-upon repository.

- Acknowledge in the publication of the research results the various viewpoints of the community on the topics researched.

- Afford the community an opportunity to react and respond to the research findings before the completion of the final report, in the final report, or even in all relevant publications.

Researcher-Practitioner: Ethical Concerns

Research into one's professional practice as a counsellor, counsellor-educator, or supervisor can improve practice by evaluating the effectiveness and value of a program, by adding to the existing body of knowledge on actual counselling training and practice, by raising standards of service, and by creating future research agendas for the counselling profession (Mills, 2000; Zinck & Littrell, 2000).

The Carlos Case

Carlos, a counsellor at a community agency, is curious about the effectiveness of his psychotherapeutic approach. Although he completed two research courses during his Master's program, he is unsure of the ethical implications of conducting research on his counselling practice.

- What are the key issues involved?
- Is ethical approval required?
- How will he explain his dual role to clients?

When counselling practitioners wish to study the outcomes of their professional practice, they need to carefully

separate what constitutes their practice from what will be conducted as part of the research. A practitioner-researcher may conduct, for example, a counselling session without obtaining a research ethics board (REB) approval; however, when the session is used as data, REB procedures must be followed. The dual use of data from professional practice requires ethical approval from institutional or organizational review boards and informed consent from participants.

Practitioner research presents unique situations that require special attention, particularly the possibility of dual relationships between researchers and participants and maintaining anonymity and confidentiality when presenting aspects of one's practice at conferences and through articles. When research is conducted within an agency or institution or within one's practice, it is challenging to protect participants' identities and the confidentiality of the information they provide. Others in the agency will likely know who participated and although data collection and analysis can be made confidential and anonymous, completely disguising data in finished reports may be problematic (Webb, Turton, & Pontin, 1998). To protect anonymity and confidentiality, ask a third party to distribute information and consent forms, to maintain confidentiality after the project is completed, and when identifying information is not possible to mask, to re-obtain participants' consent to use this identifying information (*Task Force on Research Ethics on Education*, 2005).

When counsellors conduct research on their practice or within their classrooms as educators, they must deal with "power-over" issues. The 'double-act' role (Titchen & Binnie, 1993) may cause confusion in clients or students who know the researcher in other roles and with other responsibilities. Of more concern are the inherent power differentials between researcher and participant. Coercion exists if individuals cannot refuse to participate in the research, if refusal causes a substantial loss to the participant, or if the participant believes that participation is not truly voluntary (Soldz & McCullough, 2000). For example, the counselling relationship may be viewed as an inducement that prevents participants from carefully weighing the risks and benefits of participation (Soldz & McCullough, 2000). A client who feels that the choice to not participate will have a negative impact on the counselling relationship (e.g., the counsellor-researcher will be "disappointed" in them) is likely to take greater risks and to bear greater costs to maintain the relationship.

Several steps can be taken to reduce the power-over dynamic:

- Include participants in the project when they have completed therapy, the program or practicum.

- Exclude any participants where there is a power-over relationship.

- Confirm that there is a power over relationship in the recruitment materials and informed consent forms.

- Outline in simple language how the researcher has and will address issues of inducement and coercion in the research project (*Task Force on Research Ethics in Education*, 2005).

Counsellor-Educators As Researchers

Counsellor-educators understand the status and power differential between themselves and their students and avoid, whenever possible, any dual relationship with students who participate in their research projects. Any duality of relationships should be recognized, acknowledged, and managed in a manner that clarifies the various roles and responsibilities and avoids any disadvantage to students. (CCA, 2001, p. 31)

In order for participation to be voluntary, course outlines should inform students of the research requirement and the purpose of the research. Alternative assignments are provided to satisfy the research requirement (Scott-Jones, 2000). Ra-ther than tying grades to research participation, counsellor-educators can provide alternative research-related activities such as reading and summarizing journal articles, as long as the alternatives are equivalent to the amount of time and effort required of research participation (Scott-Jones, 2000). Students should be informed that they can opt out of the research project at any time and choose an alternative assignment.

Research Publications

Counsellor-educators have multiple roles and relationships with students. Ethically, counsellor-educators need to clarify their roles, be aware of the potential problems that can ensue, and manage the assorted roles and responsibilities in a way that prevents any harm to students. As in other multiple-role relationships, there is the potential for the abuse of power by the principal investigator when students take part in research projects as research assistants. Therefore, *Standards of Practice for Counsellors* (CCA, 2001) suggest that "the primary researcher should initiate an open discussion to clarify expectations, to reach agreement as to the nature of acknowledgments for the completed research work and for any subsequent publications, and to establish procedures for managing any problems." As noted before, student grades should not be attached to research endeavours.

When a multiple-authored article is based on the student's thesis or dissertation, the student is listed as the principal author (CCA, 2006, E12). Publication credits are also given to students who contribute to the research or to the writing for publication "through joint authorship, acknowledgement, footnote statement, or other appropriate means" (CCA, 2001, p. 32). Since research collaboration is a dynamic process in which the level of contribution can change over time, the primary researcher should discuss with students any anticipated changes that would affect publication credit. The following best practice recommendation is based on Fine and Kurdek's article (1993):

> To be included as an author on a scholarly publication, a student should, in a cumulative sense, make a professional contribution that is creative and intellectual in nature, that is integral to completion of the paper, and that requires an overarching perspective of the project. Examples of professional contributions include developing the research design, writing portions of the manuscript, integrating diverse theoretical perspectives, developing new conceptual models, designing assessments, contributing to data

analysis decisions, and interpreting results. Such tasks as inputting data, carrying out data analyses specified by the supervisor, and typing are not considered professional contributions and may be acknowledged by footnotes to the manuscript. (Fine & Kurdek, 1993, p. 1145)

Duplicate submission of the same, or essentially the same, manuscript to two or more journals is unethical (CCA, 2006, E13). The central ethical concern surrounding this issue involves misrepresenting the research the author(s) has, in fact, performed. Additionally, violations of copyright law may occur. However, this standard does not prohibit the author from publishing the same data in different journals with the intent of reaching different audiences as long as acknowledgement is given through citation of the original public source.

Counsellors may be called upon to review material submitted for presentation at conferences, for publication in a journal, for a grant, or for other scholarly purposes. As reviewers, counsellors are to respect confidentiality obtained through the review process and are prohibited from using privileged and proprietary information (CCA, 2006, E10). The intention of this code is to protect the intellectual property rights of individuals who describe their ideas, research approaches, and data in unpublished materials from being used by those who participate in a peer review process.

Chapter Summary

Conducting human subjects research requires researchers to minimize harm and maximize benefit to participants in the development of scientific knowledge. The importance of following the principles outlined in the *Tri-Council Policy Statement* have been emphasized in this chapter, noting the overall responsibilities of the primary researcher in gaining research approval, in developing culturally sensitive research designs, and in leading student research teams. Questions were raised about the complexity of seeking informed consent and ensuring confidentiality.

- What will you want to tell participants about their role in participating in your research program?

- What steps will you take to obtain informed consent?

- How will you maintain confidentiality?

- What are the challenges in conducting research across cultures and what are some of the steps you can take to ensure that harms are minimized and benefits are maximized?

Conducting research about one's practice or about the training of counselling students raises other critical ethical issues. What ethical consideration should guide this type of research? As counselling students involved in publications, what ethical considerations need to be addressed if you are a co-author? While there is much to be learned about conducting ethical research and publishing its outcomes, researchers need to keep in mind that research involving human subjects should always be based on thoughtful actions based on respect for human dignity.

Learning Activities

1. *Dyads.* Imagine that you are conducting a research project to assess the effectiveness of using art in therapy with children in your counselling practice. With a partner produce a list of ethical considerations to guide your research project. Use the following questions to guide your process: What steps might you take to obtain informed consent? How will you obtain ongoing consent? How will you ensure anonymity and confidentiality? What issues must you consider when recruiting children under the age of thirteen years?

2. *Role-play.* In a small group, two members role-play participant and researcher as they are about to engage in data collection. Researchers are encouraged to use their ideas for their research projects as a basis for the role play. Observers give the researcher feedback on the following:

   a) Did the researcher ensure that participation in the project was voluntary?

   b) Did the researcher inform the participant of the purpose of the research and explain the risks and benefits of the research?

   c) Did the researcher explain how confidentiality would be guaranteed?

   d) Was the participant given an opportunity to ask clarify his or her understanding of the research and to ask questions?

3. *Small-group Role-play.* Students work in groups of two or three and brainstorm solutions to a research dilemma. One student takes on the role of a participant from a different cultural group than the researcher,

another becomes the researcher, and the others act as observers. An ethical dilemma involving the researcher making a difficult choice between two alternatives is presented. Possible topics for the researcher to address include:

a) Whether or not to change a research design that is having a negative impact on the lives of participants as the researcher is under pressure to complete his thesis

b) Whether or not to change the videotaping of a cultural activity that is central to the research project as community leaders believe that confidentiality and anonymity cannot be maintained

c) Whether or not to continue with the research project when participants are reluctant to take part in the study or drop out of the project prematurely.

The participant challenges the researcher to review his or her assumptions about the problem and to identify the ethical issue. The small group brainstorms solutions and agree on a solution.

4. *Discussion.* You and your supervisor are preparing and submitting a journal article for publication based on your supervisor's research. What ethical considerations might you need to address?

5. *Presentation.* Review Section E in the *CCA Code of Ethics* on Research and Publication. Which ethical codes would fit under the headings consequentialist and deontological? Share you list with a partner and discuss your reasoning. Present your ideas to the class by associating each code with on of the core principles (auton-

omy, justice, trust, beneficence and non-maleficence, fidelity and scientific integrity).

6. *Group work.* Take some time to review the ethics codes of the various professional organizations, for example, American Counseling Association and the British Association for Counselling and Psychotherapy (www.counseling.org/Content/ NavigationMenu/RESOURCES/ ETHICS/ACA_Code_of_Ethics.htm; www.bacp.co.uk/ethical_framework/) as they apply to research and publications. Have students work in teams to analyze the codes for similarities and differences. Given what you have read in this chapter, are there any new guidelines that you would add to the codes?

7. *Guest Speaker.* Consider inviting a researcher who conducts cross-cultural research and who is a member of a non-dominant culture to address your class on conducting culturally competent research. Possible questions for consideration might include: What do you see as the main ethical concerns in conducting research with another cultural group? What are some of the best practices in conducting this type of research? What steps can be taken to appropriately study various cultural populations? How can different understandings of ethical principles be addressed?

References

American Psychological Association (2002). American Psychological Association (2002). Rules and procedures: October 1, 2001 [Ethics Committee Rules and Procedures]. *American Psychologist*, 57, 626-645.

Ashcroft, R., Goodenough, T., Williamson, E., & Kent, J. (2003). Children's consent to research participation: Social context and personal experience invalidate fixed cutoff rules. *American Journal of Bioethics*, 3(4), 16-18.

Bäärnhielm, S., & Ekblad, S. (2002). Qualitative research, culture and ethics: A case discussion. *Transcultural Psychiatry*, 39(4), 469-483.

Beauchamp, T., Faden, R., Wallace, R. J., & Walters, L. (1982). Introduction. In T. Beauchamp, R. Faden, R. Wallace, & L. Walters (Eds.), *Ethical Issues in Social Science Research* (pp. 3-39). Baltimore, MD: John Hopkins University Press.

Bersoff, D.M., & Bersoff, D. N. (2003). Ethical perspectives in clinical research. In D. N. Bersoff (Ed.), *Ethical conflicts in psychology* (3rd ed., pp. 379-381). Washington, DC: American Psychological Association.

Bridges, D. (2002). The ethics of outsider research. In M. McNamee & D. Bridges (Eds.), *The ethics of educational research* (pp. 71-88). Oxford, UK: Blackwell Publishers Ltd.

Canadian Counselling Association (2006). *Code of ethics*. Ottawa, Ontario: Author.

Canadian Counselling Association (2001). *Standard of practice for counsellors*. Ottawa, Ontario: Author.

Christians, C. (2000). Ethics and politics in qualitative research. In N. K. Denzin & Y. S. Lincoln (Eds.), *Handbook of qualitative research* (2nd ed., pp. 133-155). Thousand Oaks, CA: Sage.

Creswell, J. W. (2005). *Educational research: Planning, conducting and evaluating quantitative and qualitative research*. Upper Saddle River, NJ: Pearson Education Inc.

Danby, S. (2002). The communicative competence of young children. *Australian Journal of Early Childhood*, 27(3), 25-30.

Etherington, K. (1996). The counsellor as researcher: Boundary issues and critical dilemmas. *British Journal of Guidance & Counselling*, 24(3), 339-348.

Fine, M. A., & Kurdek, L. A. (1993). Reflection on determining authorship credit and authorship order on faculty-student collaboration. *American Psychologist*, 48, 1141-1147.

Fisher, C. B., Hoagwood, K., Duster, T., Frank, D.A., Grisso, T., Macklin, R., et al. (2002). Research ethics for mental health science involving ethnic minority children and youth. *American Psychologist*, 57, 1024-1040.

Ford, G.G. (2001). *Ethical reasoning in the mental health professions*. Boca Raton, FL: CRC Press.

Gil, E. F., & Bob, S. (1999). Culturally competent research: An ethical perspective. *Clinical Psychology Review*, 19(1), 45-55.

Janesick, V. J. (2000). The choreography of qualitative research design: Minuets, improvisations, and crystallization. In N. K. Denzin & Y. S. Lincoln (Eds.), *Handbook of qualitative research* (2nd ed., pp. 379-399). Thousand Oaks, CA: Sage.

Kelman, H. C. (1982). Ethical issues in different social science methods. In T. L. Beauchamp, R. R. Faden, R. J. Wallace, & L. Walters (Eds.), *Ethical issues in social science research* (pp. 40-98). Baltimore, MD: John Hopkins University Press.

Kitchener, K. S. (2000). *Foundations of ethical practice, research, and teaching in psychology*. Mahwah, NJ: Lawrence Erlbaum Associates.

Macaulay, A. C., Delormier, T., Cross, E. J., Potvin, L., Paradis, G., Kirby, R. et al. (1998). Participatory research with native community of Kahnawake creates innovative code of research ethics. *Canadian Journal of Public Health*, 89, 105-108.

Madak, P. R., & MacDonald, S. L. (2000). The question of ethics in qualitative research. In W. E. Schulz (Ed.), *Counselling ethics casebook 2000* (2nd ed., pp. 219-229). Ottawa, ON: Canadian Counselling Association.

Mann, T. (1994). Informed consent for psychological research: Do subjects comprehend consent forms and understand their legal rights? In D. N. Bersoff (Ed.), *Ethical conflicts in psychology* (3rd ed., pp. 403-405). Washington, DC: American Psychological Association.

Marshall, A., & Shepard, B. (2006). Youth on the margins: Ethical conduct in focus group research with adolescents. In B. Leadbeater, E. Banister, C. Benoit, M. Jansson, A. Marshall, T. Riecken (Eds.), *Ethical Issues in Community-Based Research with Children and Youth.* (pp. 139-156). Toronto: University of Toronto Press.

McPherson, D. H., Nelson, C. H., & Rabb, J. D. (2004). *Applied research ethics with Aboriginal peoples: a Canadian dilemma.* NCEHR Communiqué CNÉRH, 12(2), 6-24.

Milgram, S. (1963).Behavioral study of obedience. *Journal of Abnormal and Social Psychology*, 67, 371-378.

Miller, T., & Bell, L. (2002). Consenting to what? Issues of access, gate-keeping and 'informed' consent. In M. Mauthner, M. Birch, J. Jessop, & T. Miller (Eds.), *Ethics in qualitative research* (pp. 53-69). London: Sage Publications.

Mills, G. E. (2000). *Action research: A guide for the teacher researcher.* Upper Saddle River: NJ: Prentice-Hall.

Morgan, D. L. (1997). *Focus groups as qualitative research* (2nd ed.) Thousand Oaks, CA: Sage.

Murphy, E., & Dingwall, R. (2001). The ethics of ethnography. In P. Atkinson, A. Coffey, S. Delamont, J. Lofland, & L. Lofland (Eds.). *Handbook of ethnography* (pp. 339-351). Thousand Oaks, CA: Sage.

Nespor, J. (2000). Anonymity and place in qualitative inquiry. *Qualitative Inquiry*, 6(4), 546-569.

Payton, C. R. (1994). Implications of the 1992 ethics code for diverse groups. *Professional Psychology: Research and Practice*, 25(4), 317-320.

Piquemal, N. (2000). Four principles to guide research with Aboriginals. *Policy Options*, 21(10), 49-51.

Piquemal, N. (2001). Free and informed consent in research involving Native American communities. *American Indian Culture and Research Journal*, 25(1), 65-79.

Pope-Davis, D. B., Liu, W. M., Toporek, R. L., & Brittan-Powell, C. S. (2001). What's missing from multicultural competency research: Review, introspection, and recommendations. *Cultural Diversity and Ethnic Minority Psychology*, 7(2), 121-138.

Potvin, L., Cargo, M., McComber, A., Delormier, T., & Macaulay, A. C. (2003). Implementing participatory intervention and research in communities: lessons from the Kahnawake Schools Diabetes Prevention Project in Canada. *Social Science & Medicine*, 56, 1295-1305.

Prilleltensky, I. (1990). Enhancing the social ethics of psychology: Toward a psychology at the service of social change. *Canadian Psychology*, 31, 310-319.

Rosenthal, R. (2003). Science and ethics in conducting, analyzing, and reporting psychological research. In D. N. Bersoff (Ed.), *Ethical conflicts in psychology* (3rd ed., 382-389). Washington, DC: American Psychological Association.

Sales, B. D., & Folkman, S. (Eds.). (2000). *Ethics in research with human participants.* Washington, DC: American Psychological Association.

Scott-Jones, D. (2000). Recruitment of research participants. In B. D Sales & S. Folkman (Eds.), *Ethics in research* with human participants (pp. 27-34). Washington: APA.

Siang, S. (1999). Researching ethically with human subjects in cyberspace. *Professional Ethics Report*, 12(4), 1, 7-8.

Sin, C. H. (2005). Seeking informed consent: Reflections on research practice. *Sociology*, 39(2), 277-294.

Smith, L. T. (1999). *Decolonizing methodologies: Research and indigenous peoples*. Dunedin, NZ: University of Otago Press.

Schnarch, B. (2004). Ownership, control access, and possession (OCAP) or self-determination applied to research. A critical analysis of contemporary First Nations research and some options for First Nations communities. *Journal of Aboriginal Health*, 1(1), pp. 80-120.

Snow, D. L., Grady, K., & Goyette-Ewing, M. (2000). A perspective on ethical issues in community psychology. In J. Rappaport & E. Seidman (Eds.), *Handbook of community psychology* (pp. 897-917). New York: Kluwer Academic/Plenum Publishers.

Snyder, L. (2002). Confidentiality and anonymity: Promises and practices. In Will C. van den Hoonaard (Ed.), *Walking the tightrope: Ethical issues for qualitative researchers* (pp. 70-78). Toronto: University of Toronto Press.

Social Sciences and Humanities Research Council (SSHRC) (2003). *Tri-council policy Statemen: Ethical conduct for research involving humans*. <http://www.sshrc.ca>

Soldz, S. & McCullough, L. (Eds.), (2000). *Reconciling empirical knowledge and clinical experience: The art and science of psychotherapy*. Washington, DC: American Psychological Association Books.

Stanley, B., Sieber, J. E., & Melton, G. B. (2003). Empirical studies of ethical issues in research: a research agenda. In D. N. Bersoff (Ed.), *Ethical conflicts in*

psychology (3rd ed., pp. 398-402). Washington, DC: American Psychological Association.

Stringer, E., & Dwyer, R. (2005). *Action research in human services*. Toronto: Pearson Education, Inc.

Task Force on Research Ethics in Education (2005). *Action research: Guidelines for teacher/practitioner research*. University of Victoria: Author.

Thompson, S. A. (2002). My research friend? My friend the researcher? My friend, my researcher? Mis/informed consent and people with developmental disabilities. In van den Hoonaard (Ed.), *Walking the tightrope: Ethical issues for qualitative researchers* (pp. 95-106). Toronto: University of Toronto Press.

Titchen, A., & Binnie, A. (1993). Research partnerships: collaborative action research in nursing. *Journal of Advanced Nursing*, 18, 858-865.

Tobin, J. (1995). Post-structural research in early childhood education. In J. Hatch (Ed.), *Qualitative research in early childhood settings* (pp. 223-241). Westport, CT: Praeger.

United Nations (1989). *Convention of the rights of the child*. Vienna: Office of the High Commissioner for Human Rights.

University of Victoria, Graduate Executive. (2003, November). *Authorship credit and ownership of access to data guidelines*. Retrieved October 5, 2005, from the University of Victoria Web site: http://web.uvic.ca/psyc/grad/grad-rules/Appendix_K.htm

van den Hoonaard, W. C. (2002). Introduction: Ethical norming and qualitative research. In van den Hoonaard (Ed.), *Walking the tightrope: Ethical issues for qualitative researchers* (pp. 3-16). Toronto: University of Toronto Press.

Walkerdine, V. (1999). Violent girls and precocious girls: Regulating childhood at the end of the millennium. *Contemporary issues in early childhood*, 1(1), 3-23.

Webb, C., Turton, P., & Pontin, D. (1998). Action research: the debate moves on. In B. Roe & C. Webb (Eds.), *Research and development in clinical nursing practice*. London: Whurr Publishers Ltd.

Wendler, D., & Shah, S. (2003). Should children decide whether they are enrolled in nonbeneficial research? *American Journal of Bioethics*, 3(4), 1-7.

Williams, D., Singer, S. M., Adrien, A., Godin, G., Maticka-Tyndale, E., & Cappon, P. (1996). Participatory aspects in the qualitative research design of phase II of the ethnocultural communities facing AIDS study. *Canadian Journal of Public Health,* 87(Suppl. 1), S15-S32.

Williamson, G. R., & Prosser, S. (2002). Action research: Politics, ethics and participation. *Journal of Advanced Nursing*, 40(5), 587-593.

Zinck, K., & Littrell, J.M.. (2000). Action research shows group counseling effective with at-risk adolescent girls. *Professional School Counseling*, 4(1), 1096-2409.

Chapter Seven

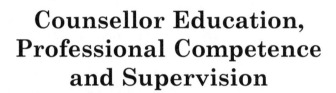

Counsellor Education, Professional Competence and Supervision

Supervisors must remain competent not only as therapists, but also as judges of another's abilities, while being competent in many facets of supervision itself. (Bernard & Goodyear, 2004, p. 63)

Chapter Objectives

The major focus of the chapter is on counsellor education, professional competence and supervision. Specific objectives are to:

- Summarize the main roles and responsibilities of counsellor-educators

- Outline the CCA standards for counsellor education programs

- Explain the value of orienting students to counsellor training programs

- Explain the importance of monitoring and evaluating the competency of counsellors-in-training

- Describe how appropriate student-faculty boundaries can be maintained

- Recognize the importance of developing and maintaining competent practice

- Clarify roles and responsibilities in supervision

- Identify and illustrate ethical considerations involved in supervision

Self-Inventory

Directions: Before reading this chapter, please use the following scale to indicate your attitudes towards issues in this chapter. For each statement, indicate the response that most closely identifies your beliefs and attitudes. Use the following code:

5 = Strong agreement with this item
4 = Agreement with this item
3 = Undecided about this item
2 = Disagreement with this item
1 = Strong disagreement with this item

___ Counsellor-educators are obligated to provide students with information about the program's expectations and evaluation processes.

___ It is unethical for counselling programs not to offer a course in ethics.

___ Counsellors-in-training have the right to know how they will be evaluated and what steps will be taken if remedial assistance is needed.

___ Selection of counsellors-in-training should be based on academic records as well as personal characteristics of effective counsellors.

___ Self-disclosure activities are a necessary component of a counselling program.

___ Supervisors need the necessary training to tailor their supervising styles and techniques to match the developmental stage of the supervisee.

___ Client protection in the supervisory relationship can best be addressed by emphasizing tape-recording and close monitoring of sessions.

___ In a supervisory relationship, the roles and responsibilities of trainees and supervisor need to be clarified.

___ One main contribution of supervision is keeping the focus on clients and their needs rather than solely on the trainee's progress.

___ Setting minimum standards of training through licensing will protect the public.

___ In order to practice ethically, counsellors must continue to upgrade their education and training.

___ Only through the process of licensing and/or certification will I continue to further my education as a counsellor.

Introduction

Counsellors who are responsible for counsellor education, training, and supervision adhere to current CCA guidelines and standards with respect to such activities and conduct themselves in a manner consistent with the *CCA Code of Ethics* (2006, F1) and *Standards of Practice for Counsellors* (CCA, 2001, p. 33).

Counsellor-educators can be viewed as gatekeepers for entry into the counselling profession. Their role as faculty members, supervisors, and trainers requires them to provide the necessary knowledge, skills, and experiences in academic programs to meet recognized standards in the counselling field. Consistent with the *CCA Standards of Practice for Counsellors* (2001), counsellor-educators are responsible for establishing respectful relationships with the students they train, educate, and supervise. Counsellor-educators are entrusted with several responsibilities, including the task of serving as role models for students by endeavouring to diminish areas in which they lack understanding or impartiality and to reduce the need for power and control over students (CCA, 2001). Additionally, counsellor-educators:

- clarify their roles, responsibilities, and appropriate relational boundaries with students

- emphasize the importance of adhering to ethical guidelines

- orient students to the counselling program and activities

- outline the limits of confidentiality

- encourage and facilitate personal exploration in relation to practice

• ensure the well-being of clients during internships and practica.

In their role as supervisors, counsellor-educators are entrusted with the responsibility for the training of the supervisee, the treatment of the supervisee's client, and the welfare of clients during the supervised practice period (Bernard & Goodyear, 2004; Haynes, Corey, & Moulton, 2003). The multiple roles played by the supervisor, including consultant, teacher, mentor, evaluator, role model, and advisor combine to form a complex structure that involves a multitude of standards and guidelines. Consequently, there are many ethical and legal standards that apply directly to supervision. Therefore, supervisors assume a wide range of responsibilities that require in-depth knowledge of the ethical standards of the profession.

This chapter explores ethical issues commonly encountered in counsellor training and supervision. The distinctive ethical issues involved in counsellor programs are outlined including responsibilities of counsellor-educators, selection of trainees, program content and accreditation standards, evaluation and remediation of students, relationship boundaries with students, and supervisor roles and responsibilities. Counselling competence is discussed in relation to CCA certification requirements and Canadian licensure initiatives.

Ethical Issues in Counsellor Training Programs

Training programs provide one of the main avenues for developing counsellor competence, an essential ingredient in protecting the public from harm. A combination of academic and personal learning interwoven with didactic and experiential approaches allows for integration of knowledge and practice (Corey, Corey, & Callanan, 2003). However, the very nature of a program that demands comprehensive knowledge of self as well as theoretical knowledge creates particular ethical issues at the level of the counsellor-educator, the program content, and not surprisingly, with faculty-student relationships.

Counsellor-Educator Roles and Responsibilities

Counsellor-educators protect and serve the future clients of counsellors-in-training and therefore act as gatekeepers to the profession (Choudhuri, 1999; Lumadue & Duffey, 1999). As trainers, supervisors, and educators, they play multiple roles in the lives of trainees. For this reason, it is essential that counsellor-educators clarify their numerous roles and responsibilities with students in order to forestall potential problems (CCA, 2006, F4). The *CCA Standards of Practice for Counsellors* (2001) summarizes the responsibilities that should be addressed with students prior to the commencement of training. They include:

• levels of counselling competence expected from students and trainees and the methods of appraisal and evaluation

• the non-grading of self-disclosure and self-growth activities

• any limits on confidentiality, including the supervisor's obligation for statutory reporting, such as in the case of child abuse

• any type of information that will be reported to the supervisor's employer, educational institution, training centre, or to a certification of licensing agency

- clarification of the supervisor's responsibility to the supervisee and to his/her clients. This should include the boundaries and responsibilities for the supervisor should there by serious concerns about the nature or quality of the counselling service being provided

- appeal procedures for students (CCA, 2001, pp. 35-36).

Counsellor-educators who are responsible for developing, putting into practice, and overseeing counsellor education programs are required to be skilled teachers and practitioners (ACA, 2005, F.6.a; CCA, 2006, F2). Because counsellor training programs are multi-faceted, emphasizing a blend of competency- and experience-based approaches, educators aim to provide programs that include:

- content and information acquisition

- skill development through systematic modeling and supervision

- process interaction in small groups

- emotional/personal development through group and self-reflective assignments

- evolution of a personal style of practice through supervised experience

- refinement of counselling interventions through feedback on videotapes (Hazler & Kottler, 1994, p. 6)

To facilitate counselling competence, counsellor-educators need to expose students to a range of pedagogical methods that meet students' various learning styles, values, and levels of development (Hazler & Kottler). For example, collaborative approaches frequently rely on Kolb's model (1984) by incorporating concrete experiences, reflective observation, abstract conceptualization, and active experimentation. This style of instruction requires counsellor-educators to be comfortable and competent in sharing their own counselling practice experiences and in demonstrating counselling skills, as personal stories and direct observation are powerful learning tools. Counsellor-educators who can share their counselling successes and challenges and articulate their knowledge provide students with valuable information not always found in textbooks. In the sharing of their counselling experiences, counsellor-educators can also impart to students current ethical responsibilities and standards of the profession as outlined in the *CCA Code of Ethics* (2006, F4) and *Standards of Practice for Counsellors* (CCA, 2001, pp. 33-39). Counsellor-educators are required to integrate their ethical considerations and decision-making processes into the courses they teach (ACA, 2005, F6d; CCA, 2001, p. 35) and to inform students and supervisors of their professional responsibilities (ACA, 2005, F6a; CCA, 2006, F4). Counsellor-educators are called upon to infuse diversity issues related to gender, sexual orientation, ethnicity, and other differences into courses and workshops (ACA, 2005, F.6.b; CCA, 2001, p. 33). This requirement places an expectation that counsellor-educators will endeavour to have self-understanding of diversity and the knowledge and experience to assist trainees in counselling in culturally sensitive ways. As can be seen, the counselling profession's *Code of Ethics* (ACA, 2005; CCA, 2006) compels counsellor-educators to meet many responsibilities.

A central responsibility of counselling faculty is to serve as role models for the profession and to impart information and techniques based on up to date empirical foundations.

How important is it to you for counsellor-educators to be current?

Can it be argued that a faculty in conflict affects the quality of education obtained by students?

The Menzies Case

For the past several years, Dr. Menzies, a counsellor-educator has focused on research and writing and during that time he has done little counselling. In the past, his practice included counselling older adults in a primarily middle-class, Caucasian community. He currently teaches two courses, one in cross-cultural counselling and the other in ethics. Students complain to the chair of the counselling department that the course material is out-dated and the instructor does not re-spect students' contributions to class discussions. Faculty members are openly critical of his lack of involvement in the counselling program.

- Using the *CCA Code of Ethics* (2006), what potential ethical issues are involved? skill development through systematic modeling and supervision

- How might conflict/disagreement among faculty members affect counselling students?

- If you were one of the students, what would you do in this situation?

- If you were the department chair, what would you do in this situation?

- How important is it for you to have faculty model healthy interpersonal behaviour?

- What are the potential risks for students not receiving current ethical and cross-cultural information and research?

Counsellors occupy a special position in the array of professional orientations. They are concerned not only with the treatment of distress but also with the development of effective preventive procedures for normally functioning and at-risk populations. They work with individual, couples, families, and other social units with the primary focus on helping persons towards achievement of their personal goals within the wider context of effective social relationships. Consideration of skill development, effectiveness of intervention, reliability of assessment, knowledge of and sensitivity to the needs of a range of diverse groups, and ethical issues are of prime importance in training counsellors. These topics must be presented both theoretically and practically, based on current research and practical experience.

According to Corey et al. (2003), "it is imperative that counsellor-educators and supervisors display cohesive relationships among themselves and treat students in a collegial manner with respect" (p. 303). In doing so, they display convincing examples about interpersonal relationships that students can incorporate into their personal and professional lives. Many students view faculty and staff members as role models for whom they have great respect and admiration. However, Kottler (1992) calls attention to how counsellor-educators, through their teaching styles and ways of interacting with students, clients, supervisees, and colleagues, practice hypocrisy by not modelling what they claim to be the most important aspects of being a counsellor; that is, displaying the core conditions of warmth, caring, respect, authenticity, and unconditional positive regard. He calls upon counsellor-educators to show their imperfections as well as their expertise and to demonstrate, through example, how to move toward growth, flexibility, and professional mastery.

> ...the greatest benefit of our profession is that we not only have the opportunity but also the imperative to combat our hypocrisies and inconsistencies. We can present ourselves as models of the potential that counselling can have when helpers apply what they know and can do to their own lives. (Kottler, p. 476)

Effective programs in Canadian institutions tend to be general in character and provide broad-based knowledge in the core course content areas and the application of counselling practices to a range of client age groups and settings. Ethical and professional conduct is typically addressed formally through a course devoted to the topic, and informally where issues and topics arise from other coursework and practicum placements.

The underlying emphasis in all courses is a balance of knowledge- and skills-acquisition and the development of practical experience. In the following sections, ethical issues involved in course content areas, student selection, self-disclosure activities, the appraisal and redressing of student deficiencies, and faculty-student interactions are outlined.

Content of Counsellor-Educator Programs

Counsellor-educators have a commitment to ensure that course requirements meet the recognized standards in the field. Since teaching can be viewed as a "process of persuasion", in which educators are socially sanctioned to influence the knowledge base and belief system of students (Friedrich & Douglass, 1998), counsellor-educators have an obligation to:

- provide students with accurate and current information (APA, 2002, 7.03b; Council on Accreditation of Counsellor Education Programs (CACEP), 2003, p. 12)

- integrate multicultural and diversity issues into course materials (ACA, 2005, F.6.b.; CACEP, p.12)

- integrate academic study and supervised practice into the program (ACA, F.6.c; CACEP, p. 13)

- infuse ethical decision-making throughout the curriculum (ACA, F.6.d; CCA, 2001, p. 35).

Accreditation of programs sets the minimal standards that training programs must meet, including requirements "with regard to institutional settings, program mission and objectives, program content, practicum experiences, student selection and advising, faculty qualifications and workload, program governance, instructional support, and self-evaluation" (CACEP, p. 1).

The Council for Accreditation of Counselling and Related Educational Programs (CACREP) was created by the American Counselling Association to implement standards of preparation for the counselling profession's graduate-level degree programs. CACREP provides leadership in promoting excellence in professional preparation through the accreditation of counselling and related educational programs (CACREP, 2001). The Canadian Counselling Association has also developed procedures and standards for counsellor education programs at the Master's level (CACEP), drawing on Canadian Psychological Association accreditation procedures for doctoral programs in psychology (1991) and the 2001 CACREP standards. The purpose of accreditation is to:

- promote high standards in the pre-service training of professional counsellors

- assist the administration and faculty of counsellor education programs to assess and improve their objectives, resources, and programs

- promote a continuing review and evaluation of existing counsellor education programs (CACEP, 2003, p. 1)

General standards include opportunities for self-appraisal and self-understanding and as such: "Counsellors who work as counsellor-educators, trainers, and supervisors, encourage and facilitate the self-development and self-awareness of students, trainees, and supervisees, so that they learn to integrate their professional practice and personal insight" (CCA, 2006, F9). Graduates are expected to display competency in the following areas:

- counselling as a profession

- ethical and legal issues in counselling

- counselling and consultation processes

- group counselling

- human development and learning

- diversity; lifestyle and career development

- assessment processes

- research methods

- program evaluation (CACEP, pp. 14-17).

The counselling program provides electives in addition to core courses. Students are required to have educational, career, and personal counselling available to them by qualified persons outside the counsellor education faculty in compliance with the *CCA Code of Ethics* (2006, F10).

Prospective students who indicate an interest in submitting an application to a counsellor education program need to be provided with information about the program.

Counsellors responsible for counsellor education programs and training activities take responsibility to orient prospective students and trainees to all core elements of such programs and activities, including to a clear policy with respect to all supervised practice components, both those simulated and real (CCA, 2006, F6).

Information brochures typically describe:

- the philosophy of the program

- admission, retention, and dismissal policies and courses of actions

- skill and knowledge achievement necessary for program completion

- the curriculum

- evaluation techniques
- training components that include self-growth and self-disclosure
- typical jobs received by graduates from the program
- required field experiences

(Herlihy & Corey, 1996; Schulz, 2000).

Selection of Trainees

Counsellor-educators are responsible for ensuring that the welfare of clients is protected by selecting and training competent students. However, Forrest, Elman, Gizara & Vacha-Haase (1999) note the "lack of clear, shared, and consistent language to represent the different types of problematic behaviours" (p. 629). Kitchener (2000) also observes that the terms incompetence, impairment, and unethical behaviour are used to describe similar as well as different concepts. In a review of the literature, Forrest et al. conclude that impairment appears to capture a wide range of incidents including "diminished professional functioning attributable to personal distress, burnout, and/or substance abuse" and may also include "unethical and incompetent professional behaviour"(p. 631-632). That is, incompetency may not be just "the result of diminished professional functioning" but rather an inability to reach a minimal acceptable standard of professional functioning" (p. 632).

Because impairment is a challenging problem to identify, the accurate screening of students entering counsellor preparation programs has been problematic. Students, as well as faculty, might be impaired when they are admitted to an institution (Witmer & Young, 1996). For this reason, the selection of students for a counsellor education program is the initial step in pre-

venting impairment (Corey et al., 2003). There are many methods of screening applicants. However, Bradey and Post (1991) find that many universities focus on letters of recommendation and academic background for screening purposes. While these measures are good predictors of academic success, they cannot predict competency or mental health. Corey et al. (2003) recommend that, along with grade-point averages and letters of recommendation, candidates write a personal essay outlining their reasons for pursuing a career in counselling, an appraisal of their strengths and weaknesses, and the work and personal experiences that they bring to counselling. Some universities and training centres also rely on group interviews involving problem-solving exercises; individual interviews by a team composed of faculty members and students; or videotaped responses to questions posed by faculty members (Schwebel & Coster, 1998).

- How should trainees be selected for admission to counsellor education programs?

- How do you establish that the candidate is mentally stable and has the personal qualities necessary to be an effective counsellor?

- How can faculty remain open to other approaches to counselling and to working with students who may challenge their approaches?

Self-Disclosure Activities

Experiential learning is often involved in counselling programs and can take a variety of forms: role-playing, coaching, and micro-counselling, for example. Self-disclosure, the process of making public information that is of a personal or sensitive nature, is frequently involved in these types of learning experiences. For example, students may act as a "client" to demonstrate counselling techniques and may, in the demonstration, reveal information that is not commonly known to other participants. Notification of self-disclosure activities should be placed in program description and course outlines with a detailed description of the activities. Ethical codes are clear as to counsellor-educator's roles and responsibilities in these situations:

> Counsellor education programs delineate requirements for self-disclosure or self-growth experiences in their admission and program materials. Counsellor-educators use professional judgment when designing training experiences they conduct that require student and supervisee self-growth or self-disclosure. Students and supervisees are made aware of the ramifications their self-disclosure may have when counsellors whose primary role as teacher, trainer, or supervisor requires acting on ethical obligations to the profession. Evaluative components of experiential training experiences explicitly delineate predetermined academic standards that are separate and do not depend of the student's level of self-disclosure. Counsellor-educators may require trainees to seek professional help to address any personal concerns that may be affecting their competency. (ACA, 2005, F7b)

Counsellors who work as counsellor-educators, trainers, and supervisors ensure that any professional experiences which require self-disclosure, and engagement in self-growth activities are managed in a manner consistent with the principles of informed consent, confidentiality, and safeguarding against any harmful effects. (CCA, 2006, F11)

Prior to engaging in an activity, counsellor-educators ensure that students have a clear understanding of the purpose of self-disclosure activities and expectations for participation. Opportunities for discussing the risks and benefits and ethical issues involved are essential components for ethical practice, as is debriefing after the activity.

- What role should self-disclosure experiences play in a counselling program?

- Should these experiences form a foundational part of the program or be merely recommended or voluntary?

- What do you see as the problems, if any, in combining experiential training with didactic course work?

- What guidelines would you like in place in regards to students' level of self-disclosure?

Evaluation and Remediation of Students

The nature of counselling work has implications for the mental health of counsellors. Helping professionals show significantly higher rates of depression, alcoholism, anxiety, and more personal relationship problems compared to individuals in the general population (Cherniss, 1995; D'Andrea & Daniels, 1992; Maeder, 1989). Students also experience the mental health concerns experienced by practitioners. Furr and

Carroll (2003) indicate that students entering their counsellor training programs are unprepared for the intense self-exploration and scrutiny required and note the emotional cost involved in learning how to counsel others. Common forms of trainee impairment noted in an extensive review of the literature include clinical deficiencies, interpersonal problems, problems in supervision, and personality disorders (Forrest et al., 1999).

In response to the question, "What do heads of graduate programs in professional psychology consider important to the well-functioning of professional psychologists?" Schwebel & Coster (1998) report top ratings for self-awareness; balanced lifestyle; relationships with spouse, partner, and family; and personal values. Further, to effectively respond to stressors, respondents indicated that students need to depend on

> their self-awareness and personal values.... to live a balanced lifestyle, enjoying vacations and physical activities and maintaining sound relationships with their spouse or partner and with friends... and when in need... turn to their peers for support and seek help, if necessary, through therapy. (p. 287)

When asked to propose ways to promote well-functioning, program heads in the study suggested:

- more careful selection of trainees and early identification of difficulties

- an orientation process that accentuates that faculty is there to work with students in helping them achieve their goals

- ongoing support groups

- faculty modeling of appropriate behaviour

- closer supervision; introduction of mentoring; and opportunities in the program "to examine how their personhood influences their professional behaviour (p. 289)

Accordingly, monitoring the competency of counsellors-in-training is a key element in training programs. *CCA Code of Ethics* (2006, B1) states, "Counsellors have a primary responsibility to respect the integrity and promote the welfare of their clients." The *Code* also notes that "Counsellors who work as counsellor-educators, trainers, and supervisors, recognize when such activities evoke significant personal issues for students, trainees, and supervisees and refer to other sources when necessary to avoid counselling those for whom they hold administrative or evaluative responsibility" (F10). Counsellor-educators are required to adhere to the ethical standards outlined by the counselling profession and must therefore be able to identify when trainees' academic and personal limitations are having an impact on their effectiveness as counsellors and take steps to secure remedial assistance for students when needed (CCA, 2001, p. 37). If counsellor-educators ignore these gatekeeping responsibilities, they "participate in creating a growing workforce of impaired counsellors" (Bradey & Post, 1991, p. 108).

> Programs that do not complete annual evaluations on all students are vulnerable on several fronts. They are not in compliance with accreditation criteria or ethical standards; documentation will not exist in situations where

future, more severe actions need to be taken; and legal challenges may result from students who claim they did not receive due process. (Forrest et al., 1999, p. 639)

Some universities have developed procedures to use in evaluating students, including defining professional competencies expected of students, developing explicit policies for working with students who need remedial assistance, and creating an evaluation instrument (Baldo, Softas-Nail, & Shaw, 1997; Frame & Stevens-Smith, 1995; Procidano, Busch-Rossnagel, Reznikoff, & Geisinger, 1995).

In a survey of Coordinators of Canadian Master's level counselling programs (Brown, 2001) to ascertain the prevalence of student-counsellor incompetence, the procedures used to identify students who may not be appropriate for counselling work, and the approach taken to manage student incompetence, coordinators of 13 of a total of 21 programs responded. Procedures used by the programs surveyed included a review of applicant's transcript (100 percent), followed by an examination of resume and previous experience (92 percent), reference letters (92 percent), and in-person interviews (46 percent). In-person interviews were reported as the most useful procedure, but lack of time and money prohibited many programs from using this procedure. In terms of frequency of student incompetence, the majority of the programs reported one or more cases in the past five years with a total incidence of 33. The most frequent types of incompetence reported included lack of response or responsiveness to supervision (21 percent), ineffective counselling skills (18 percent), and lack of personal awareness (17 percent). Methods of remediation involved counselling (92 percent) and increased practicum supervision (92 percent). Other remediation tools employed were mentoring and repeated practica. When asked to note the number of students dismissed from their programs due to competency issues, a total of eight dismissals were reported. Brown questions whether remediation efforts are so effective as to eliminate concerns or whether programs are reluctant to identify and dismiss students due to fears of retribution or lawsuits. Over half of the programs had specific written policies in place to guide faculty when addressing student incompetence outlined in course syllabi and student handbooks.

Specific program policies that protect students' rights as well as the rights and responsibilities of faculty are found in three models: Frame and Stevens-Smith model, Baldo, Softas-Nall and Shaw model, and the Lumadue and Duffey model. Frame and Stevens-Smith (1995) describe the use of nine personal characteristics used to monitor students in counsellor training programs:

- being open

- flexible

- positive

- cooperative

- willing to use and accept feedback

- aware of impact on others

- able to deal with conflict

- able to accept personal responsibility

- able to express feelings effectively and appropriately.

At midterm and at the end of each semester, the faculty assessed all students by using a five-point Likert-type scale to evaluate essential functions. A rating of three or above on each characteristic was deemed a minimum standard of behaviour. The students were all given a handbook before admission that discussed this review process. They were asked to sign an agreement stating they understood and agreed to follow the policies therein. When a problem was identified, the student was asked to meet with the professor to discuss the evaluation and to be given an opportunity for remediation. Personal therapy was a preferred choice.

Baldo et al. (1997) modified the model outlined by Frame and Stevens-Smith by implementing a four-member faculty review committee to correct potential problems rather than placing the responsibility for remediation with just one faculty member. Lumadue and Duffey (1999) blended these two models to form the Southwest Texas State University model (SWT) which begins with the admissions process and emphasizes evaluation early in the academic career of the trainee. The evaluation criteria include specific behavioural standards rather than the abstract characteristics presented by Frames and Stevens-Smith. Typical forms of remediation consist of personal therapy, as the most common strategy, and repeating coursework, repeating practicum, taking a leave of absence, increasing supervision, and leaving the program as other options (Forrest et al., 1999).

Another approach to address issues of incompetency and impairment includes the adoption of a wellness philosophy integrated into all curriculum and clinical learning experiences (Witmer & Young, 1996). Faculty and students are expected to commit to personal growth and professional competence through holistic strategies that enhance well-being. The modelling of healthy behaviour is a powerful way to teach others. Witmer and Young suggest that the following qualities might be appropriate components of a wellness community:

- a passion for caring about the well-being of all members of the community

- open, honest, and positive communication

- commitment

- leadership

- maintaining a sense of community

- creative problem solving and conflict resolution

- respect for the individuality of each member of the community.

Witmer and Young note that mentally healthy counsellors are more likely to produce mentally healthy clients.

One approach in examining behaviour and in seeking assistance involves participating in personal counselling. Dorff (1997) notes that clinical psychology students ranked personal therapy as the most effective way to cope with stressors, followed by relationships with significant others, self-care, peer support, and supervision. Corey et al. (2003) believe that personal therapy during training and throughout a counsellor's career would result in counsellors who have the ability to focus more intentionally on the welfare of their clients. Likewise, Fouad and Hains (1990) note that graduate students gain a clearer awareness of personal matters when they engage as clients in the therapeutic process. Schmidt (2002) suggests, "By seeking assistance for ourselves and exploring our own development, we illustrate our belief in the helping process and demonstrate the same courage we expect of those who someday might seek our assistance" (p. 12).

Counsellor-educators are gatekeepers, monitoring signs of impairment in counsellors-in-training. By being proactive and requiring counselling for all counsellors- in-training, counsellor-educators can take a definitive stand by recommending counselling for all incoming students to further decrease the stigma, to promote the numerous benefits of counselling, and to prevent impaired students from becoming future impaired counsellors.

For further reading in the area of remediation of counselling students, the article on trainee impairment by Forrest et al.(1999) offers a comprehensive examination of the literature regarding the recognition, remediation, and removal from programs of trainees who are unable to meet the professional standards in psychology training programs. Included in the article are responses to other counselling professionals, such as Schoener (1999) and Vasquez (1999). The well-functioning of professional psychologists has been placed on par with academic requirements by a number of researchers (Coster & Schwebel, 1997; Schwebel, Schoener, & Skorina, 1994).

Faculty-Student Relationships
A common thread found in applied programs is the importance given by students to their interactions with faculty (Casto, Caldwell, & Salazar, 2005; Hazler & Carney, 1993). At the heart of the discussion is determining appropri-

ate boundaries between counsellor-educators and students.

- How would you establish appropriate relationships with counsellor-educators in your program?

- Given that students are in a role of diminished power (Kitchener, 1988), what ethical, professional, and social boundaries need to be considered?

Hazler and Carney (1993) note that while faculty-student interactions may be important to student academic perseverance, intellectual development, personal development, and career aspirations, dual relationships between faculty and students are a matter of concern.

The *CCA Code of Ethics* (2006, F7) states, "Counsellors who work as counsellor-educators, trainers, and supervisors establish relationships with their students, trainees, and supervisees such that appropriate relational boundaries are clarified and maintained, and dual relationships avoided." Yet, students and faculty members in small graduate programs in counsellor education commonly found across Canada do form multiple relationships through academic advising where personal and career options may be examined; through the frequency and intensity of interactions in the program courses; through courses that require self-examination as in practicum classes and in supervision; and through research assistant and teaching assistant positions. When Bowman & Hatley (1995) surveyed full-time faculty and graduate students in counsellor preparation programs they found a lack of consensus regarding ethical faculty-student relationships. Women were more likely to rate actions as unethical compared to men. For example, female faculty considered attending public affairs with students as friends and sharing personal feelings with students as unethical. Female students viewed friendships among faculty and students; receiving loans from faculty; and gossiping or becoming intoxicated with faculty as unethical. Overall, female faculty and students were more cautious of situations involving student-faculty interaction.

As the student-counsellor-educator role is intrinsically asymmetrical in terms of power, because of the ability of counsellor-educators to affect student careers through evaluation, through research and professional prospects, through letters of recommendation and scholarships, and through reputation in the program and counselling community, sexual relationships are viewed as exploitative (CCA, 2001, p. 37). Sexual relationships impede the ability of the counsellor-educator to judge the student's academic and professional performance objectively and may put in jeopardy the counsellor-educator's effectiveness as a teacher or supervisor when other students in the program learn about the relationship. Additionally, the student, through threats of exposure, may be in a position to coerce the counsellor-educator regarding his or her evaluation or the evaluations of others in the program.

Based on the results of a survey of teaching psychologists and students, a portrait of an ethical professor was developed (Birch, Elliott, & Trankel, 1999/2003). According to respondents, the ethical professor avoids sexual involvement with students and if attracted to students, does not discuss that attraction with them. Ethical sexual boundaries are viewed as well-defined while attending the professor's classes, but less distinct once students are no longer members of the class. They note the lack of agreement in the expectations involved in non-sexual relationships with students including appropriate mentoring, social, and monetary interactions.

The most recent *ACA Code of Ethics* (2005) outlines the roles and relationships between counsellor-educators and students in great detail in section F.10.

> Sexual or romantic interactions or relationships with current students are prohibited. (F10a)

> Counsellor-educators do not condone or subject students to sexual harassment. (F10b)

> Counsellor-educators are aware of the power differential in the relationships between faculty and students. Faculty members foster open discussions with former students when considering engaging in a social, sexual, or other intimate relationship. Faculty members discuss with the former students how their former relationship may affect the change in relationship. (F10c)

> Counsellor-educators avoid non-professional or ongoing professional relationships with students in which there is a risk of potential harm to the student or that may compromise the training experience or grades assigned. In addition, counsellor educators do not accept any form of professional services, fees, commission,reimbursement, or remuneration from a site for student or supervisee placement. (F10d)

Counsellor-educators do not serve as counsellors to current students unless this is a brief role associated with a training experience. (F10e)

Counsellor-educators should avoid accepting gifts or other favours from students, except in cases where they are small tokens of appreciation for a special occasion or one-time event (e.g., graduation). Instructors who receive gifts are placed in an awkward situation, as the gesture may be perceived as an effort by the student to receive some academic benefit.

In recognition of the important difference in faculty-student relationships when compared to therapeutic relationships and the likelihood that many faculty and former students will interact professionally and socially in the counselling community, Lloyd (1992) suggests that rather than viewing dual relationships as unethical, attention should be given to the behaviour of those involved in such relationships. He gives the example of a professor who hires a student in financial need to perform research duties and thereby enters the dual roles of employer and instructor. Judging whether the relationship is ethical requires vigilant attention to the exact behaviours of those involved. He also notes that dual relationships within training programs can provide pertinent hands-on experience in ethical decision-making and conflict resolution, which is at the heart of the counselling profession.

The *ACA Code of Ethics* (2005) also observes the potentially beneficial relationships that can occur between counsellor-educators and students.

...If they believe a non-professional relationship with a student may be potentially beneficial to the student, they take precautions similar to those taken by counsellors when working with clients. Examples of potentially beneficial interactions or relationships include, but are not limited to, attending a formal ceremony; hospital visits; providing support during a stressful event; or mutual membership in a professional association, organization, or community. ... They discuss with students the rationale for such interactions, the potential benefits and drawbacks, and the anticipated consequences for the student. Educators clarify the specific nature and limitations of the additional role(s) they will have with the student prior to engaging in a non-professional relationship. Nonprofessional relationships with students should be time-limited and initiated with student consent. (F10f)

Students require early training in ethics with a particular focus on thinking through complex ethical dilemmas, for example, how to deal with multiple relationships. An important training strategy is the modelling provided by faculty in establishing and maintaining ethically appropriate boundaries. Counsellor-educators can gain perspective on blurred relationships with students by consulting with colleagues (CCA, 2001, p. 38).

Counsellor Competence and Counsellor Licensure

A central component of counsellor education programs is to provide the necessary knowledge and experiences students need to develop a clear understanding of the counselling field and their identity as counsellors. In Canada, counsellors have a national professional association, the Canadian Counselling Association (CCA) with chapter specialities: Career Development Chapter, Creative Arts in Counselling, Private Practitioners, Aboriginal Circle, Feminist Network, School Counsellors, and Pastoral Counsellors, as well as two provincial associations. Additionally, there are various other associations counsellors can join that are not affiliated with the Canadian Counselling Association. Despite the array of organizations available to counsellors, the counselling profession lacks a firm identity (Hanna & Bemak, 1997; Pistole & Roberts, 2002). A necessary aspect of success in the movement toward public protection, public recognition, and licensure is the building of a professional identity (Daniels, 2002; Mustaine, West, & Wyrick, 2003; Pistole & Roberts).

Specific attempts at establishing a counselling identity have included certification, developing guidelines and standards for counsellor education programs, and licensure. Certification grants the use of the title "counsellor" by verifying minimal professional standards to practice independently as a counsellor. In 1986, CCA introduced the Canadian Certified Counsellor program to oversee a non-statutory, voluntary certification process for members who meet certain qualification requirements. The certification program has several purposes, including identification to the public those counsellors who meet the necessary criteria and are thereby deemed qualified to provide counselling services. Once certified, counsellors are permitted to use the letters CCC to indicate their level of qual-

ification to practice counselling. Expectations for continuing education, adherence to the *CCA Code of Ethics*, and recommendations and discipline on issues pertaining to professional conduct are also mandated. As noted in the *Standards of Practice for Counsellors* (CCA, 2001), counsellors are involved in "regular participation in conferences and workshops in order to keep knowledge and skills current" (p. 34).

Minimal criteria for the preparation or training of professional counsellors can be set through accreditation procedures. The Council for Accreditation of Counselling and Related Educational Programs (CACREP), the chief accrediting body of counselling programs in the United States, was formed to provide an accrediting body with its own standards for training and practice independent to Psychology programs. CACREP accreditation provides recognition that the content and quality of the education offered by the accredited counselling program has been evaluated extensively and meets standards set by and for the profession. The student is reassured that included in the course of study are the appropriate knowledge and skill areas necessary for entry into the field of counselling. Furthermore, protection of the consumer of counselling services is provided as clients benefit from the appropriate training of the counsellor entering the field. Canadian educational institutions also have a set of procedures and standards for counsellor education programs at the Master's level developed by CCA (CACEP, 2003).

In order to become accredited, a counsellor education program must fulfill certain requirements or standards with regard to institutional settings, program mission and objectives, program content, practicum experiences, student selection and advising, faculty qualifications and workload, program governance, in-structional support, and self-evaluation. (p. 1)

Licensure, on the other hand, is a legislatively established process of credentialing at the provincial level which grants a practitioner the legal right to practice through law. The profession has specific responsibilities with respect to self-regulation including establishing who can be admitted to the profession and the level of competency required; creating codes of ethics and standards of practice; and dealing with formal complaints and disciplinary procedures. The principal reason for licensing counsellors is to protect the public. Without title protection and the legal definition afforded by licensure, any individual could claim the title "counsellor." The public has no means of differentiating qualified, trained practitioners from those who are untrained or distinguishing among different levels of training.

In 2006, Quebec was the only province in Canada to regulate counselling by statute. Nova Scotia, New Brunswick, and British Columbia have taken various steps towards obtaining legislated status for counsellors. While the Canadian Counselling Association offers voluntary national certification for members who have been educated at the Master's level, there is no requirement (other than in Quebec) for anyone who uses the term "counsellor" to belong to a professional organization that requires members to adhere to a professional code of ethics. The onus is on counselling programs to protect the public by ensuring that graduates are competent.

As might be expected, counsellor licensure has both positive and negative aspects. Handelsman and Uhlemann (1998) outline the issues:

> The professions may argue that the public is entitled to excellent service that can only be provided by the most highly educated and experienced practitioners who have undergone a rigorous examination process.... (H)igh levels of education and experience may not guarantee excellent practice (Handelsman, 1997; Rottenberg, 1980)...(I)t may stifle competition, raise prices, discourage innovation, and reduce access to services among those who may need the service the most (Hogan, 1979). On the other side of the continuum is the argument that government has no interest in assuring excellence. Rather, the government's only interest may be in the safety of the public....Hogan wrote, "Licensing laws are meant to protect the public from harm. A reasonable interpretation of this policy would be that even minimal competence need not be shown, so long as a practitioner could guarantee that no client would be hurt or injured" (1979, p. 101).... (T)he public retains access to a variety of services, competition is stimulated, and cost is reduced. (p. 319)

The authors pose four key questions they believe need to be answered when considering applying for statutory regulation: (1) Is it in the best interests of the public and provincial counselling organization to be regulated by statute? (2) If the counselling organization decides on statutory regulation, which general model of regulation does it think is in the best interests of the public and their organization? (3) What specific measures or regulatory functions will work most effectively to achieve the goals of the regulatory model chosen by the counselling organization? (4) Is the counselling organization willing to pay the costs (financial, professional, emotional, and political) involved in securing and working under the regulatory processes for which they are advocating? (p. 328).

In the future, the trend toward accountability may impact counsellors in a number of ways.

- Is it ethical to practice without continuing your education and training? Explain.

- How should standards be set for workshops and courses taken after graduation?

- What are the benefits and limitations of basing competency for entry-level counsellors on examinations? Should examinations be the basis for renewing credentials/licensure?

- How might licensing be limiting to the profession? What are some of the benefits of licensure?

- Some authors maintain that obtaining and maintaining a license/certification increases personal investment in the profession. What are your thoughts?

In the final section of the chapter, issues pertaining to supervision are discussed. Supervision is an essential element of therapist training in that it provides opportunities to further develop therapeutic competence and to work through "real life" ethical issues (Scott, Ingram, Vitanza & Smith, 2000). The core conditions of counselling, congruence, unconditional positive regard, and empathy are modelled in this "working alliance" (Holloway, 1995).

Ethical Issues in Supervision

The multiple levels of practice and the complexity of the process of supervision are demonstrated by the number of roles and responsibilities held by supervisors. Supervisors are required to adhere to all applicable ethical and legal guidelines that govern their profession. When taking on a supervisee, supervisors assume responsibility for supervisee compliance with these ethical and legal standards as well as his or her own actions as supervisor (CCA, 2001, p. 36). In their role of supervisor, they are responsible for instructing supervisees on ethical and legal matters and for monitoring ethical decision-making. As is the case with counsellor-educators, supervisors are representatives of the profession and therefore must behave both ethically and legally. These are all challenging tasks. To meet this challenge, supervisors must be knowledgeable and highly skilled.

Supervisor Characteristics and Competencies

Competent supervisors are empathic, genuine, open, and flexible. They are able to respect their supervisees as developing professionals and are sensitive to individual differences in terms of gender, race, ethnicity, and developmental level (Bernard & Goodyear, 2004; Haynes, Corey, & Moulton, 2003). Supervisors are knowledgeable about, and comfortable with, the evaluative functions inherent in their role and have extensive training and wide experience in counselling which gives them a broad perspective of the field (Bernard & Goodyear; Haynes et al.). An effective supervisor is able to demonstrate a range of supervision interventions and to assess the fit with the supervisee's learning needs and counselling style.

• What qualities do you look for in a supervisor?

• How is supervision similar to the counselling process? How is it different?

Supervisors need a strong theoretical and applied understanding of how to provide adequate supervision in order to facilitate the professional development of trainees (Haynes et al., 2003, p.158). Counselling itself requires a different skill set than providing an effective training environment for supervisees. A competent supervisor recognizes the interdependence in the supervisor-supervisee relationship and is able to adapt and modify his or her methods of supervision to meet the needs of the current supervisee. By continually providing well-documented written and verbal feedback to the supervisee, the supervisor not only protects for the welfare of clients, but also facilitates the self-development and empowerment of the supervisee. Competent supervisors recognize the importance of understanding and being sensitive to issues of diversity and differing worldviews (CCA, 2001, p. 34) and are well-informed about regulations, guidelines, and ethics that may surface in supervision (CCA, 2006, F3).

Currently, counsellor education programs tend to offer very limited training on the theory and practice of super-vision. Consequently, many supervisors have not received adequate training in supervision and may draw largely on personal experiences when supervising trainees. It is critical that supervisors continually seek out opportunities to educate themselves to increase their competence as supervisors, for example, by attending conferences and workshops, reading articles about supervision, reviewing ethical guidelines of supervisor-supervisee relationships (CCA, 2001, p.34). Although there is still a need to offer courses on supervision in counsellor training programs (Polanski, 2000), ultimately it is the responsibility of supervisors to seek out resources that increase their own supervision competencies.

Supervisor Roles and Responsibilities

Supervisors have many roles when training of students. Supervisors are continually required to juggle roles as a teacher, advisor, mentor, consultant, evaluator, recorder and documenter, administrator, empowerer, sounding board, and counsellor (Haynes et al., 2003). At times, supervisors may find themselves engaged in multiple roles simultaneously: teaching the supervisee a new clinical approach, evaluating the supervisee's professional development, and responding as a sounding board while allowing the supervisee to develop his or her own thinking processes. Supervisors need to be able to adapt and to modify their behaviours as they shift from one role to another (Haynes et al.). The primary role of supervisors is to focus on the professional development of supervisees. It is the responsibility of supervisors to provide supervisees with a clear understanding of objectives, procedures, and evaluation processes (Corey et al., 2003) through the co-development of a contract.

- What are the primary responsibilities of supervisors? Of supervisees?
- What is the purpose of a written supervision contract?
- Why is it important to outline duties, training philosophy, expectations and evaluation procedures at the outset of supervision?

The roles and responsibilities of supervisors and supervisees should be clearly delineated in a "Bill of Rights" (Tyler & Tyler, 1997) or a written contract. Suggested elements of the contract are:

- Purpose and goals of supervision
- Name and contact information of the clinical supervisor
- Unique qualifications for the provision of clinical supervision (licenses, coursework, certifications, etc.)
- Roles and responsibilities of supervisor and supervisee
- Frequency, time, and place where supervision will be conducted
- Supervisor's theoretical orientation and the models and methods of supervision to be used
- Documentation responsibilities of both parties
- Supervisee's agreement to follow agency policies and applicable ethical codes
- Supervisee's agreement to provide informed consent to clients. This may include the provision of a more "experienced" therapist should clients feel that they need one.

- Procedures for referral of the supervisee for counselling should it become necessary
- Evaluation strategies including due process
- Contact information of an appropriate individual should the supervisee experience a problem or dissatisfaction with supervision.

(Haynes et al., 2003, p. 198)

Supervisors are expected to use a variety of teaching methods and feedback mechanisms: responding to case study presentations, reviewing taped sessions, providing informal verbal feedback, engaging in group discussion and individual supervision, reviewing case notes, and assigning readings. Interestingly, when graduate students were asked to report their supervisors' ethical violations, the most common ethical violation pertained to supervisor evaluation (Ladany, Lehrman-Wateman, Molinaro, Wolgast, 1999, p. 457). This violation occurred when supervisors failed to provide thorough, ongoing feedback to graduate students, thereby providing minimal means for graduate students to improve their skills and competencies. This is a violation of the *CCA Standards of Practice for Counsellors* that state, "Students in counsellor education should receive on-going performance appraisal throughout their counselling program" (CCA, 2001, p.33).

Supervisees have the right to due process, a course of action that ensures that notice and hearing must be given before an important right can be removed. Substantive due process addresses the fair and consistent application of the criteria that govern a training program. Procedural due process concerns itself with the rights that counsellors have as participants in a training program:

- to be informed of the academic requirements and program regulations
- to receive notice of any deficiencies in a timely fashion
- to be evaluated regularly
- to have an opportunity to be heard.

Supervisors, through ongoing assessment and evaluation of supervisees, should be aware of any personal or professional limitations of supervisees which are likely to impede future professional performance. Supervisors have the responsibility of recommending remedial assistance to those supervisees who are unable to provide competent professional services (CCA, 2001, p. 34).

Supervisors are required to ensure that their students are knowledgeable of their ethical responsibilities according to the *CCA Code of Ethics* (2006, F3). It is the responsibility of supervisors to teach supervisees how to move through the process of making ethical decisions. That is, it is the role of supervisors to assistant supervisees in gaining practical experience by continually working through the processes of ethical decision making: identifying problems and other issues involved, reviewing the ethical code, discussing with colleagues to broaden one's perspective, identifying possible action plans, and isolating the consequences of decisions (Haynes et al., 2003, p. 156).

The major responsibilities of the supervisor are summarized by Haynes et al. (2003, pp. 30-39):

- Legal and ethical responsibility for the supervisee's actions
- Knowledge of all the supervisee's cases and clients
- Provision of regular feedback and evaluation of the supervisee's performance
- Monitoring of the supervisee's actions and decisions
- Documentation of supervisory sessions
- Supervise within one's scope of practice
- Provision of due process information and procedures
- Formulation of a written contract or understanding that clarifies expectations and parameters of the supervisory relationship
- Identification of personal issues impacting the practice of counselling
- Modelling of effective problem-solving and ethical knowledge and behaviour
- Promotion of knowledge and skills needed to be an effective counsellor.

Style and Methods of Supervision

Counsellor-educators who supervise students should be prepared in the concepts and methods of supervision (CCA, 2001, p. 33).

Clinical supervision requires a unique set of knowledge and skills which build on, but are different from, counselling knowledge and skills. Supervision models systematically attend to the development of a safe supervisory relationship, the provision of structure, the use of a variety of learning styles, management of multiple supervisory roles, and the application of effective communication skills. Knowledge of models of supervision is fundamental to ethical practice. For example, developmental approaches to supervision are based on the notion that in the process of moving toward competence, supervisees move through a series of states that are qualitatively different from each other. The behaviours of supervisors change as supervisees gain experience. Stoltenberg and Delworth (1987) describe a developmental model with three levels of supervisees: beginning, intermediate, and advanced. Particular attention is paid to (1) self-and-other awareness, (2) motivation toward development as a counsellor, and (3) amount of dependency or autonomy.

Typical development for beginning supervisees would involve dependence on supervisors to assess, understand, and explain client behaviours and attitudes, and to establish interventions. Intermediate supervisees would continue to depend on supervisors for an understanding of difficult clients, but would like to be somewhat independent when working with typical clients. At the advanced level, supervisees function independently, seek consultation when appropriate, and take responsibility for their decisions. Stoltenberg and Delworth describe eight growth areas for each supervisee:

- intervention skills
- assessment techniques
- interpersonal asssessment
- client conceptualization
- individual differences
- theoretical orientation
- treatment goals and plans
- professional ethics.

Although many counselling professionals recognize the importance of meeting the client where he or she is in a counselling session, supervisors may fail to apply this principle in the supervisor-supervisee relationship. In order for supervisors to clearly understand the stage of the supervisee's cognitive development, supervisors need to better understand the processes of developing cognitive complexity. Supervisors can tailor their teaching styles to meet the needs of the supervisee, thus creating an environment that optimizes opportunity for professional development. Bloom's taxonomy (knowledge, comprehension, application, analysis, synthesis, and evaluation) is a useful tool in moving from simple to complex levels of cognition (CITE). Early in the supervisee's training it may be appropriate to ask knowledge and comprehension questions (e.g., What was the diagnosis? What are the key elements in diagnosing depression?) to ensure that the supervisee understands the basics before moving into questions that require higher levels of cognitive functioning. Supervisors need to be able to provide appropriate feedback and evaluation to supervisees as they progress through their practicum.

It is the responsibility of supervisors to "...encourage and facilitate the self-development and self-awareness of students, trainees and supervisees, so that they learn to integrate their professional practice and personal insight" (CCA, 2001, p 39). Flexible and adaptable teaching styles encourage independence, provide ongoing professional support, and challenge supervisees (Corey et al., 2003). By encouraging supervisees to utilize their own problem-solving abilities and to become actively involved in their own self-exploration, supervisors promote individual self-development. This may mean allowing supervisees to discover some relationships on their own, engaging them in higher processes of learning rather than isolating the relationships for them.

Further information on models and styles of supervision are readily available. Bernard and Goodyear (2004) provide three approaches to supervision: psychotherapy, developmental, and social role models. Russell-Chapin and Ivey (2004) present several models including micro-counselling supervision. Haynes et al. (2003) supply a number of models in their book, including psychotherapy-based models and integrative models while Morran, Kurpius, Brack, and Brack (1995) describe a model for training supervisees in cognitive skills.

The duty of confidentiality is another key responsibility of supervisors as is the management of multiple roles. The limits of confidentiality in supervision need to be communicated to clients and to supervisees. Role relationships need to be clearly discussed with students.

Modeling Confidentiality
Confidentiality or the provision of a safe environment to disclose problems becomes more complicated to enforce in the supervision process. In the context of supervision, it is essential to inform the client that confidential communications will be shared with the supervisor, with supervisory groups and possibly with class instructors in an educational context. The client's consent should be obtained by the supervisee. Supervisees ensure that all client information is kept confidential except when used for supervision purposes. Cases should be presented with pseudonyms and audiotapes and videotapes should be kept in a locked filing cabinet and erased after

viewing.

Supervisors, too, must treat their interactions with their supervisees as confidential with some exceptions as outlined in the *CCA Standards of Practice for Counsellors* (2001, p. 38). Supervisors may have consultative discussions with colleagues related to the supervisory relationships and responsibilities. Information may be shared with persons who have some stake in their evaluation. The limits of confidentiality need to be made explicit at the beginning of the supervisory relationship so that supervisees can make informed decisions regarding what they share during supervision. Based on supervisee reports, Ladany et al. (1999) found that the most commonly violated ethical guidelines was supervisory-related confidentiality. Supervisees reported that supervisors handled issues of confidentiality inappropriately, often by not discussing the topic. If supervisors are not following ethical guidelines regarding confidentiality, it seems unlikely that supervisees will develop a clearly defined understanding about client confidentiality. Further, it is vital that supervisors educate supervisees on situations where it is their obligation to breach confidentiality.

Managing Multiple Roles
The potential for dual role-relationships is not unusual in supervision arrangements. Dual relationships are difficult to manage because the expectations and obligations of the different roles are sometimes contradictory.

The Ken Case
Ken is participating in a supervisory group in which one of the members, Dal, is a personal friend of the supervisor. In the group, the supervisor goes out of

his way to not appear to favour Dal. As a result, the supervisor comes across as quite critical in relation to Dal's work compared to the rest of the group. Ken is uncomfortable with what he views as unwarranted criticism, but does not know how to raise the issue with the supervisor who made the decision to accept Dal prior to the first meeting. In a conversation with Dal, he hears that she wants to move to another supervisory group.

- Why is this dual relationship problematic?

- What ethical guidelines are being contravened?

- What are other members in the supervisory group learning?

- Do all members of the group have the same opportunities for access to the professor's attention?

- How might future evaluation decisions be influenced

  a) if Ken speaks up?

  b) if Dal asks to be switched to another supervisory group?

- How might Dal and the supervisor manage this situation?

Supervisors need to be aware of the differences in status and power between themselves and supervisees and to consider the impact of their behaviours on the supervisor-supervisee relationship. Pre-existing friendships or the development of intimacy during the course of supervisory relationships is likely to compromise supervisory roles as teacher and evaluator.

In the case of Ken, the power differential prevents him from discussing the ethical violation and the ensuing behaviours with his supervisor. The supervisor is in a position of power because of a professional role and therefore has the duty and obligation to maintain appropriate boundaries and to take whatever steps are necessary to act in an ethical manner (CCA, 2001, p. 37). In a study of supervisory relationships, Kaberry (2000) found a number of factors that contribute to the development of an abusive supervisory relationship including:

- lack of a respectful attitude by the supervisor

- gratification of the supervisors' needs

- lack of awareness of the supervisor's own behaviours and underlying causes

- the breaking of boundaries.

Kitchener and Harding (1990) found that even benign social relationships with positive intentions can still have an adverse effect on training while Gutheil and Gabbard (1993) observed that sexual relationships with clients usually begin with the crossing of other boundaries. One solution to dealing with dual relationships caused by prior social relationships is to suspend the socializing while the professional relationship continues. This may be an adequate solution, although there is a risk that the change in roles will threaten a successful restoration of the friendship upon termination of supervision.

The decision model developed by Burian and Slimp (2000) is useful in understanding the implications of engaging in social multiple-role relationships with a supervisee. In working through the steps of the model with a colleague, the supervisor examines the professional role with the supervisee and the motivation for engaging in a social relationship at each point on the decision tree. The supervisor is then directed to proceed in various directions depending on the results of these assessments. Three main issues are assessed: reasons to be in the relationship; power difference between supervisor and supervisee; and the parameters of the social activities, including location of the social relationship. The supervisee's ability to leave the social relationship, the repercussions of leaving, and likely impact on other uninvolved supervisees and staff members is assessed using a five-point Likert scale. The model is useful for training supervisors and supervisees in ethical decision-making.

As supervisory relationships share many of the same features as therapy relationships, disclosure of personal and emotional matters by the supervisee can establish situations conducive to attraction. A supervisee who is in an intimate or sexual relationship with a supervisor may refrain from discussing issues of a sexual or intimate nature (for example, his or her attraction to clients) for fear of bringing forth an unwanted reaction from the supervisor. The supervisees may feel a range of emotions from discomfort to extreme anxiety which may impair professional or personal functioning (Corey et al., 2003, p. 338). It is the supervisor's responsibility to educate the trainee about the normalcy of attraction in counsellor-client relationships, to encourage open discussion and acknowledgment of these feelings with the supervisor, and to explain the consequences of acting on these attractions. However, Downs (2003) discovered that most supervisors and counsellor-educa-

tors are uncomfortable responding to questions about sexual attraction in clinical situations.

Chapter Summary

The *CCA Code of Ethics* (2006) devotes an entire section (Section F) to the teaching, training, and supervision of counsellors. It includes standards for counsellor-educators and supervisors, and for counsellor education programs. Along with their duty to ensure the welfare of clients, counsellor-educators also have multiple roles and responsibilities as gatekeepers for the profession. Ethical dilemmas arise when their roles and responsibilities are not clarified with trainees. Counsellor-educators need to know and to observe the *Code of Ethics* and to make sound judgements about their relationships with students.

How can counsellor competency be determined and assessed, given the variety of counsellor education and training programs across Canada? One central challenge faced by Canadian counselling programs involves developing policies and procedures in the selection of students, in the provision of remediation for students who show clinical deficiencies or interpersonal problems, and in course content and approaches to teaching or training. The procedures and standards for counsellor education programs at the Master's level (CACEP) are aimed at the development of high standards in the training of professional counsellors. Since CACEP was established relatively recently, Canadian universities are beginning to seek CCA accreditation for their counsellor education programs.

The regulation of the counselling profession through licensure or legal regulation is an emerging issue in Canada. However, just as successful graduation from a counsellor education program does not guarantee competency, the same can be said of the possession of a license. Continuing education is necessary in order to keep current and to maintain competence in counselling skills. Self-monitoring of one's effectiveness as a professional may be one method of ensuring quality of services. Consultation with other professionals is always an ethically appropriate measure to take when questions arise about effectively helping clients.

Supervision is less well-developed than counselling with regard to theory, models, and skills. However, similar issues present in the client-counsellor relationship are central to the supervisor-supervisee relationship. A critical component of supervision is ensuring that the supervisee is informed about the supervisory process. As is the case in the client-counsellor relationship, supervisees also require confidential support. Supervisors are charged with the complex task of defining and managing multiple roles and responsibilities with supervisees and self-monitoring those roles. What kinds of training and other professional experiences are vital to skilled and knowledgeable supervision? Ultimately the supervisor is held responsible for the welfare of all clients the supervisee counsels.

Learning Activities

1. *Small Groups.* Although the word supervision means "to oversee" (Merriam-Webster, 2005), clinical supervision has a more specific definition. In groups of three, generate a list of words and phrases that pertain to effective supervision. How, and in what situations, will you see these concepts play out in supervision? How would you list these words in order of importance? What ethical issues, if any, are attached to each of those words or phrases?

2. *Interview.* Interview a supervisor at a community agency in order to (a) ascertain the three most recurring ethical issues in the supervisory relationship with students and the roles and responsibilities of the supervisor in working through these ethical issues; (b) inquire about his or her ethical decision-making process; (c) determine the parameters of confidentiality in the supervisory relationship; and (d) clarify how informed consent is obtained in the supervisor-supervisee relationship.

3. *Pair-share.* Break the class into small groups of two to four students. Give each group one variation of a case. Groups have about 15 minutes to discuss their case, identify key ethical issues, and recommend a course of action. When the entire class reassembles, each group reads its case to the rest of the class. After hearing the reactions of their peers, each group describe their recommended course of action and the rationale behind their recommendations.

Variation One: After the night class on counselling theories, you often stay after class to ask questions and to talk with the counsellor-educator. One night, after the other students have left, the counsellor-educator asks you if you would like to have a drink at a nearby pub. The semester is almost finished.

Variation Two: The semester finished two weeks ago and you decide to attend evening office hours so that you can find out your final grade for the course on counselling theories. During the semester you often stayed after the evening class to ask questions and to talk with the counsellor-educator. When you visit the professor you decide to ask him (or her) to have a drink at the local pub when office hours are finished. Grades are already in.

Variation Three: The semester finished two weeks ago and you decide to attend morning office hours to find out your final grade in the counselling theories course. During the semester you often lingered after class to ask questions and to talk with the counsellor-educator. When you stop by the office you ask the instructor if he (or she) would like to have lunch at a nearby restaurant. The grades are already turned in for the semester.

Questions for the three variations: Is it ethical for the counsellor-educator to drink (to have lunch) with you? Does it matter if you are a young student or a mature student? Does it matter if you are an undergraduate or graduate student? What are the prosocializing arguments that can be made? What are the antisocializing arguments that can be made?

4. *Case Study.* Identify the nature of the dilemma and defend the therapist's decision or describe what the therapist might have done instead.

A Master's level counselling student arranges to volunteer at a local agency to gain some experience in sandtray work from the only licensed therapist in the agency. The director agrees to take on the student as a volunteer and informs the licensed therapist that the student will be helping her reduce her large case-load. The therapist points out that she needs to first interview the student to determine if they can work together and find mutually beneficial times to meet for supervision. In the interview, the student discloses that she feels competent to do the work required but does need some help in a personal area of her life. The therapist decides to go ahead and provide the student with supervision and suggests that they meet at a different time to work through the problem areas of the student's life.

5. *Dyads.* Imagine that you are about to begin your first practicum. In partners, brainstorm a list of questions you would like to ask a potential supervisor. Make a list of topics that you believe the supervisor should discuss with you.

6. *Review.* Review the handbook or brochure produced by your counselling program. Find the section on the criteria used to select candidates. Using the current criteria, establish groups of 4 to 6 students to develop further criteria for the selection of students for next years' intake. What will you require students to include with their application? What personal qualities, work, and life experiences will you be looking for? What procedures will you use in making selections? If you were to use individual or group interviews what specific questions would you ask?

7. *Role-play.* Imagine that all graduates of Canadian counselling programs are required to pass an oral examination by a licensing board. Divide the class in half. One half will take the role of examiners while the other half of the class will take the

role of new practitioners. Examiners will need to draw up a list of 15 -20 questions to present to the practitioners. Practitioners should review the *CCA Code of Ethics* prior to the class.

References

American Counselling Association (2005). *ACA code of ethics.* Alexandria, VA: Author.

American Psychological Association (2002). Rules and procedures: October 1, 2001 [Ethics Committee Rules and Procedures]. *American Psychologist,* 57, 626-645.

Baldo, T. D., Softas-Nail, B. C., & Shaw, S. F. (1997). Student review and retention in counsellor education: An alternative to Frame and Stevens-Smith. *Counsellor Education and Supervision,* 35, 245-253.

Bernard, J. M., & Goodyear, R. K. (2004). *Fundamentals of clinical supervision* (3rd ed.). Toronto: Pearson Education Incorporated.

Birch, M., Elliott, D., & Trankel, M. A. (1999/2003). Black and white and shades of gray: A portrait of the ethical professor. In D. N. Bersoff (Ed.), *Ethical conflicts in psychology* (3rd ed., pp. 436-441). Washington, DC: American Psychological Association.

Bowman, V. E., & Hatley, L. D. (1995). Faculty-student relationships: The dual role controversy. *Counsellor Education and Supervision,* 34(3), 232- 242.

Bradey, J. & Post, P. (1991). Impaired students: Do we eliminate them from counsellor education programs? *Counsellor Education and Supervision,* 31, 100-108.

Brown, J. M (2001). *Student clinical competence in master's counselling programs.* Unpublished master's thesis. Victoria, BC: University of Victoria.

Burian, B. K., & O'Connor Slimp, A. (2000). Social dual-role relationships during internship: A decision-making model. *Professional Psychology: Research and Practice,* 31(3), 332-338.

Canadian Counselling Association (1999). *Code of ethics.* Ottawa, ON: Author.

Canadian Counselling Association (2001). *Standard of practice for counsellors.* Ottawa, Ontario: Author.

Canadian Psychological Association (1991). *Accreditation manual.* Ottawa, Ontario: Author.

Casto, C., Caldwell, C., Salazar, C. F. (2005). Creating mentoring relationships between female faculty and students in counsellor education: Guidelines for potential mentees and mentors. *Journal of Counselling and Development,* 83, 331-336.

Cherniss, C. (1995). *Beyond burnout: Helping teachers, nurses, therapists, and lawyers overcome stress and disillusionment.* New York: Routledge.

Choudhuri. D. D. (1999). *Navigating the role of counsellor educator: The counsellor as teacher* (Report No. CG029574). East Lansing, MI: National Center for Research on Teacher Learning. (ERIC Document Reproduction Service No. 435881)

Corey, G., Corey, M. S., & Callanan, P. (2003). *Issues and ethics in the helping professions.* Toronto: Books/Cole.

Council for Accreditation of Counselling and Related Educational Programs [CACREP]. (2001). *CACREP accreditation standards and procedures manual.* Alexandria, VA: Author.

Council of Accreditation of Counsellor Education Programs (2003). *CCA accreditation procedures and standards for counsellor education programs at the Master's level.* Ottawa, Ontario: Canadian Counselling Association.

D'Andrea, M. & Daniels, J. (1992). *Do the leaders of counsellor education programs think graduate students should be required to participate in personal counselling: The results of a national survey.*

(Report No. CG024517). Greensboro, NC: Counselling and Personnel Services. (ERIC Document Reproduction Service No. ED349508)

Daniels, L. G. (2002). The relationship between counsellor licensure and aspects of empowerment. *Journal of Mental Health Counselling*, 24(3), 213-223.

Dorff, T. A. (1997). A needs assessment of the stressors and coping resources of graduate students in clinical psychology. *Dissertation Abstracts International*, 58 (11), p. 6231. (UMI No. AA9815234)

Downs, L. (2003). A preliminary survey of relationships between counsellor-educators' ethics education and ensuing pedagogy and responses to attractions with counselling students. *Counselling & Values*, 48(1), 2-13.

Frame, M. W. & Stevens-Smith, P. (1995). Out of harm's way: Enhancing monitoring and dismissal processes in counsellor education programs. *Counsellor Education & Supervision*, 35(2), 118-130.

Forrest, L., Elman, N., Gizara , S., & Vacha-Haase, T. (1999). Trainee impairment. A review of identification, remediation, dismissal, and legal issues. *The Counselling Psychologist,* 27(5), 627-686.

Fouad, N. A. & Hains, A. A. (1990). Factors in students' endorsement of counselling as a requirement for graduation from a counselling program. *Counsellor Education & Supervision*, 29(4), 268-275.

Friedrich, J., & Douglass, D. (1998). Ethics and the persuasive enterprise of teaching psychology. *American Psychologist*, 53, 549-562.

Furr, S. R. & Carroll, J. J. (2003). Critical incidents in student counsellor development. *Journal of Counselling & Development*, 81(4), 483-489.

Granello, D. H. (2000). Encouraging the cognitive development of supervisees: Using Bloom's taxonomy in supervision.

Counsellor Education and Supervision, 40(1), 31-46.

Gutheil, T. G., & Gabbard, G. O. (1993). The concept of boundaries in clinical practice: Theoretical and risk-management dimensions. *American Journal of Psychiatry*, 150, 188-196.

Handelsman, M. M., & Uhlemann, M. R. (1998). Be careful what you wish for: Issues in the statutory regulation of counsellors. *Canadian Journal of Counselling*, 32(4), 315-331.

Hanna, F. J., & Bemak, F. (1997). The quest for identity in the counselling profession. *Counsellor Education and Supervision*, 36, 194-206.

Haynes, R., Corey, G., & Moulton, P. (2003). *Clinical supervision in the helping professions: A practical guide*. Toronto: Nelson Thomson Learning.

Hazler, R. J., & Carney, J. (1993). Student-faculty interactions: An underemphasized dimension of counsellor education. *Counsellor Education and Supervision*, 33, 80-89.

Hazler, R. J., & Kottler, J. A. (1994). *The emerging professional counsellor. Student dreams to professional realities.* Alexandria, VA: American Counselling Association.

Herlihy, B., & Corey, G. (1996). *ACA ethical standards casebook* (5th ed.). Alexandria, VA: American Counselling Association.

Holloway, E. L. (1995). *Clinical supervision: A systems approach.* Thousand Oaks, CA; Sage.

Kaberry, S. (2000). Abuse in supervision. In B Lawton and C. Feltham (Eds.), *Taking supervision forward. Enquiries and trends in counselling and psychotherapy* (pp. 42-59). London: Sage Publications.

Kitchener, K. A. (2000). *Foundation of ethical practice, research, and teaching in psychology*. New Jersey: Lawrence Erlbaum.

Kitchener, K. & Harding S. (1990). Dual role relationships. In B. Herlihy& L. B. Golden (Eds.), *Ethical standards casebook* (4th ed.). Alexandria, VA: American Counselling Association for Counselling and Development.

Kolb, D. A. (1984). *Experiential learning.* Englewood Cliffs, NJ: Prentice-Press.

Kottler, J. A. (1992). Confronting our own hypocrisy: Being a model for our students and clients. *Journal of Counselling and Development*, 70, 475-476.

Ladany, N., Lehrman-Waterman, D., Molinaro, M., & Wolgast, B. (1999). Psychotherapy supervisor ethical practices: Adherence to guidelines, the supervisory working alliance, and supervisee satisfaction. *The Counselling Psychologist*, 27(3), 443-475.

Lloyd, A. (1992). Dual relationship problems in counsellor education. In B. Herlihy & G. Corey (Eds.), *Dual relationships in counselling* (pp. 59-64). Alexandria, VA: American Association for Counselling and Development.

Lumadue, C. A., & Duffey, T. H. (1999). The role of graduate programs as gatekeepers: A model for evaluating student counsellor competence. *Counsellor Education and Supervision*, 39(2), 101-109.

Maeder, T. (1989) Wounded healers. *The Atlantic Monthly*, January, 37-47.

Merriam-Webster (2005). *Merriam-Webster's Collegiate Dictionary* (10th ed.). Springfield, MA: Merriam-Webster Inc.

Morran, D. K., Kurpius, D. J., Brack, C. J., & Brack, G. (1995). A cognitive-skills model for counsellor training and supervision. *Journal of Counselling & Development*, 73, 384-389.

Mustaine, B. L., West, P. L., & Wyrick, B. K. (2003). Substance abuse counsellor certification requirements: Is it time for a change? *Journal of Addictions & Offender Counselling*, 23, 99-107.

Pistole, M. C., & Roberts, A. (2002). Mental health counselling: Toward resolving identity confusions. *Journal of Mental Health Counselling*, 24(1), 1-19.

Polanski, P. (2000). Training supervisors at the Masters level: Developmental consideration. *ACES Spectrum Newsletter*, 61(2), 3-5.

Procidano, M. E., Busch-Rossnagel, N., Reznikoff, M., & Geisinger, K. (1995). Responding to graduate students' professional deficiencies: A national survey. *Journal of Clinical Psychology*, 51, 426-433.

Russell-Chapin, L. A., & Ivey, A. E. (2004). *Your supervised practicum and internship. Field resources for turning theory into action.* Toronto: Brooks/Cole.

Schmidt, J. J. (2002). *Intentional Helping.* Upper Saddle River, NJ: Merrill Prentice Hall.

Schoener, G. R. (1999). Practicing what we preach. *The Counselling Psychologist*, 27(5), 693-701.

Schulz, W. E. (2000). *Counselling ethics casebook 2000* (2nd ed.). Ottawa: Canadian Counselling Association.

Schwebel, M., & Coster, J. (1998). Well-functioning in professional psychologists: As program heads see it. *Professional Psychology: Research and Practice*, 29(3) 284-292.

Scott, K. J., Ingram, K. M., Vitanza, S. A., & Smith, N. G. (2000). Training in supervision: A survey of current practices. *The Counselling Psychologist*, 28(3), 403-422.

Stoltenberg, C. D., & Delworth, U. (1987). *Supervising counsellors and therapists: A developmental approach.* San Francisco: Jossey-Bass.

Tyler, J. M., & Tyler, C. L. (1997). Ethics in supervision: Managing supervisee rights and supervisor responsibilities. In J. Lonsdale (Ed.), *The Hatherleigh guide to ethics in therapy* (pp. 75-95). New York, NY: Hatherleigh Press.

Vasquez, M. J. (1999). Trainee impairment: A response from a feminist/multicultural retired trainer. *The Counselling Psychologist*, 27(5), 687-692.

Witmer, M. J. & Young, M. E. (1996) Preventing counsellor impairment: A wellness approach. *Journal of Humanistic Education and Development*, 34(3), 141-155.

Section Two

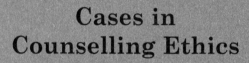

Cases in
Counselling Ethics

This section of the book provides two ethical and two unethical cases for eachof the 73 articles in the 2006 *CCA Code of Ethics*. Following the cases, a brief commentary is presented, as well as a number of questions designed to stimulate further discussion of the specific article under review.

Chapter Eight

---------- ❖ ----------

Case Studies in Professional Responsibility

---------- ❖ ----------

Counselling is a professional occupation, and some of the unique roles of the counselling profession are that members exercise independent judgment, make decisions, and provide help.

Canadian Counselling Association Code of Ethics

Ethical Guidelines for Professional Responsibility

A1 GENERAL RESPONSIBILITY
Counsellors maintain high standards of professional competence and ethical behaviour, and recognize the need for continuing education and personal care in order to meet this responsibility. (See also C1, F1)

A2 RESPECT FOR RIGHTS
Counsellors participate in only those practices which are respectful of the legal, civic, and moral rights of others, and act to safeguard the dignity and rights of their clients, students, and research participants.

A3 BOUNDARIES OF COMPETENCE
Counsellors limit their counselling services and practices to those which are within their professional competence by virtue of their education and professional experience, and consistent with any requirements for provincial and national credentials. They refer to other professionals, when the counselling needs of clients exceed their level of competence. (See also F2)

A4 SUPERVISION AND CONSULTATION
Counsellors take reasonable steps to obtain supervision and/or consultation with respect to their counselling practices and, particularly, with respect to doubts or uncertainties which may arise during their professional work. (See also B10, C4, C7)

A5 REPRESENTATION OF PROFESSIONAL QUALIFICATIONS
Counsellors do claim or imply only those professional qualifications which they possess, and are responsible for correcting any known misrepresentation of their qualifications by others.

A6 RESPONSIBILITY TO COUNSELLORS AND OTHER PROFESSIONALS

Counsellors understand that ethical behaviour among themselves and with other professionals is expected at all times.

A7 UNETHICAL BEHAVIOUR BY OTHER COUNSELLORS

Counsellors have an obligation when they have serious doubts as to the ethical behaviour of another counsellor, to seek an informal resolution with the counsellor, when feasible and appropriate. When an informal resolution is not appropriate or feasible, or is unsuccessful, counsellors report their concerns to the CCA Ethics Committee.

A8 RESPONSIBILITY TO CLIENTS

When a counsellor has reasonable grounds to believe that a client has an ethical complaint about the conduct of a CCA member, the counsellor informs the client of the *CCA Procedures for Processing Complaints of Ethical Violations* and how to access these procedures.

A9 SEXUAL HARASSMENT

Counsellors do not condone or engage in sexual harassment, which is defined as deliberate or repeated verbal or written comments, gestures, or physical contacts of a sexual nature.

A10 SENSITIVITY TO DIVERSITY

Counsellors strive to understand and respect the diversity of their clients, including differences related to age, ethnicity, culture, gender, disability, religion, sexual orientation and socio-economic status. (See also B9, D10)

A11 EXTENSION OF ETHICAL RESPONSIBILITIES

Counselling services and products provided by counsellors through classroom instruction, public lectures, demonstrations, publications, radio and television programs, computer technology and other media must meet the appropriate ethical standards consistent with this *Code of Ethics*.

Case Studies for Professional Responsibility

A1 GENERAL RESPONSIBILITY

Counsellors maintain high standards of professional competence and ethical behaviour, and recognize the need for continuing education and personal care in order to meet this responsibility. (See also C1, F1)

Improving Professional Practices (+)

An experienced elementary school counsellor, upon arriving in a new school in a different school board, realizes that many of the children in her school have problems that are a result of poor parenting. Also, due to the high number of immigrant families in this counsellor's school, she attributes some of the children's problems to their families' unfamiliarity with Canadian customs.

The counsellor spends the remainder of the year with these children researching their needs, their parents' needs and the differences in these families' cultures in comparison to Canadian ways. She works to improve her skills in cultural diversity in order that she can better serve her students.

After much research and consultation with other counsellors, she feels better qualified to facilitate evening parenting workshops for the community. Four such workshops are run throughout the school year dealing with topics such as discipline and family life education. All are highly regarded by parents, staff and administration.

Counsellor Networking (+)
A counsellor in a small rural school board organizes counsellor peer group meetings so that she can meet with her colleagues on a regular basis. This group periodically joins forces with a group of counsellors from two neighbouring school boards so that they can invite speakers from a major urban centre. The speakers keep them informed about urban counselling issues, new research and upcoming professional development opportunities. Other speakers and workshops help them upgrade their skills. In their own board meetings they are able to consult with their colleagues about their clients while still maintaining confidentiality.

Ensuring Children Receive Guidance from a Competent Counsellor (–)
An urban school board has more teachers returning from leaves than they have positions available for the upcoming school year. An extremely competent and highly regarded grade two teacher in the board returns from a two-year leave of absence. She is given a few alternatives after she notifies the superintendent of her desire to return. Yet, being a primary school teacher, the only position she feels remotely capable of accepting is a guidance and counselling position in a kindergarten through grade eight school. The school board requires that school counsellors are trained. The school with the opening is one of the toughest in the area. The previous counsellor resigned as a result of the stress he experienced from

the job, and internal advertising has resulted in no other interest from qualified staff. The superintendent awards the position to the primary school teacher despite her lack of training in counselling.

Professional Development Missing (–)
A counsellor at the Family Centre earned his Master's degree in counselling in the late 1970s. Over the next twenty years, he takes no additional course work in counselling, seldom attends counselling in-service sessions and never attends a national counselling conference.

Comments and Questions
Ethical issues facing counsellors have intensified during the past few decades. Issues related to drug use, alcohol abuse, AIDS, divorce, and sexual abuse show that this first ethical article, on the professional competence of counsellors, is very important. There is a need for high standards of professional competence, and the need for continuing education on the part of all counsellors. This article also raises several questions. Who determines a counsellor's competence? Should competence be determined by the counsellor or should it perhaps be other members? Should a client determine a counsellor's competence since it is the counsellee who can truly speak of the member's effectiveness?

Counsellors are professionals. Therefore, members and clients assume that counsellors are capable of determining their own competence. Professionals must be treated as professionals. They must be trusted to make sound judgments, to know their limitations and to know when consultation, re-training and/or additional education is necessary.

Still, counsellors are human and humans are known to make mistakes and can be misunderstood. Thus, to protect counsellors and their clients, the following two criteria are recommended before the public can enter into a counselling relationship:

• *Professional Disclosure*—Prior to beginning a counselling situation, the client is informed of the counsellor's qualifications, services offered, therapeutic process, nature of confidentiality, administrative procedures and finally, the client's own rights and   responsibilities, and

• *Written Contract*—After discussing the terms and coming to a mutual agreement of the   upcoming counselling situation, the counsellor and the client should enter into a formal contract so that there will never be future questions of what was expected or promised by   either   partner in counselling.

1. What do you believe should be the minimum standards for a professionally competent counsellor?

2. How do counsellors recognize their own competence and how do they set limitations for themselves?

3. Degrees, licensing and/or certification do not ensure competence of psychologists, social workers or counsellors, so what can clients do to ensure they are receiving the best counselling available to them?

4. Teachers are frequently assigned counselling duties without counsellor education or training. Is it ethical to hire a teacher who has no counsellor education or training for a school counselling position?

5. What are some things that counsellors could do to improve present professional practices?

6. What are some things counsellor can do with regard to their own personal care?

A2 RESPECT FOR RIGHTS
Counsellors participate in only those practices which are respectful of the legal, civic, and moral rights of others, and act to safeguard the dignity and rights of their clients, students, and research participants.

Suicide Threat (+)

Jane S. has been counselling a client for two years as part of court-mandated treatment. Jane schedules a brief appointment at 4:00 p.m. and expects to be home with her family by 5:00. During this scheduled appointment, Jane is diverted by the comment, "I don't know if I'll make it to September". Jane asks for clarification of the emotions behind the statement and determines that the client is depressed and has been contemplating suicide all week, having given hints to staff of a residential treatment centre where he has been staying for the last two months. The client has several plausible and available methods to meet his intentions. No intensive or extensive intervention has been done to that point by the facility staff.

Jane S. continues with a suicide check and is unable to move the client toward committing to living another day. She tells the client that she has no choice but to escort him to the hospital for follow-up. Jane notifies agency staff of the predicament and transports him to the hospital where a series of interviews occur and suicidal ideation diminishes. Jane remains as a support for the client during the hospital intake/treatment period.

Theft Disclosure (+)

A client discloses to his counsellor that he has stolen something from his employer. This disclosure occurs well after qualitative gains have been made in counselling. The counsellor is torn by his commitment to the client and confidentiality and the legalities of knowing about an illicit activity. The counsellor works for an agency funded by the Justice Department. The agency guidelines to counsellors indicate that all known or potential criminal activity must be reported. The counsellor encourages the client to turn himself over to authorities and indicates that he will accompany him to the police, acting as a support.

Gathering Court Data (-)

A counsellor is instructed to compile a report for the court regarding a subject charged and having pleaded guilty to sexually assaulting an 11-year-old girl. As part of the report, a victim impact statement is to be included in the report. The counsellor is required to obtain information regarding the psychological and physical damage to the victim. This agency has guidelines for interviewing any victim who may be further traumatized by having to reiterate already available information. The counsellor contacts the victim directly to arrange an interview. The interview takes place at the counsellor's office, where a series of questions is asked. Examples of these questions include:

- What emotional impact has this assault had on you?
- What physical impact has this assault had on you?
- Why did you allow the assault to occur?
- What attempts did you make to stop the assault?
- Why did you wait so long to report the assault?
- Are you sure about the assault occurring?

During the course of the interview the victim becomes overwhelmed by the focus of the questions, but the counsellor continues with the battery of questions slated for the agenda.

Inadequate Information (-)

A counsellor is employed at an agency that provides pregnancy information services to adolescents. The agency is of the opinion that clients have the right to be advised of all available resources in the community and be referred to these if they so choose. A female adolescent comes to the counsellor and requests information on different options regarding her pregnancy. The counsellor, who is pro-life, fails to provide the client with information on abortion, but provides information related to adoption and keeping her expected baby.

Comments and Questions

This ethical guideline provides a clear understanding that the professional member must demonstrate "responsible" behaviour to the client as well as to the institution or agency within which the counsellor is working. At all times, the counsellor must be respectful of the rights of others. Despite this crucial and well-meaning mandate, it would be rare to find a counsellor who has not been challenged at some level when he or she would be required to reflect on this ethical guideline and seek a creative response to remain ethical.

Counsellors invariably find conflict in responsibility to clients or the institution they serve. This may arise when an employer or institution requests a specific level of service for its clients that is not commensurate with professional standards and therefore represents a breach of responsibility. The question remains as to who is ultimately responsible: the employer who is under-funded to provide the actual number of staff or services to meet the needs of the client population, or the counsellor who acquiesces to the supervisor's advice to provide limited service to the majority of clients. It is likely that in many cases the supervisor and counsellor follow the same code of ethics, or at least, a similar series of ethical instructions. It would be easy to say that the supervisor should cut down the number of cases the agency is willing to handle. This may be appropriate for private agencies however; government agencies may not have this option. They are expected to provide services despite the lack of staff or resources.

Clients have many legal and moral rights. Counsellors need to respect these rights. One way of showing respect is for counsellors to have clear "informed consent" statements that spell out conditions of confidentiality, counsellor competencies and typical counsellor techniques and strategies.

1. List some counsellor practices where the legal, moral or civic rights of others could be jeopardized.

2. In the second case presented, what would you have done as a counsellor if the client was not willing to go to the authorities and admit his theft?

3. In the third case, what should the counsellor have done as a respectful measure in his treatment of the victim?

4. Is it realistic, with large client caseloads, to expect the counsellor to provide full services to all clients? What would you do if you were a counsellor in an agency that accepted too many clients?

5. In the fourth case, the counsellor is anti-abortion and lets his/her biases show. What would you do in this situation if your values on abortion where similar to the counsellor's in this case?

6. What type of orientation should counsellors receive with regard to the ethic of "safeguarding the rights of their clients"?

A3 BOUNDARIES OF COMPETENCE
Counsellors limit their counselling services and practices to those which are within their professional competence by virtue of their education and professional experience, and consistent with any requirements for provincial and national credentials. They refer to other professionals when the counselling needs of clients exceed their level of competence. (See also F2)

Referral (+)

A beginning school counsellor is speaking with a student about the student's recently declining grades. In the course of the discussion, they get into reasons why the student's school work is down and in a moment of disclosure the student admits to abuse in the home. The counsellor immediately recognizes that this is beyond the scope of his abilities and he notifies the proper authorities and refers the student to qualified counselling facilities specifically geared for dealing with abuse cases such as this.

Career Counsellor (+)
A graduate student at a Department of Educational Psychology in a Canadian university decides to begin her own private counselling service. In spite of the fact that many clients ask to see her for marriage counselling, she refuses all these clients, pointing out that her own training and practicum experiences are mainly in employment and career counselling.

Avoiding Teacher Lay-Offs (–)
A school board has had a declining student population for the past three years. The school superintendent makes the decision that 15 teachers will have "to be terminated". At the same time, this board makes the decision to have a school counsellor in each of their 18 elementary schools. Certified teachers with and without counsellor training apply for the counselling positions. The counselling jobs are offered to all the trained counsellors, but 12 vacant positions remain. The remaining elementary school counselling positions are offered to teachers in the board with no counsellor training. All 12 teachers accept the counselling positions for which they have no training.

No Training in Marriage Counselling (–)
An employment counsellor with eight years of experience decides to begin private counselling on a part-time basis. Her first clients are a couple who wish to receive marriage counselling. The counsellor happily accepts these clients for counselling even though she has had no training in marriage counselling.

Comments and Questions
This ethical article clearly dictates that counsellors need to evaluate their abilities and level of experience. When situations arise which are beyond the training or experience of a counsellor, it is unethical to proceed blindly into counselling. As Section B, Guideline 10 indicates (see Chapter Nine), consultation with other professionals about such situations is both ethical and recommended. Furthermore, counsellors should consider even casual discussions with colleagues an important means to determine others' experience and expertise and then should not hesitate to tap into these resources whenever the need arises.

This article suggests that counsellors provide only those services for which they are qualified. The moral principle that is important is nonmaleficence, or "do no harm". Incompetence is the leading cause of harm to clients. Counsellor preparation is the initial part of producing competent counsellors. Maintaining competence is just as important, and the responsibility rests with the counsellors themselves. Thus, a natural extension of this article is that counsellors maintain active enrolment in professional groups (determine areas of expertise among colleagues, and services available), and participate regularly in professional development activities.

Lastly, the guideline clearly states that counsellors accept only those positions for which they are professionally qualified. This means that teachers should not become school counsellors if they have not received counsellor training.

1. How do counsellors determine their "boundaries of competence"?

2. Do you believe that peer review would be a valuable and non-threatening approach to monitoring counsellor competence?

3. What should be the training of a "professionally qualified" counsellor?

4. How can counselling organizations stop the practice of school boards giving teachers (with no counsellor training) positions in counselling?

5. Is it better to offer "non-expert counselling" than no counselling at all, especially when someone is working in a remote area where referral services are limited or non-existent?

6. Should counsellors accept positions in private practice knowing that they will see clients with difficulties in areas where they have little or no expertise?

A4 SUPERVISION AND CONSULTATION
Counsellors take reasonable steps to obtain supervision and/or consultation with respect to their counselling practices and, particularly, with respect to doubts or uncertainties which may arise during their professional work. (See also B10, C4, C7)

Improving Counselling (+)
The director of a large private counselling service meets with each of her counsellors twice a year to discuss their counselling practice. The director and counsellors discuss feedback forms from clients and counselling tapes of interview sessions. There is a great deal of back-and-forth discussion of the counselling and the climate during the sessions is open and congenial. Both the director and each counsellor have opportunities to contribute to the final report that is placed in the counsellor's file.

Counselling Supervision (+)
Counsellors and therapists in one Canadian city organize a small professional organization in which they readily discuss counselling issues as well as receive feedback on their counselling. Guest speakers are invited to talk about current issues. The most valuable feature of this professional organization for many counsellors and therapists is the opportunity for each participant to present her or his counselling tape for discussion with two other counsellors. These groups of three counsellors meet four times a year to listen to each other's counselling tapes and to discuss counselling cases.

Little Professional Development (-)
In one school board where there have been severe cutbacks, resulting in fewer counsellors for many schools, the director of counselling for the board suggests that counsellors might wish to use "brief counselling", hoping to limit the total amount of time that counsellors need to help their clients. The brief counselling in-service for counsellors consists of three weekend workshops. The director makes no attempt to follow-up or evaluate the brief counselling provided by the counsellors.

Personal Problems (–)
Janice P., a counsellor, is experiencing a great deal of personal distress, including losing her mother and going through a bitter divorce. She realizes that she is just going through the motions with her clients and is not being at all helpful. She just can not

concentrate on her clients' problems since her own difficulties are so severe. When things get too overwhelming, she phones in sick. She is afraid she might lose her counselling position if she lets others know about all her personal problems.

Comments and Questions

One of the key elements of successful counselling is the trust that clients have in counsellors. This trust will be greatly enhanced when counsellors are competent practitioners. It is not possible to be competent in all areas of counselling. Counsellors who are extremely competent when they work with potential suicide clients may or may not be competent when working with young children. Other counsellors may be very effective when counselling the elderly, but not know how to work with adolescents in a junior high school. Counsellors must practice within the bounds of their competence and must be very willing to seek supervision and consultation with other professionals if they have "doubts or uncertainties" about their work with specific clients. When counsellors are learning new specialty areas in counselling (for example, brief counselling, career counselling, or crisis counselling), they need to take education or training under supervision to ensure the future competence of their work.

It is ethical counselling practice to consult with other counselling professionals when counsellors have doubts about what to do with a client. As Guideline B10, "Consulting with Other Professionals", states in Chapter Nine: "Counsellors may consult with other professionally competent persons about the client."

1. How would you determine competence for counsellors in specific areas such as schools, careers, crisis or pastoral counselling?

2. If you were the director or superintendent of counselling for a large school board, would you mandate that all counsellors be involved in a certain number of hours of professional development annually? Would you specify the type of professional development?

3. How should supervision be provided for counsellors in established counselling positions?

4. What should counsellors do when their personal concerns appear to be interfering with their counselling?

5. List some "doubts and uncertainties" that may arise in your particular type of counselling?

6. In the case entitled *Little Professional Development* counsellors are encouraged to use "brief counselling", but are given minimal training. Is it ethical to suggest one counselling approach for all counsellors?

A5 REPRESENTATION OF PROFESSIONAL QUALIFICATIONS
Counsellors do claim or imply only those professional qualifications which they possess, and are responsible for correcting any known misrepresentation of their qualifications by others.

No Master's Degree (+)

A private counselling agency hires a person with a Master's degree in Social Work. He claims to have attended a particular university in England. During the time he is employed in the agency, he becomes the assistant to the director and is expected to become director. In anticipation of his taking this position, his credentials are checked. For some reason this was not done when he was first hired. He has never attended the university and does not have a degree at all. He is fired from his position and a procedure is instituted so that all prospective employees have their credentials confirmed before they are offered a position.

Needed Referral (+)

Gail B. has counselled her client for twelve sessions with limited progress. During this time she is able to build a good rapport with her client and she feels this rapport is the strongest part of the counselling. Gail believes that the client needs treatment that is beyond the scope of her training. Although the client is given information and consent forms before counselling begins, Gail does not believe the client fully understands her qualifications. She feels she has two choices: to continue to treat her client within the limits stated on her consent form, or to refer the client to another counsellor who is known to be successful in using the treatment procedures needed by the client. Gail feels she is ethically bound to do what is best for her client and refers the client to her associate.

Cultural Differences (-)

An Aboriginal child, Nancy, is referred to Bob S. for consultation. Though he has never worked with Aboriginal clients before, Bob is confident in his ability to help Nancy work through her problems. He learns that Nancy has lived with her family on a reserve her entire life and has recently moved to the city to live with her grandmother. He also learns of the importance of cul-

ture in Nancy's life. After fifteen sessions, Bob is at a loss as to what to do. He is not making any progress with Nancy using techniques he has been successful with in the past. His success in the past has been with Caucasian, middle-class clients.

He finds it difficult to establish a relationship with Nancy due to his limited knowledge of her culture. He consults with his associates, but they do not feel confident to counsel Nancy. They encourage him to remain in the relationship as he has had a good success rate with his therapeutic process in the past. Pushing his doubts aside, Bob continues with Nancy as his client. He continues to be unsuccessful with her and is later informed that she is returning to her home reserve. Bob is relieved to discover he will not be counselling Nancy again; but at the same time he feels he should have sought help in working with Nancy or referred her to someone with experience in working with clients other than those who are Caucasian and middle-class.

Continuing Education (-)

Fred C. was licensed as a counsellor in 1965 during a time when there was much advancement being made in counselling. He often attended workshops and lectures to keep up-to-date on any developments in his field. During his career, Dr. Campbell was often asked to present at various workshops due to the success of his work and research. When he is approached to join a private practice in 1980, he does so due to his failing health.

Over the years, Fred C. continues with his private practice but he fails to keep abreast of any new developments in counselling. He feels he has devoted enough of his life to theories and wants to end his career applying those theories to clients. While discussing a rcent development presented at a workshop, Fred's associates are surprised to discover he knows nothing about this information. The associates encourage him to update his knowledge and skills, but he declines. Fred insists he has sufficient counselling knowledge to treat his clients. The associates do not force the issue and Fred continues to remain on the counselling institute's information form; a form that advises clients that all counsellors are continuing their education in counselling.

Comments and Questions

As professional counsellors become more popular and powerful in people's lives there is a greater need for guidelines to protect both counsellor and client. Canadian Counsellor Certification (CCC) is being recognized more frequently in Canada. Counsellors who are certified by the Canadian Counselling Association have a minimum of a Master's degree, extensive course work and a lengthy supervised counselling practicum. Other provincial counselling associations are requiring licensure of counsellors. Licensure is the most powerful type of credentialing since it is established by provincial law. When certified counsellors are selected by clients, they know that the certified counsellors have had supervised experience and have demonstrated knowledge and skills in counselling.

1. "Grandparenting" (allowing counsellors to continue counselling after licensure is adopted), to some extent, has resulted in keeping minimum standards for credentialing low. What do you think about the "grandparenting" concept?

2. Should it be necessary to continue training after certification to maintain qualifications?

3. Is it realistic to list specific requirements that need to be met every two to five years in order to continue practising?

4. What rights, beyond terminating counselling, does a client have if he or she discovers that the counsellor's stated or implied qualifications are inaccurate?

5. What questions should a client ask upon entering a counselling relationship?

6. If you have seen a counsellor, did she or he have an informed consent form?

A6 RESPONSIBILITY TO COUNSELLORS AND OTHER PROFESSIONALS
Counsellors understand that ethical behaviour among themselves and with other professionals is expected at all times.

Reporting Objective Data (+)

A composite high school in the city core of a large metropolitan area experiences increasing demands from government agencies for reports on specific cases. While some of these demands are internal, most come from outside the school system, as changing social conditions involve students in custody cases and with juvenile courts and child welfare agencies. The counselling department head recognizes this growing trend early in its development and engages the counsellors in establishing protocols to ensure that reports consist only of factual, objective data without breaching freedom of information acts.

Advice from the Canadian Counselling Association is sought, counsellors are in-serviced in observational skills, and a record-keeping system is devised to aid counsellors in discerning various degrees of objectivity, from scientific data to impressionistic comments. A protocol is established, ensuring that the more impressionistic observations are excluded from reports.

Ethical Behaviour Among Counsellors (+)

Six counsellors in private practice decide to open one larger counselling centre. They appoint a director for their new centre. One of the first things the director does is distribute the *Canadian Counselling Association Code of Ethics* and the *CCA Standards of Practice for Counsellors* to all the counsellors and have them work out a confidentiality policy, fee structure, and informed consent forms. The director then discusses ways to put their policies into practice.

Beyond Counselling (–)

A counsellor in private practice is asked by parents of a 12-year-old boy to counsel him due to severe behaviour problems that are causing him trouble both at school and in the community. The counsellor develops a liking for the boy and begins to see him outside of the counselling sessions, taking him to movies, etc. This practice continues as the counsellor finds that he enjoys spending time with the boy and the child seems to be responding well to the attention. The parents are also pleased with the arrangement as it provides some respite from the tensions in their home. The relationship continues to grow until the boy is spending weekends at the home of the counsellor, a single man.

Limited Responsibility to Counsellors (–)

The director of a counselling clinic, Evelyn S., has responsibility for the many volunteer counsellors who answer the telephone crisis line. She does provide the crisis counselling volunteers with some initial workshops, but since she finds that most of the volunteers are experienced counsellors, she sees no need to have more extensive training, nor to provide on-going supervision to the "telephone" crisis counsellors.

Comments and Questions

Counsellors are professionals who are ethically obliged to act in the best interests of the client. Because of the nature of the counselling relationship, counsellors are in a position of power and trust, while the clients are in a very vulnerable position. If counselling is to be an effective activity, the public must be able to trust a counsellor to avoid situations where there is a conflict between the best interests of the client and those of the counsellor. The individual counsellor must consider how his or her actions reflect upon the profession as a whole.

The trust of the public can be lost over the unethical, unprofessional or irresponsible behaviour of one member of the profession. The counsellor should endeavour to become aware of his or her own needs and how these could interfere with the counselling relationship. This does not imply that the counsellor must be without personal problems or areas that he or she needs to deal with, but that the counsellor should be aware of these issues and not bring them into the counselling relationship. Counsellors have responsibilities to themselves and their clients to seek help in dealing with problems that could interfere with their functioning within a counselling relationship, and to consult with colleagues or supervisors in cases where they are unsure about the extent to which their own needs are interfering with their ability to be effective in the counselling relationship. If counsellors become aware that they are using the counselling relationship to meet their own needs rather than the needs of the client, counsellors have a responsibility to refer clients to another counsellor and to terminate the relationship.

Counsellors are also ethically required to work with other counsellors in a professional manner. Speaking negatively about a colleague, not consulting with more experienced counsellors, and not working with other counsellors to obtain supervision and additional professional development, are all questionable ethical practices.

1. What are some personal needs you or others might have that could interfere with being an effective counsellor?

2. What political considerations might occur which would pressure the counsellor to tell less than "the truth, the whole truth, and nothing but the truth" in reporting counselling results to other professionals?

3. What biases, institutional and personal, might come into play to limit the counsellor's ability to work effectively with other counsellors?

4. Should counsellors deliberately keep somewhat distant from clients to avoid any possibility of too much intimacy in the counselling relationship?

5. What responsibilities do you have to other non-counselling professionals that you work with?

6. In the case **Beyond Counselling** the counsellor is acting unethically. What would you do if this counsellor in private practice was a colleague of yours?

A7 Unethical Behaviour by Other Counsellors

Counsellors have an obligation when they have serious doubts as to the ethical behaviour of another counsellor, to seek an informal resolution with the counsellor, when feasible and appropriate. When an informal resolution is not appropriate or feasible, or is unsuccessful, counsellors report their concerns to the CCA Ethics Committee.

Reporting of Abuse (+)

After an appointment with a school counsellor, a 15-year-old male student seeks an interview with another counsellor who discovers during the conversation, through student disclosure and physical evidence, that the student has been physically abused by his guardian the previous evening. The student volunteers further information that indicates that he is no longer permitted to enter his home and that no action has been taken by the first counsellor to secure his safety and well-being. Following guidelines for legal responsibilities and school board protocol, the second counsellor contacts Child and Family Services to report suspected abuse, informs the principal of this action, then seeks out the first school counsellor to advise him of the actions that have been taken. Once approached on the issue of abuse, the counsellors discuss the school policy regarding ethical responsibilities and the importance of reporting information to proper authorities.

Mentorship Program (+)

A high school principal acknowledges that some of the new counsellors he has recently hired are having difficulty integrating the CCA ethical guidelines, the school's policies and procedures, and the provincial laws. In order to address this issue, he implements a mentorship program whereby experienced counsellors are paired with novice counsellors. The ultimate goal of the program is to promote and encourage ethical behaviour within the classroom and within the school. Through modeling, supervision, and consultation, the experienced and exemplary counsellors guide the novice counsellors to resolve ethical dilemmas as they occur naturally.

Conduct of an Associate (-)

During a routine counselling session prior to graduation, a distraught grade 12 student confides to her counsellor that one of her teachers has abruptly ended an intimate relationship with her. She indicates that her life is "falling apart" and she doesn't know what she is going to do after graduation. The student requests that no action be taken since she would be graduating in two weeks and she does not want to harm anyone's reputation. The counsellor consoles the student and the request by the student for no further action is granted.

Losing a Friend? (-)

A community counselling centre employs 10 to 12 full-time counsellors. One of the counsellors, Ben, regularly conducts "growth" groups. Ben's friend and associate, Larry, realizes that on numerous occasions, when members are leaving after a group session, they seem quite distraught and some are openly crying. Larry talks to Ben about

his observation, and Ben tells him that he thinks the group members will resolve their issues more quickly if he "opens them up, and then lets them go to fend for themselves for a week". Ben tells Larry that he disagrees with this treatment of clients but Larry does not change his methods. Ben chooses to remain silent, fearing that he will be losing a friend if he reports Larry's conduct.

Comments and Questions

This ethical guideline is a mandate to guide counsellors in their everyday conduct and in the resolution of ethical dilemmas. It assists in the evaluation of questionable behaviour by colleagues. The basic principles underlying this guideline are respect for the dignity and integrity of persons, responsible caring in counselling relationships, and responsibility to society. Two of the principles from the *CCA Code of Ethics* are beneficience (promoting good for others) and nonmaleficence (avoiding doing harm). This means that it is every counsellor's responsibility not only to do good and to do no harm, but also to see to it that colleagues do good and no harm.

Doubts should be raised as to the ethical or non-ethical behaviour of professional associates, both members and non-members, in situations where:

- the welfare of a student is at risk
- the reputation of a school or agency could be compromised
- confidence in the counselling profession could be diminished.

1. In the last case, *Losing a Friend?*, the counsellor chose not to report questionable practices on the part of a colleague. What would you have done in this situation?

2. This ethical guideline refers to counsellor obligations when other counsellors are not acting ethically. Do the same guidelines apply to colleagues such as teachers? What would you do in the third case entitled **Conduct of an Associate**?

3. What are some common feelings and/or thoughts experienced when a counsellor has serious doubts about the ethical behaviour of a colleague?

4. Has the CCA set up guidelines to follow when unethical behaviour is suspected? If so, what are the guidelines?

5. What is the protocol for reporting known unethical behaviour of a colleague?

6. What are the likely short-term, ongoing, and long-term risks and benefits (i.e., consequences) of each course of action (e.g., reporting, not reporting) on the individual(s)/ group(s) involved or likely to be affected (e.g., student, school, colleague, profession, society, self)?

A8 **RESPONSIBILITY TO CLIENTS** When a counsellor has reasonable grounds to believe that a client has an ethical complaint about the conduct of a CCA member, the counsellor informs the client of the CCA Procedures for Processing Complaints of Ethical Violations and how to access these procedures.

Counsellor Dan (+)

Kiera K. had barely closed the door to her counselling office when her new client, Sandra, blurts out her experience with her last counsellor. Sandra explains that initially when she saw "Counsellor Dan" he seemed attentive and caring, but gradually he became overly friendly, gave her too long hugs, and made several inappropriate sexual comments. As Sandra said, "He was definitely coming on to me!"

After getting more details Kiera urges Sandra to read the *CCA Procedures for Processing Complaints of Ethical Violations* and to let the CCA Ethics Committee know about the unethical behaviour of her former counsellor.

Lack of Training (+)

"When I started seeing a counsellor at Milestone Counselling Centre, he told me that he had excellent counsellor training and years of successful counselling experience." Bill then continues to tell his friend Joe, a school counsellor, more about his experiences with the counsellor at Milestone Counselling Centre. Bill mentions that he did not like the constant references that the counsellor made about the need for religion, Christianity, and prayer. Bill further investigates the counsellor's credentials and learns that he had only taken one counselling course during his Bachelor of Theology degree program. He is quite amazed that the counsellor's resume indicates that he is a member of CCA. Joe encourages Bill to contact the CCA office in Ottawa to learn what he should do. Joe gives Bill both the telephone number and the e-mail address for CCA.

Friendship? (–)

A counsellor at an employment and career centre realizes that his friend and colleague is not correctly interpreting the results of a new personality test that the company is using. The counsellor knows that his friend has not taken any training on the use of the personality test. He also knows he would probably lose a friend if he told his colleague that he was not interpreting the personality test accurately. The counsellor decides not to do anything, even though some clients will be affected by the faulty test interpretations.

Gossip (–)

A beginning school counsellor feels it is important to connect well with other professionals in her school, including administrators, teachers and paraprofessionals. As a result, she makes it a practice to have coffee and lunch in the staff room, so that she can also get to know her colleagues socially. She is amazed at the amount of gossip that goes on about students between teachers. Even the other two counsellors in the school tell stories about the students they are counselling. She doesn't know what to do, since she feels it is important to maintain relationships with her colleagues. She feels that as a beginning counsellor she might jeopardize her relationship with colleagues if she mentions the unethical behaviour she observes almost on a daily basis. She knows that revealing the names of clients (students) that the counsellors are seeing, as well as openly discussing the content of the sessions, is unethical and detrimental to clients. Yet, as a beginning counsellor she is reluctant to "rock the boat". She remains quiet.

Comments and Questions

Too often, counsellors are reluctant to get involved in what other counsellors are doing. This ethical article clearly demands that clients need to be protected and that it is the ethical, professional responsibility of counsellors to help clients deal with the ethical violations of counsellors. Stated in the introduction to the *CCA Procedures for*

Processing Complaints of Ethical Violations is the following mandate:

> "If someone is not satisfied with the practices or behaviour of a CCAmember, they have the opportunity to complain to the CCA Ethics Committee."

Briefly, the procedures for submission of complaints to the CCA Ethics Committee are as follows:

• Whenever feasible, and appropriate, the complainant is encouraged to approach the counsellor directly to discuss and resolve the complaint.

• In cases where a resolution is not forthcoming following personal contact with the CCA member, and in instances when personal contact is not feasible and/or inappropriate, the complainant, after receiving complaint procedures from the CCA Ethics Committee chairperson, shall prepare a formal written statement of the complaint, stating the details of the alleged violation and shall submit it to the Ethics Committee Chairperson.

1. What would you do if you were Kiera K. in the case of **Counsellor Dan**?

2. In the case entitled **Lack of Training**, Bill can make the decision to get another counsellor. Should he do more, and contact the CCA Ethics Committee, regarding the counsellor at Milestone Counselling Centre?

3. What are your experiences with counsellors who do not keep client information confidential?

4. What would you do if you were the counsellor in the **Friendship** case?

5. Do you agree with the process used by the CCA for reporting ethical violations? How might this process be improved?

6. What are the possible negative results of complaining to the CCA Ethics Committee about another CCA member?

A9 SEXUAL HARASSMENT
Counsellors do not condone or engage in sexual harassment, which is defined as deliberate or repeated verbal or written comments, gestures, or physical contacts of a sexual nature.

Not Condoning (+)

At a junior high school, the school counsellor has a number of female students coming to see him regarding a certain science teacher on staff. This staff member has always taken a great interest in promoting science interest among girls and encouraging the girls to become actively involved in their own science education. To this end, he has set up a special science club for the girls in his classes, and has made participating in the club a graded requirement. He has club meetings after school and has each of the girls in the club working on a project, for marks. Recently, he has suggested that some of the girls see him on an individual basis for extra help with their projects. He has given the girls various reasons; for example, one girl was told she had exceptional abilities and he wanted to help her develop these talents. Another was told she was not going to pass science unless she came for extra help. All of the girls report that in these individual meetings, Mr. X becomes overly friendly, sitting very close to the students, sometimes touching their arms or putting an arm around their shoulders. The girls

feel very uncomfortable about this, but nothing overtly improper in nature has occurred. The school counsellor decides to have a talk with Mr. X to inform him of the concerns of the female students, and to let him know that his behaviour could be construed as sexual harassment.

The counsellor suggests to Mr. X that he should probably cease insisting on having private meetings with female students after school hours, and if a student requires help, he should have the meeting in a more public forum, such as the office or library, rather than in his classroom. The counsellor also informs Mr. X that she will continue to check in with the students in question, to ensure they are feeling more comfortable in Mr. X's science classes. Privately, she makes a notation of the date and nature of the conversation, as well as making a plan to check with the students periodically to ensure that there are no further incidents. She decides that should she have any more complaints, she would make a report to her department head and the administration.

Education (+)

The school counsellor at a high school has become increasingly concerned about the issue of sexual harassment, and knows that while many staff members are aware of the issue, most are not knowledgeable about the type of behaviours that could be construed as sexual harassment. He decides to approach the administration of the school about holding a workshop at the upcoming school in-service. He plans to invite speakers to explain to staff members what types of actions or comments constitute sexual harassment, how to respond to student concerns regarding the behaviour of fellow students or teachers, and how to handle situations in which they (teachers) feel they are the victims of harassment, by both students or other people with whom they may come in contact. His rationale for suggesting the in-service presentation is that once teachers have clear guidelines for proper behaviour, they will be less likely to find themselves in a compromising position, and hopefully, they will pass their new knowledge on to their students, who in turn will become more aware of behaviours that may make others uncomfortable.

Condoning (–)
In a junior high school, the physical education teacher, who also happens to be the school counsellor, notices a problem developing in one of the co-educational gym classes. One of the students, a boy named Justin, has been harassing some of the more physically mature girls during the ten-minute run at the start of every class. He began by staring overtly at their chests as they ran past him, and has now progressed to making suggestive comments. The girls are clearly uncomfortable with the attention, and have become increasingly resistant to doing the run. The physical education teacher feels that Justin is just being a typical adolescent boy, preoccupied with his sexuality, and that this behaviour will pass in time. On the other hand, he feels that the girls are over-reacting to a situation that they will have to get used to anyway, since boys will be boys, and he lets the girls know that he will impose penalties if they refuse to participate in the ten-minute run at the beginning of the class.

Student Discomfort (–)
The school counsellor in a high school

has been asked to teach the new "Life Skills" course to all grade ten students. The course includes a unit on human sexuality, and is designed to be taught in co-educational classes. The counsellor believes students get the most out of classes if they are made to feel as though they are active participants, and follows this philosophy in teaching the human sexuality component of the course. He begins the unit by having each student fill out an explicit questionnaire on his/her sexual maturation, asking such questions as when the girls first started to menstruate, and when the boys first noticed they were maturing sexually. He then uses the results to compare students to one another in a discussion of how maturation occurs at different times for different members of the class. Even when he notices some of the students are embarrassed at having such personal details revealed in the class, he persists in making reference to the questionnaire results at various times during the ensuing weeks. He continues to make sexual comments about specific students despite the students being openly uncomfortable with his sexual descriptions.

Comments and Questions
Harassment has been defined as disturbing or troubling another person by persistent, repeated attacks. This guideline is clear - members do not condone or engage in sexual harassment. Members of a professional counselling association are expected to do something about colleagues involved in sexual harassment. This action may consist of confronting a colleague on her or his sexual harassment, and it may mean reporting continued harassment to appropriate authorities.

1. What is your definition of sexual harassment? Give some specific examples.

2. What assistance or resources are available for members who must deal with sexual harassment?

3. What are some of the risks involved in reporting a case of sexual harassment? What are the benefits?

4. If a colleague appears to be sexually harassing another person, would you confront the individual or would you report the individual? Comment.

5. What is the counsellor's responsibility if he or she senses sexual attraction on the part of the client?

6. Clients are in vulnerable positions when they come for help. Counsellors greatly abuse their power and influence by sexually harassing clients in any way. List some forms of sexual harassment that are too often overlooked.

A10 SENSITIVITY TO DIVERSITY
Counsellors strive to understand and respect the diversity of their clients, including differences related to age, ethnicity, culture, gender, disability, religion, sexual orientation and socio-economic status. (See also B9, D10)

Counselling Services (+)

At a board meeting of administrators and school counsellors, the counsellors submit to the administration that their schools must make every attempt to provide students with as many options as possible. The submission includes recommendations regarding the equitable hiring of qualified male and female counsellors, providing each student with the opportunity to seek counsel from someone they feel comfortable approaching, regardless of their gender. It is also suggested that the school board expand the current facilities to allow for the increase in personnel and the appropriate confidential space required by each counsellor.

Sexual Stereotyping (+)

During a grade eight team meeting, teachers, administrators and counsellors examined the results of the eighth grade on the *Canadian Tests of Basic Skills*. Comments are made about the low scores in mathematics by many of the female staff members. One male teacher claims that these results are not unexpected and that "girls never do as well as boys in mathematics" since they don't understand mathematics. Several teachers agree. The counsellor feels that this comment is unfair to the girls and talks to the group about their attitudes towards females and mathematics.

Cultural Stereotype (–)

An employment/career counsellor working with Human Resources Canada has a client, Joe, who is now a foreman in a construction company. Joe is a highly respected carpenter, but is concerned that as he gets older he may not be able to meet the demands of the heavy work he is doing. Also, he has the opportunity to buy into a small company. The employment counsellor focuses entirely on Joe's carpentry skills and encourages him to stay with the other workers who know him very well, and are mainly of the same ethnic culture as Joe. The employment counsellor ignores Joe's skills as a foreman and the possibility that he may very well be a good manager of his own company.

Discriminatory Counselling (–)

During a rash of break and entry crimes in a small town, local authorities suggest that the high school provide guidance and counselling for the student body to discuss the problem as well as outline the possible outcomes of such behaviours. The school agrees and the counsellor proceeds to organize group counselling sessions for the aboriginal students within the student population. The session is announced over the school's public address system as being mandatory for all aboriginal students, but no provisions are made for counselling other students because it is assumed that they would probably not be involved in the break and entry crimes.

Comments and Questions

With the global community gradually becoming a reality, the importance of multiculturalism in counselling is increasingly important. *The Canadian Charter of Rights and Freedom* does not allow for discrimination and guards the rights of all Canadians. Racial and sexual stereotypes and discrimination must not be allowed. Counsellors can not be "culturally encapsulated" and rely on stereotypes when working with culturally diverse clients.

Most counsellor education programs in Canada now include some training in multiculturalism and diversity. Counsellors-in-training have an opportunity to examine their attitudes and beliefs about issues of gender, culture, race and sexual orientation. In addition, counsellors both in training and in practice need to have knowledge about working with diversity. Multicultural or cross-cultural skills include the ability to converse appropriately with many types of clients, to exercise skills helpful for various cultures, to consult with tra-ditional healers and spiritual leaders, and to teach diverse clients about their specific approach to helping.

1. What efforts are being made in your counselling centre to promote non-traditional work for women and men?

2. Is it the responsibility of counsellors to educate others regarding sexual and racial stereotyping?

3. What are the more subtle forms of racial and sexual stereotyping that counsellors must guard against?

4. Should re-education or education of counsellors on multicultural issues be mandatory?

5. Is the provision of specific ethnic or cultural counsellors for specific ethnic or cultural groups a form of discrimination?

6. Are the core conditions of Carl Rogers (empathy, respect and genuineness) relevant for all cultures?

A11 EXTENSION OF ETHICAL RESPONSIBILITIES
Counselling services and products provided by counsellors through classroom instruction, public lectures, demonstrations, publications, radio and television programs, computer technology and other media must meet the appropriate ethical standards consistent with this Code of Ethics.

Boundaries of Competence (+)

A school counsellor is a guest on a radio program and receives a call from a listener asking for advice about her troubled marriage. The counsellor has very little experience in marriage counselling and explains that he is not qualified to comment, but refers the caller to an appropriate agency for information and help.

Professional Qualifications (+)

A family counsellor is prepared to speak at a public lecture. The counsellor is introduced by the lecture coordinator who gives a short personal history of the counsellor and lists the counsellor's qualifications and experience. The counsellor realizes that her educational qualifications have been incorrectly stated and corrects the error for the audience before starting her lecture.

Post-Secondary Career and Educational Information (-)

The post-secondary career and educational information in one high school is provided by the counselling department. This information is placed on display and is available for viewing by the entire school body. Unfortunately, the information available only applies to a small percentage of students, those wishing to attend university. The information does not apply to vocational training or job training for those students not aspiring to university. Also, the counselling offered about this information is only available to those students meeting requirements for university.

Psychodrama (–)

A counsellor-educator is invited to demonstrate several new psychodrama techniques in front of a large audience. She asks for volunteers with whom to demonstrate the techniques. The demonstration begins without any arrangements having been made regarding confidentiality, audience involvement, or follow-up.

Comments and Questions

Counsellors should make every attempt to provide accurate information during counselling, when making presentations to others, in their print materials and when giving information on radio or television. Counsellors should not exaggerate their education or experience. Counsellors should not use their institution's name when giving personal opinions on issues. Print materials should be well-suited to the readership they are intended to serve; that is, counsellors need to ensure that media materials are:

- appropriate for the reading level and maturity of the audience

- accurate, unbiased and gender and culture fair

- distributed with appropriate explanations

- giving a fair representation of all sides of an issue.

1. What range of materials should be available in a high school, junior high school, and elementary school counselling office regarding sensitive life issues, future education options, and future job opportunities?

2. How can educators and counsellors increase the availability of culturally sensitive media materials?

3. What factors would you need to consider when using media materials to discuss a cultural issue?

4. What precautions should be taken to make sure that all media meet ethical standards?

5. What are some of the possible ethical concerns regarding counselling and the Internet?

6. What arrangements should the counsellor in the case entitled **Psychodrama** have made before, during and after his demonstration?

Chapter Nine

---❖---

Case Studies in Counselling Relationships

---❖---

Counsellors must be aware that, at all times, their primary obligation is to help their clients. Counsellors must recognize that they have limited confidentiality and must always inform clients of counselling conditions.

Canadian Counselling Association Code of Ethics

Ethical Guidelines for Counselling Relationships

B1 PRIMARY RESPONSIBILITY
Counsellors have a primary responsibility to respect the integrity and promote the welfare of their clients. They work collaboratively with clients to devise integrated, individualized counselling plans that offer reasonable promise of success and are consistent with the abilities and circumstances of clients.

B2 CONFIDENTIALITY
Counselling relationships and information resulting therefrom are kept confidential. However, there are the following exceptions to confidentiality:
(i) when disclosure is required to prevent clear and imminent danger to the client or others;
(ii) when legal requirements demand that confidential material be revealed;
(iii) when a child is in need of protection.
(See also B15, B17, E6, E7, F8)

B3 DUTY TO WARN
When counsellors become aware of the intention or potential of clients to place others in clear or imminent danger, they use reasonable care to give threatened persons such warnings as are essential to avert foreseeable dangers.

B4 CLIENT'S RIGHTS AND INFORMED CONSENT
When counselling is initiated, and throughout the counselling process as necessary, counsellors inform clients of the purposes, goals, techniques, procedures, limitations, potential risks and benefits of services to be performed, and other such pertinent information. Counsellors make sure that clients understand the implications of diagnosis, fees and fee collection arrangements, record-keeping, and limits of confidentiality. Clients have the right to participate in the ongoing counselling plans, to refuse any recommended services, and to be advised

of the consequences of such refusal. (See also C5, E5)

B5 CHILDREN AND PERSONS WITH DIMINISHED CAPACITY
Counsellors conduct the informed consent process with those legally appropriate to give consent when counselling, assessing, and having as research subjects children and/or persons with diminished capacity. These clients also give consent to such services or involvement commensurate with their capacity to do so. Counsellors understand that the parental or guardian right to consent on behalf of children diminishes commensurate with the child's growing capacity to provide informed consent.

B6 MAINTENANCE OF RECORDS
Counsellors maintain records in sufficient detail to track the sequence and nature of professional services rendered and consistent with any legal, regulatory, agency, or institutional requirement. They secure the safety of such records and create, maintain, transfer, and dispose of them in a manner compliant with the requirements of confidentiality and the other articles of this *Code of Ethics*.

B7 ACCESS TO RECORDS
Counsellors understand that clients have a right of access to their counselling records, and that disclosure to others of information from these records only occurs with the written consent of the client and/or when required by law.

B8 DUAL RELATIONSHIPS
When Counsellors make every effort to avoid dual relationships with clients that could impair professional judgment or increase the risk of harm to clients. Examples of dual relationships include, but are not limited to, familial, social, financial, business, or close personal relationships. When a dual relationship can not be avoided, counsellors take appropriate professional precautions such as role clarification, informed consent,

consultation, and documentation to ensure that judgment is not impaired and no exploitation occurs. (See also B11, B12, B13, C5, C7, F10)

B9 RESPECTING DIVERSITY
Counsellors actively work to understand the diverse cultural background of the clients with whom they work, and do not condone or engage in discrimination based on age, colour, culture, ethnicity, disability, gender, religion, sexual orientation, marital, or socio-economic status. (See also D10)

B10 CONSULTING WITH OTHER PROFESSIONALS
Counsellors may consult with other professionally competent persons about the client. However, if the identity of the client is to be revealed, it is done with the written consent of the client. Counsellors choose professional consultants in a manner which will avoid placing the consultant in a conflict of interest situation.

B11 RELATIONSHIPS WITH FORMER CLIENTS
Counsellors remain accountable for any relationships established with former clients. Those relationships could include, but are not limited to those of a friendship, social, financial, and business nature. Counsellors exercise caution about entering any such relationships and take into account whether or not the issues and relational dynamics present during the counselling have been fully resolved and properly terminated. In any case, counsellors seek consultation on such decisions.

B12 SEXUAL INTIMACIES
Counsellors avoid any type of sexual intimacies with clients and they do not counsel persons with whom they have had a sexual relationship. Counsellors do not engage in sexual intimacies with former clients within a minimum of three years after terminating the counselling relationship. This prohibition is not limit-

ed to the three year period but extends indefinitely if the client is clearly vulnerable, by reason of emotional or cognitive disorder, to exploitative influence by the counsellor. Counsellors, in all such circumstances, clearly bear the burden to ensure that no such exploitative influence has occurred, and to seek consultative assistance.

B13 MULTIPLE CLIENTS
When counsellors agree to provide counselling to two or more persons who have a relationship (such as husband and wife, or parents and children), counsellors clarify at the outset which person or persons are clients and the nature of the relationship they will have with each person. If conflicting roles emerge for counsellors, they must clarify, adjust, or withdraw from roles appropriately.

B14 MULTIPLE HELPERS
If, after entering a counselling relationship, a counsellor discovers the client is already in a counselling relationship, the counsellor is responsible for discussing the issues related to continuing or terminating counselling with the client. It may be necessary, with client consent, to discuss these issues with the other helper.

B15 GROUP WORK
Counsellors have the responsibility to screen prospective group members, especially when group goals focus on self-understanding and growth through self-disclosure. Counsellors inform clients of group member rights, issues of confidentiality, and group techniques typically used. They take reasonable precautions to protect group members from physical and/or psychological harm resulting from interaction within the group, both during and following the group experience. (See also Appendix B.)

B16 COMPUTER USE
When computer applications are used as a component of counselling services, counsellors ensure that: (a) client and counsellor identities are verified; (b) the client is capable of using the computer application; (c) the computer application is appropriate to the needs of the client; (d) the client understands the purpose and operation of client-assisted and/or self-help computer applications; and (e) a follow-up of client use of a computer application is provided to assist subsequent needs. In all cases, computer applications do not diminish the counsellor's responsibility to act in accordance with the CCA Code of Ethics, and in particular, to ensure adherence to the principles of confidentiality, informed consent, and safeguarding against harmful effects. (See also D5)

B17 DELIVERY OF SERVICES BY TELEPHONE, TELECONFERENCING, AND INTERNET
Counsellors follow all additional ethical guidelines for services delivered by telephone, teleconferencing, and the Internet, including appropriate precautions regarding confidentiality, security, informed consent, records and counselling plans, as well as determining the right to provide such services in regulatory jurisdictions.

B18 REFERRAL
When counsellors determine their inability to be of professional assistance to clients, they avoid initiating a counselling relationship, or immediately terminate it. In either event, members suggest appropriate alternatives, including making a referral to resources about which they are knowledgeable. Should clients decline the suggested referral, counsellors are not obligated to continue the relationship.

B19 **TERMINATION OF COUNSELLING**
Counsellors terminate counselling relationships, with client agreement whenever possible, when it is reasonably clear that: the goals of counselling have been met, the client is no longer benefiting from counselling, the client does not pay fees charged, previously disclosed agency or institutional limits do not allow for the provision of further counselling services, and the client or another person with whom the client has a relationship threatens or otherwise endangers the counsellor. However, counsellors make reasonable efforts to facilitate the continued access to counselling services when services are interrupted by these factors and by counsellor illness, client or counsellor relocation, client financial difficulties and so forth.

Case Studies for Counselling Relationships

B1 **PRIMARY RESPONSIBILITY**
Counsellors have a primary responsibility to respect the integrity and promote the welfare of their clients. They work collaboratively with clients to devise integrated, individualized counselling plans that offer reasonable promise of success and are consistent with the abilities and circumstances of clients.

Respect for the Client (+)
A counsellor comes highly recommended to a woman whose marriage is in trouble due to many factors, but most significantly due to emotional and verbal abuse from her husband. The abuse has gone on for several years without the wife being able to persuade the husband to seek any kind of help. The counsellor recognizes the hurt the woman is feeling and that she has a plan which she seems to have difficulty carrying out. The counsellor does not tell her what to do or question whether what she reveals to him are her true inner feelings. He seems to accept what she is saying and to recognize that the feelings that she displays are real to her. This counsellor makes the woman feel comfortable; the rapport between the two that is established during their first session is so positive that it leaves the door wide open for more revelations.

The counsellor's genuineness is picked up by the woman early on in the first session. He shows understanding of the inner conflicts the woman has regarding whether or not she and her children should remain in the abusive situation. The counsellor is able to explain the cycle of abuse and the consequences of remaining in the situation, and to restate the alternatives the woman has decided are open to her. Most importantly, the counsellor helps her to see that the time has come for her to make a decision.

Disclosure in a Group (+)
In a group session involving six students, all of whom come from non-abusive alcoholic homes, one of the students confides that he "can not take any more". He is 16 years old and is intending to take his father's car and run away to the nearest big city. He has no money, no skills, and no friends or relatives with whom to stay. It is his intention to live on the street. He is aware that many people his age live this way and he feels it is better than the life he is currently living. Despite all arguments against this course of action from the other members of the group and the counsellor, the boy staunchly adheres to his position. Knowledge of the family situation leads the counsellor to believe that apart from the concern for the stolen car, little will be done for the student if parents were notified. The coun-

sellor calls Child and Family Services and requests their help in working with the student and his family.

Alone (–)

A male teacher, Frank, who is in his early forties, comes home one day to learn that his wife has taken their two children and left him. In the subsequent divorce case, his wife is given custody of the children. Frank has been seeing a counsellor for weekly sessions for several months. He continues to express much anger, pain and loneliness during his hourly sessions. During the last session, the counsellor stops the session after ten minutes and tells Frank that he is "behind schedule" even though Frank has made his usual hourly appointment.

Doubting Counsellor (–)

In a small, remote community, a 14-year-old grade nine student, Mary, tells her female school counsellor that she desperately needs to talk to her in confidence as soon as possible. The counsellor feels that the student is probably overreacting about something and does not meet with her immediately. A week later, the student once again approaches her counsellor and explains that she has been sexually abused by her stepfather. The counsellor is not convinced that the student is speaking the truth, and feels the student's motive is to attack her stepfather with these allegations. The counsellor tells the student that she will look into the matter, but never reports it to the proper authorities for further investigation.

Comments and Questions

Counselling is a personal matter that involves personal relationships. Honesty, sincerity, acceptance, understand-ing, and spontaneity are basic ingredients for a successful relationship between the counsellor and counsellee. The degree of caring, counsellor interest and ability in helping the counsellee, and counsellor genuineness are all factors that influence this relationship and enhance the positive aspects of this ethical guideline. These characteristics are definitely lacking in the two negative cases.

Group counselling gives clients a place to express conflicting feelings, explore self-doubts and come to the realization that they may share these concerns with their peers. A group may allow counsellees to openly question their values and to modify those that may need to be changed.

In a group setting, if members are to drop their defences and reveal their "selves", they need assurances that the group is a safe place in which to do this.

It is the responsibility of counsellors to ensure that they "promote the welfare of counsellees", whether this is in individual or group counselling. This guideline has been placed first in this counselling relationship section; first, because counsellors must never forget that their primary obligation is to help their clients. It is necessary that counsellors act in ways that further the best interests of clients. Counsellors must:

- be willing to consult with colleagues

- keep themselves informed about laws affecting counselling practice

- keep current

- reflect on the impact their values have on counselling

- be willing to engage in honest self-evaluation.

This important article incorporates

many aspects of the six ethical principles of CCA:

- Beneficence—being proactive in promoting the client's best interests

- Fidelity—honouring commitments to clients and maintaining integrity in counselling relationships

- Autonomy—respecting the right of clients to self-determination

- Nonmaleficence—not wilfully harming clients and refraining from actions that risk harm

- Justice—respecting the dignity and just treatment of all persons

- Societal Interest—respecting the need to be responsible to society.

1. Where might "societal interest" come in conflict with "autonomy"?

2. In the two cases, *Alone* and *Doubting Counsellor*, what would you have done as counsellor?

3. What do you do when the school or agency that you work for has policies that do not appear to be helpful for your client?

4. What are some ways in which counsellors can enhance the welfare of clients?

5. Can you 'promote the welfare' of a client by breaking confidentiality? Explain.

6. How can group leaders protect group members from "physical and psychological" harm?

B2 CONFIDENTIALITY
Counselling relationships and information resulting therefrom are kept confidential. However, there are the following exceptions to confidentiality:
(i) when disclosure is required to prevent clear and imminent danger to the client or others;
(ii) when legal requirements demand that confidential material be revealed;
(iii) when a child is in need of protection. (See also B15, B17, E6, E7, F8)

What's Happening? (+)

Fred D. is a counsellor in a family counselling agency. One day he receives a phone call from the wife of one of the clients he is counselling. The wife indicates that she has seen some changes in her husband and asks the counsellor for information regarding what her husband is saying during counselling. The counsellor, in a kind but firm manner, explains to the woman that the matters discussed during counselling are confidential.

Limited Confidentiality (+)

Fifteen-year-old Sally has been referred to the high school counsellor, Ms. S. by her English teacher because her grades are falling and she is very inattentive in class. Her teacher fears that Sally will fail the course if she doesn't do something to pull up her grades. During the conversation between Sally and Ms. S., it becomes evident that Sally's performance in her other classes is similar to her performance in her English class and that she is likely to fail several courses if she isn't able to improve her performance.

Sally discloses to the counsellor that she has been feeling depressed lately and cannot seem to concentrate on her school work. After further probing, it becomes evident to Ms. S. that Sally is being sexually abused by her father. Sally admits to the abuse but says she is afraid of what might happen to her if her father finds out she has disclosed this information to anyone. Ms. S. tells Sally that she is required to report the matter to Child and Family Services and assures her that it is in Sally's best interest that she do so. Ms. S. then uses the school protocol to call Child and Family Services and waits with Sally for the social worker to arrive.

Inappropriate Chatter (–)

An anger management group at a local high school is co-led by two counsellors. At a social gathering one evening, one counsellor is the focus of attention as he shares antics and incidents that have occurred during the group sessions.

Breaking Confidentiality (–)

Sixteen-year-old Mary Lou has an appointment with Ms. J., the high school counsellor, to discuss what courses she should take in grade 12 to prepare for entering university the following year. During the course of their conversation, Mary Lou discloses to Ms. J. that she is having problems with her mother because her mother is always trying to control her life. Because she believes that whatever she tells Ms. J. is strictly confidential, she further discloses that she has been lying to her mother, telling her that she is studying at the library evenings when in fact she is spending time with a young man whom, she feels, her mother would disapprove of. Shortly after the session ends, Ms. J. telephones Mary Lou's mother to inform her of Mary Lou's involvement with the young man and how she has been lying to her. Ms. J. hopes she is helping Mary Lou by informing her parents.

Comments and Questions

Confidentiality protects clients from unauthorized disclosures and is the foundation upon which trust between the counsellor and client is built. Confidentiality is crucial to establishing and maintaining a strong counsellor/client relationship. With confidentiality, counsellors not only respect clients' ability to control their own lives, but also respect all human relationships. Confidentiality is useful to the community as a whole since clients are much more likely to seek the help of a counsellor knowing that what is said in counselling is confidential.

Counsellors agree that the material of a counselling session belongs to the client. Confidentiality is, nevertheless, not absolute. There are times when confidentiality must be broken, and there are other times when breaking confidentiality remains unclear. Some of the exceptions to confidentiality include:

- The client is a danger to self or others

- The court orders release of counselling information

- Support staff who process information and papers

- Legal and clinical consultation

- During clinical supervision of counsellors.

1. What are additional exceptions to confidentiality?

2. How can counsellors increase the chances of confidentiality in a group?

3. What is your responsibility as a counsellor when you hear other staff members discussing clients over coffee?

4. How should counsellors explain to clients that there are limits to their confidentiality?

5. Should the limits of confidentiality be listed on counsellors' informed consent forms?

6. How would you deal with the last two cases, *Inappropriate Chatter* and *Breaking Confidentiality*?

B3 **DUTY TO WARN**
When counsellors become aware of the intention or potential of clients to place others in clear or imminent danger, they use reasonable care to give threatened persons such warnings as are essential to avert foreseeable dangers.)

Threat Assessment (+)
George regularly attends addictions counselling as part of his court-ordered sentence. He likes his counsellor, Allan S., and gradually discloses more and more about his past and present actions. He has been physically abusive to several neighbourhood adolescents who have teased him about going to a counsellor, and his anger is escalating.

One day George sees his counsellor and is still furious with another teenager, Frank, who has again teased him. He is so angry that he blurts out, "One day I'm going to kill Frank. I hate him so much. I should just get my blade and stuff him the next time I see him."

Allan S. determines that George's threat is certainly possible. He informs George of the need to inform authorities to protect people from harm, and that he will stay with George until a threat to safety is no longer an issue. He uses the Threat Assessment Protocol to contact the head counsellor who then arranges for contact with the local police and Frank, as well as immediate

intervention by the Threat Assessment Team

Potential Suicide (+)
A suicide note is left by a Jessica, grade seven student indicating her intention of suicide. The note is brought to the attention of the guidance department head since the girl's counsellor is out of the building at the time. The department head speaks briefly to Jessica to determine her level of safety and tells her that she has called her counsellor to return to the building. The department head contacts Jessica's parents regarding the note, but they do not seem too concerned, although they do agree to telephone the counsellor or school principal if help is needed.

Once the counsellor returns, she meets with Jessica and talks to her about her note and her suicidal intentions. It seems that she has considered suicide, but has not thought of how to carry out the plan. She has a very close friend; someone she trusts and feels that she could talk to at all times. The counsellor checks that this person is reliable and stable, then creates a safety plan with Jessica and gives her the telephone number of a suicide prevention centre, as well as her own home telephone number to call if the safety plan does not work.

Informing Others (–)
A 15-year-old student has begun to see the counsellor at the local drop-in centre because of problems he is having with his girlfriend. The counsellor enjoys the relationship he has with the students at the centre and feels that he has gained their trust and respect. During one of these sessions, the boy expresses to the counsellor that many of the students trust him and feel that he

is really on their side. He also tells the counsellor that he and his girlfriend have tried "crack" on several occasions. She had first been hesitant to try the drug but after some pressure she gave in and in fact enjoys it. The counsellor discusses the dangers of the drug as well as the strain the boy is putting on his girlfriend and their relationship.

The counsellor debates whether he should inform the girl's parents or his supervisor, but feels that the trust he has gained among the youth is very important. He decides to continue his sessions with the boy and does not inform the responsible authorities. He is informed several days later that the girl has nearly died of an overdose of drugs at a party on the weekend. The counsellor is given a short-term suspension from his position at the centre for not following their policy on reporting drug use.

Selling Drugs (–)
Alan tells his counsellor that his friend Joe told him about a big drug deal that is going to go down that evening at the arcade. He mentions Darryl, a good-looking, well-dressed, senior student who is always surrounded by a group of friends, as being the person who will purchase a large amount of "crack". Alan says Darryl plans to sell the drugs to the other students at school. The counsellor knows Darryl's parents, his father is a teacher, and feels that this could not be true. Alan, however, insists that he knows all of the details of the transaction from Joe, and he wants the counsellor to do something. The counsellor continues to listen to Alan and reflects his concerns about the situation, but he tells Alan that he can not get involved in something that is only hearsay evidence.

Comments and Questions
It is important for counsellors to inform clients, at the beginning of their sessions, of their obligation and responsibility to break confidentiality when counsellors feel that their clients or others are in potential danger. By informing clients of their limited confidentiality, counsellors can alleviate the sense of betrayal that clients may feel if they are under the impression that anything said to the counsellor will be kept confidential. Warning of danger must be presented in such a way that it is seen as a caring act on the part of the counsellor.

The famous *Tarasoff* court decision has helped counsellors to understand how to act in situations where there is danger to a third party. Counsellors have a legal obligation to third parties who are at risk from dangerous clients. As with other situations where confidentiality must be broken, counsellors should tell their clients that they have a legal responsibility to warn people in danger. Counsellors should then inform their supervisor, the police and the intended victim.

Counsellors should be aware that there may be certain repercussions that result from informing responsible authorities. There is the danger that other clients may feel that the counsellor cannot be trusted, or the client may even feel a sense of anger or betrayal toward the counsellor.

Counsellors must be aware of institutional or agency policies and the responsible parties to whom they have an obligation to contact when they feel the client or others are in danger. Parents have a right to be informed if their child may be harmed, and parents should be informed of additional resources within the community, or professional organizations, that can help with a potentially dangerous situation.

1. Do you agree with the *Tarasoff* decision that counsellors have a "duty to warn" people in danger? Discuss.

2. What can be done to alleviate a possible sense of betrayal that the clients may feel if they become aware of the counsellor breaking confidentiality?

3. Under what circumstances and in what situations should the counsellor assume responsibility for the counsellee's actions?

4. If there is a case in which the counsellor has been made aware of a possible danger to the client or others, but does not feel that the danger is probable, is there still an obligation to inform responsible authorities?

5. Are counsellors legally obliged to inform responsible authorities of their clients' involvement in illegal activities if counsellors feel that it would be detrimental to the clients? Counsellors may feel they have a better chance of helping clients by encouraging them to stop their involvement in illegal activities within the framework of their counselling relationship.

6. What would you have done in the last two cases?

B4 CLIENT'S RIGHTS AND INFORMED CONSENT
Counsellors When counselling is initiated, and throughout the counselling process as necessary, counsellors inform clients of the purposes, goals, techniques, procedures, limitations, potential risks and benefits of services to be performed, and other such pertinent information. Counsellors make sure that clients under-stand the implications of diagnosis, fees and fee collection arrangements, record-keeping, and limits of confidentiality. Clients have the right to participate in the ongoing counselling plans, to refuse any recommended services, and to be advised of the consequences of such refusal. (See also C5, E5.)**

A Plan of Action (+)
Jane is a 14-year-old grade eight student who comes to the school counsellor in a panic, thinking she is pregnant. The counsellor is a long-time staff member and is well-liked by the student. Given the rapport between the two, it is not too long before the student is calm and rational enough to listen to the counsellor. The counsellor indicates there are ways to confirm pregnancy and the plan of action would depend on whether the pregnancy test show a positive or negative result. If negative, the counsellor would help Jane to educate herself to avoid future unplanned pregnancies. If positive, Jane would have one of three choices: keep the baby, offer the baby for adoption, or end the pregnancy, and the consequences of each choice would be discussed. Furthermore, Jane's parents would have to be informed. Should this moment arrive, the counsellor offers to provide emotional support and, based on Jane's decision, either to tell Jane's parents himself or to be with Jane when she tells them. Jane decides to work through her problem with the guidance of her counsellor, beginning with determining whether she is pregnant.

Informed on Confidentiality (+)
Joyce meets with her school counsellor and tells the counsellor that she has a very serious concern, but before she will tell the counsellor, Joyce insists that

the counsellor keep everything she says in strictest confidence. The counsellor carefully explains that she will keep matters confidential, but that there are limits to her confidentiality. The counsellor explains what these limits are. The counsellor then encourages Joyce to talk more about her demand for absolute confidentiality, and to then decide if she wishes to tell the counsellor her concerns despite the limits that the counsellor has placed on confidentiality.

Secret Phone Call (–)

During the course of several counselling sessions, a counsellor discovers that part of the reason for a boy's aggression in class toward his teacher and peers is the fact that he has been physically abused by his father. The counsellor contacts a Child Guidance Clinic to give them this information. But because he is afraid the child and the child's mother will want to stop the counselling to protect the father, the counsellor does not indicate to either the boy or his mother that he has contacted the Child Guidance Clinic.

Principal's Orders (–)

Jocelyn, a grade 11 student, is referred to the counsellor by a teacher who was having difficulty "controlling Jocelyn and her disruptive behaviour in the classroom." Jocelyn and the counsellor establish a good relationship, but the disruptive behavior continues and the principal is called in to take more severe action. The principal tells the counsellor that he will be taking action in this situation and he asks the counsellor to submit any records of her meetings with Jocelyn to him, so that he can get a better understanding of the situation. Despite the fact that the counsellor has shown Jocelyn a counselling consent form that promises confidentiality (except when there is danger to the client or to others), the counsellor gives the principal all her private documentation of her meetings with Jocelyn.

Comments and Questions

All clients have the right to know what counsellors typically do during their counselling. Obtaining consent from clients beforehand is good counselling practice and an ethical way to proceed. Informing clients about counselling and the roles both the counsellor and client will have, helps clients to realize that counselling is a sort of partnership, where both counsellor and client will work together to help the client.

Counsellors should prepare a personal, written statement (informed consent) on their counselling. Such an informed consent form would contain a short statement about the counselling sessions, the nature and length of the counselling, and the type of follow-up used. This informed consent form would also contain information on the counsellor's qualifications and experience. An informed consent form would also contain a statement on confidentiality and its limitations. Clients would learn that they have the right to obtain information about case notes, the right to refuse any recommended services and the right to participate in ongoing counselling plans.

1. If it is true that the majority of school counsellors and employment counsellors do not have informed consent forms, what do you think are the reasons for this?

2. Other than the areas mentioned in the preceding comment, what other

items should be part of a counsellor's personal statement?

3. Should group facilitators have different consent forms than individual counsellors?

4. What are some limitations that may result in the discontinuance of counselling? Should this information be part of the consent form?

5. Should the fee structure be part of the informed consent form?

6. Should the counsellor's theoretical orientation (in lay language) be part of the informed consent form?

B5 CHILDREN AND PERSONS WITH DIMINISHED CAPACITY

Counsellors conduct the informed consent process with those legally appropriate to give consent when counselling, assessing, and having as research subjects children and/or persons with diminished capacity. These clients also give consent to such services or involvement commensurate with their capacity to do so. Counsellors understand that the parental or guardian right to consent on behalf of children diminishes commensurate with the child's growing capacity to provide informed consent.

Research with Children (+)

A child psychologist at a university receives a research grant to investigate the play behaviour of children in kindergarten. The psychologist plans to observe children in three different schools in one school board. After receiving permission from the school board, school and teachers, the psychologist-researcher contacts all the parents and guardians with children in the three classrooms, and, after fully explaining her research, she asks parents and guardians to sign permission forms for their children to be involved in the study.

Children with Special Needs (+)

The school psychologist is aware that there are many children with special needs in the middle years school in which she is working. She wants to find out as much as possible about these children so that she can work with the teachers to help them in school. The psychologist explains to all the students in each classroom that she will be visiting regularly and observing their behaviour. She also obtains permission from the parents and/or guardians of all the children in the classroom, including those without special needs, for her proposed work.

No Consent (-)

A school psychologist, Francis C., thinks that she will be able to help two students that she is working with if she has a better idea of their behavior in the classroom and playground. The teachers involved tell the psychologist to "come in anytime you want to", and so the psychologist does. When students in the classroom ask her why she is visiting, she says that she is interested in the classroom behaviour of children.

Secret Data Gathering (-)

A counselling student works at a crisis centre as part of his counselling practicum for his Master's program. He realizes that many of the clients coming for help are having emotional problems related to family relationships. He begins to gather data with the intent of using the information for a paper that he plans to write.

Comments and Questions

Informed consent is a basic right for clients and when counsellors are working with children and/or persons with diminished capacity, they need to conduct the informed consent process with parents or legal guardians. It is important that guardians have every opportunity to ask questions and that the information provided is totally understandable.

Counsellors are frequently faced with the dilemma of providing children with confidentiality, but also wanting to respect the legal responsibilities to parents and guardians. *The American Counseling Association Code of Ethics* asks that counsellors "act in the best interests" of children and that counsellors may include parents and guardians in the counselling process "as appropriate". In short, counsellors are expected to use professional judgement to act in the best interests of children and those of diminished capacity.

1. What can be done to enhance the professional judgement of counsellors?

2. Is record-keeping even more important when working with children or persons with diminished capacity?

3. In the case entitled *No Consent*, is it better to tell a "little white lie" than to let the class know the psychologist is observing one or two students?

4. How would you handle the situation in *No Consent*?

5. How would you deal with the situation in *Secret Data Gathering*?

6. Collaborative narrative inquiry is research for counselling rather than on counselling. Would you use this research method with children?

B6 **MAINTENANCE OF RECORDS** **Counsellors maintain records in sufficient detail to track the sequence and nature of professional services rendered and consistent with any legal, regulatory, agency, or institutional requirement. They secure the safety of such records and create, maintain, transfer, and dispose of them in a manner compliant with the requirements of confidentiality and the other articles of this** *Code of Ethics.*

Counsellor Files (+)

In a family counselling agency, records are kept of all the clients coming to the agency for counselling. These individual files contain only basic biographical information. Each counsellor at the agency keeps personal files on all clients that she or he is counselling. These personal counsellor files contain interview notes and are intended only for the use of the counsellor who is counselling a particular client.

Tape Recordings in a Practicum (+)

In a counselling practicum, students are required to submit audio- and video-tapes of counselling sessions with clients. The practicum instructor develops appropriate forms that explain the purposes of the audio- and video-recordings. All clients and student counsellors sign the forms giving permission for the practicum instructor and counselling student to view the tapes for learning purposes. After the viewing, the tapes are erased.

The Police Are Calling (–)

A marriage counsellor is contacted by the police regarding one of her clients. The police ask for any information the counsellor can offer from the interviews with a particular client. The counsellor, realizing the police are asking, goes to her files and tells the inquiring police officer the essence of the interviews.

The Principal's Policy (–)

The policy of one school principal is to have one set of files in his school. He insists that all counsellors write interview notes for each client that they see, and that these notes be placed in the school files. As a result of the protests from counsellors, the principal has "compromised" by telling counsellors that their interview notes "may be brief", but that they must submit a report on each student interviewed. In spite of the fact that the files are accessible to all the teachers, secretaries and clerks in the school, the counsellors continue to file their interview notes in the school files.

Comments and Questions

Client records belong to the client. These records include test data, letters of correspondence, any video- or audio-recordings and the counsellor's interview notes. These materials belong to the client and are for the use of the client and counsellor. These personal records "are not part of the official records of the institution or agency in which the counsellor is employed." Permission from the client is necessary before these "client records" are shared with others.

There are, however, exceptions to confidentiality of records, particularly for students in schools. The regulations for record-keeping vary from province to province. In one province, Manitoba, counsellors need to be aware of guidelines and regulations such as:

- *Manitoba Pupil File Guidelines,*
- *The Freedom of Information and Protection of Privacy Act*

- *The Personal Health Information Act*
- *The Public School Act*
- *Education Administration Act*
- *Youth Criminal Justice Act,* and
- *The Guidelines on the Retention and Disposition of School Division/District Records.*

Counsellors are well-advised to become familiar with agency or school regulations for record-keeping.

Special attention should also be focused on the maintenance of records. Interview notes should be recorded at the time service is provided, and they should be factual, objective, legible and well-organized. Any observations and personal impressions should be identified as those of the person producing the records.

1. What are the main policies or legislation governing record-keeping for counsellors in your province?

2. What type of record-keeping policy is in place at your counselling centre?

3. Do some schools have records policies similar to those of the principal depicted in the last case?

4. Should counsellors-in-training be allowed to keep their audio- or video-recordings of clients?

5. Should counsellors give police or lawyers records of their interviews?

6. Should parents have access to the counselling records of their school-aged children?

B7 ACCESS TO RECORDS
Counsellors understand that clients have a right of access to their counselling records, and that disclosure to others of information from these records only occurs with the written consent of the client and/or when required by law.

Confidential Files (+)
A counsellor in private practice keeps detailed records of all her clients, including the dates of all sessions, a summary of each counselling session, commentary on counselling progress, and tentative plans for future sessions. All the records are kept in a locked file. Clients are informed at the beginning of counselling that the counselling records are kept confidential unless ordered to be released by the courts.

Client Records (+)
After almost a year of counselling, Janice Z. begins to wonder whether she should continue seeing the counsellor. She discusses the matter with her counsellor and feels she would be in a better position to make her decision if she could see all the records that the counsellor has made of their counselling sessions. After reading the records, Janice realizes more clearly the degree of progress that she is making, and so she makes the decision to continue counselling.

Provincial Mandate (–)
The Ministry of Education from one Canadian province distributes guidelines on the school records of students. The new guidelines indicate that all records, including those of counsellors, social workers and psychologists, are to be open to parents and guardians upon request. Although there are a few exceptions to this guideline, little guidance is given to counsellors and other

school personnel on how to challenge this guideline.

Releasing Counselling Records (–)
The police arrive at the adolescent treatment centre and explain that they have arrested Bob F., because they suspect him of selling drugs to other young people at the centre. Bob indicates to the police that he frequently spoke to his counsellor about many things. The police tell the director of the treatment centre that their case would be much stronger if they knew more about what Bob was saying to the counsellor. The director tells the counsellor to immediately provide the police with his counselling records. The counsellor gives the police his records.

Comments and Questions
Clients have a right of access to their counselling records. Records must be written so that clients can understand what the records say. What is less clear to counsellors are the appropriate actions to take when parents or legal guardians request the counselling records of their children. Although parents may legally see the records of their children, counsellors must use their professional judgment as to whether the best interests of the child are being served by showing parents or guardians the records. Children, like adults, are protected by *The Canadian Charter of Rights and Freedoms*.

1. "Just because children are favoured in some areas of the law does not mean that they can't have the same rights as adults in other areas of the law." Discuss.

2. What do you think about the mandate presented in the *Provincial Mandate* case?

3. What would you do if you were the counsellor in the case *Releasing Counselling Records*?

4. Do you think that clients would understand the diagnosis and notes that counsellors record?

5. What should school counsellors do if their administrator insists that all records must be kept in the school pupil (cumulative) file?

6. What do you think about using counselling records in the way described in the case of *Client Records*?

B8 **DUAL RELATIONSHIPS**
When Counsellors make every effort to avoid dual relationships with clients that could impair professional judgment or increase the risk of harm to clients. Examples of dual relationships include, but are not limited to, familial, social, financial, business, or close personal relationships. When a dual relationship can not be avoided, counsellors take appropriate professional precautions such as role clarification, informed consent, consultation, and documentation to ensure that judgment is not impaired and no exploitation occurs. (See also B11, B12, B13, C5, C7, F10)

Referrals (+)
When two close friends of a marriage counsellor decide to divorce, they both seek their counsellor-friend for counselling. The counsellor, knowing the ethical boundaries of dual relationships, decides not to mix her personal relationship with a professional relationship. The counsellor explains her dilemma to the couple and makes appropriate referrals to other marriage counsellors.

Counselling Students? (+)
A counsellor-educator is asked by one of her graduate students to help her with her severe depression. The counsellor-educator explains to the student that she is her teacher and evaluator of her work and that it would be inadvisable for them to have a counselling relationship as well. The counsellor-educator recommends several counsellors who she feels could help the graduate student.

Counselling a Relative (–)
A counsellor is approached by his niece regarding her personal problem. She is under pressure from her family to leave the man she is dating, and who wishes to marry her. The man she is dating is of a different culture, and her family strongly disapproves. The counsellor begins to counsel his niece, since she has come to him with her concerns. Although he attempts to help his niece with her dilemma, his professional judgement becomes influenced. He tells his niece that she should leave her boyfriend and find a man from within her own culture.

Counselling Co-Workers (–)
The director of a counselling centre with ten counsellors is approached by one of the counsellors for help with her own marital problems. The two counsellors are good friends, even though the director of the centre is required to send annual reviews of each counsellor to a board of directors. Despite the different roles that the director has, she agrees to counsel her friend and co-worker.

Comments and Questions
Dual relationships occur when counsellors take on several roles with clients seeking help. Sometimes it is difficult to define clear boundaries in relation-

ships with clients. School administrators who may have to discipline students are in a dual relationship if they take on counselling responsibilities with students. Marriage and family counsellors who work with couples who are their friends may encounter ethical dilemmas in their dual relationship. There are many additional boundary issues: bartering with a client for goods or services, counselling and supervising counsellor trainees, or counselling the son or daughter of a close friend. It is very difficult to balance a professional relationship with a personal or social relationship outside of counselling. Dual relationships continue to be controversial because not all dual relationships are harmful and some dual relationships are difficult to avoid. Boundary issues need to be discussed so that potential harm can be avoided. To reduce this potential harm, counsellors should:

• have a discussion of the boundary issues with other professionals

• offer explanations of boundary issues when counsellor educators supervise counsellor candidates

• prepare a detailed informed consent form

• document all the details of a troublesome boundary issue or dual relationship, and

• involve the client in setting boundaries.

1. Counsellors in remote areas can face the dilemma of friends receiving either no counselling or counselling with them. What would you do?

2. Whose needs are being met when a counsellor counsels a close friend or relative?

3. What is the best way to avoid getting into a counselling relationship with friends?

4. When it is difficult or impossible to refer a potential client (with whom you have a supervisory or administrative relationship) to another counsellor, what are some precautions you should take in this counselling relationship?

5. Is it possible that counselling a friend will enhance the friendship?

6. Should counselling students be allowed to have their counselling practicum in a school where they formerly worked?

B9 RESPECTING DIVERSITY
Counsellors actively work to understand the diverse cultural background of the clients with whom they work, and do not condone or engage in discrimination based on age, colour, culture, ethnicity, disability, gender, religion, sexual orientation, marital, or socio-economic status. (See also D10)

Differences in Values (+)

Fred F., a counsellor in private practice, is very aware of the general differences in values between "mainstream" Canadians and immigrants coming from Asia. He has found that many of his Asian clients are used to a more authoritarian relationship with parents and family and are generally more compliant and cooperative. When an Asian client tells him about his unhappiness regarding his family's wishes for him to get an engineering degree, Fred realizes that both the family wishes and his client's interest must be considered. They spend many sessions discussing this dilemma and finally decide to have a session with key family members present.

Multicultural School (+)

A counsellor working in a middle years school realizes that there are literally dozens of ethnic and cultural groups in her school. She makes every effort to learn more about the various minority groups and at all times attempts to demonstrate equal respect, warmth and genuineness to all the students she sees. She realizes that she needed to carefully monitor any assumptions she makes about students, regardless of their cultural background.

"Melting Pot" Philosophy (–)

Frank W. is tired of "all the multicultural awareness brainwashing" he is constantly receiving from his colleagues and the director of the counselling clinic where he works. He still has his 1970s "Perls Prayer" on the wall and relates to the line "I do my thing, and you do your thing..." He counters his colleagues' suggestions for multicultural education by telling them that his Rogerian attitudes of empathy, respect and genuineness for all clients is all he needs. "As well," Frank states, "immigrants have to learn how to fit into Canadian society."

Western Values (–)

Susan P. often complains to her counselling associates about clients from another culture who "take forever to say what they want or what's wrong." She says she can understand that these clients will have some trouble with the language, but dislikes the fact that she seldom can have eye contact with them, that she has to ask a lot of closed questions and that she receives little positive feedback from them for her efforts to help. Often she suggests that the quiet, conforming, dependent clients join her evening group on assertiveness training.

Comments and Questions

Many research studies have shown that counsellor involvement with others who are different in terms of "age, colour, culture, ethnicity, disability, gender, religion, sexual orientation, marital or socio-economic status", will result in greater respect for diversity. There is, therefore, a need for counsellors who come from a majority culture to learn more about other cultures and to be sensitive to cultural values, and attitudes different than their own. Counsellors must educate themselves and learn how their own experiences, education, values and attitudes have affected them. They must look beyond North American counselling approaches and accept the fact that something can be learned from all ethnic and cultural groups.

1. In the third case, Frank W. believes empathy, respect, and genuineness are sufficient. What do you think?

2. In the last case, what should Susan do to increase her multicultural acceptance?

3. Should counsellors help people from minority groups learn the normative behaviour of majority groups? If so, how?

4. What are some ways in which counsellors can learn more about diverse cultures?

5. Should counsellors work with clients against whom they have some biases or prejudices (e.g., clients who are gay, lesbian, old, disabled, etc.)?

6. Would you encourage the use of "same culture" counsellors? For example, should schools that have a large number of Asian or Aboriginal students, have Asian or Aboriginal

counsellors for Asian or Aboriginal students?

B10 CONSULTING WITH OTHER PROFESSIONALS

Counsellors may consult with other professionally competent persons about the client. However, if the identity of the client is to be revealed, it is done with the written consent of the client. Counsellors choose professional consultants in a manner which will avoid placing the consultant in a conflict of interest situation.

Consultation With Consent (+)

David has been counselling Marty for several weeks without making much progress. He feels that Marty's home situation has much to do with his problems in school. David feels it would be beneficial if he consulted with another professional about Marty. David concludes that the social worker in the community would be a professionally competent person with whom to consult. David approaches Marty with his intentions of consulting with the social worker. Marty gives his consent to this, and David then consults with the social worker.

Consultation With Another Counsellor (+)

Janice has been counselling Miguel, a grade six student, for several sessions. Miguel and his mother recently moved to Canada to live with his aunt and uncle. Miguel likes his new home but he really misses his home and his family. School is very different for Miguel, and he is having some difficulty adjusting to this new environment. He has made no close contacts or friendships with other students. He maintains a distance between himself and others.

Janice is concerned about Miguel's situation. She has counselled others similar to Miguel before, but Miguel has made little progress and she feels she needs advice from someone more experienced in this field. Janice feels that it would be beneficial if she consulted with another professional who has more experience with immigrant children.

Murray is a very experienced counsellor who has done extensive counselling with recent immigrants. Janice feels that he would be able to give some evaluation and advice on Miguel's situation and her counselling action.

Janice approaches Murray to ask him if he would be willing to consult with her on one of her cases. Murray is willing to help. Janice explains Miguel's situation and her concerns to Murray. He gives Janice his opinions and ideas, and they discuss the situation. Miguel's identity is not revealed in this consultation.

Client Uninformed (−)

Through counselling sessions with Jamie W., Tanya, a junior high student, has shown some improvements in her attitudes toward school. As counselling continues, Tanya begins to disclose more, and she makes reference to her involvement in "hanging out" with high school age students and drinking and doing drugs. The counsellor feels that she should consult with Tanya's teacher concerning Tanya's situation. She feels that by consulting and collaborating with the teacher, she can get further insight into the Tanya's situation and devise a plan of action that would be more helpful.

Once Jamie W. decides that this consultation should be the next step, she goes immediately to the teacher to discuss Tanya's situation. Tanya is not made aware of this consultation, and does not consent to such action.

Uninvolved "Client" (–)

An English teacher in an urban high school contacts one of the school counsellors about the strange behaviour of one of her students. She also tells the counsellor that in a recent autobiographical paper that the student submitted, the student has written that it "would be wonderful not to be in this world anymore." Without stopping to talk to the student, the counsellor immediately contacts his department head, the school principal, and the parents of the student.

Comments and Questions

Consultation needs to be an integral part of counselling. Counsellors must realize their own attitudes and limitations in working with clients. Consulting with a professionally competent person can present new ideas and attitudes, and offer new ways of thinking to the counsellor. Often, when working with a problem in a certain manner, counsellors may not easily recognize another effective approach. Consultation can provide a varied array of approaches and ideas. Counsellors may also receive needed reinforcement, support, or evaluation of their ideas and practices through consultation.

Counsellors must remember that their primary obligation is to the client and any additional help from another professional may help the client.

It is crucial that when consulting another person, the counsellor maintain the highest ethical standards. In terms of ethical guidelines regarding consultation, the counsellor must not reveal the identity of the client unless the client is aware of the consultation.

1. Do you believe that written consent is necessary every time a counsellor wants to confer with another professional about an identified client?

2. What does a counsellor do if the client refuses consent for consultation?

3. Do you agree that with most consultation it is not necessary to reveal the name of the client?

4. How best can a counsellor avoid a conflict of interest situation when consulting with teachers?

5. What are some situations where a consultant can be put into a conflict of interest situation?

6. In the last case, *Uninvolved "Client"*, what should the counsellor have done?

B11 RELATIONSHIPS WITH FORMER CLIENTS

Counsellors remain accountable for any relationships established with former clients. Those relationships could include, but are not limited to those of a friendship, social, financial, and business nature. Counsellors exercise caution about entering any such relationships and take into account whether or not the issues and relational dynamics present during the counselling have been fully resolved and properly terminated. In any case, counsellors seek consultation on such decisions.

Business Opportunity (+)

Several weeks after Louise W.'s client suddenly terminates counselling, she receives a call inviting her to become involved in one of the businesses that her former client owns. The financial arrangements appear attractive, and Louise knows her former client is a wealthy, successful business woman. Louise politely rejects the offer since she feels that not all the counselling issues have been resolved.

Can't We Be Friends? (+)

Approximately a year after completing counselling with Alvin, George R. meets Alvin in a shopping mall. They strike up a conversation and since they are next to a coffee shop, decide to have coffee together. Both of them are ardent hockey fans and when Alvin says that he has four season tickets and one of the men in their group can't come to the next game, and would George be interested in coming to the game, George gladly accepts. Later on, George thinks about ethical guidelines related to seeing former clients, so he telephones a colleague to get his opinion regarding the invitation. Both agree the counselling of the past is no longer an issue and George's colleague supports his acceptance of the invitation to a hockey game.

After Hours (–)

After group counselling sessions, the group facilitator often goes for a few drinks with some of the members of the group. Invariably, discussions begin about some of the things that are happening in the group.

Personal Relationships (–)

Tanis H. is seeing a couple who are exploring the possibility of a marriage separation. After a few sessions, the woman stops coming to counselling, feeling she wants a marriage separation. Her husband, Eric, continues to see Tanis for counselling. Both Tanis and Eric soon realize that they have strong feelings for each other and Tanis stops the counselling relationship. A few weeks later, Tanis and Eric begin seeing each other socially.

Comments and Questions

It is wise to avoid potentially harmful relationships with former clients, but many relationships with former clients are not harmful or unethical. If a professor is very impressed with the research skills of a former graduate student, should it be unethical for the professor to hire the student to work on a research project? If counsellor and former client belong to the same tennis club, is it all right to strike up a friendship and go for coffee? If a former client is an electrician, is it ethical to hire him to do some electrical work? Most counsellors would find these relationships ethical. Counsellors should realize however, that it is difficult to discern when a past counselling relationship is no longer a factor. Consequently, it is important that counsellors seek consultation regarding decisions to have financial, social or other relationships with former clients.

1. Is it acceptable to establish social or sexual contact with a former client?

2. In *After Hours*, the group facilitator meets with some of the group members. What would make this situation acceptable?

3. Should individuals who have been clients always remain clients?

4. What guidelines would you establish regarding relationships with former clients?

5. With former clients, is there a difference among relationships that are financial, business, social or friendship?

6. In the case *Personal Relationships*, what does the *CCA Code of Ethics* state regarding the behaviour of Tanis and Eric?

B12 SEXUAL INTIMACIES

Counsellors avoid any type of sexual intimacies with clients and they do not counsel persons with whom they have had a sexual relationship. Counsellors do not engage in sexual intimacies with former clients within a minimum of three years after terminating the counselling relationship. This prohibition is not limited to the three year period but extends indefinitely if the client is clearly vulnerable, by reason of emotional or cognitive disorder, to exploitative influence by the counsellor. Counsellors, in all such circumstances, clearly bear the burden to ensure that no such exploitative influence has occurred, and to seek consultative assistance.

Counselling Relationship Explained (+)

Bryan A. is an employment counsellor at a large employment counselling centre. A woman, seeking to re-enter the workforce after having stayed home to raise three children, greatly appreciates the time and effort Bryan takes on her behalf. He spends many sessions with her, helping her to gain confidence in her ability to take on a job. Since the woman has recently left her husband, she feels she needs much emotional support. Thinking that Bryan A. is also attracted to her, she suggests they meet for dinner. Bryan, in a kind but firm way, explains that their meeting socially would interfere with their counselling relationship and that intimate behavior with clients is unethical.

Just Say No (+)

A female counsellor in a high school setting works regularly with a 17-year-old male student. During one session, the student places his hand on the counsellor's leg and leaves it there. The counsellor removes the student's hand, informs him that his action is inappro-

priate, and advises him that if it happens again she will have to terminate their counselling relationship and refer him to another counsellor in the school.

Boundaries I (–)

A male elementary school counsellor frequently gives his students pats on the back or hugs, recognizing how deprived of affection many of them are. One of his clients is an attractive, 13-year-old girl whose father has recently deserted the family. During one session, the girl breaks down and begins to cry. The counsellor attempts to comfort her and she ends up sitting on his lap as he strokes her back. Although the counsellor recognizes that he is being sexually stimulated by this contact, he does nothing to end it, and in fact encourages her to come back any time she needs a shoulder to cry on.

Boundaries II (–)

A male counsellor in private practice has a female client whose marriage has recently ended. He is seen to be a caring, compassionate counsellor who regularly holds clients' hands or gives hugs when he feels it is helpful. On one occasion with this client, the hug becomes more than simply an affectionate gesture. At present, although they have not engaged in actual intercourse, a certain amount of sexual activity is now a regular part of each counselling session. The therapist justifies his actions by claiming that the client is a consenting adult and that his attention to her physical needs is part of the healing process for her.

Comments and Questions

This ethical guideline is an absolute mandate for counsellors to avoid any type of sexual intimacy or sexual relationship with clients. It is important that counsellors recognize and accept that sexual attractions are human responses, but it is just as important that counsellors are aware of other options such as the following:

- modelling sensitive but non-exploitive behavior

- willingness to consult with colleagues

- recognizing and dealing with their own issues of sexuality

- recognizing the distinction between having sexual feelings and acting on them.

1. Does CCA need clearer standards banning potentially detrimental relationships? Clarify.

2. If you were aware that a counselling colleague was the male counsellor in **Boundaries I** and **Boundaries II**, what would you do?

3. What feelings or thoughts might be experienced by the client if you were sexually attracted to him/her?

4. What feelings or thoughts would you experience if a client were sexually attracted to you?

5. What approach would you take in either case?

6. What training would be helpful for you as a counsellor to assist you ethically in potential, sexually intimate situations?

B13 **MULTIPLE CLIENTS**
When counsellors agree to provide counselling to two or more persons who have a relationship (such as husband and wife, or parents and children), counsellors clarify at the outset which person or persons are clients and the nature of the rela-

tionship they will have with each person. If conflicting roles emerge for counsellors, they must clarify, adjust, or withdraw from roles appropriately.

Clarifying Goals (+)

Five counsellors working at a crisis clinic have a number of issues that seem to be getting in the way of a good working relationship. They decide to all see a counsellor-mediator to discuss their concerns. Since one of the five counsellors also works as a part-time director of the small counselling unit, the counsellor-mediator carefully established the goals and relationships at the beginning of the first session. All the counsellors, including the director, agree that they should be seen as five equal professionals in a crisis clinic.

Informed Consent (+)

A marriage and family counsellor, Wayne A., receives a request for counselling from Stuart. Stuart is married to Belinda and they have two children, aged eight and eleven years. Stuart tells Wayne that he thinks the many verbal fights he is having with his wife has got to stop, since the children appear to be affected by all the negativity in the home. He wants some counselling for the family, and since his wife believes all the fighting is his fault, will not come for counselling; but she does believe it would be a good idea for Stuart and the children to have some counselling. After some thought, Wayne calls Stuart and tells him he is willing to work with the family, and if he and the children agree, he will phone Belinda and will encourage her to come to one session where he will explain his typical process in family counselling. Wayne is prepared to work with Stuart and the children without Belinda.

A Family Divided (–)

A family therapist is working with a family consisting of the parents and three adolescent children. Not much progress is being made, since the three children feel that their parents will never change their autocratic, dictatorial ways of dealing with them. The therapist decides he can help matters by working separately with the children for a while, and helping them plan a strategy that he feels would get the parents to be "less bossy" with their children. He tells the children his plan will work best if the parents do not know about the strategy. He then calls the family together, but does not inform the parents of his strategy.

Taking Sides (–)

At the beginning of counselling, Bev outlines to the couple seeking marriage counselling that they will set goals together and that she feels her job is to help them decide what is best for them. As she listens to each partner share perspectives on the marriage, Bev cannot help feeling that the husband is the real villain in this marriage and that his wife has every reason to be very upset, and even desire to end the marriage. Bev does not share her feelings, but it is obvious that she begins to side almost exclusively to the woman's views on the marriage during the counselling sessions.

Comments and Questions

Many marriage and family counsellors are aware of additional issues when working with multiple clients, since the help given to one client may be non-helpful or even detrimental to the other client. Conflicting roles can readily appear when working with multiple clients and, as this guideline suggests, counsellors must take the time to clarify, modify, and adjust their roles. They need to have answers to questions such as the following:

- To whom do I have primary responsibility?

- What will I do if the goals of my multiple clients are different?

- Are family interests the most important, or the interests of individuals?

- What will I do if my values are very different from those of my multiple clients?

- Will I be able to keep from telling my clients how they should change?

1. Can the counselling goals be the same when working with multiple clients?

2. How do family counsellors deal with biases they might have regarding family life and child-rearing practices?

3. Can family and marriage counsellors be successful with others when their own commitment to marriage and family is not present?

4. What should Bev do in the *Taking Sides* case?

5. What should the counsellor have done in the *Family Divided* case?

6. Would you have counselled Stuart and his children in the case entitled *Informed Consent*?

B14 MULTIPLE HELPERS
If, after entering a counselling relationship, a counsellor discovers the client is already in a counselling relationship, the counsellor is responsible for discussing the issues related to continuing or terminating counselling with the client. It may be necessary, with client consent, to discuss these issues with the other helper.

Permission to Counsel (+)

Frank O. has been seeing a counsellor in private practice for several months. Frank decides to go back to university to finish the last year of his degree, a degree program that he interrupted for eight years. He learns of the counselling service at the university and sees a counsellor about some educational/career matters. When the university counsellor learns of Frank receiving counselling elsewhere, she says that she needs permission from the counsellor in private practice before she can continue counselling Frank. Frank agrees to this request and upon receiving permission, the university counsellor and Frank continue their counselling relationship.

Group and Individual Counselling (+)

Freyda asks a group leader about joining her confidence-building group. In the ensuing screening interview, the group leader learns that Freyda is currently under the care of a local psychiatrist. With Freyda's permission, the group leader contacts the psychiatrist regarding Freyda's request to join her group. The psychiatrist feels that the group experience may be very helpful to Freyda and encourages her entering the confidence-building group.

Counselling Plus (–)

Joan and Bob have been seeing a marriage counsellor for over six months. One day Joan learns from her good friend about a counsellor who is very good. Besides seeing the marriage counsellor with her husband Bob, Joan also begins seeing the counsellor, Joyce R., that her friend recommended. When Joyce R. learns that Joan is also seeing a marriage counsellor, she asks Joan for permission to discuss this dual counselling with the marriage counsellor. Joan tells Joyce that she does not want the other counsellor to know. She also tells Joyce how much she is gaining from their individual counselling sessions. Joyce decides to continue their counselling.

Two Counsellors For Bobby (–)

Bobby has been in trouble with the law regarding drug use, and his parents arrange for him to see a counsellor with experience working with adolescents who abuse drugs. Since Bobby is on the volleyball team, he establishes a close relationship with the coach who is also the school counsellor. Bobby begins seeing the school counsellor. Even though both counsellors are aware that they are both counselling Bobby, neither counsellor makes any attempt to discuss the issue of "two counsellors for Bobby".

Comments and Questions

It is important that counsellors do not work at cross purposes with a client. To help avoid any problems that might arise if two or more counsellors are working with the same client, it is vital that counsellors discuss issues related to multiple helpers. The client must give permission for counsellors to contact each other, and if this permission is not granted, counselling by at least one of the counsellors should be terminated.

1. What are some possible benefits of a client having multiple helpers?

2. What are some of the problems that can arise if a client is seeing two counsellors at the same time?

3. If both counsellors agree, should a client see two counsellors?

4. Many counsellors would see the Counselling Plus case as an ethical 'grey area'. What do you think?

5. Is it the counsellor's responsibility to ensure that her or his client is not receiving other counselling?

6. What would you do as a counsellor if you were convinced that you were helping a client; the client said that you were being helpful; the client did not want to stop seeing another helpful counsellor; you discussed the issues with the other "first" counsellor, and he insisted that you stop seeing his client?

B15 **GROUP WORK**
Counsellors have the responsibility to screen prospective group members, especially when group goals focus on self-understanding and growth through self-disclosure. Counsellors inform clients of group member rights, issues of confidentiality, and group techniques typically used. They take reasonable precautions to protect group members from physical and/or psychological harm resulting from interaction within the group, both during and following the group experience.

Screening Prospective Group Members (+)

A counsellor about to start a social skills group in her school meets with the students individually to talk with them about the goals and expectations of the group. During the screening interviews, the counsellor and one of the students, Elaine, discuss areas in which Elaine wishes to focus. It becomes evident that Elaine is having a major problem with another child also referred to the group. Elaine is reluctant to participate in the same group since she feels the conflict cannot be resolved at this time. Since several of these social skills groups are being facilitated by the counsellor, it is possible to separate these two students yet allow them both to experience group counselling. The counsellor arranges for the two students to be in separate groups.

Prior Screening (+)

Several weeks before the group begins to meet, the counsellor interviews each member individually. He determines why the prospective members want to be a part of the group, if they have ever been involved with a group before, and how they think this group will benefit them. On one occasion the counsellor is challenged by a potential group member regarding the need for a screening. The counsellor decides not to include this person in a group whose goals were self-understanding through self-disclosure.

Insufficient Screening (–)

A teacher refers a student, Susan, to a counselling group focused on building empathy and anger control. Susan is an extremely angry acting out student who has not learned to accept responsibility for her actions. Whenever she is in trouble, she diverts the blame elsewhere. Susan does not admit she has difficulty dealing with anger. Although a limited screening interview takes place prior to placement of the child in the group, no discussion regarding goals of the group takes place. Susan is unaware that she is expected to talk about her anger in this group setting. When she is confronted with her anger during one session, the results are traumatic for her and the other members of the group.

Group Follow-Up Counselling Needed (–)

Darren, a young boy in an elementary school, refuses to attend a counselling group after having a conflict with another member. The conflict arises after another boy in the group becomes extremely angry over home issues. He takes his anger out on Darren, who appears to come from a stable, caring environment. The group leader feels rejected by this Darren's refusal to come to the group. As a result, he ignores the child and does not arrange for counselling to assist him in dealing with the issues he is experiencing.

Comments and Questions

This ethical guideline denotes a responsibility for the counsellor to screen prospective group members, particularly when the group goals focus on self-understanding through self-disclosure, and for the counsellor to ensure that there is professional assistance available to any one who needs assistance both during and following the group session.

Group members should be informed of their responsibility when entering the group. These responsibilities might include taking risks, self-disclosure, giving and receiving feedback, and keeping confidentiality. Group members should be made aware of the possible advantages and disadvantages of participating in a group. They need to know the possible psychological risks and how the group might disrupt their lives. They need to be informed that often friends and families may not support the changes they make.

It is extremely important to ensure that there is professional assistance available during and following the group experience. Individual group members may need assistance coming to terms with painful issues resulting from the group process or other events in their lives. Sometimes these issues are of a highly complex and personal nature and it is not appropriate to deal with them in a group setting. Furthermore, upon conclusion of the group, referrals should be made when and if group members have issues they wish to discuss further.

1. What types of questions should be asked during a group screening interview?

2. What behaviours or comments in a screening interview would keep you from including a person in your group?

3. What type of professional assistance would you arrange if you were planning to lead a personal growth group?

4. What types of follow-up activities are needed for group members?

5. What are the special issues related to confidentiality when doing group work?

6. What are the issues related to group pressure, inappropriate self-disclosure and equal treatment of group members? Discuss.

B16 COMPUTER USE

When computer applications are used as a component of counselling services, counsellors ensure that: (a) client and counsellor identities are verified; (b) the client is capable of using the computer application; (c) the computer application is appropriate to the needs of the client; (d) the client understands the purpose and operation of client-assisted and/or self-help computer applications; and (e) a follow-up of client use of a computer application is provided to assist subsequent needs. In all cases, computer applications do not diminish the counsellor's responsibility to act in accordance with the CCA Code of Ethics, and in particular, to ensure adherence to the principles of confidentiality, informed consent, and safeguarding against harmful effects. (See also D5)

Computerized Career Information (+)

At one employment counselling centre, a computerized career information system is used to help clients make career decisions. The director of this centre insists that all counsellors are thoroughly familiar with the computer system, and that all clients receive at least an initial and follow-up session so that counsellors can both explain the computer counselling tool and can discuss the results with the clients afterwards.

High School Career Information (+)

At a large high school in a large city in Eastern Canada, all the students in their final year of high school are given the opportunity of spending an hour or more on the computer terminal and work with an interactive career information program designed to help them explore future career directions. The high school has a full-time guidance technician who assists the students with the computerized program. Following this session with the computer, all the students are scheduled for an appointment with one of the counsellors of their choice to make any additional plans regarding their possible career directions.

Open Computer Access (–)

In a small remote northern town, the area employment office is equipped with the latest in computer equipment. The manager makes sure that all the information on each client — biographical, work history, and counselling interview information — is stored in the computer. All of this data in the computer, including the counselling interview material, are accessible to all the staff members, including secretarial staff and clerks.

Emotional and Career Needs (–)

In a career counselling program designed to help middle-aged women (with limited education and formal work experience) enter or re-enter the world of work, one counselling outreach program has designed a program that consists mainly of computer interactions. Although some of the women are interested in "what the computer says", many others have other counselling needs that require attention prior to sitting in front of a computer terminal and examining career information.

Comments and Questions

As more and more use is being made of technology, particularly e-mail and the World Wide Web, a whole new set of ethical articles are needed in addition to the *CCA Code of Ethics* (See Appendix C for *The Practice of Internet Counseling, NBCC*). The information available on the Internet for both counsellors and clients can be overwhelming, and counsellors need to make clients aware of the fact that much of what is on the Internet is not controlled for quality or content. Recommended sites need to be reviewed regularly. Counsellors should also know that as computer applications become more sophisticated there is the danger that the "computer becomes the counselling", rather than a tool to help the counsellor help clients. Computer-ized career guidance programs must be restricted to those clients who can truly benefit from such programs. Besides making sure that clients fully understand computer applications, counsellors must guarantee that follow-up counselling is provided after clients use computerized counselling programs.

1. Do you feel that the ethical articles for Internet counselling from The National Board for Certified Counselors (See Appendix C) are adequate? Discuss.

2. How do counsellors typically determine whether computer applications are appropriate to the needs of the client?

3. What are the implications of computers and the Internet with reference to confidentiality, informed consent, and records?

4. In a school or employment counselling centre, should counsellors store interview data in the computer?

5. What data is appropriate to store in a counselling computer system?

6. How long should client information be stored in the computer?

B17 DELIVERY OF SERVICES BY TELEPHONE, TELECONFERENCING, AND INTERNET
Counsellors follow all additional ethical guidelines for services delivered by telephone, teleconferencing, and the Internet, including appropriate precautions regarding confidentiality, security, informed consent, records and counselling plans, as well as determining the right to provide such services in regulatory jurisdictions.

Preparing for Internet Counselling (+)

Florence H. has a Master's degree in counselling and is certified as a counsellor by the Canadian Counselling Association. Florence has two preschool children at home and decides to set up Internet counselling from her home, rather than going to an office that she shares with another counsellor at a counselling agency. Before letting her clients know about her new approach to counselling, Florence spends several months studying the ethical standards for counselling on the Internet, online record-keeping, site security regulations, counselling without visual and auditory cues, interpersonal issues, and the difficulties with relationship-building.

Providing Local Assistance (+)

Many of Jack's Internet clients live in other areas and Jack is concerned that not all of his clients will have an experienced and trained counsellor nearby who can provide crisis counselling if needed. Jack spends some time contacting counsellors in the same areas as each of his clients. As well, Jack ensures that each of his Internet counselling clients knows their local emergency telephone numbers and crisis telephone numbers.

Not Prepared for the Internet (–)
Hart J. is aware that the wireless router that he uses with his laptop computer makes confidentiality somewhat difficult. Hart is not familiar with encryption methods and so has unsecured communication on the Internet. Unfortunately, he does not have procedures in place regarding record-keeping and forwarding information on the Internet. Hart continues to work with eight to ten clients who ask for counselling via the Internet.

Unexpected e-mail Counselling (–)
Evelyn works as a counsellor for a large counselling agency. Since nearly all her clients have computer access, Evelyn encourages the clients to contact her via e-mail. Soon Evelyn finds that several clients are sending her lengthy personal messages. Not wanting to discourage the clients in any way, Evelyn responds to their very personal messages without first clarifying issues of confidentiality, record-keeping and informed consent.

Comments and Questions
In the last decade, much attention has been focused on standards for the ethical practice of Internet counselling. Both the American Counseling Association (ACA) and the National Board for Certified Counselors (NBCC) have ethical standard and articles governing ethical counselling on the Internet. NBCC recommends that Internet counsellors observe the following standards of practice:

- Verifying the identity of Internet clients through the use of code words or numbers.

- Clients who are minors need parental/guardian consent.

- Internet counsellors explain to clients how they can be reached when they are off-line and how frequently they check their e-mail messages.

- Internet counsellors explain to clients the possibility of technology failure and discuss alternative modes of communication.

- As part of the orientation process, Internet counsellors explain how to cope with potential misunderstandings when visual cues do not exist.

- Clients are informed of available local counsellors and emergency phone numbers.

- Clients are informed of free public access points for receiving assessment, information, and instructional resources.

- Internet counsellors have an obligation to make their website a barrier-free environment for clients with disabilities.

- Internet counsellors are aware of diversity in culture and language.

- Encryption methods should be used whenever possible.

- Internet counsellors inform clients of their record-keeping procedures.

- Internet counsellors follow appropriate procedures regarding the release of information.

- Internet counsellors review pertinent legal and ethical codes on the practice of Internet counselling and supervision.

- The Internet counsellor's website provides links to websites of all appropriate certification bodies (e.g. Canadian Counsellor Association) to facilitate consumer protection.

1. Can a trusting relationship be built between an Internet counsellor and client? Discuss.

2. Should minors (with parental/guardian permission) be permitted to use Web-based counselling?

3. Should counsellors such as Hart J. (*Not Prepared for the Internet*) be cited for ethical violations and have their certification suspended?

4. Internet counsellors increase accessibility of counselling services for many people, yet many client messages can be missed with Internet counselling. Do you see Internet counselling as "second best" counselling?

5. Should all Internet counsellors in Canada be required to have Canadian counsellor certification (CCC) before being allowed to do Web counselling?

6. The majority of Web counselling sites do not last very long. Why do you believe this is the case?

B18 **REFERRAL**
When counsellors determine their inability to be of professional assistance to clients, they avoid initiating a counselling relationship, or immediately terminate it. In either event, members suggest appropriate alternatives, including making a referral to resources about which they are knowledgeable. Should clients decline the suggested referral, counsellors are not obligated to continue the relationship.

Aggressive Client (+)

A counsellor has had four sessions with a client. With each succeeding session the client becomes more aggressive, hostile and verbally abusive towards the counsellor. The counsellor decides to terminate the counselling relationship after the client refuses to cease the verbal abuse directed toward the counsellor. The counsellor suggests further expertise is required and offers to make a referral. The client agrees and the case is appropriately referred.

Intoxicated Client (+)

A counsellor is working with a client concerning alcohol dependency. It becomes apparent after three sessions that the client attends the counselling sessions intoxicated. The counsellor informs the client he cannot work with his client under these conditions, but recommends a referral to an agency skilled in the area of alcohol abuse. The client refuses to accept the referral. The counsellor then explains he must terminate the relationship and follows through with this decision.

Referral Refused (–)

After counselling a client for several months concerning issues of intense grief, loss, and abandonment, the counsellor decides that she can be of little further help and recommends that the client receive intense grief therapy with a specialist in this area. After discussing this decision with her client, the client refuses the suggestion and states that she views this recommendation as further rejection and abandonment. She reproaches the counsellor for even suggesting a referral. The counsellor, not wishing to upset her client any further, forgets the referral and continues working with her client.

Unresolved Counsellor Issues (–)

A counsellor who is recently separated carries unresolved marital issues and over-identifies with a recently separated client. The counsellor is unable to be objective and is not performing her role competently. There is no clear differentiation of boundaries between client and counsellor. The counsellor continues the therapeutic relationship despite the circumstances.

Comments and Questions

This ethical guideline provides a clear mandate for counsellors to recognize their own boundaries of professional competence and personal limitations. It is necessary for counsellors to keep in mind that their primary obligation is to the client. Counsellors must maintain a relationship with the client only if it is beneficial to the client. Being always accountable to the client, counsellors must at all times evaluate their own abilities as counsellors. When and if counsellors are in situations where they lack competence, they must recognize this and refer the client to a specialist or terminate the therapy. Counsellors should be aware of the services and resources in their community in order to refer clients when necessary. Counsellors should also be aware of their own abilities and limitations and share their struggles with their supervisors and colleagues. Most importantly, they should realize that referring clients or terminating therapy when necessary is sound judgment. Ethically, members must admit to themselves and to their clients when they are not competent to continue the therapy. When the client refuses the referral or termination, the counsellor is still obligated to terminate the relationship. This guideline makes counsellors accountable to clients and to themselves. Continual self-awareness is the key to effective counselling.

1. How can counsellors be sure that they are not referring clients to other services too soon? Should counsellors "hang in there" a little longer than the client expects them to?

2. How can a counsellor know when to terminate counselling?

3. Would you continue counselling a client if he or she refused your referral?

4. Is counselling that does not seem to be accomplishing anything better than no counselling at all? (See *Referral Refused*).

5. How can counsellors determine if they are being of "professional assistance"?

6. What should the counsellor have done in the case entitled *Unresolved Counsellor Issues*?

B19 TERMINATION OF COUNSELLING
Counsellors terminate counselling relationships, with client agreement whenever possible, when it is reasonably clear that: the goals of counselling have been met, the client is no longer benefiting from counselling, the client does not pay fees charged, previously disclosed agency or institutional limits do not allow for the provision of further counselling services, and the client or another person with whom the client has a relationship threatens or otherwise endangers the counsellor. However, counsellors make reasonable efforts to facilitate the continued access to counselling services when services are interrupted by these factors and by counsellor illness, client or counsellor relocation, client financial difficulties and so forth.

Awareness of Skills (+)

A client that a counsellor has been counselling regarding the death of a parent discloses that he is drinking heavily and realizes that it is a problem that is getting worse. Upon discussion with the client, the counsellor and client agree that referral to Alcoholics Anonymous would be advisable in order to monitor his progress in this area, and to join a support group.

Strong Personal Bias (+)

A teenager comes for counselling and discloses that she is pregnant and wants an abortion. After discussion with the client, the counsellor refers the girl to a pregnancy information centre due to strong pro-choice feelings on the part of the counsellor and the inability to be objective in her professional assistance.

Referral Required (–)

A family counsellor has just moved to a new city and joined a family counselling centre. He has worked with a client for several sessions when he learns of the client's problems of dealing with alcohol abuse in her family. The family counsellor, unaware of an excellent alcohol counselling program in the city, continues the counselling, despite his total inexperience with addictions counselling.

Suicidal Tendencies (–)

Kayla T. has just graduated with a Master's degree in counselling psychology. Her total counselling experience consists of an eight-month field experience in an elementary school, working with an elementary school counsellor. Kayla joins a three-person counselling service and begins her private practice.

One of her first clients is a young man who tells her of his "useless life", his feelings of "hopelessness", and his envy for his cousin who has recently committed suicide. Kayla, in her zeal to begin counselling, never questions her own ability to help her client, despite her total lack of training in helping suicidal clients. She continues her once-a-week, Rogerian-like sessions, and after the third session she learns that her client has had an unsuccessful suicide attempt.

Comments and Questions

As stated in the first guideline in this section, "counsellors have a primary responsibility to respect the integrity and promote the welfare of their clients." This means that counsellors want clients to function without their help and, thus, when it appears that the clients' goals have been met, counselling will be discontinued. This guideline also states that when the client is no longer benefiting from counselling, counsellors will terminate counselling, or will make efforts to have counselling or other services continue with other professionals.

This guideline also encourages counselling professionals to make every effort to have counselling continue for clients if they are relocated, cannot counsel due to illness, or when clients do not maintain their financial obligations.

1. How can counsellors know if the goals of counselling have been met if they are using counselling approaches that are less cognitive and behavioural?

2. How would you determine if a client is no longer benefiting from your counselling?

3. Would you discontinue counselling for a client who has not paid her or his counselling fees for the last two sessions? Explain.

4. What do you think about the policy of some employee assistance programs that do not allow for more than four to six sessions of counselling?

5. Do most counsellors terminate counselling when research suggests other services may be superior to individual counselling (for example, Alcoholics Anonymous has been shown to be more beneficial than one-on-one counselling)?

6. In the case **Strong Personal Bias**, do counsellors need to refer clients if they are open to clients about their biases? Discuss.

Chapter Ten

---------- ❖ ----------

Case Studies in
Consulting and
Private Practice

---------- ❖ ----------

Counselling is a professional business and
as such is governed by legal and ethical regulations. Counsellors, both in private practice
and as consultants, need to be aware of their
additional responsibilities in relationship to
advertising, contracts and business.

Canadian Counselling Association Code of Ethics

Ethical Guidelines for Consulting and Private Practice

C1 GENERAL RESPONSIBILITY
Counsellors provide consultative services only in those areas in which they have demonstrated competency by virtue of their education and experience.

C2 UNDIMINISHED RESPONSIBILITY AND LIABILITY
Counsellors who work in private practice, whether incorporated or not, must ensure that there is no diminishing of their individual professional responsibility to act in accordance with the *CCA Code of Ethics*, or in their liability for any failure to do so.

C3 ACCURATE ADVERTISING
Counsellors, when advertising services as private practitioners, do so in a manner that accurately and clearly informs the public of their services and areas of expertise.

C4 CONSULTATIVE RELATIONSHIPS
Counsellors ensure that consultation occurs within a voluntary relationship between a counsellor and a help-seeking individual, group, or organization, and that the goals are understood by all parties concerned.

C5 INFORMED CONSENT
Counsellors who provide services for the use of third parties, acknowledge and clarify for the informed consent of clients, all obligations of such multiple relationships, including purpose(s), entitlement to information, and any restrictions on confidentiality. Third parties include: courts, public and private institutions, funding agencies, employees, and so forth.

C6 RESPECT FOR PRIVACY
Counsellors limit any discussion of client information obtained from a consulting relationship to persons clearly involved with the case. Any written and oral reports restrict data to the purposes of the consultation and, every effort is made to protect client identity and to avoid undue invasion of privacy.

C7 CONFLICT OF INTEREST
Counsellors who engage in consultation avoid circumstances where the duality of relationships, or the prior possession of information could lead to a conflict of interest.

C8 SPONSORSHIP AND RECRUITMENT
Counsellors present any of their organizational affiliations or membership in such a way as to avoid misunderstanding regarding sponsorship or certification. They also avoid the use of any institutional affiliation to recruit private practice clients

Case Studies for Consulting and Private Practice

C1 GENERAL RESPONSIBILITY
Counsellors provide consultative services only in those areas in which they have demonstrated competency by virtue of their education and experience.

Referral Resources (+)
John S., a member of a small consulting firm, is asked to help a large electrical and electronics wholesaler with a research project that demands both knowledge of complex statistical procedures and an understanding of a number of standardized group tests. John S., who is quite knowledgeable in the area of testing, accepts the job with the provision that he will be using the statistical expertise and computer software of another consulting firm.

Skill Awareness (+)
Joan S., a career consultant, has many contacts in business and industry. She is asked to be a consultant for a firm owned by a good friend of hers. The work is mainly in conflict management. Ms. S. informs her friend that although her knowledge of career counselling and consulting has made her familiar with conflict management, she does not feel that she has enough expertise in the area to take on this job.

Mediation Services (-)
Nolan H. sees an advertisement on learning about mediation skills. He attends the two-weekend workshop and feels he has some understanding of mediation. He plans to take a practicum in the area of mediation and conflict resolution in the near future. Before he can do this, he is contacted by a large insurance company (for whom he has done consulting work in career decision-making in the past) to help management and workers establish a program for mediation of disputes. Nolan takes the consulting contract, feeling this would give him much needed experience in mediation.

Lacking Resource Knowledge (-)
A counsellor/consultant moves to a new city and opens a one-person counselling and consulting firm. Because of past associations with several national firms, he is able to obtain a lucrative consulting contract from one of the firms. Much of the work consists of community liaison, and knowledge of community resources is a definite asset to any consultant taking on this job. The consultant, although new to the city, feels he would quickly learn about available resources and makes no mention of his limited knowledge of the

city's community resources.

Comments and Questions
The first case illustrating this ethical guideline shows a consultant who is aware of his own competencies (in this case, a knowledge of tests), who is not at all reluctant to admit to his limited resources in computer software for statistical analysis, and who is willing to use the expertise of another firm that has the appropriate resources. Consultants may have a great deal of expertise in many areas, but few consultants can be knowledgeable in all areas related to counselling. It is sound practice for consultants to admit shortcomings, but also to look for further education and supervision as they develop additional areas of expertise.

1. In the *Mediation Services* case presented, what can the consultant do to make her or his consulting contract more ethical?

2. Is "on the job" training acceptable for consultants?

3. Is it appropriate for consultants to accept contracts from former employers?

4. How should consultants advertise their skills or competencies?

5. Will it be seen as a shortcoming if and when a consultant uses the services of other consultants?

6. The cultural context in which consultation takes place is very important. How should a consultant balance the norms of mainstream society with the cultural norms of consultees?

C2 UNDIMINISHED RESPONSIBILITY AND LIABILITY
Counsellors who work in private practice, whether incorporated or not, must ensure that there is no diminishing of their individual professional responsibility to act in accordance with the *CCA Code of Ethics*, or in their liability for any failure to do so.

Values Awareness (+)
Joseph O., a consultant in a large Canadian city, is approached to help a provincial agency make decisions regarding funding for several pregnancy information organizations. Joseph is very aware of his values regarding abortion and other issues, and feels his strong Pro Life stance would get in the way of being fair to organizations appealing for funds for abortion counselling. He does not take the job.

Getting Set (+)
Richard retires from his job as a counsellor with a mental health agency, and decides to see clients privately in his home. He checks the zoning by-laws with the city, and purchases the necessary license to operate. He also purchases liability insurance, and a locking filing cabinet for client files. He ensures that clients have a private waiting room off the main entrance where they will not be readily seen by clients who are leaving. He prepares informed consent forms listing the ethical and legal exceptions to confidentiality and his fee schedule, consent forms for the release of information (for cases that may require consultation with other professionals), and an information sheet on how client information will be kept secure and how clients can access their personal information. Richard contacts professionals in his community with whom he can consult, when necessary,

about challenging cases within his area of expertise.

No Respect for Privacy (–)

Francis A., a member of CCA, has recently started to take on consulting work in addition to his small, one-person private counselling business. One of his consulting contracts includes of his writing a detailed report on how an in-house counsellor might benefit workers and management. Francis interviews dozens of workers and management staff and learns about concerns and issues. He learns about the people who are receiving counselling. In his report to management, Francis provides detailed information, including some of the names of people receiving counselling. Management shares the details of the report with all workers.

Unprofessional practice (–)

Dan leaves his job as a child and youth counsellor to open a private practice. One of the things Dan disliked the most about his prior job was the bureaucracy and red tape, which he felt constrained him in his work. Dan wants a more relaxed approach, so he doesn't use informed consent forms, doesn't have a fee schedule, and doesn't issue receipts to clients. Generally, Dan thinks that "being his own boss" means he can run his private practice with very little in the way of structure and protocol.

Comments and Questions

Not all Canadian provinces have legislation that allows counsellors and consultants to incorporate. In fact, in 2005 most provinces did not have such provisions. The *Standards of Practice for Counsellors* (CCA, 2001) provides some advice for CCA counsellors establishing a private counselling/consulting agency:

- CCA members must abide by the articles of the *CCA Code of Ethics* and *Standards of Practice for Counsellors*.

- The employment arrangements should be with the individual counsellor rather than the agency.

- It is up to the CCA member to ensure that the employer does not act in any way to limit a member's professional responsibility and liability to counselling services.

- CCA members respect privacy and limit discussion of client information obtained from a consulting relationship to persons clearly involved with the case. Written and oral reports should protect client identity.

1. Should professional liability insurance available to CCA members be made to individuals or to the consulting agency?

2. Should liability insurance for counsellors in private practice be higher than for counsellors working for agencies, schools or institutions?

3. Is it ethical for consultants to take contracts for work they do not know much about, but hope to prepare by contacting other professionals with expertise in the required area?

4. Who is liable for counsellors or consultants working for a large organization with many counsellors and/or consultants?

5. Should all consultants be required to be members in a professional organization like CCA?

6. What can be done in the last two cases to change the unethical behaviour to ethical behaviour?

C3 ACCURATE ADVERTISING
Counsellors, when advertising services as private practitioners, do so in a manner that accurately and clearly informs the public of their services and areas of expertise.

Business Card (+)
A recent graduate from a doctoral program in general and family counselling establishes his own private counselling service. After joining CCA, he applies for Canadian Counsellor Certification and is accepted. His business card read as follows:

John Smith, Ph.D.
Canadian Certified Counsellor
111 Chestnut Road (204) 555-4567
(residence)
Winnipeg, Manitoba (204) 555-4321
(business)
personal counselling
family counselling

Private Practitioner (+)
A private practitioner receives a Master's degree in counselling psychology, and has specialized in family counselling. Both in his advertising and his informed consent forms, he carefully points out that typical counselling sessions would consist of relationship building, discussion of concerns, decision-making, and formulating plans of action.

False Advertising (–)
A counsellor in private practice has received her Master's degree from a Faculty of Education in the Department of Educational Psychology. Many of the courses she has taken in her Master's program are in school counselling. In her advertising for her private counselling services in the Business Telephone Directory, she indicates that her degree is in Counselling Psychology. The Faculty of Education that she graduated from offers no degree in counselling psychology.

Deceptive Advertising (–)
A recent advertisement in a paper reads, in part, as follows:

...trained counsellor specializing in family counselling...

This counsellor has received a degree in theology from a non-accredited university and his counsellor training consists of a weekend workshop on "family reconstruction."

Comments and Questions
The gist of this ethical guideline is that members accurately inform the public of their "services, expertise and techniques of counselling." Too often, the expertise of the member is glowingly described or implied through the listing of paper credentials, but the detailed description of services and techniques are neglected.

The *Standards of Practice for Counsellors* (CCA, 2001) provides additional guidelines for advertising in private practice. Counsellors should not use testimonials by clients or former clients, or by relatives or friends of clients, or former clients. Testimonials from organizations or businesses may be acceptable. Counsellors should state their professional services in a straightforward way, avoiding jargon and embellishment of training and experience.

Counsellors may participate in advertisements for publications of which the counsellor is an author or editor, and in other publications of which the counsellor is a reviewer. Except for advertising their own professional services, counsellors do participate in advertising that, either directly or implicitly, suggests they are endorsing a particular product brand name for use in the provision of counselling services. Finally, counsellors do not permit their name to be associated with other advertising in such a way that it is implied that the counsellor's professional expertise or professional status is relevant to the service or product being advertised.

1. What are some examples of misleading advertising of counsellor services of which that you are aware?

2. What is your responsibility once you become aware of misleading or false advertising of counsellor services?

3. How should counsellors advertise their "techniques of counselling"?

4. Since so much of advertising exaggerates positives, can we expect counsellors to inform accurately or realistically?

5. Should counsellors advertise the fact that they are members of professional organizations such as CCA?

6. Should counsellors advertise that they have Canadian certification (CCC) and what that means?

C4 CONSULTATIVE RELATIONSHIPS Counsellors ensure that consultation occurs within a voluntary relationship between a counsellor and a help-seeking individual, group, or organization, and that the goals are understood by all parties concerned.

Collaborative Action (+)
A guidance and counselling coordinator in a British Columbia school district has been asked by the principal in another school district to help the counsellors in his school reorganize a guidance and counselling program that meets the needs of students, teachers, parents and administrators. The coordinator meets with students, teachers, parents and administrators and then verifies the goals and techniques with the principal to confirm continuing support. He then begins the work of reorganizing the program, making sure that counsellors, parents, teachers, administrators and students are consulted.

Group Leadership Skills (+)
Human Resources Development Canada begins a long-term program in which all their employment counsellors are trained in group leadership skills. The final goal is to have personnel from within the organization provide the training to other employment counsellors. Several university counsellor-educators are hired as consultants over the initial years to work with Human Resources to get the project under way and to provide the preliminary group leadership training. After a few years, the training program is well established and the consultants are no longer directly involved.

Further Consulting Offered (–)
A counsellor/consultant is hired to help prepare counsellors to organize and to train students in their schools for peer-helper programs. After a two-week program, the consultant indicates that his services are available to each of the participants in the program to help them actually start peer-helper programs in the schools. The consultant explains that his years of experience are needed to start the programs effectively. The counsellors had been led to believe that the two-week program would prepare

them to do the organizing of the peer-helper programs by themselves.

Ready for Self-Direction (–)

A consultant is hired by an employment agency to help employment counsellors with the skills of conflict management. The participants are eager and skilful counsellors and after a few days of professional development appear ready to use their newly developed skills. The consultant, knowing she is being paid a per diem of $500 per day, decides to spend another five days of professional development with the employment counsellors, repeating much of the same material.

Comments and Questions

In this guideline, counsellors are reminded that consultative relationships are voluntary and that the goals established should be fully understood by all participants. It is important that all the people involved in a consultative relationship have the opportunity to ask any questions, and have all pertinent information given to them in language they can fully understand, so that informed decisions can be made by all. Generally, goals, aspects of the relationship, and limits relating to confidentiality will be put in writing.

1. How could the duality of relationships interfere with a consultative relationship?

2. How can consultants ensure that all participants are involved voluntarily?

3. What happens when there is a disagreement regarding the goals among participants?

4. Should the interventions that the consultant may use be approved by the participants?

5. Discuss how you would deal with the case *Further Consulting Offered*.

6. What should the consultant have done in *Ready for Self-Direction*?

C5 | **INFORMED CONSENT**
Counsellors who provide services for the use of third parties, acknowledge and clarify for the informed consent of clients, all obligations of such multiple relationships, including purpose(s), entitlement to information, and any restrictions on confidentiality. Third parties include: courts, public and private institutions, funding agencies, employees, and so forth.

Directives to the Consultant (+)

A large company has counselling services for their employees, and they most frequently use the services of one consulting counsellor, Norman A.. The company is having real difficulty with one employee who frequently gets into arguments with his co-workers. The manager of this employee phones Norman A. and strongly suggests to him that he see the employee for counselling and to encourage him to seek a job elsewhere. Norman A. realizes that the possible client has not received sufficient information and he informs the manager that he would be violating his code of ethics regarding services for a third party by not informing him of the goals and/or purposes of the counselling.

Confidentiality (+)

A psychologist is hired by Human Resources Development, Canada to provide education and training for any employees who are experiencing "burn out" or stress on the job. The psychologist informed all the participants that he would be reporting back to management any aspects of their work that they feel contribute to their burn out or stress. He also informs the participants that he will describe the stressful situations but that no names will be revealed to management. The psychologist also explains these conditions to management.

Consultant's Report (–)

A consultant who is eager for additional business has been asked by a school board to make recommendations for several schools that are renovating classrooms into guidance and counselling areas, with individual offices for counsellors, and a waiting room/resource area for students. The consultant, who is very familiar with guidance and counselling areas, draws up a tentative plan, but then asks building consultants for their advice regarding structure, lighting and heating. The building consultants indicate that building codes have changed and there would be many additional costs if the whole area is brought to present day electrical standards. The consultant talks to the school superintendent about this. The consultant agrees not to mention the coding deficiencies in his report, after the superintendent assures him that their divisional electricians would look after things.

Not Enough Consulting (–)

A consultant's report shows her recommendations for a good counselling area design for a number of employment counsellors working in a career centre. She has been hired to design the area after counsellors asked their manager to address problems with the current design. The consultant listens to the manager's ideas but does not arrange any meetings with the counsellors

before submitting her report.

Comments and Questions

When counsellors act as consultants to third parties, they must remember that obtaining informed consent from all people involved is a basic right of third parties. Sometimes it is difficult to anticipate all the goals, procedures, relationships and restrictions that might arise, but with thorough, careful planning many of the obligations of informing third parties can be met.

Consultants working with third parties can be put into conflict with issues of confidentiality. The degrees or limits of confidentiality must be discussed beforehand. There must be protection for participants, and there may be times when it is not the best practice to say that everyone involved should receive feedback.

1. When would a consultant likely limit her or his feedback to all participants?

2. Are there times when informed consent is not needed?

3. How can consultants deal most effectively with differences in status and power among participants?

4. Is a consultant ever justified in trying to change the people who hired her or him?

5. What are the special conditions of informed consent as it pertains to the courts and funding agencies?

6. Should consultants attempt to encourage management (the management that hired them) to share all the results of their final reports? Discuss.

C6 RESPECT FOR PRIVACY
Counsellors limit any discussion of client information obtained from a consulting relationship to persons clearly involved with the case. Any written and oral reports restrict data to the purposes of the consultation and, every effort is made to protect client identity and to avoid undue invasion of privacy.

Conscientious Consultant (+)

Terry is a trauma counsellor who has been contracted by a school district to do some trauma counselling with students after a shooting incident at a high school. Terry is given a small office in which to see individual students privately. She makes it clear to students before they begin that a summary of their work together will be forwarded to the school counselling office, but that no one other than the counsellors will have access to it. When Terry writes her summary reports after sessions, she includes only those details relevant to the incident.

Confidential Consulting (+)

Sam is hired to do conflict resolution work with the staff and management of a local company. After completing the contract, Sam asks whether he can list the company name on his curriculum vitae. Sam is told that the company would prefer to not have it known that they hired someone to do conflict resolution work with them, and they would prefer not to be included on his list. Sam respects their wishes.

Idle Speculation (–)

Alex is hired as a consultant to work with the management of a private business college to improve their communication and active listening skills. On the second day of the workshop, Alex is having lunch with a member of the teaching staff who expresses interest in the workshop. The person begins to speculate about which management members would have the most difficulty learning the communications skills and asks for Alex's opinion. Alex says he can't go into detail, but that the teacher's guesses are "very accurate."

Invasion of Privacy (–)

Heather is hired to do a workshop on stress management for the staff of a local company. In a discussion about the stresses of parenting, one participant announces that she and her husband are ending their marriage and that she is finding their discussions of custody very stressful. Without asking the participant's permission, Heather makes a point of taking a member of the management aside after the workshop to tell her about the pending divorce, in case the woman needs "extra support through her difficult time."

Comments and Questions

This ethical guideline, much like the guidelines on confidentiality, clearly states that counsellors and consultants need to keep client information private. Counsellors and consultants are encouraged to adapt existing guidelines on privacy to their own practice. The 1995 *Canadian Standards Association's Model Code for the Protection of Personal Information* consists of ten principles related to privacy:

- Accountability
- Identifying purposes
- Consent
- Limiting Collection
- Limiting Use
- Accuracy
- Safeguards

- Openness
- Individual Access
- Challenging Compliance

1. Is there a "grey area" between counsellors talking about clients with other professionals over coffee and when they make a more formal consultation request?

2. In the case *Confidential Consulting*, is it ethical for Sam to tell possible future clients that he has done consulting work for the "local company"?

3. Should Alex (*Idle Speculation*) be censored for his comments? What would you say to Alex?

4. In *Invasion of Privacy*, Heather wants to be helpful. Do her obvious attempts to be helpful supercede the "participant's" right to privacy?

5. Where and when in your counselling organization is privacy not always observed?

6. Are there some additional principles related to privacy that you would add? Discuss.

C7 CONFLICT OF INTEREST
Counsellors who engage in consultation avoid circumstances where the duality of relationships, or the prior possession of information could lead to a conflict of interest.

Avoiding Conflicts of Interest (+)

A counsellor-consultant with a small but thriving practice is also a member of the local school board. The board decides to offer leadership training for all administrators in the school board. The counsellor-consultant, who has offered similar types of workshops throughout the province, excuses himself from the board meeting while any discussions or decisions are made regarding who will provide the leadership training.

Avoiding Dual Relationships (+)

Samuel P. is a consultant who has experience helping personnel deal with on-the-job stress. While working with a large firm, he realizes that much of the stress for some of the workers comes from personal problems at home. Samuel recommends individual and group counselling would be helpful for many of the stressed workers. He does not suggest in any way that his counselling/consulting agency be given the contract for this suggested counselling.

Recruiting Clients (–)

A consultant is hired by a university to offer a counselling skills course for the Continuing Education Division of the university. Students are strongly encouraged to seek their own counselling in order to experience the feelings clients might have. The part-time instructor is also a partner in a private counselling service and suggests that the practicum students might wish to receive counselling at his counselling service. He would see to it that his partners would offer students favourable counselling fees.

Dual Role (–)

A counselling foundation receives a large contribution. Part of the money is to be used to offer career development workshops throughout Canada. One member of the foundation board knows about this requirement and without letting others know, takes on the work himself.

Comments and Questions

More ethical guidelines are needed for consultants since they work in many different areas and are affiliated with a wide range of professional organizations (or none at all). Consultants must be particularly careful regarding multicultural considerations and the varying expectations from clients related to consultants' roles. As well, consultants are often seen as having more power, and they must be careful that they develop independence in clients rather than dependence.

Conflicts of interest also arise when there are hidden agendas or dual relationships. For example, when a consultant is hired by the manager of a firm to improve relationships among staff, but then asks the consultant after the workshops to supply the names of the employees who seem to be detrimental to his firm's climate. All of these potential problems underscore the importance of confidentiality and informed consent in consulting.

1. In the case *Avoiding Conflicts of Interest*, should the consultant accept a contract if the board offered him one?

2. In *Avoiding Dual Relationships*, the consultant does not steer counselling to his own firm. Would it be ethical for him to suggest that he would like his agency to be considered if individual and group counselling were initiated for the workers?

3. What are some ways that the power imbalance between consultant and client can be diminished?

4. Where might you experience a conflict of interest if you were asked to

be a consultant?

5. How could the conflict outlined in *Recruiting Clients* be resolved?

6. What elements would you include in an informed consent form to help avoid conflict of interest situations?

C8 SPONSORSHIP AND RECRUITMENT
Counsellors present any of their organizational affiliations or membership in such a way as to avoid misunderstanding regarding sponsorship or certification. They also avoid the use of any institutional affiliation to recruit private practice clients

---

Non-Faculty Member (+)

A counselling consultant, who has a four-person consulting firm, frequently teaches courses at a nearby university. Even though the consultant is frequently introduced as teaching at the university, she quickly clarifies by saying she has her own consulting firm, has on occasion taught a course for the university, but is not a faculty member at the university.

CCA Member Only (+)

Bob R., a counsellor in a rural high school, becomes a member of the Canadian Counselling Association. At a divisional meeting of counsellors, where counsellor certification is being discussed, most of the counsellors assume Bob is certified since he has been accepted for membership by CCA. Bob points out that he is only a member of CCA and has not applied for counsellor certification through CCA.

Recruitment (–)

One university uses a number of supervisors in the field to help them with their counselling practica. This practice has worked well. However, when the counselling department becomes accredited by CCA, the hours of supervision need to be increased. The counselling department decides to charge students for extra supervision and provides a list of supervisors willing to do extra supervision. One supervisor, knowing of this plan, writes a letter to counselling students offering his services at a reduced rate.

Misleading Business Cards (–)

Tom A., a counsellor in a high school, is hired by the university in his city to teach a summer school course for beginning counsellors. While at the university, he has a thousand business cards created with the university logo. He feels this university affiliation will help him in future consulting and counselling work.

Comments and Questions

It is obvious that in the case of Tom A. and his *Misleading Business Cards*, little or no attention is paid to important guidelines in advertising counselling services. Advertising should not imply full association with an established organization when someone is hired only to work for a short period of time for an organization. Many members of the public do not understand that membership in a professional organization does not mean that the member is skilled or certified as a counsellor. Using CCA on a business card is unethical if it is intended to imply endorsement as a counsellor. Canadian Counsellor Certification (CCC) was established to show that an individual meets certain graduate training criteria, and the designation "CCC" can be used on business cards and letterhead.

1. Should business cards be reviewed by a lawyer to ensure accuracy in advertising counselling services?

2. Should business cards be reviewed by the CCA Ethics Committee?

3. Can you provide some examples of inaccurate sponsorship?

4. Is there a "fine line" between being a member of a university and recruiting clients for private practice (as in the *Recruitment Case*)?

5. Should counsellor-educators at universities involved in practicum supervision have their own private counselling practice?

6. How can consultants best avoid any implied affiliation with a professional organization or an institution?

Chapter Eleven

❖

Case Studies in Evaluation and Assessment

❖

In the articles and cases presented in this chapter, counsellors are encouraged to familiarize themselves with proper test administration and interpretation procedures.

Canadian Counselling Association Code of Ethics

Ethical Guidelines for Evaluation and Assessment

D1 GENERAL ORIENTATION
Counsellors adequately orient and inform clients so that evaluation and assessment results can be placed in proper perspective along with other relevant information.

D2 PURPOSES AND RESULTS OF EVALUATION AND ASSESSMENT
Counsellors take responsibility to inform clients about the purpose of any evaluation and assessment instruments and procedures and the meaning of evaluation and assessment results.

D3 EVALUATION AND ASSESSMENT COMPETENCE
Counsellors recognize the limits of their competence and offer only those evaluation and assessment services for which they have appropriate preparation and which meet established professional standards.

D4 ADMINISTRATIVE AND SUPERVISORY CONDITIONS
Counsellors ensure that evaluation and assessment instruments and procedures are administered and supervised under established conditions consistent with professional standards. They note any departures from standard conditions and any unusual behaviour or irregularities which may affect the interpretation of results.

D5 USE OF TECHNOLOGY
Counsellors recognize that their ethical responsibilities are not altered, or in any way diminished, by the use of technology for the administration of evaluation and assessment instruments. Counsellors retain their responsibility for the maintenance of the ethical principles of privacy, confidentiality, and responsibility for decisions regardless of the technology used.

D6 APPROPRIATENESS OF EVALUATION AND ASSESSMENT
Counsellors ensure that evaluation and assessment instruments and procedures are valid, reliable, and appropriate to both the client and the intended purposes.

D7 REPORTING EVALUATION AND ASSESSMENT RESULTS
Counsellors ensure that when reporting evaluation and assessment results to clients and other individuals care is taken to provide, in an appropriate manner, accurate and sufficient information for an understanding of any conclusions and recommendations made, and to identify the basis for any reservations which might exist.

D8 RELEASE OF EVALUATION AND ASSESSMENT DATA
Counsellors ensure that evaluation and assessment data are released appropriately and only to the client and persons qualified to interpret and use them properly.

D9 INTEGRITY OF EVALUATION AND ASSESSMENT INSTRUMENTS AND PROCEDURES
Counsellors who use psychological tests and other assessment instruments, the value of which depends on their novelty to the client, ensure that they are limited to and safeguarded by those with the professional interest and competence to do so.

D10 SENSITIVITY TO DIVERSITY WHEN ASSESSING AND EVALUATING
Counsellors proceed with caution when judging and interpreting the performance of minority group members and any other persons not represented in the group on which the evaluation and assessment instruments and procedures were standardized. They recognize and take into account the potential effects of age, ethnicity, disability, culture, gender, religion, sexual orientation and socio-economic status on both the administration of, and the interpretation of date from, such instruments and procedures.

D11 SECURITY MAINTENANCE
Counsellors ensure the integrity and security of evaluation and assessment instruments and procedures consistent with any legal and contractual obligations. They refrain from appropriating, reproducing, or modifying established evaluation and assessment instruments without the expressed permission and adequate recognition of the original author, publisher and copyright holder.

Case Studies for Evaluation and Assessment

D1 GENERAL ORIENTATION
Counsellors adequately orient and inform clients so that evaluation and assessment results can be placed in proper perspective along with other relevant information.

Recognizing Language Differences (+)
Richard D. is an immigrant who recently decided to leave his home in France to move to Winnipeg. He is fluent in the oral communication of English and is able to communicate well verbally. However, he has a problem in interpreting written English. He is required to take a employment evaluation test at a placement centre for the unemployed. Both a written and oral form of the test are available. The counsellor, who is informed of Richard's weakness, administers the test orally to Richard and writes exactly what Richard says for each test question.

Orientation (+)
A counsellor decides that in order to help his client, Heather, she needs a personality assessment. Before conducting the test, the counsellor holds an

orientation meeting with Heather. During this meeting, Heather is told the purpose of the test, ways in which the counsellor will use the test and some of the limitations of personality testing. During this meeting, the counsellor answers any questions or concerns Heather has about the test. At the end of the meeting, the counsellor feels that Heather is comfortable taking the test.

Standardized Tests for Placement (–)
An American aptitude test battery is used for the placement of students at an inner city high school. There are no Canadian or local norms for the tests. Based on the results of these tests, as well as school grades, students are placed in various educational streams in the school. There are large numbers of recently immigrated students in this school. Most students score very low in the aptitude test and most have not achieved well in school, due to their weaknesses in English. As a result of low scores, most of these immigrant students are placed in "high school leaving" streams.

The Test Says... (–)
In a private career counselling office, one counsellor regularly uses the Strong Interest Inventory to help clients make career decisions. After clients complete the inventory and the computer print-out of results is returned, the counsellor tells clients, "The test says you should go into one of the following occupations...." Little or no time is taken to consider other relevant factors in career decision-making; factors such as aptitude, personality, socio-economic and job outlook.

Comments and Questions
Certain guidelines and procedures must be followed when administering a test and interpreting test results. Before a counsellor administers a test to an examinee, the following matters should be considered:

- the counsellor previews in advance the language, ethnic and culture differences of examinee(s) and selects the appropriate assessment or makes necessary adjustments to ensure differences are recognized

- the counsellor obtains consent from the examinee before any test is administered or information about the examinee is shared

- examinee(s) are informed of the purpose of testing and confidentiality and limitations are explained

- examinee(s) are informed of the availability of test results, interpretations made and explanation of interpretations

- the counsellor ensures the examinee understands that these test results are only one factor from a variety of data used when making a counselling or personal decision.

1. In the case of **Standardized Test for Placement**, what should the administration in the high school do in order to be fair to all students?

2. If you were an examinee, what questions might you want to ask about the nature of the test?

3. Should standardized tests be the main criterion used for placement and college/university selection?

4. What would you do to make an examinee feel more at ease prior to taking a test, especially if you

noticed outward signs of being over-anxious?

5. How should the examinee be notified of test results? How should the test results be given to the examinee? (Written or verbal)

6. As a counsellor who administers tests, how should the test results be used and should anybody else in your department have access to them?

D2 PURPOSES AND RESULTS OF EVALUATION AND ASSESSMENT
Counsellors take responsibility to inform clients about the purpose of any evaluation and assessment instruments and procedures and the meaning of evaluation and assessment results.

The Purpose of Testing (+)
The counsellor informs students, class by class, of the purposes of the *Differential Aptitude Tests*. The counsellor explains carefully the information booklet making sure all questions are answered and all information is provided. The test administration is explained by the counsellor. Students are made aware of the test's possible significance and how the results can be used in helping to make future educational and career decisions. Students are also informed that all test interpretations will be done on an individual basis so that other relevant information can be considered.

Test Orientation (+)
In a university counselling service, the counsellors organize and teach regular testing orientation sessions. Every effort is made to help clients understand the purposes and uses of any standardized tests that are used. In addition, clear instructions are given regarding the individual interpretation that will follow test administration and scoring.

Results for the Files (–)
Frank N., a high school counsellor, learns that most of the high schools are administering the *Differential Aptitude Tests (DAT)* to grade nine students. With his administration's agreement, he schedules two morning meetings in the gymnasium for all grade nine students to complete the *DAT*. Students are asked to complete the test in order for the school to have their scores on file.

Unstated Purpose for Testing (–)
As a regular practice, a school principal asks the teachers in her elementary school to administer the *Canadian Tests of Basic Skills* to all grade four and five students. One year, after the scores are known, two of the grade five teachers receive very negative reports on their teaching from the principal. Upon inquiring about these negative reports, two grade five teachers were told that the students in their classes have not progressed sufficiently (one grade equivalency higher) since their testing in the previous year when the students were in grade four.

Comments and Questions
This ethical guideline requires that those individuals who are in charge of testing must delineate the purpose of testing to the examinees, consider the examinees' welfare, have explicit prior understanding with tests, and acknowledge the examinees' right to know the testing results, the interpretations made, and other aspects of the testing results. In other words, clients need informed consent. Informed consent implies that clients understand the full

purpose of testing as well as how the interpretation will be done and how the results will be used. Testing provides clients and counsellors with additional information so that more realistic decisions can be made. It is very important that counsellors realize that it is their responsibility to see that tests serve the best interests of clients.

1. What are some things a counsellor can do to make the testing experience a more collaborative venture?

2. How could a counsellor explore examinees' reasons for taking tests, as well as their past experience with tests?

3. What are the major purposes of testing?

4. Who should introduce the idea of standardized testing, the client or the counsellor? Why?

5. What are some ways in which the counsellor can explain beforehand how interpretations, conclusions and recommendations will be made for interest and personality inventories, intelligence tests, diagnostic tests, achievement batteries and aptitude tests?

6. In the case entitled **Results for the Files**, what would you have done to make the *DAT* results meaningful for students?

D3 EVALUATION AND ASSESSMENT COMPETENCE

Counsellors recognize the limits of their competence and offer only those evaluation and assessment services for which they have appropriate preparation and which meet established professional standards.

Art Therapy (+)

A beginning counsellor sees that the art work of one student consistently depicts scenes of violence involving children and adults. Recognizing that there may be psychological significance in this art work, and acknowledging the limitations of his own expertise, the counsellor hands over the collection to the guidance department head, a counsellor with many years of experience, and some knowledge of art therapy.

Staff Orientation (+)

At the beginning of a school year, a counsellor at a high school holds an orientation workshop with school administration and teaching staff at which the counsellor's education background, training, experience and competencies are outlined. Participants become familiarized with the range of tests which can be accessed and ones which are beyond the competence of the counsellor to administer. The counsellor makes clear that for these situations the services of a school psychologist should be enlisted.

Score Misinterpretation (–)

A procedure of one small community high school is to administer the *Canadian Test of Basic Skills* to all new students entering the school with a view to determining an estimate of functional levels in language and mathematics. The school counsellor administers the tests and makes the grade equivalent scores available to teachers. No attempt is made to interpret the scores with the teachers or to make conversions to percentile ranks. Teachers take the grade equivalent scores into account in assessing functional levels and developing individual programs, often misinterpreting both the meaning and intent of grade equivalency scores.

Limited Information (–)

Art interpretation happens to be a recently discovered interest of a department head through some journal articles she has read. She has even discovered a neatly packaged technique including a test to verify the findings. She then applies the test to the client. From the test results, she concludes family violence to be the root cause of the problem. Based on her findings, she proceeds to get social workers involved to start the necessary investigations.

Comments and Questions

It is incumbent upon the counselling practitioners to engage in constant self-scrutiny and self-evaluation regarding knowledge of, skills, and competence in testing.

It is both a duty and a responsibility to remain current on test availability, the latest testing techniques, the norming schemes, and the accurate interpretation of results. This can be achieved through professional reading, attendance at seminars and workshops, maintaining contact with colleagues, and enrolling in upgrading and refresher courses.

Counsellors should convey to clients the range of testing services within and outside their sphere of competence. There must be a willingness to refer to a more competent authority when cases arise that require services outside counsellors' levels of ability or training.

1. Increasingly, tests and inventories are available on the internet. What are some of the pitfalls of using tests from the internet?

2. What are the disadvantages of using grade or age equivalency scores?

3. What criteria should be used to determine the testing competence of counsellors?

4. To what extent should a practitioner attempt to upgrade and keep current on up-to-date test availability, techniques, and results interpretations?

5. Should a counsellor's experience and training in assessment and evaluation be part of her or his informed consent form?

6. What specific information about one's background and competencies should one divulge to prospective clients?

D4 ADMINISTRATIVE AND SUPERVISORY CONDITIONS

Counsellors ensure that evaluation and assessment instruments and procedures are administered and supervised under established conditions consistent with professional standards. They note any departures from standard conditions and any unusual behaviour or irregularities which may affect the interpretation of results.

Counsellor Competence (+)

A counsellor decides to use a test designed to measure attitudes and values with a particular client. The counsellor has extensive knowledge about this type of test and about whether it is suitable and appropriate for his client. The counsellor is qualified to give this test. He carefully administers the test exactly as prescribed in the administration manual.

Irregularities Noted (+)

John E. is qualified to administer a large number of standardized tests. During the administration of a group aptitude test, the electricity in the room goes off for three or four minutes. John carefully notes this irregularity since he feels the test results and subsequent interpretations could be affected.

Consultant Job Placement through the Mail (–)

A counsellor with a career consulting firm sends out brochures advertising career aptitude inventory tests that can be purchased through the mail from his firm. The advertisement claims that if you buy the test you can give yourself the test to determine career suitability. These tests have not been designed or standardized to be self-administered or self-scored.

Prescribed Material Shortage (–)

A counsellor in an elementary school is administering a test to a group of students. Due to budget cuts the counsellor is unable to purchase the prescribed computer answer sheets that accompany the test booklets. Therefore, the counsellor has the students write out the answers on a sheet of paper and then marks and scores them himself.

Comments and Questions

This ethical guideline is a mandate for counsellors and any other qualified professionals who administer tests to do so only as prescribed in the administration manual. The only exception to changing test administration regulations would be for research, and then only if the changes are in accordance with professional standards. The counsellor must note and report any unusual behaviour or irregularities during the testing session which may affect the interpretation of the test scores. Great caution must be taken in using tests and inventories from the internet.

Tests that are published must be purchased. Computer software related to testing must also be purchased. This purchasing refers to all aspects of the test or inventory: the answer sheets, manuals, test and norms.

1. Should test users be able to document appropriate education and experience in the areas of testing in which they are engaged?

2. What qualifications would you expect to have as a counsellor before giving any tests or battery of tests?

3. In addition to understanding the prescribed methods in any given administration manual, counsellors need to be able to clarify the purposes of the test and to point out any limitations for any particular client. How can this be done?

4. What are some irregularities that might occur during testing that should be reported?

5. Explain whether do you believe it is ethical to self-administer and self-score interest inventories?

6. Would you allow more time to complete a test for someone who has difficulty with the language?

D5 USE OF TECHNOLOGY
Counsellors recognize that their ethical responsibilities are not altered, or in any way diminished, by the use of technology for the administration of evaluation and assessment instruments. Counsellors retain their responsibility for the maintenance of the ethical principles of privacy, confidentiality, and responsibility for decisions regardless of the technology used.

On-Line Counselling (+)

Sara B. prepares carefully before deciding to do a limited amount of on-line counselling for clients in remote areas. She is a certified counsellor with many years of experience. She ensures all data received during counselling is secure. As well, she allows herself adequate time to process on-line counselling interactions after each session. When testing is a part of the counselling, Sara ensure that tests are valid and reliable, and that time is spent on qualitative data collection as well.

Sending Confidential Faxes (+)

The counsellor, Adrian C., realizes that the fax machine in their counselling centre is centrally located and many people have access to all the faxes that are sent daily. Before receiving confidential information by fax, Adrian ensures that a phone call is made just before sending the fax so that he can immediately pick up the confidential fax.

Secret Password (–)

Joe, a college senior, notes the word HELPER taped to the side of the computer of one of the counsellors in the college counselling centre. He has already seen the computer account number left on the desk of the counsellor. When Joe returns to his own computer, he uses this information to look at the case notes that the counsellor has made on her clients.

Computer Test Results (–)

A very busy counsellor decides he could see more clients in a shorter period of time if he relies more on his personal computer, particularly when he is counselling clients with career concerns. Clients sit at the computer and complete a battery of tests. They also receive computer-generated results of the tests. Counsellor and client then discuss the test results. The counsellor makes no attempt to check the data entries of the client, or to add qualitative data to the computer-generated data.

Comments and Questions

The use of technology in counselling continues to increase at a rapid pace. Computers are now being used not only to score tests but also to administer tests, provide statistical comparisons and to print out computer-generated assessments. Computerized assessments are now possible on such highly sophisticated tests as the *Wechsler Adult Intelligence Scale*, the *Wonderlic Personnel Test*, the *Minnesota Multiphasic Personality Inventory* and the *16 Personality Factor Test* (to name a few). The benefits of computerized tests include rapid retrieval of information and easy storage of data. As well, with computers it is possible to tailor tests for the test-taker.

Counsellors must, however, also be aware of limitations of technology and assessment. Sound testing practices include observing clients during test-taking. Will counsellors rely too much on the computer, and not take the time for observation? Furthermore, there is the danger of the computer-generated assessment results and reports becoming the major focus of the counselling, rather than as an adjunct to the counselling. There may also be a need for new information on validity, reliability and normative data for using well-known standardized tests on the computer.

1. What safeguards should be put in place to guarantee the confidentiality of tests and records?

2. Should test results be placed on a college- or university-wide computer networks?

3. What are some of the strengths and limitations of computer-generated assessment results and reports?

4. How frequently should passwords be changed?

5. What can counsellors do to make sure that clients do not buy into the perceived "magic" of computer-generated results and suggestions?

6. In what situations could you ethically use computer tests or inventories?

D6 APPROPRIATENESS OF EVALUATION AND ASSESSMENT

Counsellors ensure that evaluation and assessment instruments and procedures are valid, reliable, and appropriate to both the client and the intended purposes.

Placement Policy (+)

A school district has a policy that all senior high students who transfer in from out-of -province must complete a standardized achievement test battery. Much time is taken by district counsellors and psychologists in selecting a test battery that is appropriate for out-of-province students. Each year the appropriateness of the test is re-evaluated.

Test Appropriateness (+)

The manager of an employment centre asks the counsellors in his office to recommend an aptitude test that will be helpful in determining the mechanical aptitude of clients. After careful examination of *Buros Mental Measurement Yearbook* and the examination of the technical data available on several aptitude tests, the counsellors recommend an aptitude test that appears to be appropriate, reliable and valid.

Language Deficiencies (–)

A high school student, Sophie, has recently moved from predominantly French-speaking Quebec City to an English language high school in Edmonton. Although Sophie can read

and speak English, she is not at the same linguistic level as other students in her grade. When Sophie completes an aptitude test, the counsellor uses the regular normative data and makes no allowances for Sophie's language deficiencies.

Finding Students who are Gifted and Talented (–)

A program for educating children who are gifted and talented is being rushed into place by a school division that seems to be responding more to parental pressure than to any clearly defined educational goal or research to substantiate the advisability of such a program. To select students for the "gifted and talented" program, the school superintendent asks counsellors to use a group intelligence test that measures verbal ability, numerical ability, and abstract reasoning. The test is twenty years old and no data is available suggesting that the test is appropriate for the selection of students who may be gifted or talented.

Comments and Questions

This ethical guideline clearly states the importance and need to be knowledgeable and skilled in test selection and use. There must be a purpose for giving tests and standards should be followed for evaluating tests. The publication, *Standards for Education and Psychological Tests*, is a comprehensive guide for both test developers and test users. These standards set out information that should be included in test manuals; information on technical adequacy and information on how to use tests. As well, test users will find an extensive review of tests in *O.K. Buros's Mental Measurements Yearbook*.

Several factors should be considered

when selecting either norm-referenced or criterion-referenced tests. Validity is the most important factor. This means that the test must measure what it claims to measure and what the user wants it to measure. Reliability coefficients must meet acceptable standards and there should be a relatively small standard error of measurement. To make sure the test is appropriate, the population on whom the test was normed should include people like the ones to be tested. These and other considerations are to be adhered to before selecting tests for use.

1. What questions would you be prepared to discuss with your administrator if the required tests do not show evidence of sufficient validity in their test manuals?

2. If a test is a "big seller", does this imply that the test is valid? Explain.

3. How would you counter the argument, "The use of an inadequate device is better than the use of no test at all"?

4. Explain why it is realistic to demand very high standards of reliability when using tests for decision-making?

5. How can you ensure greater test appropriateness with clients from minority groups?

6. Do you believe there is such a thing as a "culture-free" or "culture-fair" standardized test? Clarify.

D7 **REPORTING EVALUATION AND ASSESSMENT RESULTS**
Counsellors ensure that when reporting evaluation and assessment results to clients and other individuals care is taken to provide, in an appropriate manner, accurate and sufficient information for an understanding of any conclusions and recommendations made, and to identify the basis for any reservations which might exist.

Tests and Counselling (+)
Bob, a first year engineering student, is not enjoying his program of studies. He decides to take an interest inventory at the university counselling centre to see if his interests really are in engineering. After the results of the interest inventory are known, the counsellor discusses the results with Bob. The interest inventory scores do not support his field of study, but the counsellor points out that a standardized interest inventory is only one factor among many others that should influence his career decision. The counsellor and Bob then discuss some of the other factors.

Effective Test Interpretation (+)
With the consent of the student, a school counsellor telephones the parents of John in order to communicate a concern about his behavioural change over the last several months. John appears sullen, non-communicative with all school personnel and the frequency of skipping of classes is increasing.

After talking further with the counsellor, John reveals that he feels hopelessly lost in most of his subjects. He agrees to some diagnostic testing to determine more specifically what the major problems might be. Since his parents are very concerned and willing to help, the counsellor asks John's permission to include them in the discussion of the test results and in future remedial learning plans.

Parental Request for Information (–)

In November of Jamie's grade six year, her parents notice that she appears to be regressing in mathematics and not progressing in her reading ability. Her parents know that special testing is done for some students at the beginning of each year by the resource teacher and counsellor. After learning that Jamie had been tested several months earlier, the parents request the results of the tests. The results indicate dramatic drops in performance, yet the results had not been communicated to the parents and remedial action was not implemented to correct or work with Jamie. The present classroom teachers were not informed of the child's problems or what teaching strategies might help her learning.

Inadequate Test Interpretation (–)

A counsellor is researching self-concept in adolescent females. A standardized test on self-concept is administered to all students in one middle years school. After the test results are interpreted, the counsellor intends to meet with the students individually to discuss the test results. Due to lack of time, only half of the students are provided with this opportunity. With the rest of the students, the results are handed back to each classroom, generally to groups of thirty-five, with a short period of time to answer any questions students might have. As there are no questions asked, no further interpretation is provided.

Comments and Questions

This ethical guideline emphasizes that test results must be accompanied by adequate interpretation and where it is felt to be necessary, by counselling as well. Many of the tests that counsellors use are fairly easy to administer and interpret. This is true for a number of interest inventories and some aptitude tests. Nevertheless, clients will usually not be familiar with the meaning of the scores provided and counsellors need to take the time to make sure that results are communicated in an understandable way. If possible, test interpretations should be provided as only one piece of information and related to other information available to the counsellor and client.

1. Is it appropriate for interpretation of test results to be done in small groups or should all interpretation be done individually?

2. Should all tests be subject to a "User Qualification Form" to ensure that only qualified people are administering the tests?

3. Who is qualified to determine whether or not a test administrator is in fact qualified to interpret the results of the test? Does a particular degree really determine whether or not the user is qualified to interpret the results and communicate them in an ethical fashion?

4. Should test interpretation practica or workshops be required for all counsellors-in-training?

5. In the case entitled **Parental Request for Information**, no test information was given to parents or teachers. What should the counsellor have done in this case?

6. In the case entitled **Inadequate Test Interpretation**, inadequate test results interpretation is given. What should the counsellor, with limited time, have done in this situation?

D8 RELEASE OF EVALUATION AND ASSESSMENT DATA

Counsellors ensure that evaluation and assessment data are released appropriately and only to the client and persons qualified to interpret and use them properly.

Discussion of Test Results (+)

Mrs. J., the parent of an elementary school student, asks for the results of the *WISC-R* taken by her daughter. The psychologist sets up an appointment and carefully interprets the test results so that Mrs. J. understands the scores from the *WISC-R*.

Student Cumulative Files (+)

Cumulative files are kept on all students attending public schools. These cumulative files include medical alerts, past grades, home addresses and telephone numbers and other information. Psychological test results are placed in the psychologist's clinical files and are only released to counsellors and others who are qualified to interpret the results of each specific psychological test. A counsellor in Snow Valley School Division is familiar with these policies on student files, and when he asks to see the test score results of the *WISC-R* for one of his clients, he shows the psychologist his university transcript and course outline of his successfully completed course on advanced testing.

Access to Test Scores (–)

In a middle years school, all students' cumulative files can be accessed by teachers, the student, and his or her parents. When psychological assessments are sent to the school, they are also placed in the students' cumulative files.

Reporting to Outside Agencies (–)

Counsellors are in frequent contact with agencies such as Child and Family Services and Child Guidance Services regarding particular students. These outside agencies may request further information about psychological tests performed in the school. One busy counsellor assigns the job of sending test results to outside agencies to the school secretary. Since the school secretary has a good friend at one of the outside agencies, she frequently reports test results verbally over the telephone to her friend.

Comments and Questions

The Supreme Court of Canada has ruled that every person has the legal right to know what is written about them. This includes government documents, school files and medical records. The records must be written in such a manner that the person can understand the information, as in the case of school cumulative files. If the records are not written as such, a qualified person must be on hand to interpret the information.

1. How does one determine if the person to whom test scores are released is truly qualified to interpret and use the test scores properly?

2. What is the difference between 'psychological test scores' and 'interpreted test results'?

3. What are your organization's regulations regarding the storing of test results in clients' files?

4. Should secretaries have access to psychological test scores?

5. Where should psychological reports and standardized test score results be kept?

6. Have you included a statement in your informed consent form on the release of testing information? Discuss.

D9 INTEGRITY OF EVALUATION AND ASSESSMENT INSTRUMENTS AND PROCEDURES

Counsellors who use psychological tests and other assessment instruments, the value of which depends on their novelty to the client, ensure that they are limited to and safeguarded by those with the professional interest and competence to do so.

Test Security (+)
Professor Jonathan S. is quite concerned that many standardized tests in the Faculty of Education, where he works, are not being properly safeguarded. He receives permission from the Dean and his Department Head to draft a policy on the 'safeguarding of tests'. This policy results in some inventories being kept in the library and some tests being kept in locked filing cabinets in professors' offices.

Graduate Record Examinations (+)
Joan F. is concerned about all the manuals that are available to help potential graduate students prepare for their *Graduate Record Examinations (GRE)*. As well, several workshops are advertised purporting to help students score higher on their *GRE*. She contacts the *GRE* office and is reassured to find that the GRE tests are constantly being revised and that *GRE Preparation Manuals* and special workshops might help students somewhat, but this preparation is taken into consideration when norms are established.

Test Item Coaching (–)
In one urban school, students are placed into a "gifted" program if they have demonstrated outstanding achievement in earlier grades or if they score at the 98th percentile or above on several sub-tests of the *Differential Aptitude Test (DAT)*. One counsellor, whose daughter attends this school, takes the *DAT* home and has her daughter familiarize herself with some of the test items. Not surprisingly, her daughter gets into the gifted program based on her *DAT* scores.

Test Familiarity (–)
Bob C. is the employee counsellor at a large savings and loan company. Management tells him that they are planning to promote several people to management positions. As part of their evaluation of prospective candidates for promotion, candidates will complete several leadership and self-concept tests. Bob decides to help two of the employees whom he has counselled in the past by providing them with sample items from the standardized tests that will be used in the assessment process.

Comments and Questions
Test users employ tests appropriately and are responsible for safeguarding the use of tests. If the tests are to be valid and reliable, they must, in most instances, be "new" to the person taking the test. Any prior information or coaching that clients receive invalidate test results and normative data.

1. Is it considered a dual relationship when counsellors give standardized tests to relatives, close friends or business associates? Clarify.

2. Should professors or teachers be allowed to reproduce interest inventories when the inventories are simply being used to explain a model?

3. This guideline states that psychological tests must be given by persons with professional competence. How should this professional competence be developed?

4. How are special manuals with sample questions and preparation for testing workshops different from the "prior information" and "coaching" mentioned in this guideline?

5. Should some adjustment be made to scores for students who have taken many standardized tests during their school years? Or for students who are taking their first-ever standardized test?

6. What safeguards for standardized tests are in place in your organization?

D10 SENSITIVITY TO DIVERSITY WHEN ASSESSING AND EVALUATING
Counsellors proceed with caution when judging and interpreting the performance of minority group members and any other persons not represented in the group on which the evaluation and assessment instruments and procedures were standardized. They recognize and take into account the potential effects of age, ethnicity, disability, culture, gender, religion, sexual orientation and socio-economic status on both the administration of, and the interpretation of date from, such instruments and procedures.

Student Placement (+)
An immigrant student who has only lived in Canada for a year completes several standardized tests to help school officials make placement decisions. The test results suggest placement in the stream for "slower learners." The home room teacher says that she will develop other, more appropriate ways of determining this immigrant

student's academic potential. She does this, and after the student performs at an above average level, the student is placed in the appropriate educational stream.

Score Adjustments (+)
Several counsellors, in a school division that has many students who are from minority groups, decide to do something about the fact that many of the minority group students do not perform well on a particular standardized test. They carefully research the literature on this issue and learn how to adjust the scoring on their standardized test so that a more accurate score is derived for minority group students.

Miller's Analogies Test (–)
The *Miller's Analogies Test* is used as a major criterion for admission to one university graduate program. Many foreign students who apply do not have a strong English background and because of low scores are not admitted to the graduate program.

Non-Representative Norm Group (–)
A counsellor, working in a remote northern community, administers tests of mental ability (I.Q.) to all the students in the school. He uses an American group I.Q. test and uses the American norms. When interpreting the test scores, the counsellor pays no attention to the fact that most of the students speak English as an additional language and that most of the students are not represented in the norms.

Comments and Questions
This ethical guideline states that all counsellors and researchers examine carefully the performance of minority groups on standardized tests. The following issues should be kept in mind:

- Standardized tests provide only an estimate of an individual's performance in standard English as compared to a cross-section of American (sometimes Canadian) persons of the same age or grade.

- Culturally diverse populations are typically under-represented in normative data.

- Are there culturally appropriate tests available?

- Testing is one aspect of counselling. Members must acquire competencies in multicultural counselling when interpreting tests for minority groups.

1. What is the policy among counsellors in your school, college, or agency regarding the avoidance of cultural bias in tests and in test interpretation?

2. What provisions are made for school counsellors, agency counsellors, career counsellors and counsellors in private practice to acquire competencies in multicultural counselling to help them with clients of different ethnicities?

3. Since culture is not fair, can we or should we expect counsellors to use "culture-fair" tests?

4. Even though minority groups are under-represented in normative data, can we expect counsellors to develop their own norms?

5. Is what we expect of minority groups in Canada different than in the United States (cultural mosaic versus melting pot)?

6. Do minority group members want special consideration?

D11 SECURITY MAINTENANCE Counsellors ensure the integrity and security of evaluation and assessment instruments and procedures consistent with any legal and contractual obligations. They refrain from appropriating, reproducing, or modifying established evaluation and assessment instruments without the expressed permission and adequate recognition of the original author, publisher and copyright holder.

Reproducible Interest Inventories (+)

Every year, Frank N., a high school counsellor, is faced with a limited budget. He finds it worthwhile to use several self-scoring interest inventories when helping students with their future career planning. To help off-set the costs of buying a new supply of the standardized tests each year, Frank N. asks the students to contribute a portion of the costs of the readily-reproducible interest inventories.

Aptitude Tests (+)

During high school, students often take an aptitude test to give them ideas about careers that relate to their aptitudes. Before the test, the counsellor explains to the students that the test measures aptitude in areas such as verbal reasoning, mechanical reasoning, abstract reasoning and so forth. These aptitudes are later related to possible careers. It is stressed to the students that the results of the test are to be viewed only as suggestions. Students are made aware that just because the aptitude test does not suggest a certain career does not mean that the student would not do well in it, or should not consider it.

Canadian or American Social Studies? (–)

A board of education makes the decision to test the basic knowledge of middle years students in the area of social studies. A number of standardized tests are reviewed for this purpose and the one chosen is American and uses American norms. When the testing is announced to the public, as well as when the results are returned, teachers state that the test is intended to measure students' knowledge of social studies, and that the students are being compared to students in the same age bracket. There is no reference to the fact that the tests are American and that a few of the "most glaring" American questions have been changed. (For example, a question about George Washington is changed to a question about Laura Secord). The lack of information given leaves most parents with the impression that the test scores reflect their child's knowledge of Canadian social studies.

New Norm Group (–)

A Canadian test publisher decides to enlarge the norm group for one popular Canadian achievement test. These changes are carefully explained in the technical manual. As a result of the new norm group, students in many school divisions score considerably higher. Since the publisher does not include the technical manual with the package of materials sent to schools, teachers and counsellors are left with the impression that students are scoring higher.

Comments and Questions

This ethical guideline is similar to guideline D9, "Integrity of Evaluation and Assessment Instruments and Procedures", in that counsellors must see to it that procedures for test-taking are similar for all people taking the standardized instrument. In addition, changes should not be made to any standardized test "without permission and adequate recognition of the original author, publisher, and copyright holder." Changing an instrument without permission is not only unethical, but also has the effect of changing the validity, reliability and normative data of the standardized test.

1. What can counsellors do to increase the likelihood of administering test consistent with published procedures?

2. What are your ethical obligations when you notice that a colleague has copied an interest inventory for her or his class?

3. Are local norms necessary in order to provide test-takers with accurate information? Explain.

4. Should teachers and professors be allowed to duplicate standardized tests for instructional purposes only for the classroom?

5. Should students in school pay for the costs of standardized tests used in member of a university and recruiting clients for private practice (as in the **Recruitment Case**)?

5. Should counsellor-educators at universities involved in practicum supervision have their own private counselling practice?

6. How can consultants best avoid any implied affiliation with a professional organization or an institution?

Chapter Twelve

---------- ❖ ----------

Case Studies in Research and Publication

---------- ❖ ----------

Some of the critical ethical issues in research and publication relate to: informed consent, cultural diversity, qualitative research, publication, research sponsors, confidentiality, voluntary participation, subject welfare and research responsibilities.

Canadian Counselling Association Code of Ethics

Ethical Guidelines for Research and Publications

E1 RESEARCHER RESPONSIBILITY
Counsellors plan, conduct, and report on research in a manner consistent with relevant ethical principles, professional standards of practice, federal and provincial laws, institutional regulations, cultural norms, and standards governing research with human subjects.

E2 SUBJECT WELFARE
Counsellors are responsible for protecting the welfare of their research subjects during research, and avoid causing injurious psychological, physical or social effects to persons who participate in their research activities.

E3 PRINCIPAL RESEARCHER RESPONSIBILITY
Counsellors, when in the role of principal researcher are responsible for ensuring that appropriate ethical research practices are followed and, with respect to research involving human subjects, for obtaining an independent and appropriate ethical review before proceeding with the research. Research associates involved in the research activities share ethical obligations and full responsibility for their own actions.

E4 VOLUNTARY PARTICIPATION
Counsellors ensure that participation in research is voluntary. However, involuntary participation may be appropriate when it can be shown that participation will have no harmful effects on subjects, is essential to the research, and meets ethical review requirements.

E5 INFORMED CONSENT OF RESEARCH SUBJECTS
Counsellors inform all research subjects of the purpose(s) of their research. In addition, subjects are made aware of any experimental procedures, possible risks, disclosures and limitations on confiden-

tiality. Subjects are also informed that they are free to ask questions and to discontinue at any time.

E6 RESEARCH CONFIDENTIALITY
Counsellors ensure that research information on subjects is confidential and the identity of participants is protected unless otherwise authorized by them, consistent with all informed consent procedures.

E7 USE OF CONFIDENTIAL INFORMATION FOR DIDACTIC OR OTHER PURPOSES
Counsellors do not disclose in their writings, public presentation, or public media, any personally identifiable information obtained in confidence about clients, research participants, students, or organizational clients unless (1) there is legal authorization to do so, (2) reasonable steps are taken not to identify the person or organization, or (3) the person or organizational client has given informed written consent.

E8 FURTHER RESEARCH
Counsellors have an obligation to collaborate with colleagues by making available original research data to qualified researchers who may wish to replicate or verify the research.

E9 RESEARCH SPONSORS
Counsellors, when conducting research, obtain informed consent from sponsors and institutions and ensure that sponsors and institutions are given feedback information and proper acknowledgement.

E10 REVIEW OF MANUSCRIPTS
Counsellors who review material submitted for publication, research or other scholarly purposes respect the confidentiality and proprietary rights of those who submitted the research.

E11 REPORTING RESULTS
In reporting research results, counsellors mention any variables and conditions that might affect the outcome of the investigation or the interpretation of the results, and provide information sufficient for others who might wish to replicate the research.

E12 RESEARCH CONTRIBUTIONS
Counsellors give due credit through joint authorship, acknowledgement, footnote statements, or other appropriate means to those who have contributed significantly to the research and/or publication, and to those who have done previous work on the topic. For an article that is based mainly on a student thesis or dissertation, the student is listed as principal author.

E13 SUBMISSION OF PUBLICATIONS
Counsellors do not submit the same manuscript or one essentially similar in content for simultaneous publication consideration by two or more journals. In addition, manuscripts published in whole or in substantial part in another journal or published work should not be submitted for publication without acknowledgement and permission from the previous publication.

Case Studies for Research and Publication

E1 RESEARCHER RESPONSIBILITY
Counsellors plan, conduct, and report on research in a manner consistent with relevant ethical principles, professional standards of practice, federal and provincial laws, institutional regulations, cultural norms, and standards governing research with human subjects.

Responsible Practice (+)
A department of counselling psychology has establishes an ethics committee to evaluate all research proposals, and particularly those proposals involving

research with human subjects. In one research proposal, university student volunteers will be used to compare the results of three treatment processes for dealing with depression. Before approving the research proposal, the ethics committee consults with experts on each of the treatment processes to consider possible harmful side effects to student subjects.

Research in Schools (+)
Several university researchers plan to study the possible effects single parent families have on the school success of their children. They need the cooperation of many schools to obtain anecdotal information, standardized test scores and school grades. They plan meetings with school superintendents, school principals and teacher representatives to explain their research, the possible benefits for educators and their plans for confidentiality and publishing of results.

Protecting the Client (–)
One private counselling centre receives many referrals for counselling from various large companies that provide counselling services as part of their employee benefits. One of the companies asks for an evaluation report on all the counsellors in the counselling centre so that they could determine whether or not they would continue to refer employees to the centre. The head of the counselling centre asked for a videotaped counselling session from each counsellor so that she could show examples of good counselling to the company asking for feedback on counsellor effectiveness. The counsellors at the centre each submitted a videotape.

Obtaining Research Approval (–)
Several school counsellors in a large city school board agree to administer a questionnaire to their guidance classes in order to help a colleague, Sally S., collect data for her Master's thesis. The questions on the questionnaire are very "low key" (to use the words of the researcher) and do not invade the privacy of any of the students. Sally realizes that her school board has a policy on getting school board approval for her research, but because of the weeks, if not months, of delay to get approval, and because of the totally harmless nature of her questionnaire, she collects the data with the help of her colleagues in counselling.

Comments and Questions
Counsellors doing research must be educated in research methodologies and should, at all times, attempt to answer research questions professionally and ethically. Research subjects should have confidence in researchers and their ability to "plan, conduct, and report" research with high professional standards of practice.

Confidentiality and informed consent are key responsibilities of the researcher. There must be:

- detailed explanations of the purposes and procedures of the research

- identification of any experimental procedures

- identification of risks and benefits of the research

- willingness to discuss any questions that participants pose

- confidentiality of all tape recordings, verbal disclosures, records, and tests

- an understanding that participation is voluntary at all times.

1. What are the research guidelines for the organization or institution where you work?

2. Is it a violation of research ethics when student teachers complete a university assignment that calls for some classroom observation? Discuss.

3. In the case of **Protecting the Client**, what needs to be done to make this situation ethical?

4. Are there times (see **Obtaining Research Approval**) when it should not be necessary to go through all the channels for obtaining research approval?

5. What cultural norms might affect how a research project would be conducted?

6. Do you believe that many school boards discourage research by asking researchers to submit their detailed research proposals to review panels? Discuss.

E2 SUBJECT WELFARE
Counsellors are responsible for protecting the welfare of their research subjects during research, and avoid causing injurious psychological, physical or social effects to persons who participate in their research activities.

Ethics Committee (+)

All graduate students and professors conducting research must submit any research proposal dealing with human beings to an ethics committee. Part of the responsibility of this ethics committee is to ensure that proper procedures are in place to safeguard the welfare of all the subjects in the research experiment.

Research on Streaming (+)

One school principal has asked the divisional researcher to study the advantages and disadvantages of streaming in the school. After observing many of the classes in the school and talking to the teachers, the researcher is convinced that the procedures needed to examine streaming will be highly disruptive to students and teachers. The researcher informs the principal that the research design that they had hoped to use will have to be changed in order to better protect students and teachers from any harmful effects.

Strenuous Exercises (–)

A physical education teacher, Butch C., is working on his Master's research thesis and is gathering information on his study from students in his physical education classes. One part of his study includes checking the amount of time it takes students' heartbeats to return to normal after a strenuous series of exercises. No mention is made to students of the study and no precautions are taken with regard to the strenuous exercises before the study begins.

Confidentiality Missing (–)

Although students enrolled in an introductory psychology course are given a detailed handout of what will be expected from them when volunteering for any experiment, there is no mention made that names of people who participate in the experiments will be included in the results. When experiment results are released, each student is identified by first name and student number.

Comments and Questions

This ethical guideline states that subjects who participate in research experiments should not be exposed to injurious psychological, physical or social effects. This guideline needs to be considered each time a subject participates in an experiment or research situation. It should not be assumed that subjects know this guideline. The guideline needs to be discussed fully with all subjects. As well, parental permission is necessary for students to be research subjects.

Prior to participating in a research experiment, each subject should receive a detailed outline of what to expect. Some of the information contained in the outline would include:

- a description of the research experiment

- the purpose of the research

- that participation was voluntary

- permission for subjects to withdraw from the research at any time

- the date, time and how long the research would take

- where the experiment would be held

- that each student that participated in the test situation would receive results and that their names would not be identified

- assurances of confidentiality of all information gathered

- explanations of research results for subjects.

Researchers should be guided by the following ethical principles:

Respect for
- human dignity
- informed consent
- confidentiality and privacy
- vulnerable persons,
- justice and diversity

- the need to minimize harm and to maximize benefits.

1. What additional ethical principles would you add to the list of six principles listed above?

2. In addition to presenting ethical guidelines, what are some other ways to prevent harm to research subjects?

3. What are some well-known research experiments that have caused psychological or physical harm to the subjects?

4. Should the availability of counselling for subjects after the research has ended be part of all research designs?

5. When new counselling techniques or methods are used in research, can the psychological and social effects on clients be predicted?

6. The social effects of certain research practices are sometimes overlooked by researchers. What are some negative social effects that might result from certain research practices?

E3 PRINCIPAL RESEARCHER RESPONSIBILITY

Counsellors, when in the role of principal researcher are responsible for ensuring that appropriate ethical research practices are followed and, with respect to research involving human subjects, for obtaining an independent and appropriate ethical review before proceeding with the research. Research associates involved in the research activities share ethical obligations and full responsibility for their own actions.

Divisional Research Study (+)

The coordinator of guidance and counselling for a school division organizes a task force to do research on the issue of AIDS education in junior high and senior high schools in her area. The task force consists of parents, teachers, counsellors, administrators, and family life educators. Some of the issues discussed by the task force are age appropriateness, content, availability, and presentation of the material. Before the research on AIDS education begins, the coordinator discusses the various ethical issues related to the study and the need for everyone to look out for the welfare of students.

Mainstreaming Research (+)

The superintendent of a large urban school district allowed a researcher and his team to study the effects of mainstreaming of students in all classrooms. Teachers were asked for their help and cooperation with the study. Before agreeing to work with the researcher, the teachers invite a professor from the university, who is very knowledgeable about research and ethics, to help them examine the ethical and practical issues related to the study.

Videotaping Interviews (–)

The head of a counselling psychology department allows all counsellor-educators in the department to have counsellors-in-training record both audio- and videotape sessions with clients. Although clients are aware they are being taped, and that the tapes will be seen by others, no guidelines or regulations have been established by the department head regarding who has access to the tapes, where they will be stored, or when they will be erased.

Little Direction (–)

A researcher obtains a large grant to study cross-cultural counselling. Several of his graduate students are interested in doing the research. The researcher is extremely busy on several other projects and so, he gives the graduate students complete control of subject selection, interview questions, and safeguards for confidentiality. He does insist on being the principal researcher.

Comments and Questions

All members involved in a research project have the responsibility of being familiar with guidelines related to research, and the obligations of adhering to the guidelines. Graduate students doing research under the supervision of a professor are responsible for their own ethical actions. When research is being done with human subjects, the principal researcher must receive an independent ethical review of the research proposal before proceeding with the research. The principal researcher has the added responsibility of making sure that all participation in research is voluntary, that no harm will be done to research subjects, that research subjects are fully informed of the purposes of the research, and that the identity of research subjects is protected.

1. What should the process be in an independent review of a research proposal involving human subjects?

2 What can the principal researcher do to ensure ethical research practice?

3. Should there be more explicit guidelines on videotaping? What might these guidelines be?

4. In the last case presented, what should the principal researcher have done?

5. Should the principal researcher be responsible for teaching associate

researchers about ethical practices in research?

6. What are the ethical guidelines for doing research at your school, college, university or agency?

E4 VOLUNTARY PARTICIPATION
Counsellors ensure that participation in research is voluntary. However, involuntary participation may be appropriate when it can be shown that participation will have no harmful effects on subjects, is essential to the research, and meets ethical review requirements.

Identity Protected (+)

A research counsellor in a large Canadian urban centre is gathering information on sexual abuse/incest obtained from records of adult survivors of such abuse. Information required is age of onset, gender, perpetrator's status in the family/community, intervention (if any), years between last incident and seeking help, marital history of survivor, etc.

Clients' permission is not sought for use of this information, but no identification of individuals is attached to the statistics gathered. The purpose of the research is initial information gathering on sexual abuse/incest survivors. This information provides a base for further study of such abuse which would hopefully lead to the development of early intervention strategies.

The long-term educational plan is the development of workshops by school counsellors for the in-servicing of school personnel division-wide on the issues/concerns of child abuse intervention strategies.

Voluntary Participation (+)

Elementary and junior high school counsellors in a large Canadian urban centre where grades are structured kindergarten to grade six, grades seven to nine, and grades ten to twelve, develop a longitudinal study on children with learning disabilities. The purpose of the study is to research factors that contribute to a positive or negative transition from elementary school to the junior high school level.

Information gathering begins at grade four and the study continues to grade nine. The framework is both objective and subjective. Criteria for entry into the study are established by the resource team who determine the definition of a learning disability.

The study involves family (parents/siblings) and student participation. The research instruments are surveys and interviews. Participants are solicited through presentation of accurate information of the study including interviews, and written explanations. Written consent from both parents and students is mandatory. In addition, participants are free to withdraw from the study at any time.

The desired outcome is (a) the development of intervention strategies which would promote successful social transitions from one school level to the next, and (b) the maintenance of this success throughout the upper level for students with their particular defined special needs.

Non-Voluntary Participation (−)

A research project on the reaction of teenagers to their parents' separation and divorce is being conducted at a university by a candidate for a Ph.D. in counselling psychology. The purpose of the study is to provide information and analysis for teachers, counsellors, and social workers who work with teenagers. The premise of the study is that the information would:

- help to highlight individuals who are at risk from the experience

- lead to intervention before crisis.

Names of prospective participants are attained randomly from the divorce dockets. Sixty teens and either one of their parents are required for the study. The time commitment is four individual sessions of forty-five minutes over a six month period.

One interviewer, a counselling student in the department of counselling psychology, becomes aware at a first session that one individual, a fifteen-year-old male, is very reluctant to be in the study. He is verbally abusive to his father during the initial session, and distant and abrupt in his communications with the interviewer. She does not suggest that they consider withdrawing from the study. The reluctant behaviour continues for the remaining three sessions.

Unaware Participants (–)
A drop-in centre's counsellor initiates a small group on the developmental issues of peer pressure relating to sexuality. The group consists of six girls between the ages of twelve and fourteen years. These students are not aware that they are being videotaped by a research counsellor. This particular researcher has requested the taping for the purpose of presenting it to counselling students who are studying adolescent sexual development.

Comments and Questions
This ethical guideline underscores that:

- Written consent of all voluntary participants must be mandatory

- Written explanation of the research,

including purposes of the study and techniques to be used, must be presented to all voluntary participants

- Voluntary participants must be clearly advised that they can choose to refuse to participate

- Voluntary participants must be advised in writing that they can withdraw from the study at any time.

1. Can involuntary research participation ever be justified?

2. Should explicit rights of participants (voluntary/involuntary) be protected legally by legislation?

3. Describe the consequences that should be in place for researchers who:

   - knowingly cause psychological/ emotional or physical damage to participants

   - do not honestly inform participants about essential components of the study which could influence their consent to participate

   - deliberately mislead the participants.

4. In what types of counselling research would it be advantageous to have non-voluntary participants?

5. In the case entitled **Non-Voluntary Participation**, should the researcher have met with the fifteen-year old male to discuss his behaviour? Discuss.

6. In the last case presented, **Unaware Participants**, can a case be made that this taping will "have no harmful effects" on the young girls?

E5 INFORMED CONSENT OF RESEARCH SUBJECTS

Counsellors inform all research subjects of the purpose(s) of their research. In addition, subjects are made aware of any experimental procedures, possible risks, disclosures and limitations on confidentiality. Subjects are also informed that they are free to ask questions and to discontinue at any time.

New Approach to Family Life (+)

A school counsellor decides to use his class for a research project as part of a university course in which he is enrolled. The project involves testing a new approach to teaching a unit in family life. The teacher and professor set up the project together.

A letter is composed to parents describing the project in general. The letter is sent home at the beginning of the family life unit and the students are informed about the project and its purpose. Parents and/or students are given the option of being part of the project. At the completion of the project, and following an analysis of the results, a summary is composed and sent to students and parents. Several parents respond with telephone calls to the counsellor and others make comments at the parent-teacher conference which follows the project. Parents are interested in the nature and results of the study.

Discipline Project (+)

A school principal and guidance counsellor set up a project in which Reality Therapy is taught to a whole school staff as a discipline approach. Teachers are informed of the purpose of the study and are given a chance as staff to opt into the program. Parents are also informed of the project and training sessions are provided for them as well.

Students are taught the major tenets of Reality Therapy. Throughout the year, records are kept of the discipline infractions and comparisons are made to the previous year. Following the completion of the project, a summary of the results is published and circulated along with the results of a survey given to teachers, parents and students.

Self-Concept Research (–)

In a research project, some guidance counsellors and parents are trained to work directly with students in the school and in the home on enhancing students' self-concept. Magic circle, active listening, and a classroom meeting are some of the procedures taught. There are three groups involved. The experience of the first group of students includes training for both counsellor and parents. The experience of the second group involves the training of the counsellor only. The third group is a control group in which no training is involved. A series of tests designed to measure improvement in self-concept is administered to all three groups.

No plan is in place to inform students or their parents of this research, either before or after the completion of the project. Parents of the first group are exposed to the information, but neither parents nor students of the second group are aware of the project. Nothing is planned to inform the control group of the research project.

Uninformed Students (–)

A high school counsellor, John S., invites grade twelve students to participate in a research project involving the research of students' backgrounds and relating this information to their academic success throughout their high school years. Students are asked to participate in this project, and are given credit in the form of term marks for participating. No mention is made of the purpose of the study to the students.

The questionnaire takes from one to two hours to complete and includes specific items related to family background. These items, if answered in the affirmative, indicate criminal acts of abuse. The purpose of the project is intended to parallel research on the effects of abuse and its relationship to academic progress.

Comments and Questions

This guideline states that all research subjects should be informed of the purpose of the study or project. Researchers must take the time to explain carefully these purposes before subjects volunteer to be part of the study.

In the two positive cases presented, all parties involved are informed of the purposes of the projects. As well, results of the studies are made available. In the last case presented, the researcher, John S., places himself in a very difficult position if an actual case of abuse were revealed by the questionnaire. To use marks as an incentive for participation in a project of this type is placing pressure on students to participate and reveal personal information that they might not otherwise disclose.

1. As a counsellor, how might you participate in or initiate research on abuse in your school?

2. In the first case, *New Approach to Family Life*, the counsellor is researching a new approach to teaching a unit on family life. How would a researcher carry out this project if family life were a controversial topic in the community?

3. What are the advantages/disadvantages of providing informed consent in a group? To individuals?

4. How should counsellors handle resistance to research projects from other teachers?

5. What are some research projects where withholding information about the project is necessary?

6. To capture the spirit of informed consent, what can researchers do to encourage subjects to feel free to ask questions and to discontinue at any time?

E6 **RESEARCH CONFIDENTIALITY**
Counsellors ensure that research information on subjects is confidential and the identity of participants is protected unless otherwise authorized by them, consistent with all informed consent procedures.

Subject Disclosure (+)

A researcher in counselling psychology uses direct observation and videotaping to study the anxiety subjects may show when asked to elaborate on traumatic childhood experiences. Before the first session with each subject begins, the researcher informs the subjects of the purpose of the research study and counselling session. The researcher makes sure that each subject fully understands the purposes and obtains written consent from each subject willing to participate and be videotaped. At the end of the study, all videotapes of sessions are erased.

Case Study Research (+)

A university researcher contacts a large child guidance centre for information on reports of child abuse. The researcher asks that these reports be given to him without any identifying material regarding the subjects.

Videotaping (–)

Gayle J. has second thoughts about a videotape of a session that she initially consented to and she asks the researcher to erase the tape of the session. Gayle is concerned about having other people see the tape and learn about her personal problems. The researcher weighs the options of erasing the tape for the subject's benefit or keeping it because it could prove useful research for the researcher's benefit. He decides to meet his own needs and keeps a copy of the subject's videotaped session. The researcher feels safe because he still has the subject's initial written consent form. The researcher allows others to see the videotape.

Subject Confidentiality (–)

A counsellor-researcher walks into the university cafeteria and overhears four of his counsellor trainees discussing counsellee subjects by name. He decides to ignore the students' conversation.

Comments and Questions

Before supplying data to others or reporting the results on specific subjects, researchers must get informed consent from the subjects involved, disguise identities, or otherwise protect the identities of these subjects. If these measures are not taken, researchers can be held ethically and legally liable by their professional organization, employer, and/or the court system. The foremost questions researchers should ask themselves before disclosing information on specific subjects are:

- Can the research subject be hurt in any way in this study?

- Is the subject aware of the research and has she or he given consent to participate?

- Has every effort been taken to disguise or otherwise protect the identity of the research subjects?

1. What are the added difficulties of research confidentiality when doing research in schools and with students?

2. Should a subject's identity be disguised or otherwise protected if she or he is found to have been abused?

3. Should a subject's identity be disguised or otherwise protected if he or she disclosed a criminal act?

4. Should researchers disguise or otherwise protect the identity of subjects in a qualitative research study? Explain.

5. Is it ever possible to disguise or otherwise protect the identity of subjects who are part of a study while they are attending an institution (prison, school, group home, etc.)?

6. In the last case, *Subject Confidentiality*, how would you deal with the counsellor trainees discussing the research, including the names of people who are subjects in the study?

E7 USE OF CONFIDENTIAL INFORMATION FOR DIDACTIC OR OTHER PURPOSES
Counsellors do not disclose in their writings, public presentation, or public media, any personally identifiable information obtained in confidence about clients, research participants, students, or organizational clients unless (1) there is legal authorization to do so, (2) reasonable steps are taken not to identify the person or organization, or (3) the person or organizational client has given informed written consent.

Non-Disclosure (+)

At a public meeting, Joyce B. is asked to explain counsellors' roles and functions at her community-based, government-funded counselling centre. In her well-prepared talk, Joyce explains her career and that of her colleagues very well. The session ends with a question period. She is asked to give some specific examples of counselling cases at the community centre. Joyce explains that she could provide a few hypothetical examples, but since she is not sure that she could disguise the identity of actual clients from the community, and since she has not received permission to reveal information about clients, she would not talk about actual cases at the community counselling centre.

Research Client (+)

Robert K. has completed a large research project on the effectiveness of individual counselling funded by Employee Assistance Programs. At a counselling conference he presents many details of his research. To explain the counselling process and to show examples of improved client well-being, Dr. K. details the progress of two clients in particular. He acknowledges their willingness to help, identifies the clients, and assures his conference audience that both clients in the research project have given him written permission to identify them and to talk about the counselling they received.

Too Much Disclosure (–)

A professor has completed a research study which includes many of his students from the psychology courses that he teaches. He has much data on each of his student subjects, including names, intelligence test scores, results form the *Minnesota Multiphasic*
Personality Inventory, and other personal information. When a friend and colleague from another university asks the professor for details of his study, the professor sends him all the material. He asks his friend to keep the material confidential.

Identifiable School Division (–)

In a doctoral dissertation, Bev P. describes the many changes that occured in a small, rural school division as a result of a major industry closing down. Many administrators and teachers gave interviews, and many of their comments became part of the dissertation. Although Bev P. made every attempt to change names and places, some people did speculate as to who had said what, and why. Few, if any, major industries had closed in the province and so, many people felt they knew the real name of the school division being researched.

Comments and Questions

Researchers are responsible for the welfare of the research participants. To make sure that participants are not harmed in any way, researchers must respect the confidentiality of participants, must ensure that participation is voluntary and must obtain informed consent from all the research participants. This ethical article focuses on the need for confidentiality. Participants in research studies have a right to expect confidentiality. This article emphasizes that when case studies or other research information is described, all identifying details are disguised or otherwise protected, unless there is legal requirement to identify the person or organization, or if written informed consent has been given by participants.

1. Should a research project be funded if it is nearly impossible to hide the identity of the human subjects involved?

2. Is it ethical to review the records of clients (for research purposes) without securing the consent of the clients?

3. If the importance of the research seems invaluable to research participants, is it justifiable to not obtain consent?

4. Would it ever be acceptable to give research data on human subjects to another professional, even though the subjects did not give permission to release the date on them?

5. Are there examples that members in your group can give of when not enough effort was made to disguise the identity of clients or research subjects? Discuss.

6. In the case entitled *Identifiable School Division*, the researcher, Bev P., does disguise names and places. What else should Ms. P. have done?

E8 FURTHER RESEARCH Counsellors have an obligation to collaborate with colleagues by making available original research data to qualified researchers who may wish to replicate or verify the research.

Collaboration with Colleagues (+)
A university professor reports on her study that refutes some commonly held ideas regarding learning theory. The study is published in a highly regarded professional journal. A professor in educational psychology from another university requests to see a copy of the original data. A copy of the data is provided the following week, along with some additional comments.

Available Raw Data (+)
The department head of a department of educational psychology establishes a policy that all the data for each thesis or dissertation published by graduate students in the department must be made available to any interested faculty member or graduate student. This policy also includes guidelines on confidentiality issues related to research subjects.

Non-Collegial (–)
A well-known Canadian counsellor-educator publishes an article that strongly supports a particular counselling technique that he favours. In this article, he also points out how this technique is far superior to many other well-established counselling techniques. When several counsellor-educators contact him regarding the more detailed original data, he ignores their requests for more information.

Confidentiality Lacking (–)
A high school counsellor is in the process of completing her Master's thesis on teenage pregnancy and abortions. She is using the school records and her position as one of the school guidance counsellors to obtain data for her research. She has received the school administration's permission and her fellow counsellors' support in doing her study. The girls are made aware of her study and are promised complete confidentiality.

The counsellor successfully defends her thesis and her work is made available to other university faculty and students. It is also reported in the education section of the local newspaper.

Mrs. O., the chairperson of the Pro-Life Council and a powerful school board member who is trying to shut down the local abortion clinic, indicates that she wants to examine the data some more and need to know the names of the students. The counsellor, fearing the loss of her promotion, supplies the names to Mrs. O.

Comments and Questions

This ethical guideline indicates that members have an obligation to collaborate with colleagues by making original research available to qualified others. There is no place for selfishness, secrecy and petty jealousies in the pursuit of knowledge. An open, collegial, cooperative attitude provides the greatest benefit to the profession and to the knowledge base.

Collaboration with colleagues encourages:

• a high level of scientifically verifiable research

• use of acceptable research methods

• honesty and accuracy in interpreting and reporting research

• a faster pace of knowledge acquisition.

1. What are some reasons why researchers might be reluctant to share details of their research?

2. What effect does this guideline have on client confidentiality and informed consent?

3. Does cost and time factors, and a concern for the use to be made of the data, enter into the decision to make original research available?

4. Do personal feelings about your colleagues influence decisions about

making research available?

5. What, if any, effect does reputation, power, position, or money have on decisions to request or provide original research? Who is to be considered a qualified other?

6. How can university tenure and promotion guidelines affect research collaboration with colleagues?

E9 RESEARCH SPONSORS
Counsellors, when conducting research, obtain informed consent from sponsors and institutions and ensure that sponsors and institutions are given feedback information and proper acknowledgement.

Acknowledgment of Sponsors (+)

A counsellor in a high school requires additional funding for a research project she is doing. She writes to several local businesses, explains her project, and asks for some funding. All contribute small amounts to her project. She explains the sponsorship to all her research subjects, and then undertakes her research. When the research is completed and the paper is written, the sponsors are included in the acknowledgments.

Informed Consent of Sponsors (+)

Fourteen colleges and universities in one Canadian province decide to support a study that provides high school students with more information about each of the colleges or universities. The major researcher informs each college and university of the type of questions she will be asking and that comments will be solicited from present college/university students. She receives written permission to use the data collected, and at the end of the project all the colleges and universities are given full details on the results of the study, and are all acknowledged as contributing sponsors of the study.

Unacknowledged Sponsor (–)

A university professor receives a small amount of funding from a university's innovations grants to develop a new course in counselling. In his promotional material for the course, the professor does not acknowledge the money received from the university's innovations grants. Neither does he acknowledge the work done by a graduate student who was paid from the grant money.

Inappropriate Feedback (–)

A parents' group in a wealthy suburban area feel that newspaper reports of alcohol and drug use in the city are not relevant for their area. They decide to ask the schools to conduct a survey of alcohol and drug abuse in the two divisional high schools. Alcohol and drug abuse are found to be quite widespread. Since this information would upset the parents' group, the researchers report the results as being "inconclusive."

Comments and Questions

In a recent newspaper account, a journalist pointed out the real ethical dilemma faced by researchers, who had found that users of a certain product had slightly more incidence of cancer. The makers of the product had recently contributed 10 million dollars to the university where the researchers worked. This case, and other similar cases, point to the importance of informed consent for sponsors, the need for clear directions on feedback, and the publishing of all research results. Sponsors and institutions should be given the same respect as individual

participants in research; namely, the opportunity for giving informed consent.

On the other hand, sponsors or institutions should not expect any control over research results simply because they have funded the research. As with all research, whether sponsored or not, results of research should be reported accurately and clearly and acknowledgment should be given to all contributors.

1. Should a sponsor who funds an entire research study have control over the results of the study?

2. If sponsors request that their financial contributions be kept anonymous, should this request be honoured? Are there exceptions?

3. Are there situations in which research results should not be given to sponsors or institutions? Clarify.

4. What would you have done in the case study entitled *Inappropriate Feedback*?

5. Is it adequate to give sponsors and institutions verbal feedback? Should researchers always attempt to publish their results, even though they are being discouraged from doing so by sponsors or institutions?

6. Do you know of any situations where pressure was put on researchers not to publish their results? Clarify.

E10 **REVIEW OF MANUSCRIPTS**
Counsellors who review material submitted for publication, research or other scholarly purposes respect the confidentiality and proprietary rights of those who submitted the research.

Reviewing Manuscripts (+)

Professor J., a member of the CCA, publishes widely and successfully. He is asked to be a reviewer for the *Canadian Journal of Counselling*. When he receives manuscripts from the editor, he promptly reviews the manuscripts following all the guidelines provided by the editor on confidentiality, feedback, and process.

Editorial Review Board (+)

In establishing a board of reviewers for a major counselling journal, Sue T., the editor, makes sure she has reviewers with expertise in a wide range of counselling areas. Manuscripts for review are then sent only to reviewers with specific expertise related to the research topic of the manuscript.

Breaking Confidentiality (–)

A professor in a university, who regularly reviews manuscripts for journals, receives a manuscript that deals with a novel approach to using solution-focused brief therapy. Receiving the manuscript is very timely, since the professor is speaking on "innovations in solution-focused counselling" in the next week. In his speech the next week, the professor includes some of the ideas from the manuscript.

Reviewing the Manuscripts of Known Writers (–)

The manuscript Dr. John J. receives for reviewing purposes could only have come from his good friend at another university in the same city. John J. is very familiar with the research and the many obstacles his friend has encountered in finally getting his results finalized. There are both procedural errors and some gaps in the data in the manuscript under review. Dr. J. decides his friend needs all the help he can get, and spends the majority of his review emphasizing the positive aspects of the study.

Comments and Questions

In smaller research communities it is sometimes difficult to disguise the identity of researchers. This puts all the more emphasis on the need for confidentiality of manuscripts submitted for publication.

Until a manuscript is published, the contents of the manuscript, as well as the identity of the authors, should remain confidential. The authors of manuscripts have all proprietary rights to their manuscripts and any and all use or reference to the manuscripts belongs to the authors.

In addition to respecting confidentiality and the proprietary rights to those submitting manuscripts for review, counsellor-reviewers make publication decisions based on accepted standards. As well, counsellors review only those manuscripts that are within their area of expertise.

1. Can reviewers avoid their own personal biases when reviewing manuscripts for publication?

2. In the case on **Breaking Confidentiality**, what should the professor have done if he wanted to use the ideas from an unidentified writer?

3. "I'm about ready to give up submitting research for publication. The last two times I submitted something, I had to wait eighteen months the first time and about a year the second time." What can and should be done to process manuscripts quicker?

4. Should manuscripts for journals resulting from theses or dissertations be evaluated the same way as

other submissions?

5. What are some safeguards that can be up into place to guard the "proprietary rights" of unidentified writers?

6. What needs to be done in the last case to change the behaviour of John J. to more ethical behaviour?

E11 REPORTING RESULTS
In reporting research results, counsellors mention any variables and conditions that might affect the outcome of the investigation or the interpretation of the results, and provide information sufficient for others who might wish to replicate the research.

Ethnic Variables (+)
A school psychologist recognizes the ethnic diversity of the student population at a high school he is testing as a whole. When reporting the results, he includes a detailed description of the school population. He describes the number of recent immigrant students, the many transfer students, their ages, grade levels, and the length of time living in Canada.

Sex Survey (+)
A very powerful parent committee in a small rural town of ten thousand people seeks the assistance of the guidance and counselling department to survey students at the local high school to determine their degree of sexual activity. The counsellor reports that the results are significantly lower than the national average and neighbouring towns and city. In writing his report, the counsellor explains that the results might reflect the students' awareness that the survey was prompted by the parents' committee and that the results would be given to them. Possibly, students were not entirely forthcoming due

to anxiety, or possible stricter curfews, of restrictions to social functions, and the possibility of parents finding out who was sexually active.

Superficial Study (–)
The head of a divisional counselling association conducts a study to examine students' social values. He obtains the assistance of one counsellor from each of the high schools to help him administer the study to a number of students in each school. The results are then compiled, representing the school division as a whole. The results are published in the divisional newsletter. Absent from the report are any details on the number of subjects from the vastly different high schools in this large school division. As well, no mention is made of the fact that no attempt at random selection of students was made.

Jumping the Gun (–)
At a case conference meeting, which includes all the counsellors of the high school, the school social worker, and the psychologist, an eighteen-year-old male student becomes the focus of attention. The student in question has become an increasing behaviour problem at school in addition to his decreasing academic performance. A personality test has been administered to the student by the psychologist and the report is being shared at this meeting. The team makes recommendations based on the test without consideration of the effects that the recent break up of the student's parents and death of a grandparent in a car accident might have had on the results of a personality test.

Comments and Questions
If research is to be of any real value and benefit, researchers must report any conditions or variables that may have

affected the outcome of interpretation of the results. Not reporting a variable that may have affected the research results leaves the research impotent, and casts a shadow on the validity of the research findings. A few of the conditions or variables that could affect the outcome and interpretation of results are:

- cultural backgrounds (norms, values, beliefs) of the subjects

- socio-economic influences especially if results are being groups or compared to another social class

- religious influences of the subjects, such as customs, values and beliefs

- personal, social, and medical histories of the subjects, where appropriate and ethical.

1. In the **Sex Survey** case study, the counsellor explains that the results of the study may have been influenced by the knowledge that the students' parents would get the results. Knowing this to be the case, how could this research study have been improved?

2. What are the ethical considerations that were overlooked in the case of **Superficial Study**?

3. Do you feel that it is a realistic expectation that all variables and conditions that may affect results be identified?

4. Under what circumstances, if any, do you feel it is ethical to disclose a subject's medical or personal history when reporting variables and conditions that may affect results?

5. Do you feel that our own values, beliefs and biases are variables and conditions that may affect research results?

6. What are some additional variables that could affect research results?

E12 **RESEARCH CONTRIBUTIONS**
Counsellors give due credit through joint authorship, acknowledgement, footnote statements, or other appropriate means to those who have contributed significantly to the research and/or publication, and to those who have done previous work on the topic. For an article that is based mainly on a student thesis or dissertation, the student is listed as principal author.

Appropriate Acknowledgment (+)
A counsellor in a relatively small high school requires additional data for a research paper she is writing. She writes to three nearby schools that can help her with the data collection. When the research is completed and the paper is written, the three schools and their counsellors are included in the acknowledgements.

Joint Authorship (+)
A counsellor is asked to write an article explaining the school's guidance program. Recently, the school principal and the counsellor had written a similar paper for another organization. After receiving the principal's approval and making some minor adjustments to the paper, the counsellor asks for permission from the publisher of the original article to submit this similar article. After receiving permission, the counsellor submits the adapted manuscript for publication. Both the principal and counsellor are listed as authors.

Unethical Behaviour (–)
During a conversation with a colleague, a counsellor is given significant information pertaining to a paper he is writing. The counsellor uses the discussion

as the basis for the paper and includes many of his colleague's ideas. When the paper is completed, the colleague's name is not acknowledged in any way.

Footnoting (–)

A counsellor uses an entire section of a colleague's unpublished paper within the body of a manuscript she is writing. The unpublished work is not referenced and used as the counsellor's own ideas.

Comments and Questions

It is important to give due credit to any person or group who gives information, written or verbal, or who assists a researcher significantly. Knowing where information comes from gives researchers credibility and helps to substantiate their ideas and statements. Another reason for giving due credit is to assist future researchers. It helps them to find background information and check specific data.

Major contributions to research should be given joint authorship. This includes help with writing a paper or with the actual research or testing. For example, an assistant who helps to design a test and formulates procedures should be given joint authorship. Minor contributions should be acknowledged through references or footnotes.

1. If, for business reasons, a major sponsor asks not to be credited for sponsoring your research, do you abide by the sponsor's wishes? Discuss.

2. When do the ideas of others become your own? Many ideas come from someone, whether they are known or not. Where is the line between one's own idea and someone else's?

3. Is it unethical to use what you think are your own ideas if you have not checked to see whether these ideas

have not been presented elsewhere?

4. If you pay someone to collect data for you, does he or she need to be acknowledged in a subsequent research article?

5. When graduate students publish parts of their theses or dissertations as articles, should they acknowledge the members of their thesis or dissertation committee?

6. When joint research is conducted, is it possible to agree beforehand the order of author credit and list of acknowledgments? Discuss.

E13 SUBMISSION OF PUBLICATIONS
Counsellors do not submit the same manuscript or one essentially similar in content for simultaneous publication consideration by two or more journals. In addition, manuscripts published in whole or in substantial part in another journal or published work should not be submitted for publication without acknowledgement and permission from the previous publication.

Single Submission (+)

A graduate student in a department of counselling psychology wrote her thesis on reasonable behaviour on the part of counsellors in dealing with confidentiality in a counselling situation. After having her advisor read the thesis, she was encouraged to submit it for publication. The student obtained a list of the current journals on counselling psychology, and reviewed the most recent publications. The author chose to submit the thesis to one counselling journal that had recently published other articles related to confidentiality and other ethical issues.

Acknowledgment and Permission from a Previous Publication (+)

A professor in the department of educational psychology submits a lengthy manuscript to a professional journal. The editors of the journal agree to publish one major part of the manuscript. Various colleagues advise the professor that they find the article useful to their courses, and wish to read more about the subject. The professor is advised to submit the article in whole to another publication. He subsequently contacts the previous publisher and requests acknowledgment and permission to submit the manuscript to another publisher in order that it might be published in its entirety.

Publisher Does Not Respond (–)

At a university, one professor writes a manuscript regarding the timely issue of AIDS education in the schools. He feels that time is of the essence for publication due to the rising epidemic of sexually transmitted diseases among youth. The professor is aware that it could take up to three months for a publisher to respond to a manuscript submission. Due to time constraints, the author chooses not to wait for an answer to his submission, and after a six-week period, he submits the work to another publisher.

Embarrassment Caused (–)

An author submits the same manuscript to three publications simultaneously. Two of the three publications accept the manuscript. The author contacts the editors of the less prestigious journals and informs them that he is withdrawing his manuscript for publication. The other journal publishes the manuscript.

Comments and Questions

This ethical guideline states that an author must not submit a manuscript to two or more journals simultaneously for publication consideration. As well, when an author chooses to submit a manuscript that has been published in part by another publisher, it is his or her obligation to get permission from the previous publisher to allow the manuscript to be published in another journal.

Due to the costs incurred and the time required to read all manuscripts that are submitted to a publication, there are no journal publishers who accept manuscripts from an author if it comes to their attention that there are multiple submissions. Counsellors and researchers should be aware of the validity of this concern by editors. It is not ethical practice to have a manuscript, or portion thereof, submitted to, or published in, more than one journal without acknowledgement. Even in the event of a time constraint which the author may deem to be unreasonable, it would not be ethical to submit the work again at any time, without the written notification to, and the permission of, the first publisher.

1. What are some ways in which the whole review process of manuscripts can be improved?

2. Should reviewers of manuscript be paid a small honorarium on the condition that they review a manuscript within one week?

3. Do you believe that authors should be permitted to send manuscripts to more than one publisher if a letter accompanied the manuscript stating "multiple submissions"?

4. What are the advantages and disad-

vantages of allowing for multiple submissions of manuscripts?

5. Is it realistic to expect a publication to respond to you regarding acceptance or refusal of your submitted manuscript within a reasonable and agreed-upon time limit, for example, a period of six to eight weeks?

6. If a journal has not given a response to authors of manuscripts after two months, should the author or authors be permitted to send the manuscript elsewhere?

Chapter Thirteen

---◆---

Case Studies in Counsellor Education, Training and Supervision

---◆---

Counsellor-educators are in a unique position of not only teaching and discussing ethical articles, but also modelling ethical responsibilities. These ethical responsibilities are presented in the cases, discussions, and questions.

Canadian Counselling Association Code of Ethics

Ethical Guidelines for Counsellor Education, Training, and Supervision

F1 GENERAL RESPONSIBILITY
Counsellors who are responsible for counsellor education, training and supervision adhere to current CCA guidelines and standards with respect to such activities and conduct themselves in a manner consistent with the *CCA Code of Ethics and Standards of Practice for Counsellors*.

F2 BOUNDARIES OF COMPETENCE
Counsellors who conduct counsellor education, training and supervision have the necessary knowledge and skills to do so, and limit their involvement to such competencies.

F3 ETHICAL ORIENTATION
Counsellors who are responsible for counsellor education, training and supervision have an obligation to make their students, trainees, and supervisees aware of the ethical responsibilities as expressed in the *CCA Code of Ethics and Standards of Practice for Counsellors*.

F4 CLARIFICATION OF ROLES AND RESPONSIBILITIES
Counsellors who engage in counselling supervision of students or trainees take responsibility for clarifying their respective roles and obligations.

F5 WELFARE OF CLIENTS
Counsellors who engage in counselling supervision of students or trainees take steps to ensure the welfare of clients during the supervised practice period, and intervene, when necessary, to ensure that this obligation is met.

F6 PROGRAM ORIENTATION
Counsellors responsible for counsellor education programs and training activities take responsibility to orient prospective students and trainees to all core elements of such programs and activities, including to a clear policy with respect to all supervised practice components, both those simulated and real.

F7 RELATIONAL BOUNDARIES
Counsellors who work as counsellor educators, trainers, and supervisors establish relationships with their students, trainees and supervisees such that appropriate relational boundaries are clarified and maintained, and dual relationships avoided.

F8 OBLIGATION TO INFORM
Counsellors who work as counsellor educators, trainers, and supervisors take steps to inform students, trainees, and supervisees, at the beginning of activities associated with these roles, of all reasonably foreseeable circumstances under which confidentiality may be breached during such activities.

F9 SELF-DEVELOPMENT AND SELF-AWARENESS
Counsellors who work as counsellor educators, trainers and supervisors, encourage and facilitate the self-development and self-awareness of students, trainees and supervisees, so that they learn to integrate their professional practice and personal insight.

F10 DEALING WITH PERSONAL ISSUES
Counsellors responsible for counsellor education, training, and supervision recognize when such activities evoke significant personal issues for students, trainees, and supervises and refer to other sources when necessary to avoid counselling those for whom they hold administrative, or evaluative responsibility.

F11 SELF-GROWTH ACTIVITIES
Counsellors who work as counsellor educators, trainers, and supervisors, ensure that any professional experiences which require self-disclosure, and engagement in self-growth activities are managed in a manner consistent with the principles of informed consent, confidentiality, and safeguarding against any harmful effects.

Case Studies for Counsellor Education, Training, and Supervision

F1 GENERAL RESPONSIBILITY
Counsellors who are responsible for counsellor education, training and supervision adhere to current CCA guidelines and standards with respect to such activities and conduct themselves in a manner consistent with the *CCA Code of Ethics and Standards of Practice for Counsellors.*

CCA Position Paper (+)
A counsellor-educator telephones the CCA headquarters in Ottawa, indicating that her department is reorganizing their counsellor education program and they want to have the latest position of CCA on training. The counsellor-educator is informed that the CCA *Position Paper for the Provision of Counselling Services* would be mailed to her. She is also told to check the CCA website (www.ccacc.ca) to receive information on accreditation of counsellor education programs in Canada. She is also told that Canadian Counsellor Certification requirements consist of a graduate degree in counselling, a counselling theories course, a supervised counselling practicum, and graduate course work in any six of the following areas: communication and relationship skills, group counselling, career development, assessment and testing, research and

evaluation, consultation methods, learning and human development, psychological education, counselling intervention strategies, counselling girls and women, multicultural counselling, counselling in specialized settings, and professional ethics.

CCA Accreditation (+)

An American student, familiar with accreditation of university programs, applies to several Canadian counsellor education programs. When he asks whether the counselling program is accredited, he learns that accreditation of counselling programs is just beginning in Canada and that only one university is accredited by CCA, although a number of other universities are applying for accreditation. The potential student is encouraged to contact CCA headquarters in Ottawa and to visit the "accreditation" website for CCA (www.ccacc.ca).

Counselling Practicum (–)

One university with a small number of counsellor-educators admits many graduate students to its counselling program. Nearly all the students are teachers or counsellors who plan to take all the courses during the summer months when they have vacation. Since a counselling field experience is not offered during the summer, these counsellors complete their program of studies without ever being supervised in an actual counselling situation.

Program Philosophy (–)

A counsellor interested in graduate studies, telephones the department head of a counsellor education program in a neighbouring province regarding the philosophy, admission requirements, and other program specifics.

The department head provides some information regarding admission and courses, but when asked whether their program is accredited by CCA, and whether their graduates are eligible for certification by CCA, the department head indicates that he is not familiar with CCA accreditation or certification.

Comments and Questions

CCA now has both certification and accreditation policies. The main purpose for Canadian Counsellor Certification (CCC) is to establish a Canadian certification process, to identify counsellors who have obtained certification, and to maintain a register of certified counsellors. To obtain certification, counsellors must satisfy certain education standards: a graduate degree with evidence of graduate course work in counselling theory, a supervised counselling practicum, and additional course work in six areas of thirteen listed areas (for example, group counselling, research and evaluation).

Accreditation is intended to promote high standards in education of counsellors, and to promote review and evaluation of counsellor education programs. In order to become accredited by CCA, university counsellor education programs must fulfil standards related to "student selection and advising, faculty qualifications and workload, program governance, instructional support, and self-evaluation" (CCA, date).

1. Should all university departments offering degree programs in counsellor education offer programs that reflect the course work and practica specified in *Accreditation of Counselling Programs* articles?

2. What are your opinions regarding accreditation of counsellor training

programs in Canada?

3. Are certification and accreditation specifications too general? Do they help clarify the position for specific groups of counsellors such as family and marriage counsellors, school counsellors, or career counsellors?

4. Do you agree with the CCA certification requirements? Should the counselling course work be more specific?

5. What do you believe will happen to smaller counsellor education programs that do not meet the extensive practica criteria and the full-two year Master's program requirements?

6. What additional counselling areas would you add to the present Canadian Counsellor Certification list of fifteen areas?

F2 BOUNDARIES OF COMPETENCE
Counsellors who conduct counsellor education, training and supervision have the necessary knowledge and skills to do so, and limit their involvement to such competencies.

Improved Teaching (+)
Because of complaints of poor teaching in a particular department of counselling psychology, the department head invites several professors known to be excellent teachers from different departments to offer a series of lectures and demonstrations on effective college teaching.

Counselling Skills (+)
A professor has just been granted a year-long sabbatical leave. In applying for this leave, he has had some difficulty convincing the university administration that he wants to devote time during this year not only to research

and to publish, but also to improve his skills as a counselling practitioner. He is convinced that if he improves his counselling skills by becoming involved in counselling others and receiving feedback on his counselling, he will be in a better position to help students in subsequent years when he teaches the counselling skills courses.

Out-Dated (–)
A professor in counsellor education regularly teaches an introductory course on the role, function, and services of high school counsellors. Since this professor has seldom been in a high school after leaving her high school counselling position twenty years ago, she continues to talk about the role and function of counsellors in the seventies and early eighties. All of her examples are drawn from what she did in her high school many years ago.

Lack of Specialized Skills (–)
A counselling department begins teaching courses and offering a supervised practicum in the area of family and marriage counselling. The backgrounds of the three counsellor-educators in the department are all in other areas such as career, school, or crisis counselling. Nevertheless, the department head assigns one of the counsellor-educators to teach and supervise the practicum in family counselling.

Comments and Questions
Many counsellor-educators and professors in general bemoan the fact that there is no career payoff for teaching well. It is true that professors with mediocre teaching records, but good research records, receive tenure and get promoted. A professor with excellent teaching credentials and a poor

research record, has little or no chance of being promoted. The result is that few poor or mediocre professors take advantage of university teaching services designed to improve teaching. These professors feel their time is better spent on getting a research grant or on publishing an additional article.

Nevertheless, it is of vital importance that counsellor-educators not only become competent teachers, but that they are successful practitioners who can demonstrate their counselling skills and can give personal examples of counselling effectiveness. Research or study leaves for counsellor-educators are readily available in most Canadian universities, but typically counsellor-educators decide, during their leaves, to do research rather than to improve their teaching or practitioner skills.

1. In smaller counsellor-education departments, counsellor educators through necessity may be required to teach outside their area of expertise. Is this acceptable?

2. What should universities do to encourage better teaching?

3. What recommendations would you make regarding the improvement of the practitioner skills of counsellor-educators?

4. Should counsellor-educators be required to be practitioners as well?

5. When hiring new counsellor-educators, what can search committees do to ensure that they are getting skilled teachers and practitioners?

6. The case of **Counselling Skills** is a situation that happened in a large Canadian university. Should sabbatical leaves to improve teaching be as readily available as leaves for research?

F3 **ETHICAL ORIENTATION**
Counsellors who are responsible for counsellor education, training and supervision have an obligation to make their students, trainees, and supervisees aware of the ethical responsibilities as expressed in the *CCA Code of Ethics and Standards of Practice for Counsellors*.

Course in Ethics (+)
A university introduces a new course entitled "Legal and Ethical Issues in Counselling." The course is compulsory for all students in counselling. The course is taught by an acknowledged expert in the area of legal and ethical counselling issues.

Ethics Workshop (+)
A university provides all students with the *CCA Code of Ethics* (2006) during the first class of its compulsory introductory course in counselling. As well, a three-hour workshop is provided which includes small group discussion on such issues as 'confidentiality' and 'danger' to self and others, an opportunity to discuss other guidelines in the *CCA Code of Ethics*, and a chance to examine ethical cases of interest to the students.

Ethics De-emphasized (–)
The counselling program at one Canadian university does not have any course on ethical issues in counselling. Nor is the topic of ethics discussed or presented in any of the other counselling and related courses. Students are encouraged, however, to read the chapter on ethics in their introductory counselling course – "although", says the professor, "it will not be on your final test."

Practicum Experience (–)

A graduate student in a counselling practicum informs her practicum supervisor at the university of some of the practices of the counsellor she is working with in a high school. The male school counsellor at times gives female students back and neck massages in his office. The practicum supervisor does not discuss this with the graduate student and dismisses the issue by saying it is the school's business.

Comments and Questions

Stated in the preamble to the *CCA Code of Ethics* (2006) is the following:

> Members of CCA have a responsibility to ensure that they are familiar with this *Code of Ethics*, understand its application to their professional conduct, and strive to adhere to its principles and values. Counsellors should also be familiar with other sources of information which will assist them in making informed professional decisions. These include: the laws, regulations, and policies which are professionally relevant to their working environment.

Counsellor-educators have the further responsibility of teaching counselling students the issues around counselling ethics. Basic principles upon which the *Code of Ethics* is based, must be examined and understood. These principles are:

a) Beneficience—being proactive in benefiting clients.

b) Fidelity—honouring client commitments and having integrity in client-counsellor relationships.

c) Autonomy—respecting clients' freedom of choice.

d) Nonmaleficence—not willfully harming others and refraining from actions that risk harm to others.

e) Justice—respect for the equal treatment of all persons.

f) Societal Interest—respecting the need to be responsible to society.

1. In 2005, the ethical principles were re-written and adopted for the revised *Code of Ethics*. If you were asked to rank these principles would your ranking remain the same for most issues? What would your most frequent ranking be?

2. Which ethical principles (just listed) would you want to change?

3. Should all counsellor education programs offer a required course or courses in ethics?

4. What are the best ways of educating students regarding their ethical responsibilities and the standards of the counselling profession?

5. What values would you wish to maximize in any given situation?

6. Can or should values and principles in ethical decision-making be prioritized?

F4   **CLARIFICATION OF ROLES AND RESPONSIBILITIES**
Counsellors who engage in counselling supervision of students or trainees take responsibility for clarifying their respective roles and obligations.

Supervisor's Role (+)

Manny L., a counsellor educator in a Canadian university, is supervising his first group of counselling students in a practicum. He takes to heart what he recalls from his own training; namely, that as supervisor he is ultimately responsible for all the practicum trainees. Before the first practicum class, he contacts all the students and informs them of his expectations of them and his own supervisory procedures. Among the things discussed are his training objectives, the amount and type of feedback, assessment procedures, caseload requirements, classroom expectations, and evaluation criteria.

Supervised Practicum (+)

One counsellor-educator feels it is extremely important for students to have a good understanding of counselling philosophy, counselling theory, psychological assessment, and counselling techniques before students are placed in a supervised counselling practice situation. To make sure that he will have time to do intensive supervision of counselling practice, he arranges for all these aforementioned academic subjects to be scheduled in the first semester so that he can devote most of his time in the second semester for on-site supervision of students. He arranges weekly meetings for each student as well as a seminar for the whole practicum group, where students can discuss their philosophies and theories in light of the realities of their practice.

No Clarification of Supervisory Roles (–)

Evelyn D., a counsellor-educator, appears to be much more interested in her research project than she is in meeting her obligations in supervising her students in the counselling practicum. She asks the six students in her practicum class to arrange their own supervision in the field and to do the type of counselling being done at the counselling centre that accepts them.

Counsellor or Supervisor (–)

Jill F. is a new collaborating counsellor for counsellor trainees from the major university in her city. She devotes much time in getting to know her counselling student, Samantha. As trust grows between the two, Samantha tells Jill about many personal problems she is facing in her family and many difficulties she is experiencing with the man with whom she is living. Samantha is very upset when Jill, in her formative report to her university supervisor, writes that "relationship problems with her family and boyfriend are getting in the way of Samantha being an effective counsellor."

Comments and Questions

The last case presented illustrates the difficulties that can arise when the roles of trainees, counsellor-educators, and collaborating counsellors in the field are not clearly stated. Close, trusting relationships should not get in the way of the responsibility that a supervisor has in evaluating trainees. On the other hand, using the personal problems that a trainee has as the reason for an inferior counselling report does a great disservice to the trainee. The roles and responsibilities of trainees, counsellor-educators and collaborating counsellors need to be clarified and understood by all before the practicum begins. Trainees need to understand the:

- knowledge and skill level required to complete the training program
- evaluation criteria that are used, and stated in measurable terms
- amount of time or number of clients they must counsel
- type of supervisory setting
- dismissal policies and procedures

- counsellor education components that encourage self-disclosure.

1. In the first case, ***Supervisor's Role***, the counsellor educator says that he is "ultimately responsible for all the practicum trainees." What do you think?

2. What would you do if you were the head of this counsellor educator's department in the third case, ***No Clarification of Supervisory Roles***?

3. What are the professional obligations of counsellor trainees?

4. What would you have done if you were Jill (***Counsellor of Supervisor***)?

5. What are the major obligations of supervisors of counselling trainees?

6. This article focuses mainly on the role and responsibility of the counselling supervisor. Counsellors-in-training also have responsibilities. For example, what is a trainee's responsibility when she or he has personal problems?

F5 **WELFARE OF CLIENTS** **Counsellors who engage in counselling supervision of students or trainees take steps to ensure the welfare of clients during the supervised practice period, and intervene, when necessary, to ensure that this obligation is met.**

Relationship Skills Lacking (+)

In a counselling practicum situation, co-taught and co-supervised by two counsellor-educators, one of the counsellors-in-training does not appear to relate very well to clients. Both counsellor-educators observe her in videotaped counselling situations and are not satis-fied with her progress. Helpful suggestions are given to the trainee, but a month later her relationships with clients remain cool and distant. The counsellor-educators clearly tell the trainee that her skills in relating with clients must improve if she hopes to be a counsellor.

Pre-Practicum (+)

During the first semester of a counsellor training program, all counselling students are required to take a pre-practicum, laboratory course, designed to help students develop their communication skills, but also to help staff determine whether or not a student should be recommended for the counselling practicum. At least two supervisors observe each student and write detailed evaluations of each student's communication and relationship skills. Students are informed that one of the main reasons for the pre-practicum is to make sure that future clients will not experience negative results by being counselled by trainees.

Supervision Lacking (–)

A counselling practicum supervisor receives a telephone message from a school counsellor that the practicum student, Joyce S., does not seem to be working out very well. Several students that she has counselled have complained to the school counsellor that "Miss S. just doesn't seem to be very interested", and "She didn't even remember what I said earlier." The practicum supervisor returns the telephone message and asks the school counsellor to be patient because he is sure that Joyce, given a little more time and experience, will be a fine counsellor.

No Guidelines for Collaborating Counsellors (–)

In one university counsellor training program, full-time counselling students are placed in a community counselling program within two weeks of starting their one-year Master's program. Although some of the collaborating counsellors in the field gradually introduced the counselling trainees into counselling, other counsellors immediately have the trainees begin one-on-one counselling with the clients. The university does not provide specific guidelines for the collaborating counsellors.

Comments and Questions

The first two cases presented demonstrate ethical behaviour on the part of the counsellor-educators. They are willing to evaluate the performance of counsellors-in-training, and are prepared to screen from the program trainees who do not appear to be suitable future counsellors. Counsellor-educators must keep in mind at all times that they are responsible for the actions of their counsellors-in-training, and the welfare of clients must be the main concern. Counsellor-educators are in a position to model, by professional supervision of trainees, ethical, legal, and professional standards of counselling.

1. What would you have done in the case entitled **Supervision Lacking**?

2. In the last case, what guidelines should collaborating counsellors receive?

3. When counselling trainees are counselling their first few clients, should a collaborating counsellor be present during the counselling session? Discuss.

4. What criteria should be established to determine which trainees could be detrimental to clients?

5. What are the preferred methods of evaluation and appraisal for counsellors-in-training?

6. How often should a counselling supervisor meet with a counsellor-in-training? Should supervision be individual or in groups?

F6 **PROGRAM ORIENTATION**
Counsellors responsible for counsellor education programs and training activities take responsibility to orient prospective students and trainees to all core elements of such programs and activities, including to a clear policy with respect to all supervised practice components, both those simulated and real.

Student Information (+)

A department of counselling psychology sends a very detailed booklet to each graduate student applicant in counselling. Included in the booklet is material on admission requirements, programs of study, course expectations, student expectations and typical jobs received by graduates from this counselling psychology department.

Orientation (+)

Several weeks before class registration, the department head of a department of counsellor education organizes an extensive orientation program. Various professors discuss the advantages and disadvantages of the thesis versus the practicum route; other professors give detailed outlines of the core courses in counselling as well as the elective courses; and former graduate students comment on their present jobs and field questions regarding their former programs of study at this university.

Professor Leaves (–)

At one small department of educational psychology (which includes counsellor education) several good courses in consulting have been developed by a professor who specializes in the area of consultation. Several graduate students are attracted to this university and department because of their desire to learn a great deal about counselling and consulting. When registration for courses begins, the graduate students learn that the professor scheduled to teach the consulting courses has moved to another university and the consulting courses have been cancelled.

No Graduate Follow-Up (–)

Although the university department of counsellor education stipulates the basic program expectations, no attempt is made to link the skills of counselling to specific courses or even the total program. At no time in the last ten years have any efforts been made to follow-up with graduates of the program to give prospective students some idea of the employment prospects.

Comments and Questions

This ethical guideline suggests that counsellor education departments clearly delineate their program expectations, the basic counselling skills that must be developed and the supervisory practices of the department. This has not always been done, but in recent years more and more counselling departments are developing not only detailed brochures and other materials, but are offering extensive, in-person orientation programs to students prior to registration.

As a minimum, the orientation materials that prospective students receive should contain information on the following:

- admission requirements, including not only minimum admission requirements, but the typical grades and other criteria that recently admitted students obtained

- complete descriptions of program and course expectations. This would include detailed course outlines for all courses. These outlines would indicate the nature of the course, teaching format, assignments and a grading system

- skills and attitudes that students are expected to develop

- supervisory practices of the counsellor-educators.

1. What questions would you ask a department head if you were considering a graduate program in counselling in her/his department?

2. Is it realistic to expect counsellor education departments to know and report on employment prospects of counselling graduates?

3. What would you include in an in-person orientation session prior to registration?

4. What materials would you include in the materials you would send to students who were interested in your counsellor education program?

5. Would you include dismissal policies and procedures in your orientation sessions or print materials? How can a balance be found between being supportive and setting high standards?

6. Should students be screened before admission into a graduate counselling program?

F7 RELATIONAL BOUNDARIES
Counsellors who work as counsellor educators, trainers, and supervisors establish relationships with their students, trainees and supervisees such that appropriate relational boundaries are clarified and maintained, and dual relationships avoided.

Counselling Internship (+)
It is the practice of one university to offer several counselling internships to doctoral students in the university's counselling centre. A great deal of planning has gone into making this field placement a positive learning experience for the counselling interns. At the beginning of the year, a meeting is held with the interns, the counselling director, and all the counsellors in the centre. All individuals are made aware of the goals and expectations of the interns. As well, the counsellors are all encouraged to help provide clients for the interns and to arrange some discussion time with the interns. A schedule of supervision and evaluation procedures is also presented at this time.

Teamwork Supervision (+)
One counselling practicum supervisor sees the real need for cooperation among the students in training the cooperating counsellors in the field and the university counsellor education department. The supervisor meets with all cooperating counsellors before the field placements are made. Not only does she determine their willingness to supervise student counsellors, but she develops a contract specifying the goals and objectives for the cooperating counsellor and the student in training.

University Residence Hall Counsellors (–)
One practicum supervisor arranges for all the doctoral students in his practicum to spend one semester counselling undergraduate students in university residence halls. The doctoral students are told to spend five hours a week at the university residence hall and attempt to "drum-up some business." No suggestions are given as to how to get potential student clients involved in counselling and no guidelines are given as to interview structure or feedback. Furthermore, many of the doctoral students have friends and classmates in residence.

Professor and Group Facilitator (–)
In a small counsellor education department, one professor is responsible for teaching most of the course work for counsellors-in-training as well as supervising practica. One of the major assignments for the group counselling course that the professor teaches is to be a participant in a "growth group" led by the professor teaching the course. The professor assigns a grade to each student based on their attendance, verbal participation, and openness during the group experience.

Comments and Questions
As indicated in this guideline, there is a need for counsellor-educators, trainers, and supervisors to clearly state the expectations and roles of counsellors-in-training. Clear instructions must be provided on the boundaries between cooperating counsellors in the field, counselling supervisors and course instructors. Dual relationships are a violation of ethical standards and can take many forms, including socializing, becoming emotionally or sexually involved, combining the role of counsellor-educator and counsellor and combining the role of supervisor and coun-

sellor. These types of relationships can impair judgement and have the potential for conflicts of interest. On the other hand, counsellor-educators must be aware of the importance of beneficial interactions with counsellors-in-training. These might include providing support during stressful times, membership in a local counselling association, or visiting a trainee in a hospital.

1. What are some situations where dual relationships among counsellor-educators, supervising counsellors in the field and counsellors-in-training could result in conflicts of interest?

2. Should counsellor-educators, responsible for practica, have their friends in the field (skilled in supervision of trainees) be collaborating counsellor supervisors?

3. Should collaborating counsellors assign grades to counsellors-in-training?

4. What should be stated in a field placement policy guide?

5. What should be the supervisor's role in the field?

6. What would you include in a statement on relational boundaries among counsellor-educators, supervisors, and counsellor trainees?

F8 OBLIGATION TO INFORM
Counsellors who work as counsellor educators, trainers, and supervisors take steps to inform students, trainees, and supervisees, at the beginning of activities associated with these roles, of all reasonably foreseeable circumstances under which confidentiality may be breached during such activities.

Obligation to Protect (+)

Tony Z., a counsellor trainee, has been counselling a high school student for several sessions when a student reveals to him that her uncle has on occasion touched her inappropriately. The student asks Tony what she should do to make her uncle stop his sexual advances. She does not want to tell her parents because she does not think that they would believe her, and, even if they did, it would "destroy the family." Tony remembers the informed consent form that his counsellor-educator helped him prepare and the legal requirement to report children in need of protection. He points out to his client that he needs to break confidentiality because he has an obligation to protect her from further harm. He contacts the appropriate authorities using the established protocol of the high school in which he is practicing.

Ethics Course (+)

At a Canadian counsellor training program, no trainees are allowed to work with clients until they have completed a course on ethics in counselling; a course that includes students having to develop an appropriate "informed consent" form that includes a statement on the limits of confidentiality and a duty to warn others of dangers to the client and others.

Limitless Confidentiality (–)

A counsellor-in-training begins her practicum at a local crisis centre soon after beginning her Master's program in counselling. At the beginning of her counselling sessions she tells clients a little about herself and assures them that everything they say will be kept strictly confidential. She has been told by her counselling practicum supervisor of the importance of confidentiality and telling clients about the confidentiality of everything said during counselling sessions.

Not Explaining Confidentiality (–)

Before sending trainees to their counselling sites, the practicum instructor tells them "remember to keep things confidential unless your clients are in danger to themselves or others." No discussion is held regarding other limits of confidentiality such as court-ordered disclosures, fatal diseases, or client waivers.   .

Comments and Questions

Counsellor-educators, trainers, and counselling supervisors have the responsibility to inform all the counsellors-in-training of exceptions to confidentiality. The ethical guidelines B2 and B3 are very clear about these exceptions:

i)   when disclosure is required to prevent clear and imminent danger to the client or others;

ii) when legal requirements demand that confidential material be revealed; and

iii) when a child is in need of protection.

Not only must trainees be aware of these ethical guidelines, but they must fully understand them. It is the responsibility of the trainers to assure that the limits of confidentiality are understood by providing trainees with explanations and case studies that illustrate counsellor practice when exceptions to confidentiality are required.

1. In the *CCA Code of Ethics* (2006), Articles B2 and B3 clearly state exceptions to confidentiality. What are some other circumstances where confidentiality might be broken?

2. What should the counsellor in *Limitless Confidentiality* do to rectify the dilemma she may get into?

3. What are the ways in which counsellor-educators can inform trainees of exceptions to confidentiality?

4. Should ethics courses be mandatory at Canadian universities that provide training for counsellors?

5. In the case *Obligation to Report*, would you have done what Tony did?

6. Would you break confidentiality (and inform parents) with an adolescent who had an eating disorder?

F9 SELF-DEVELOPMENT AND SELF-AWARENESS

Counsellors who work as counsellor educators, trainers and supervisors, encourage and facilitate the self-development and self-awareness of students, trainees and supervisees, so that they learn to integrate their professional practice and personal insight.

Performance Objectives (+)

Soon after two new members join a small department of five counsellor-educators, the chairperson sees this as an opportune time to get all members involved in evaluating and modifying their counsellor education program. At the end, course objectives are written for all courses and performance standards for counsellors are presented in clear, measurable terms.

Group Leadership Skills (+)

In a group counselling course offered in a Master's program in counselling, the course instructor requires all course members to lead a group to demonstrate interaction skills such as linking, process observing, and limiting. At the end of the practice session, each student leader receives feedback on the specific leadership skills from the course instructor.

Research Emphases (–)
A potential graduate student seeks information from six different Canadian universities regarding their Master's programs in counsellor education. After studying the written materials from each of the universities, he applies and is accepted into one university program that seems to promise training both in research and in counselling skills. Too late, the graduate student is disappointed to learn that the practicum is cancelled for that year, but he is allowed to substitute additional courses in research and statistics. He graduates with his Master's degree without having taken a counselling practicum.

Practicum Supervision (–)
One professor is assigned to teach and supervise a counselling practicum for eight graduate students. This practicum course is described in the university calendar as consisting of practice and supervision of counselling skills for participants. The professor assigns each practicum student to a school and his 'supervision' consists of the occasional phone call to the school. No directions are given as to the counselling skills that are to be practiced or supervised. At the end of the course, all eight practicum students are awarded grades of "A".

Comments and Questions
Opportunity must be provided for counselling students not only to relate their professional practice to relevant coun-

selling theory, but also to have time for personal development, insight and self-awareness as individuals in a helping profession. The revised counsellor certification regulations of CCA recognize this need by recommending graduate course work not only in specific areas like group work, career development, and counselling theory, but also in more personal growth areas such as communication and relationships, learning and human development, and multicultural counselling. Specifically, the revised certification criteria indicate the following:

A. CCA Membership
All persons who are members in good standing of the Canadian Counselling Association are eligible for certification.

B. Graduate Training
A graduate degree, or equivalent, in counselling or a related field from a CCA-recognized higher education institution is required, showing evidence of GRADUATE work in:

- *Counselling Theory*
  A study of basic counselling theories, models of counselling, principles and techniques of counselling.

- *Supervised Counselling Practicum*
  A supervised counselling experience in an appropriate work setting of at least 120 hours should be spent in direct client contact.

and GRADUATE course work in *six* of the following areas:

- *Communication and Relationship Skills*
  A study of counsellor/client relationship skills.

- *Group Counselling*
  A study of group leadership, types of groups, group practices, group methods and techniques, and group dynamics.

- *Career Development*
  A study of areas such as career development theory, career choice and lifestyle, educational, and career information and decision-making.

- *Assessment and Testing*
  A study of individual and group assessment and testing, case study approaches, individual differences, and methods of data collection and interpretation.

- *Research and Evaluation*
  A study of research design, statistics, evaluation, and types of research.

- *Consultation Methods*
  A study of consultation theory research and practice. Topics include the process or stages of consultation, ethical issues, and approaches to consultation.

- *Learning and Human Development*
  A study of the nature and needs of individuals at all developmental levels. Included would be topics such as learning theory, human behaviour, studies of change, and personality theory.

- *Psychological Education*
  A study of topics in psychology such as personality, growth, development, attitude formation, and socialization.

- *Counselling Intervention Strategies*
  Theory and practice in planning and implementing client change interventions in counselling.

- *Counselling Girls and Women*
  A study of sex role development, stereotyping and social roles, and corresponding counselling theories and counselling approaches.

- *Multicultural Counselling*
  An examination of cross cultural issues in counselling, influence of social and cultural contexts on client problems, and relevant counselling theories and counselling approaches.

- *Counselling in Specialized Settings*
  A study of issues, applied theory, and relevant counselling approaches pertaining to a special client population or setting, (e.g., families, rehabilitation, schools, disabled clients, etc.)

- *Professional Ethics*
  A study of code of ethics and standards of practice.

1. Which part of your counsellor education program do you believe will be most helpful to you in gaining greater self-awareness? Comment.

2. This particular ethical guideline suggests that academic study should be integrated with supervised practice. How can this best be done?

3. What areas of graduate course work would you add or delete from the list of fifteen areas for CCA certification?

4. Do you believe more of the areas should be compulsory? For example, should all counsellors have compulsory course work in group counselling, research and evaluation, and communication skills?

5. Should more than 120 hours of "direct client contact" during a counselling practicum be required?

6. What skills, knowledge, self-awareness and self-understanding activities, and practicum requirements would you include in a counsellor education program?

F10 DEALING WITH PERSONAL
           ISSUES

Counsellors responsible for counsellor education, training, and supervision recognize when such activities evoke significant personal issues for students, trainees, and supervises and refer to other sources when necessary to avoid counselling those for whom they hold administrative, or evaluative responsibility.

Avoiding a Dual Relationship I (+)

A counselling professor teaches counselling courses and supervises one section of a counselling practicum. He also has a small private practice in counselling. One of his practicum students phones him at his private counselling office to arrange for some personal counselling. The professor tells the student of the conflict with his supervisory duties and recommends several other counsellors to his student.

Avoiding a Dual Relationship II (+)

A counsellor in private practice agrees to supervise a trainee from the university counsellor education program. Both the counsellor and trainee feel good about the supervisory relationship that is established between them during the first semester. During the second semester however, the trainee begins to ask for help in some of the things that are unresolved in her personal life. The counsellor points out that she would like to be helpful but is faced with the problem of being both her supervisor and counsellor. She explains to the trainee that a dual relationship between them might result in her being compromised in her first obligation, that of supervising the trainee's counselling.

Growth Group Revelations? (–)

One professor in a small counsellor education program teaches both the group counselling course and supervises four practicum students. Two of the practicum students are in his group counselling course. In this course, students are required to be part of a personal growth group and are encouraged to talk freely about themselves, their counselling program, and anything else that is important to them. The two students who are also being supervised by the professor are very reluctant to talk about their counselling practicum issues in fear that it might influence the professor's evaluation of them. No alternative assignment to being part of the growth group is offered.

Relative Problem (–)

Mark H. is enrolled in a counselling practicum being taught and supervised by his father. Mark does not like the alternative; namely, to move out of his parent's home and take a counselling program in another university.

Comments and Questions

The issue of dual relationships raises many questions. What should the boundaries be between practicum supervisor and trainee? How can it be determined whether dual relationships will be harmful? Should a professor be friends with the students he supervises? If a student needs counselling, and no other counsellor is readily available, is it acceptable for a counsellor-educator to counsel the student? Some dual relationships fall in the "grey area" between ethical and unethical and will need careful examination. It is generally accepted that supervision and counselling have different purposes and supervisors of counselling should leave the counselling for counsellors. At times, in smaller counsellor education programs, counselling supervisors will be advisors, teachers, and supervisors. If this situation cannot be avoided, great care must be taken to explain the expectations and responsibilities of each role.

1. If you were a colleague of the professor in the case, **Relative Problem**, what would you advise him to do?

2. How can the situation in **Growth Group Revelations**? be resolved?

3. Was the counselling supervisor in **Avoiding a Dual Relationship II** being too careful? Could she not have tried to be helpful with some of the trainees' personal issues?

4. What are the boundaries between counsellor-educators and counselling students with regard to social relationships?

5. Can you define the line or boundary between being a supportive, helpful supervisor and being a counsellor?

6. What other situations can you think of that might compromise a counselling supervisor's role as a supervisor?

F11 SELF-GROWTH ACTIVITIES Counsellors who work as counsellor educators, trainers, and supervisors, ensure that any professional experiences which require self-disclosure, and engagement in self-growth activities are managed in a manner consistent with the principles of informed consent, confidentiality, and safeguarding against any harmful effects.

Dealing With Group Pressure (+)

In a counselling practicum class, all students are required to practice their counselling skills for one day per week at a school or agency. In addition, the students in this class meet for three hours weekly with their practicum instructor to discuss counselling issues, their counselling experiences and their own personal development as counsellors. During one class, seven of the eight students in the class share some of their personal development as counsellors. There is a silence as the class members wait for the last member to say something. The practicum instructor, sensing the reluctance of this last person to say something at this time, interjects and points out that all disclosures are completely voluntary and she does not want anyone to feel any pressure to say something simply because everyone else has. The instructor then introduces a new topic for discussion.

Informing Graduate Student Applicants (+)

At a university in Western Canada, all graduate students are provided with detailed brochures and statements from the counsellor education department regarding the expectations and challenges that are part of the training program before admission. These materials contain comments on ethical standards, non-sexist language, involvement in personal growth group experience, and personal counselling expectations.

Group Counselling (–)
Prior to students beginning an advanced group counselling course, they are unaware that they are required to become part of a growth group where they will be under both group leader and group member pressure to reveal personal aspects of their lives. Furthermore, they are given a grade for this 'growth group assignment' portion of the course.

Personal Counselling (–)
During their first counselling practicum seminar, students learn for the first time that one requirement of their practicum is for each of them to receive counselling by one of the counsellors at the university counselling centre. No substitute for this "assignment" is allowed.

Comments and Questions
Most Canadian counsellor education programs pay some attention to this article, namely to ensure that self-growth activities are consistent with the principles of informed consent, confidentiality, and safeguarding against any harmful effects. Some universities however, may not be providing sufficient information to counsellors-in-training. It is expected that course outlines, including teaching approaches, assignments and student expectations are provided and clarified. As well, in group counselling courses and practica, students are informed that they will be expected to share counselling tapes, to role-play counselling situations, to discuss personal information, and to be part of a personal growth group.

In some university counsellor education programs, students are not informed of these types of expectations prior to admission, although many graduate students in counselling welcome the opportunity to be involved in personal counselling and to be part of a growth group experience.

1. What information were you given regarding disclosure of personal information, role-playing and possible involvement in a growth group, prior to beginning your counsellor education program?

2. What should counsellor-educators do when students become highly emotional during a practicum or group counselling course?

3. Are students given enough information if they are informed of the need for personal disclosures at the beginning of the course?

4. How legitimate are the personal disclosure activities as part of counsellor training?

5. Will counsellor-educators allow personal growth activities to be voluntary?

6. Should all personal growth activities be voluntary?

Appendices

Appendix A

CCA Code of Ethics

This *Code of Ethics* expresses the ethical principles and values of the Canadian Counselling Association and serves as a guide to the professional conduct of all its members. It also informs the public which they serve of the standards of ethical conduct for which members are to be responsible and accountable. The *Code* reflects such values as integrity, competence, responsibility and an understanding of and respect for the cultural diversity of society. It is part of a social contract, based on attitudes of mutual respect and trust by which society supports the autonomy of the profession in return for the commitment of its members to act ethically in the provision of professional services.

Members of CCA have a responsibility to ensure that they are familiar with this Code of Ethics, to understand its application to their professional conduct, and to strive to adhere to its principles and values. Counsellors should also be familiar with the *CCA Standards of Practice for Counsellors* (2001), as well as with other sources of information which will assist them in making informed professional decisions. These include the laws, regulations, and policies which are professionally relevant to their working environment.

Members are accountable to both the public and their peers and are therefore subject to the complaints and disciplinary procedures of the Canadian Counselling Association. Violations of this *Code*, however, do not automatically imply legal liability. Such a determination can only be made by legal and judicial proceedings. This peer review process is intended to enable the Association to advise and to discipline its members in response to substantiated complaints originating either with peers or the public.

Although a Code of Ethics is essential to the maintenance of ethical integrity and accountability, it cannot be a substitute for the active process of ethical decision-making. Members increasingly confront challenging ethical demands and dilemmas in a complex and dynamic society to which a simple and direct application of this code may not be possible. Also, reasonable differences of opinion can and do exist among members with respect to how ethical principles and values should be rank-ordered when they are in conflict. Therefore, members must develop the ability and the courage to exercise a high level of ethical judgement. For these reasons, the *Code* includes a section on ethical decision-making.

This *Code* is not a static document but will need revisions over time because of the continuing development of ethical knowledge and the emergence of consensus on challenging ethical issues. Therefore, members and others, including members of the public, are invited to submit comments and suggestions at any time to CCA.

The CCA Process of Ethical Decision-Making

This brief overview of approaches to the process of ethical decision-making is provided so that counsellors will have some direction when making ethical decisions and resolving ethical dilemmas.

1. Principle-Based Ethical Decision-Making

Step One—What are the key ethical issues in this situation?

Step Two—What ethical articles from the CCA Code of Ethics are relevant to this situation?

Step Three—Which of the six ethical principles are of major importance in this situation? (This step also involves securing additional information, consulting with knowledgeable colleagues or the CCA Ethics Committee, and examining the probable outcomes of various courses of action.)

Step Four—How can the relevant ethical articles be applied in this circumstance and any conflict between principles be resolved and what are the potential risks and benefits of this application and resolution?

Step Five—What do my feelings and intuitions tell me to do in this situation? (Counsellors may consider "2. Virtue-Based Ethical Decision-Making" at this point).

Step Six——What plan of action will be most helpful in this situation?

2. Virtue-Based Ethical Decision-Making

The virtue ethics approach is based on the belief that counsellors are motivated to be virtuous and caring because they believe it is the right thing to do. Virtue ethics focus on the counsellor as an ethical agent with the capacity to make complex ethical decisions. Although there is no step-by-step methodology for virtue ethics, the following questions may help the counsellor in the process of virtue-based ethical decision-making.

1. What emotions and intuition am I aware of as I consider this ethical dilemma and what are they telling me to do?

2. How can my values best show caring for the client in this situation?

3. How will my decision affect other relevant individuals in this ethical dilemma?

4. What decision would I feel best about publicizing?

5. What decision would best define who I am as a person?

3. Quick Check

1. **Publicity**—Would I want this ethical decision announced on the front page of a major newspaper?

2. **Universality**—Would I make the same decision for everyone? If every counsellor made this decision, would it be a good thing?

3. **Justice**—Is everyone being treated fairly by my decision?

For a more comprehensive treatment of Ethical Decision-Making, members are directed to the CCA publication, *Counselling Ethics: Issues and Cases*, available from the CCA National Office.

Canadian Counselling Association Code of Ethics

Ethical Guidelines for Professional Responsibility

A1. General Responsibility
Counsellors maintain high standards of professional competence and ethical behaviour, and recognize the need for continuing education and personal care in order to meet this responsibility. (See also C1, F1)

A2. Respect for Rights
Counsellors participate in only those practices which are respectful of the legal, civic, and moral rights of others, and act to safeguard the dignity and rights of their clients, students, and research participants.

A3. Boundaries of Competence
Counsellors limit their counselling services and practices to those which are within their professional competence by virtue of their education and professional experience, and consistent with any requirements for provincial and national credentials. They refer to other professionals, when the counselling needs of clients exceed their level of competence. (See also F2)

A4. Supervision and Consultation
Counsellors take reasonable steps to obtain supervision and/or consultation with respect to their counselling practices and, particularly, with respect to doubts or uncertainties which may arise during their professional work. (See also B10, C4, C7)

A5. Representation of Professional Qualifications
Counsellors do claim or imply only those professional qualifications which they possess, and are responsible for correcting any known misrepresentation of their qualifications by others.

A6. Responsibility to Counsellors and other Professionals
Counsellors understand that ethical behaviour among themselves and with other professionals is expected at all times.

A7. Unethical Behaviour by Other Counsellors
Counsellors have an obligation when they have serious doubts as to the ethical behaviour of another counsellor, to seek an informal resolution with the counsellor, when feasible and appropri-

ate. When an informal resolution is not appropriate or is not feasible, or is unsuccessful, counsellors report their concerns to the CCA Ethics Committee.

A8. Responsibility to Clients
When a counsellor has reasonable grounds to believe that a client has an ethical complaint about the conduct of a CCA member, the counsellor informs the client of the CCA Procedures for Processing Complaints of Ethical Violations and how to access these procedures.

A9. Sexual Harassment
Counsellors do not condone or engage in sexual harassment, which is defined as deliberate or repeated verbal or written comments, gestures, or physical contacts of a sexual nature.

A10. Sensitivity to Diversity
Counsellors strive to understand and respect the diversity of their clients, including differences related to age, ethnicity, culture, gender, disability, religion, sexual orientation and socio-economic status. (See also B9, D10)

A11. Extension of Ethical Responsibilities
Counselling services and products provided by counsellors through classroom instruction, public lectures, demonstrations, publications, radio and television programs, computer technology and other media must meet the appropriate ethical standards consistent with this Code of Ethics.

Ethical Guidelines for Counselling Relationships

B1. Primary Responsibility
Counsellors have a primary responsibility to respect the integrity and promote the welfare of their clients. They work collaboratively with clients to devise integrated, individualized counselling plans that offer reasonable promise of success and are consistent with the abilities and circumstances of clients.

B2. Confidentiality
Counselling relationships and information resulting therefrom are kept confidential. However, there are the following exceptions to confidentiality:
(i) when disclosure is required to prevent clear and imminent danger to the client or others;
(ii) when legal requirements demand that confidential material be revealed;
(iii) when a child is in need of protection.
(See also B15, B17, E6, E7, F8)

B3. Duty to Warn
When counsellors become aware of the intention or potential of clients to place others in clear or imminent danger, they use reasonable care to give threatened persons such warnings as are essential to avert foreseeable dangers.

B4. Client's Rights and Informed Consent
When counselling is initiated, and throughout the counselling process as necessary, counsellors inform clients of the purposes, goals, techniques, procedures, limitations, potential risks and benefits of services to be performed, and other such pertinent information. Counsellors make sure that clients understand the implications of diagnosis, fees and fee collection arrangements, record-keeping, and limits of confidentiality. Clients have the right to participate in the ongoing counselling plans, to refuse any recommended services, and to be advised of the consequences of such refusal. (See also C5, E5)

B5. Children and Persons with Diminished Capacity

Counsellors conduct the informed consent process with those legally appropriate to give consent when counselling, assessing, and having as research subjects children and/or persons with diminished capacity. These clients also give consent to such services or involvement commensurate with their capacity to do so. Counsellors understand that the parental or guardian right to consent on behalf of children diminishes commensurate with the child's growing capacity to provide informed consent.

B6. Maintenance of Records

Counsellors maintain records in sufficient detail to track the sequence and nature of professional services rendered and consistent with any legal, regulatory, agency, or institutional requirement. They secure the safety of such records and create, maintain, transfer, and dispose of them in a manner compliant with the requirements of confidentiality and the other articles of this Code of Ethics.

B7. Access to Records

Counsellors understand that clients have a right of access to their counselling records, and that disclosure to others of information from these records only occurs with the written consent of the client and/or when required by law.

B8. Dual Relationships

Counsellors make every effort to avoid dual relationships with clients that could impair professional judgment or increase the risk of harm to clients. Examples of dual relationships include, but are not limited to, familial, social, financial, business, or close personal relationships. When a dual relationship can not be avoided, counsellors take appropriate professional precautions such as role clarification, informed consent, consultation, and documentation to ensure that judgment is not impaired and no exploitation occurs. (See also B11, B12, B13, C5, C7, F10)

B9. Respecting Diversity

Counsellors actively work to understand the diverse cultural background of the clients with whom they work, and do not condone or engage in discrimination based on age, colour, culture, ethnicity, disability, gender, religion, sexual orientation, marital, or socio-economic status. (See also D10)

B10. Consulting With Other Professionals

Counsellors may consult with other professionally competent persons about the client. However, if the identity of the client is to be revealed, it is done with the written consent of the client. Counsellors choose professional consultants in a manner which will avoid placing the consultant in a conflict of interest situation.

B11. Relationships with Former Clients

Counsellors remain accountable for any relationships established with former clients. Those relationships could include, but are not limited to those of a friendship, social, financial, and business nature. Counsellors exercise caution about entering any such relationships and take into account whether or not the issues and relational dynamics present during the counselling have been fully resolved and properly terminated. In any case, counsellors seek consultation on such decisions.

B12. Sexual Intimacies

Counsellors avoid any type of sexual intimacies with clients and they do not counsel persons with whom they have had a sexual relationship. Counsellors do not engage in sexual intimacies with former clients within a minimum of three years after terminating the counselling relationship. This prohibition is not limited to the three year period but extends indefinitely if the client is clearly vulnerable, by reason of emotional or cognitive disorder, to exploitative influence by the counsellor. Counsellors, in all such circumstances, clearly bear the burden to ensure that no such exploitative influence has occurred, and to seek consultative assistance.

B13. Multiple Clients

When counsellors agree to provide counselling to two or more persons who have a relationship (such as husband and wife, or parents and children), counsellors clarify at the outset which person or persons are clients and the nature of the relationship they will have with each person. If conflicting roles emerge for counsellors, they must clarify, adjust, or withdraw from roles appropriately.

B14. Multiple Helpers

If, after entering a counselling relationship, a counsellor discovers the client is already in a counselling relationship, the counsellor is responsible for discussing the issues related to continuing or terminating counselling with the client. It may be necessary, with client consent, to discuss these issues with the other helper.

B15. Group Work

Counsellors have the responsibility to screen prospective group members, especially when group goals focus on self-understanding and growth through self-disclosure. Counsellors inform clients of group member rights, issues of confidentiality, and group techniques typically used. They take reasonable precautions to protect group members from physical and/or psychological harm resulting from interaction within the group, both during and following the group experience.

B16. Computer Use

When computer applications are used as a component of counselling services, counsellors ensure that: (a) client and counsellor identities are verified; (b) the client is capable of using the computer application; (c) the computer application is appropriate to the needs of the client; (d) the client understands the purpose and operation of client-assisted and/or self-help computer applications; and (e) a follow-up of client use of a computer application is provided to assist subsequent needs. In all cases, computer applications do not diminish the counsellor's responsibility to act in accordance with the CCA Code of Ethics, and in particular, to ensure adherence to the principles of confidentiality, informed consent, and safeguarding against harmful effects. (See also D5)

B17. Delivery of Services by Telephone, Teleconferencing, and Internet

Counsellors follow all additional ethical guidelines for services delivered by telephone, teleconferencing, and the Internet, including appropriate precautions regarding confidentiality, security, informed consent, records and counselling plans, as well as determining the right to provide such services in regulatory jurisdictions.

B18. Referral
When counsellors determine their inability to be of professional assistance to clients, they avoid initiating a counselling relationship, or immediately terminate it. In either event, members suggest appropriate alternatives, including making a referral to resources about which they are knowledgeable. Should clients decline the suggested referral, counsellors are not obligated to continue the relationship.

B19. Termination of Counselling
Counsellors terminate counselling relationships, with client agreement whenever possible, when it is reasonably clear that: the goals of counselling have been met, the client is no longer benefiting from counselling, the client does not pay fees charged, previously disclosed agency or institutional limits do not allow for the provision of further counselling services, and the client or another person with whom the client has a relationship threatens or otherwise endangers the counsellor. However, counsellors make reasonable efforts to facilitate the continued access to counselling services when services are interrupted by these factors and by counsellor illness, client or counsellor relocation, client financial difficulties and so forth.

Consulting and Private Practice
C1. General Responsibility
Counsellors provide consultative services only in those areas in which they have demonstrated competency by virtue of their education and experience.

C2. Undiminished Responsibility and Liability
Counsellors who work in private practice, whether incorporated or not, must ensure that there is no diminishing of their individual professional responsibility to act in accordance with the CCA Code of Ethics, or in their liability for any failure to do so.

C3. Accurate Advertising
Counsellors, when advertising services as private practitioners, do so in a manner that accurately and clearly informs the public of their services and areas of expertise.

C4. Consultative Relationships
Counsellors ensure that consultation occurs within a voluntary relationship between a counsellor and a help-seeking individual, group, or organization, and that the goals are understood by all parties concerned.

C5. Informed Consent
Counsellors who provide services for the use of third parties, acknowledge and clarify for the informed consent of clients, all obligations of such multiple relationships, including purpose(s), entitlement to information, and any restrictions on confidentiality. Third parties include: courts, public and private institutions, funding agencies, employees, and so forth.

C6. Respect for Privacy
Counsellors limit any discussion of client information obtained from a consulting relationship to persons clearly involved with the case. Any written and oral reports restrict data to the purposes of the consultation and, every effort is made to protect client identity and to avoid undue invasion of privacy.

C7. Conflict of Interest

Counsellors who engage in consultation avoid circumstances where the duality of relationships, or the prior possession of information could lead to a conflict of interest.

C8. Sponsorship and Recruitment

Counsellors present any of their organizational affiliations or membership in such a way as to avoid misunderstanding regarding sponsorship or certification. They also avoid the use of any institutional affiliation to recruit private practice clients.

Evaluation and Assessment

D1. General Orientation

Counsellors adequately orient and inform clients so that evaluation and assessment results can be placed in proper perspective along with other relevant information.

D2. Purposes and Results of Evaluation and Assessment

Counsellors take responsibility to inform clients about the purpose of any evaluation and assessment instruments and procedures and the meaning of evaluation and assessment results.

D3. Evaluation and Assessment Competence

Counsellors recognize the limits of their competence and offer only those evaluation and assessment services for which they have appropriate preparation and which meet established professional standards.

D4. Administrative and Supervisory Conditions

Counsellors ensure that evaluation and assessment instruments and procedures are administered and supervised under established conditions consistent with professional standards. They note any departures from standard conditions and any unusual behaviour or irregularities which may affect the interpretation of results.

D5. Use of Technology

Counsellors recognize that their ethical responsibilities are not altered, or in any way diminished, by the use of technology for the administration of evaluation and assessment instruments. Counsellors retain their responsibility for the maintenance of the ethical principles of privacy, confidentiality, and responsibility for decisions regardless of the technology used.

D6. Appropriateness of Evaluation and Assessment

Counsellors ensure that evaluation and assessment instruments and procedures are valid, reliable, and appropriate to both the client and the intended purposes.

D7. Reporting Evaluation and Assessment Results

Counsellors ensure that when reporting evaluation and assessment results to clients and other individuals care is taken to provide, in an appropriate manner, accurate and sufficient information for an understanding of any conclusions and recommendations made, and to identify the basis for any reservations which might exist.

D8. Release of Evaluation and Assessment Data

Counsellors ensure that evaluation and assessment data are released appropriately and only to the client and persons qualified to interpret and use them properly.

D9. Integrity of Evaluation and Assessment Instruments and Procedures

Counsellors who use psychological tests and other assessment instruments, the value of which depends on their novelty to the client, ensure that they are limited to and safeguarded by those with the professional interest and competence to do so.

D10. Sensitivity to Diversity when Assessing and Evaluating

Counsellors proceed with caution when judging and interpreting the performance of minority group members and any other persons not represented in the group on which the evaluation and assessment instruments and procedures were standardized. They recognize and take into account the potential effects of age, ethnicity, disability, culture, gender, religion, sexual orientation and socio-economic status on both the administration of, and the interpretation of date from, such instruments and procedures.

D11. Security Maintenance

Counsellors ensure the integrity and security of evaluation and assessment instruments and procedures consistent with any legal and contractual obligations. They refrain from appropriating, reproducing, or modifying established evaluation and assessment instruments without the expressed permission and adequate recognition of the original author, publisher and copyright holder.

Research and Publications

E1. Researcher Responsibility

Counsellors plan, conduct, and report on research in a manner consistent with relevant ethical principles, professional standards of practice, federal and provincial laws, institutional regula-

tions, cultural norms, and standards governing research with human subjects.

E2. Subject Welfare

Counsellors are responsible for protecting the welfare of their research subjects during research, and avoid causing injurious psychological, physical or social effects to persons who participate in their research activities.

E3. Principal Researcher Responsibility

Counsellors, when in the role of principal researcher are responsible for ensuring that appropriate ethical research practices are followed and, with respect to research involving human subjects, for obtaining an independent and appropriate ethical review before proceeding with the research. Research associates involved in the research activities share ethical obligations and full responsibility for their own actions.

E4. Voluntary Participation

Counsellors ensure that participation in research is voluntary. However, involuntary participation may be appropriate when it can be shown that participation will have no harmful effects on subjects, is essential to the research, and meets ethical review requirements.

E5. Informed Consent of Research Subjects

Counsellors inform all research subjects of the purpose(s) of their research. In addition, subjects are made aware of any experimental procedures, possible risks, disclosures and limitations on confidentiality. Subjects are also informed that they are free to ask questions and to discontinue at any time.

E6. Research Confidentiality

Counsellors ensure that research information on subjects is confidential and the identity of participants is protected unless otherwise authorized by them, consistent with all informed consent procedures.

E7. Use of Confidential Information for Didactic or Other Purposes

Counsellors do not disclose in their writings, public presentation, or public media, any personally identifiable information obtained in confidence about clients, research participants, students, or organizational clients unless (1) there is legal authorization to do so, (2) reasonable steps are taken not to identify the person or organization, or (3) the person or organizational client has given informed written consent.

E8. Further Research

Counsellors have an obligation to collaborate with colleagues by making available original research data to qualified researchers who may wish to replicate or verify the research.

E9. Research Sponsors

Counsellors, when conducting research, obtain informed consent from sponsors and institutions and ensure that sponsors and institutions are given feedback information and proper acknowledgement.

E10. Review of Manuscripts

Counsellors who review material submitted for publication, research or other scholarly purposes respect the confidentiality and proprietary rights of those who submitted the research.

E11. Reporting Results

In reporting research results, counsellors mention any variables and conditions that might affect the outcome of the investigation or the interpretation of the results, and provide information sufficient for others who might wish to replicate the research.

E12. Research Contributions

Counsellors give due credit through joint authorship, acknowledgement, footnote statements, or other appropriate means to those who have contributed significantly to the research and/or publication, and to those who have done previous work on the topic. For an article that is based mainly on a student thesis or dissertation, the student is listed as principal author.

E13. Submission for Publication

Counsellors do not submit the same manuscript or one essentially similar in content for simultaneous publication consideration by two or more journals. In addition, manuscripts published in whole or in substantial part in another journal or published work should not be submitted for publication without acknowledgement and permission from the previous publication.

Counsellor Education, Training and Supervision

F1. General Responsibility

Counsellors who are responsible for counsellor education, training and supervision adhere to current CCA guidelines and standards with respect to such activities and conduct themselves in a manner consistent with the *CCA Code of Ethics and Standards of Practice for Counsellors.*

F2. Boundaries of Competence

Counsellors who conduct counsellor education, training and supervision have the necessary knowledge and skills to do so, and limit their involvement to such competencies.

F3. Ethical Orientation
Counsellors who are responsible for counsellor education, training and supervision have an obligation to make their students, trainees, and supervisees aware of the ethical responsibilities as expressed in the CCA Code of Ethics and Standards of Practice for Counsellors.

F4. Clarification of Roles and Responsibilities
Counsellors who engage in counselling supervision of students or trainees take responsibility for clarifying their respective roles and obligations.

F5. Welfare of Clients
Counsellors who engage in counselling supervision of students or trainees take steps to ensure the welfare of clients during the supervised practice period, and intervene, when necessary, to ensure that this obligation is met.

F6. Program Orientation
Counsellors responsible for counsellor education programs and training activities take responsibility to orient prospective students and trainees to all core elements of such programs and activities, including to a clear policy with respect to all supervised practice components, both those simulated and real.

F7. Relational Boundaries
Counsellors who work as counsellor educators, trainers, and supervisors establish relationships with their students, trainees and supervisees such that appropriate relational boundaries are clarified and maintained, and dual relationships avoided.

F8. Obligation to Inform
Counsellors who work as counsellor educators, trainers, and supervisors take steps to inform students, trainees, and supervisees, at the beginning of activities associated with these roles, of all reasonably foreseeable circumstances under which confidentiality may be breached during such activities.

F9. Self-Development and Self-Awareness
Counsellors who work as counsellor educators, trainers and supervisors, encourage and facilitate the self-development and self-awareness of students, trainees and supervisees, so that they learn to integrate their professional practice and personal insight.

F10. Dealing with Personal Issues
Counsellors responsible for counsellor education, training, and supervision recognize when such activities evoke significant personal issues for students, trainees, and supervises and refer to other sources when necessary to avoid counselling those for whom they hold administrative, or evaluative responsibility.

F11. Self-Growth Activities
Counsellors who work as counsellor educators, trainers, and supervisors, ensure that any professional experiences which require self-disclosure, and engagement in self-growth activities are managed in a manner consistent with the principles of informed consent, confidentiality, and safeguarding against any harmful effects.

Association for Specialists in Group Work Best Practice Guidelines

Approved by the ASGW Executive Board, March 29, 1998
Prepared by: Lynn Rapin and Linda Keel
ASGW Ethics Committee Co-Chairs

Appendix B

The Association for Specialists in Group Work (ASGW) is a division of the American Counseling Association whose members are interested in and specialize in group work. We value the creation of community; service to our members, clients, and the profession; and value leadership as a process to facilitate the growth and development of individuals and groups.

The Association for Specialists in Group Work recognizes the commitment of its members to the Code of Ethics and Standards of Practice (as revised in 1995) of its parent organization, the American Counseling Association, and nothing in this document shall be construed to supplant that code. These Best Practice Guidelines are intended to clarify the application of the ACA Code of Ethics and Standards of Practice to the field of group work by defining Group Workers' responsibility and scope of practice involving those activities, strategies and interventions that are consistent and current with effective and appropriate professional ethical and community standards. ASGW views ethical process as being integral to group work and views Group Workers as ethical agents. Group Workers, by their very nature in being responsible and responsive to their group members, necessarily embrace a certain potential for ethical vulnerability. It is incumbent upon Group Workers to give considerable attention to the intent and context of their actions because the attempts of Group Workers to influence human behavior through group work always have ethical implications. These Best Practice Guidelines address Group Workers' responsibilities in planning, performing and processing groups.

Section A: Best Practice in Planning

A.1. Professional Context and Regulatory Requirements

Group Workers actively know, understand and apply the ACA Code of Ethics and Standards of Best Practice, the ASGW Professional Standards for the Training of Group Workers, these ASGW Best Practice Guidelines, the ASGW diversity competencies, the ACA Multicultural Guidelines, relevant state laws, accreditation requirements, relevant National Board for Certified Counselors Codes and Standards, their organization's standards, and insurance requirements impacting the practice of group work.

A.2. Scope of Practice and Conceptual Framework

Group Workers define the scope of practice related to the core and specialization competencies defined in the ASGW Training Standards. Group Workers are aware of personal strengths and weaknesses in leading groups. Group Workers develop and are able to articulate a general conceptual framework to guide practice and a rationale for use of techniques that are to be used. Group Workers limit their practice to those areas for which they meet the training criteria established by the ASGW Training Standards.

A.3. Assessment

- a. Assessment of self. Group Workers actively assess their knowledge and skills related to the specific group(s) offered. Group Workers assess their values, beliefs and theoretical orientation and how these impact upon the group, particularly when working with a diverse and multicultural population.

- b. Ecological assessment. Group Workers assess community needs, agency or organization resources, sponsoring organization mission, staff competency, attitudes regarding group work, professional training levels of potential group leaders regarding group work; client attitudes regarding group work, and multicultural and diversity considerations. Group Workers use this information as the basis for making decisions related to their group practice, or to the implementation of groups for which they have supervisory, evaluation, or oversight responsibilities.

A.4. Program Development and Evaluation

- a. Group Workers identify the type(s) of group(s) to be offered and how they relate to community needs.

- b. Group Workers concisely state in writing the purpose and goals of the group. Group Workers also identify the role of the group members in influencing or determining the group goals.

- c. Group Workers set fees consistent with the organization's fee schedule, taking into consideration the financial status and locality of prospective group members.

- d. Group Workers choose techniques and a leadership style appropriate to the type(s) of group(s) being offered.

- e. Group Workers have an evaluation plan consistent with regulatory, organization and insurance requirements, where appropriate.

- f. Group Workers take into consideration current professional guidelines when using technology, including but not limited to Internet communication.

A.5. Resources
Group Workers coordinate resources related to the kind of group(s) and group activities to be provided, such as: adequate funding; the appropriateness and availability of a trained co-leader; space and privacy requirements for the type(s) of group(s) being offered; marketing and recruiting; and appropriate collaboration with other community agencies and organizations.

A.6. Professional Disclosure Statement
Group Workers have a professional disclosure statement which includes information on confidentiality and exceptions to confidentiality, theoretical orientation, information on the nature, purpose(s) and goals of the group, the group services that can be provided, the role and responsibility of group members and leaders, Group Workers; qualifications to conduct the specific group(s), specific licenses, certifications and professional affiliations, and address of licensing/credentialing body.

A.7. Group and Member Preparation
- a. Group Workers screen prospective group members if appropriate to the type of group being offered. When

selection of group members is appropriate, Group Workers identify group members whose needs and goals are compatible with the goals of the group.

- b. Group Workers facilitate informed consent. Group Workers provide in oral and written form to prospective members (when appropriate to group type): the professional disclosure statement; group purpose and goals; group participation expectations including voluntary and involuntary membership; role expectations of members and leader(s); policies related to entering and exiting the group; policies governing substance use; policies and procedures governing mandated groups (where relevant); documentation requirements; disclosure of information to others; implications of out-of-group contact or involvement among members; procedures for consultation between group leader(s) and group member(s); fees and time parameters; and potential impacts of group participation.

- c. Group Workers obtain the appropriate consent forms for work with minors and other dependent group members.

- d. Group Workers define confidentiality and its limits (for example, legal and ethical exceptions and expectations; waivers implicit with treatment plans, documentation and insurance usage). Group Workers have the responsibility to inform all group participants of the need for confidentiality, potential consequences of breaching confidentiality and that legal privilege does not apply to group discussions (unless provided by state statute).

A.8. Professional Development

Group Workers recognize that professional growth is a continuous, ongoing, developmental process throughout their career.

- a. Group Workers remain current and increase knowledge and skill competencies through activities such as continuing education, professional supervision, and participation in personal and professional development activities.

- b. Group Workers seek consultation and/or supervision regarding ethical concerns that interfere with effective functioning as a group leader. Supervisors have the responsibility to keep abreast of consultation, group theory, process, and adhere to related ethical guidelines.

- c. Group Workers seek appropriate professional assistance for their own personal problems or conflicts that are likely to impair their professional judgement or work performance.

- d. Group Workers seek consultation and supervision to ensure appropriate practice whenever working with a group for which all knowledge and skill competencies have not been achieved.

- e. Group Workers keep abreast of group research and development.

A.9. Trends and Technological Changes

Group Workers are aware of and responsive to technological changes as they affect society and the profession. These include but are not limited to changes in mental health delivery systems; legislative and insurance industry reforms; shifting population demographics and client needs; and technological advances in Internet and other communication and delivery systems. Group Workers adhere to ethical guidelines related to the use of developing technologies.

Section B: Best Practice in Performing

B.1. Self Knowledge

Group Workers are aware of and monitor their strengths and weaknesses and the effects these have on group members.

B.2. Group Competencies

Group Workers have a basic knowledge of groups and the principles of group dynamics, and are able to perform the core group competencies, as described in the ASGW Professional Standards for the Training of Group Workers. Additionally, Group Workers have adequate understanding and skill in any group specialty area chosen for practice (psychotherapy, counseling, task, psychoeducation, as described in the ASGW Training Standards).

B.3. Group Plan Adaptation

- a. Group Workers apply and modify knowledge, skills and techniques appropriate to group type and stage, and to the unique needs of various cultural and ethnic groups.

- b. Group Workers monitor the group's progress toward the group goals and plan.

- c. Group Workers clearly define and maintain ethical, professional, and social relationship boundaries with group members as appropriate to their role in the organization and the type of group being offered.

B.4. Therapeutic Conditions and Dynamics

Group Workers understand and are able to implement appropriate models of group development, process observation and therapeutic conditions.

B.5. Meaning

Group Workers assist members in generating meaning from the group experience.

B.6. Collaboration

Group Workers assist members in developing individual goals and respect group members as co-equal partners in the group experience.

B.7. Evaluation

Group Workers include evaluation (both formal and informal) between sessions and at the conclusion of the group.

B.8. Diversity

Group Workers practice with broad sensitivity to client differences including but not limited to ethnic, gender, religious, sexual, psychological maturity, economic class, family history, physical characteristics or limitations, and geographic location. Group Workers continuously seek information regarding the cultural issues of the diverse population with whom they are working both by interaction with participants and from using outside resources.

B.9. Ethical Surveillance

Group Workers employ an appropriate ethical decision making model in responding to ethical challenges and issues and in determining courses of action and behavior for self and group members. In addition, Group Workers employ applicable standards as promulgated by ACA, ASGW, or other appropriate professional organizations.

Section C: Best Practice in Group Processing

C.1. Processing Schedule

Group Workers process the workings of the group with themselves, group members, supervisors or other colleagues, as appropriate. This may include assessing progress on group and member goals, leader behaviors and techniques, group dynamics and interventions; developing understanding and acceptance of meaning. Processing may occur both within sessions and before and after each session, at time of termination, and later follow up, as appropriate.

C.2. Reflective Practice

Group Workers attend to opportunities to synthesize theory and practice and to incorporate learning outcomes into ongoing groups. Group Workers attend to session dynamics of members and their interactions and also attend to the relationship between session dynamics and leader values, cognition and affect.

C.3. Evaluation and Follow-Up

- a. Group Workers evaluate process and outcomes. Results are used for ongoing program planning, improvement and revisions of current group and/or to contribute to professional research literature. Group Workers follow all applicable policies and standards in using group material for research and reports.

- b. Group Workers conduct follow-up contact with group members, as appropriate, to assess outcomes or when requested by a group member(s).

C.4. Consultation and Training with Other Organizations

Group Workers provide consultation and training to organizations in and out of their setting, when appropriate. Group Workers seek out consultation as needed with competent professional persons knowledgeable about group work.

The Practice of Internet Counselling

National Board for Certified
Counselors, Inc.
and
Center for Credentialing and
Education, Inc.
3 Terrace Way, Suite D
Greensboro, NC 27403

Appendix C

This document contains a statement of principles for guiding the evolving practice of Internet counseling. In order to provide a context for these principles, the following definition of Internet counseling, which is one element of technology-assisted distance counseling, is provided. The Internet counseling standards follow the definitions presented below.

A Taxonomy for Defining Face-To-Face and Technology-Assisted Distance Counseling

The delivery of technology-assisted distance counseling continues to grow and evolve. Technology assistance in the form of computer-assisted assessment, computer-assisted information systems, and telephone counseling has been available and widely used for some time. The rapid development and use of the Internet to deliver information and foster communication has resulted in the creation of new forms of counseling. Developments have occurred so rapidly that it is difficult to communicate a common understanding of these new forms of counseling practice.

The purpose of this document is to create standard definitions of technology-assisted distance counseling that can be easily updated in response to evolutions in technology and practice. A definition of traditional face-to-face counseling is also presented to show similarities and differences with respect to various applications of technology in counseling. A taxonomy of forms of counseling is also presented to further clarify how technology relates to counseling practice.

Nature of Counseling

Counseling is the application of mental health, psychological, or human development principles, through cognitive, affective, behavioral or systemic intervention strategies, that address wellness, personal growth, or career development, as well as pathology.

Depending on the needs of the client and the availability of services, counseling may range from a few brief interactions in a short period of time, to numerous interactions over an extended period of time. Brief interventions, such as classroom discussions, workshop presentations, or assistance in using assessment, information, or instructional resources, may be sufficient to meet individual needs. Or, these brief interventions may lead to longer-term counseling interventions for individuals with more substantial needs. Counseling may be delivered by a single counselor, two counselors working collaboratively, or a single counselor with brief assistance from another counselor who has specialized expertise that is needed by the client.

Forms of Counseling

Counseling can be delivered in a variety of forms that share the definition presented above. Forms of counseling differ with respect to participants, delivery location, communication medium, and interaction process. Counseling *participants* can be **individuals, couples, or groups**. The *location* for counseling delivery can be **face-to-face or at a distance** with the assistance of technology. The *communication medium* for counseling can be what is **read** from text, what is **heard** from audio, or what is **seen** and heard in person or from video. The *interaction process* for counseling can be **synchronous** or **asynchronous**. Synchronous interaction occurs with little or no gap in time between the responses of the counselor and the client. Asynchronous interaction occurs with a gap in time between the responses of the counselor and the client.

The selection of a specific form of counseling is based on the needs and preferences of the client within the range of services available. Distance counseling supplements face-to-face counseling by providing increased access to counseling on the basis of **necessity** or **convenience**. Barriers, such as being a long distance from counseling services, geographic separation of a couple, or limited physical mobility as a result of having a disability, can make it **necessary** to provide counseling at a distance. Options, such as scheduling counseling sessions outside of traditional service delivery hours or delivering counseling services at a place of residence or employment, can make it more **convenient** to provide counseling at a distance.

A *Taxonomy of Forms of Counseling Practice.* Table 1 presents a taxonomy of currently available forms of counseling practice. This schema is intended to show the relationships among counseling forms.

Table 1

A Taxonomy of Face-To-Face and Technology-Assisted Distance Counseling

Counseling
- Face-To-Face Counseling
  - Individual Counseling
  - Couple Counseling
  - Group Counseling

- Technology-Assisted Distance Counseling
  - Telecounseling
    - Telephone-Based Individual Counseling
    - Telephone-Based Couple Counseling
    - Telephone-Based Group Counseling
  - Internet Counseling
    - E-Mail-Based Individual Counseling
    - Chat-Based Individual Counseling
    - Chat-Based Couple Counseling
    - Chat-Based Group Counseling
    - Video-Based Individual Counseling
    - Video-Based Couple Counseling
    - Video-Based Group Counseling

Definitions

Counseling is the application of mental health, psychological, or human development principles, through cognitive, affective, behavioral or systemic intervention strategies, that address wellness, personal growth, or career development, as well as pathology.

Face-to-face counseling for individuals, couples, and groups involves synchronous interaction between and among counselors and clients using what is seen and heard in person to communicate.

Technology-assisted distance counseling for individuals, couples, and groups involves the use of the telephone or the computer to enable counselors and clients to communicate at a distance when circumstances make this approach necessary or convenient.

Telecounseling involves synchronous distance interaction among counselors and clients using one-to-one or conferencing features of the telephone to communicate.

Telephone-based individual counseling involves synchronous distance interaction between a counselor and a client using what is heard via audio to communicate.

Telephone-based couple counseling involves synchronous distance interaction among a counselor or counselors and a couple using what is heard via audio to communicate.

Telephone-based group counseling involves synchronous distance interaction among counselors and clients using what is heard via audio to communicate.

Internet counseling involves asynchronous and synchronous distance interaction among counselors and clients using e-mail, chat, and videoconferencing features of the Internet to communicate.

E-mail-based individual Internet counseling involves asynchronous distance interaction between counselor and client using what is read via text to communicate.

Chat-based individual Internet counseling involves synchronous distance interaction between counselor and client using what is read via text to communicate.

Chat-based couple Internet counseling involves synchronous distance interaction among a counselor or counselors and a couple using what is read via text to communicate.

Chat-based group Internet counseling involves synchronous distance interaction among counselors and clients using what is read via text to communicate.

Video-based individual Internet counseling involves synchronous distance interaction between counselor and client using what is seen and heard via video to communicate.

Video-based couple Internet counseling involves synchronous distance interaction among a counselor or counselors and a couple using what is seen and heard via video to communicate.

Video-based group Internet counseling involves synchronous distance interaction among counselors and clients using what is seen and heard via video to communicate.

Standards for the Ethical Practice of Internet Counseling

These standards govern the practice of Internet counseling and are intended for use by counselors, clients, the public, counselor educators, and organizations that examine and deliver Internet counseling. These standards are intended to address practices that are unique to Internet counseling and Internet counselors and do not duplicate principles found in traditional codes of ethics.

These Internet counseling standards of practice are based upon the principles of ethical practice embodied in the NBCC Code of Ethics. Therefore, these standards should be used in conjunction with the most recent version of the NBCC ethical code. Related content in the NBCC Code are indicated in parentheses after each standard.

Recognizing that significant new technology emerges continuously, these standards should be reviewed frequently. It is also recognized that Internet counseling ethics cases should be reviewed in light of delivery systems existing at the moment rather than at the time the standards were adopted.

In addition to following the NBCC® Code of Ethics pertaining to the practice of professional counseling, Internet counselors shall observe the following standards of practice:

Internet Counseling Relationship

1. In situations where it is difficult to verify the identity of the Internet client, steps are taken to address impostor concerns, such as by using code words or numbers.

2. Internet counselors determine if a client is a minor and therefore in need of parental/guardian consent. When parent/guardian consent is required to provide Internet counseling to minors, the identity of the consenting person is verified.

3. As part of the counseling orientation process, the Internet counselor explains to clients the procedures for contacting the Internet counselor when he or she is off-line and, in the case of asynchronous counseling, how often e-mail messages will be checked by the Internet counselor.

4. As part of the counseling orientation process, the Internet counselor explains to clients the possibility of technology failure and discusses alternative modes of communication, if that failure occurs.

5. As part of the counseling orientation process, the Internet counselor explains to clients how to cope with potential misunderstandings when visual cues do not exist.

6. As a part of the counseling orientation process, the Internet counselor collaborates with the Internet client to identify an appropriately trained professional who can provide local assistance, including crisis intervention, if needed. The Internet counselor and Internet client should also collaborate to determine the local crisis hotline telephone number and the local emergency telephone number.

7. The Internet counselor has an obligation, when appropriate, to make clients aware of free public access points to the Internet within the community for accessing Internet counseling or Web-based assessment, information, and instructional resources.

8. Within the limits of readily available technology, Internet counselors have an obligation to make their Web site a barrier-free environment to clients with disabilities.

9. Internet counselors are aware that some clients may communicate in different languages, live in different time zones, and have unique cultural perspectives. Internet counselors are also aware that local conditions and events may impact the client.

Confidentiality in Internet Counseling

10. The Internet counselor informs Internet clients of encryption methods being used to help insure the security of client/counselor/supervisor communications.

Encryption methods should be used whenever possible. If encryption is not made available to clients, clients must be informed of the potential hazards of unsecured communication on the Internet. Hazards may include unauthorized monitoring of transmissions and/or records of Internet counseling sessions.

11. The Internet counselor informs Internet clients if, how, and how long session data are being preserved.

Session data may include Internet counselor/Internet client e-mail, test results, audio/video session recordings, session notes, and counselor/supervisor communications. The likelihood of electronic sessions being preserved is greater because of the ease and decreased costs involved in recording. Thus, its potential use in supervision, research, and legal proceedings increases.

12. Internet counselors follow appropriate procedures regarding the release of information for sharing Internet client information with other electronic sources.

Because of the relative ease with which e-mail messages can be forwarded to formal and casual referral sources, Internet counselors must work to insure the confidentiality of the Internet counseling relationship.

Legal Considerations, Licensure, and Certification

13. Internet counselors review pertinent legal and ethical codes for guidance on the practiceof Internet counseling and supervision.

Local, state, provincial, and national statutes as well as codes of professional membership organizations, professional certifying bodies, and state or provincial licensing boards need to be reviewed. Also, as varying state rules and opinions exist on questions pertaining to whether Internet counseling takes place in the Internet counselor's location or the Internet client's location, it is important to review codes in the counselor's home jurisdiction as well as the client's. Internet counselors also consider carefully local customs regarding age of consent and child abuse reporting, and liability insurance policies need to be reviewed to determine if the practice of Internet counseling is a covered activity.

14. The Internet counselor's Web site provides links to websites of all appropriate certification bodies and licensure boards to facilitate consumer protection.

Appendix D

CCA Procedures for Processing Complaints of Ethical Violations

Approved by the CCA BOD on May 24, 2003
Revised byCA Board of Directors November 27, 2004
Revised by CCA Board of Directors January 12, 2006

A. Introduction

The Canadian Counselling Association (CCA) promotes professional conduct and counselling practices that are consistent with its Code of Ethics and Standards of Practice for Counsellors. If someone is not satisfied with the practices or behaviour of a CCA member they have the opportunity to complain to the CCA Ethics Committee. This Committee assists in the arbitration and resolution of ethical complaints. As well, the CCA Ethics Committee receives and processes questions regarding ethical issues and standards of practice.

CCA is not regulated by statute and therefore its disciplinary procedures are not subject to the same administrative principles as are tribunals established by legislation. CCA is, however, committed to the principle of fairness and the procedures outlined herein are intended to ensure complaints are processed in an equitable fashion having regard to the interests of all parties and the geographical and financial limitations involved.

The Committee will not deal with complaints while the subject matter of the complaint is part of a legal proceeding or when such a proceeding is pending. However, a complaint may be appropriate after any such proceedings are concluded.

A complaint must be lodged within three (3) years of the event which forms the substance of the complaint. This limitation will not apply if legal proceedings have commenced within that time frame.

When the Ethics Committee is made aware of criminal charges against a member that involve the relationship with his or her clients, the Committee may require the member to accept a limitation on his or her practice, accept supervision, or may impose other limitations deemed reasonable and appropriate under the circumstances and until the charges are dealt with.

When the Chair of the Ethics Committee becomes aware that a member has been convicted of an offence under the Criminal Code or a similar penal statute of another country, or has been suspended by a governing body of an occupational group in a province or territory of Canada or another country for reason of professional misconduct, conduct unbecoming a member of the professional group or professional incompetence, this information shall be acted on by the Ethics Committee as if it were a complaint.

Once a complaint has been received, the Chairperson of the Ethics Committee will notify the complainant as to CCA procedures for processing complaints of ethical violations and will also notify the member of receipt of the complaint. The Chairperson will notify other members of the Ethics Committee of the complaint within two (2) weeks after receiving it.

The substance of the complaints will be communicated to the fewest people necessary to implement the complaint procedures, and documentation will be confidential to those people and destroyed after three (3) years from the completion of the complaint procedures.

B. Procedures for Submitting Complaints

The CCA Ethics Committee will act only on those complaints where the member complained against is also a member of the CCA or was a member at the time of the alleged violation.

Complaints can be made by a member of the public who has received services provided by a CCA member, and a complaint can also be made by a member of CCA. The CCA Ethics Committee acts only on written, signed complaints, with one type of exception; an anonymous complaint will be acted on if the Committee itself can independently and readily observe the basis for such a complaint, such as, a complaint about a counsellor's website, print material, media presentation, and so forth.

The procedures for submission of complaints to the CCA Ethics Committee are as follows:

1. Whenever feasible, and appropriate, the complainant is encouraged to approach the counsellor directly to discuss and resolve the complaint.

2. CCA members report their concerns about the conduct of another member to the CCA Ethics Committee when they fail to achieve satisfactory resolution of the matter with the counsellor concerned, or because the nature of the suspected violation warrants this direct action.

3. Members of the public and CCA members are reminded that suspected statutory violations by a member, such as, child abuse, should be reported both to the appropriate local authorities and to the CCA Ethics Committee.

4. In cases where a resolution is not forthcoming following personal contact with the CCA member, and in instances when personal contact is not feasible and/or inappropriate, the complainant, after receiving complaint procedures from the CCA Ethics Committee Chairperson, shall prepare a formal written statement of the complaint, stating the details of the alleged violation and shall submit it to the Ethics Committee Chairperson.

5. Written statements must include:

   a) a statement explaining the attempts made to resolve the issues personally or, if not, an explanation of why this step was not feasible or appropriate;

   b) the name of the individual being complained against;

   c) a very detailed and specific statement about the alleged unethical conduct; and

   d) the dates of the alleged violation.

6. All complaints shall be mailed to:

   Chairperson
   CCA Ethics Committee
   Canadian Counselling Association
   16 Concourse Gate, Suite 600
   Ottawa, ON
   K2E 7S8

   The enveloped must be marked "Confidential."

C. Procedures for Processing Complaints

The procedures for processing complaints are as follows:

1. Within two weeks after a written complaint is received at the CCA (National Office) the complaint is sent to the Chairperson of the CCA Ethics Committee. CCA staff verification of membership for the member complained against shall be included among the documents sent to the Ethics Committee Chairperson.

2. Within two weeks of receipt of the written statement of the alleged violation of ethical practices, the Chairperson will decide if there are reasonable grounds for the complaint and if further investigation is warranted. In the event the complaint is dismissed at this point, the Chairperson will notify the complainant of this decision in writing.

3. If it is determined that further investigation is warranted, the Chairperson of the CCA Ethics Committee shall:

   a. direct a letter to the complainant acknowledging receipt of the complaint, informing the complainant that the complaint will be investigated by the Committee, and outlining the procedures to be followed in the investigation;

   b. direct a letter to the member complained against informing the member of accusations lodged against her or him, asking for a response and requesting that relevant information be submitted to the Chairperson within thirty (30) days; and

   c. notify members of the CCA Ethics Committee of the case.

Note: A member's response to the Chairperson pursuant to subparagraph 2(b) shall be in writing and signed by the member. The failure of a member to comply with a request by the Chairperson under subparagraph 2(b) may be acted on by the Ethics Committee as a separate complaint.

4. Within sixty (60) days of notification of the complaint, the CCA Ethics Committee may exercise one or more of the following powers:

   a. refer the complaint to the Chair of the Ethics Committee for investigation, and when appropriate, resolution of the complaint to which both the complainant and member agree. Whenever such a resolution is achieved, it shall be referred back to the Ethics Committee for consideration and approval;

   b. conduct an investigation itself, by way of a teleconferenced meeting of members of the Ethics Committee. During such an investigation, the Ethics committee shall discuss the information received from the complainant and the member complained against, and, at their discretion, interview the complainant and the member complained against, in an attempt to reach a resolution to which both parties can agree, the Committee may seek agreement to any of the sanctions as listed in the Disposition and/or Resolution Options section of this document; or

   c. when the CCA Ethics Committee is of the opinion there are no reasonable grounds to believe the member has acted unethically, the Committee shall dismiss the complaint and give notice in writing of the dismissal to the complainant and the member;

   d. when the complaint is not dismissed by the Ethics Committee and when a satisfactory resolution cannot be reached, the Ethics Committee shall refer the complaint to a three member Adjudication Panel.

D. Adjudication Panel

The Chair of the CCA Ethics Committee shall take steps to constitute a three (3) member Adjudication Panel from the five (5) CCA members who have previously agreed to serve in this capacity, and then will refer the unresolved ethical complaint to it. The Adjudication Panel shall conduct itself as follows:

1. It will require the member to participate in a hearing before the Panel, by way of teleconference, to answer the complaint;

2. Neither the member nor the complainant will be entitled to legal representation before the Panel during a teleconferenced hearing, however, each will be entitled to have a support person present who may, where appropriate, speak on their behalf.

3. The Panel hearing will normally follow this sequence:

   a. the Chair of the Panel invites the complainant to present a short verbal summary;

   b. the Chair invites the member complained against to present summary of his or her response to the complaint;

   c. the complainant and the member complained against are allowed to ask each other questions;

   d. the Panel members ask questions and seek clarification;

e. the Panel may hear witnesses for both the complainant and the member complained against and all present may question the witnesses;

f. at the end, the complainant and member complained against have an opportunity to summarize their position;

g. following a hearing, the Adjudication Panel shall decide whether or not a member's conduct is unethical and dispose of the matter in accordance with the

h. following Disposition and/or Resolution Options and shall communicate its decision to the member, the complainant, and the Chair of the Ethics Committee, within ten (10) days.

E. Disposition and/or Resolution Options

1. Where the Adjudication Panel is of the opinion there are no reasonable grounds to believe the member has acted unethically, it shall dismiss the complaint and give notice in writing of the dismissal to the complainant, the member, and the Chair of the Ethics Committee.

2. Where the Adjudication Panel is of the opinion that the complaint is justified and that the member's conduct is unethical, the Panel shall notify the member and the complainant of this determination, and ask the member to cease and desist the practice either with or without the imposition of further sanctions. Should the Panel determine that further sanctions are necessary, such sanctions could include:

a. the issuance of a time-limited reprimand with recommendations for corrective action, subject to review by the Adjudication Panel;

b. the placement of the member on probation for a specified period of time, subject to review by the Adjudication Panel;

c. the placement of the member on probation and the specification of conditions that must be met before the probation is lifted. These conditions could include one or more of the following:

   i. make restitution to the complainant or other persons affected by the conduct of the member;

   ii. obtain appropriate help, that may include medical treatment, counselling, treatment for substance abuse, and so forth;

   iii. engage in a continuing education program;

   iv. restrict the member's counselling practice or permit continuing practice under certain conditions, such as supervision;

   v. require the member to report on compliance with the condition and to authorize others involved in his or her treatment or supervision to report on it.

d. the imposition of other conditions that are just and reasonable in the circumstances;

e. the withdrawal of membership in the CCA, and/or certification for a specified period of time;

f. the expelling of the member from the CCA permanently.

3. At the conclusion of the deliberations of the Adjudication Panel, the Chairperson shall notify the member, the complainant, and the Chair of the Ethics Committee, of the Panel's decision, in writing. All of the written evidence and a summary of the decision of the Panel, as well as that of the Ethics Committee, shall be forwarded to, and secured at, the CCA National Office.

F. Appeal Procedures

Both the member, as well as the complainant, have the right to appeal decisions of the CCA Ethics Committee and the Adjudication Panel. However, appeals will be heard only when substantive evidence is presented that could call into doubt the appropriateness of a decision and/or that there could have been a failure with procedures consistent with the principles of natural justice.

The following procedures shall govern appeals:

1. A three (3) member Appeal Committee is established, composed of the President, President-Elect and Past-President of CCA.

2. The appeal, with supporting documentation, must be made in writing within sixty (60) days to the President of the CCA and indicate the basis upon which it is made.

3. The Appeal Committee shall review all materials considered by the CCA Ethics Committee or the Adjudication Panel. The Appeal Committee can, at its discretion, interview the member complained against and the complainant.

4. Within sixty (60) days the Appeal Committee shall submit a written decision regarding the appeal from the following alternatives:

    a. support the decision of the CCA Ethics Committee or Adjudication Panel;

    b. reverse the decision of the CCA Ethics Committee or Adjudication Panel;

    c. impose a different disposition or resolution.

5. The parties to the appeal shall be advised of the action in writing.

G. Procedures for Submitting and Interpreting Questions of Ethical Conduct

1. Whenever possible, the questioner is first advised to consult other colleagues when seeking an explanation or interpretation to questions regarding some appeal of the CCA Code of Ethics and/or Standards of Practice for Counsellors or its application to a particular circumstance.

2. If a national level response is deemed appropriate, the questioner shall prepare a written statement, detailing the matter in question. Statements should include a detailed description of the concern. Questions are forwarded to CCA National Office to be sent to the Ethics Committee Chairperson.

3. The Ethics Committee Chairperson shall direct a letter to the questioner acknowledging receipt of the question, informing the member that the question will be answered by the CCA Ethics Committee, and outlining the procedures to be involved in the development of a response.

4. The CCA Ethics Committee will review and develop a response to the question and, if requested by the questioner, make recommendations for appropriate conduct.

H. Composition of the Adjudication Panel

The President of the Canadian Counselling Association (CCA) or his/her designate will appoint five CCA members who agree to serve on an Adjudication Panel when requested to do so by the Chair of the CCA Ethics Committee.

1. Of the five CCA members first appointed to serve on the Adjudication Panel, three will be appointed for a period of two years and two for a period of one year and all subsequent appointments will be for a period of two years.

2. Notwithstanding the expiry of his or her term, a member appointed to serve on the Adjudication Panel continues to be a member until he or she is reappointed or a replacement is appointed.

3. Persons appointed to serve on the Adjudication Panel may be reappointed.

4. For the purpose of dealing with a complaint referred to it by the CCA Ethics Committee, the Adjudication Panel will be constituted by any three members from the five members appointed as per clause 1 agreeing to serve on the Panel.

5. The Adjudication Panel shall select its Chairperson.